Canto is a paperback imprint which offers a broad range of titles, both classic and more recent, representing some of the best and most enjoyable of Cambridge publishing.

AZTECS

an interpretation

Inga Clendinnen

CAMBRIDGE
UNIVERSITY PRESS

PUBLISHED BY THE PRESS SYNDICATE OF THE UNIVERSITY OF CAMBRIDGE
The Pitt Building, Trumpington Street, Cambridge, United Kingdom

CAMBRIDGE UNIVERSITY PRESS
The Edinburgh Building, Cambridge CB2 2RU, UK   http://www.cup.cam.ac.uk
40 West 20th Street, New York, NY 10011-4211, USA   http://www.cup.org
10 Stamford Road, Oakleigh, Melbourne 3166, Australia
Ruiz de Alarcón 13, 28014 Madrid, Spain

First published 1991
Reprinted 1991, 1992
First paperback edition 1993
Reprinted 1993
Canto edition 1995
Reprinted 1999, 2000

Printed in the United States of America

A catalog record for this book is available from the British Library

Library of Congress Cataloging in Publication data is available

ISBN 0 40093 7 hardback
ISBN 0 521 44695 3 paperback
ISBN 0 521 48585 1 Canto paperback

Credits for literary material and illustrations appear on page 397.

Cover illustration: Quetzalcoatl and Tezcatlipoca. *Borbonicus 22.*

TO

PROFESSOR MAX CRAWFORD

AND TO

JOHN

Contents

PART IV. THE CITY DESTROYED

Illustrations: Artefacts

(following page 240)

Acknowledgements

In preparing this manuscript I have enjoyed close to ideal working conditions, for a period of leave at the Institute for Advanced Study, Princeton, between August and December 1987, and at La Trobe University, which has supplied questioning but responsive students and colleagues, the expertise and generous good will of the staff of the Borchardt Library, and the small grants-in-aid from the School of Humanities which best carry this kind of long-term project along. The photographic material was elegantly prepared by Russel Baader and Lindsay Howe of the La Trobe University Reprography section. My colleague John Barrett and his wife Margaret came to my rescue at a time of crisis. Throughout I have been sustained by my publisher Frank Smith from Cambridge University Press, a deeply humane man in a profession not usually regarded as remarkable for that quality. I thank them all.

This being essentially an essay in interpretation, it rests heavily on the work of other scholars in a range of fields. Having no better than a nodding acquaintance with Nahuatl, I am especially indebted to Miguel León-Portilla and his students, and to North American scholars like Frances Karttunen and James Lockhart for their readiness to share the fruits of their most taxing labours. My greatest debts are to Charles Dibble and Arthur Anderson, who gave years of exemplary and generous scholarship to the translation of the Nahuatl version of Fray Bernardino de Sahagún's *General History of the Things of New Spain,* so rendering that incomparable text generally accessible. But my debts are multiple, as I hope the notes and bibliography will make clear.

At all times I have taken courage from the writings of Clifford Geertz and E. P. Thompson as never-failing sources of instruction and delight.

Over the years June Philipp, Rhys Isaac, Greg Dening, Donna Merwick, Sandra Lauderdale Graham, and more recently William Taylor have combined loving friendship with heartless criticism: a rare and invigorating combination. Despite the pressure of their own work, Rhys Isaac, Sandra Lauderdale Graham and William Taylor somehow found time to read and to comment on the whole first draft, and I am deeply grateful to them.

Throughout our years together my husband John has been the best of companions, in this as in all other pursuits. In the dedication of this book I join his name to that of Professor Max Crawford, the man who introduced me to the study of his kind of history more than thirty years ago, and whose depth of wisdom I am still discovering.

Antipodean Australia can seem very remote from Mesoamerica and the centres of Aztec studies to the north. But as I sit at my typewriter facing south towards the penguins, I comfort myself that distance too has its advantages. At least it gives a long perspective.

NOTE ON NAHUATL

The Aztecs, or more properly the 'Culhua Mexica', together with most of the peoples of Central Mexico, spoke the language called Nahuatl. Names of places and persons as written here will no more than approximate complex Nahuatl sounds. Readers will notice variations in spellings between different scholars cited, but the variations are minor, and ought not impede understanding. I will call the ruler of Tenochtitlan 'Moctezoma', a most imperfect but recognizable approximation of the Nahuatl pronunciation. Nahuatl words will be italicized only for their first appearance. The accent, which commonly falls on the second-to-last syllable, will not be marked. Pluralizations will not follow Nahuatl practice, but our own.

The basic pronunciation rules are simple. Each vowel is given its full value. Single consonants have approximately the same values as in English, for example, as in 'Cihuacoatl', excepting the following:

h is pronounced *hw* as in 'Huitzilopochtli'

qua, quo is pronounced *kw* as in 'Etzalqualiztli'

que, qui is pronounced *k*, as in 'Quetzalcoatl', 'Panquetzaliztli', 'Coyolxauq(h)ui'

tl is pronounced like the English 'atlas', as in 'Tlaxcala', 'Tlaloc', 'Tlatelolco'

x is pronounced *sh*, as in 'Xipe Totec', 'Coyolxauqhui', 'Xilonen'

z is pronounced *s* as in 'sat'.

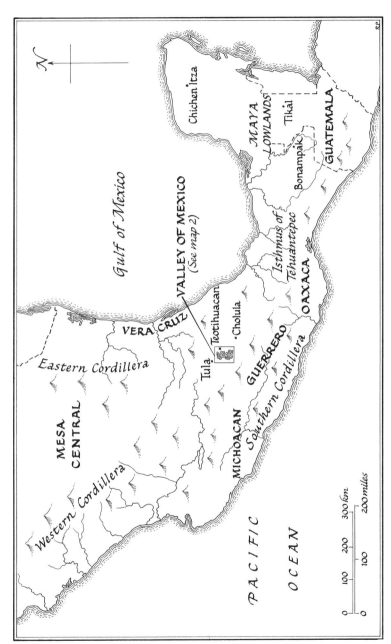

Map 1. Mexico.

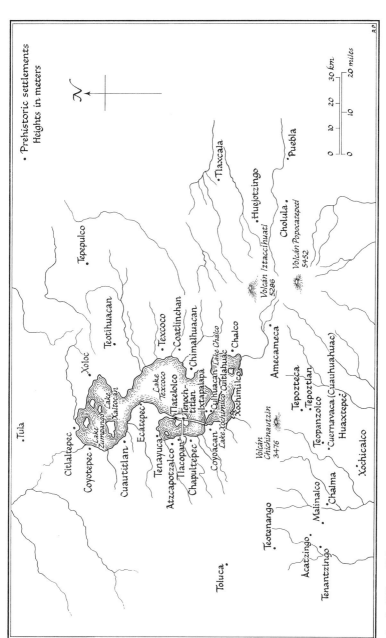

Map 2. Valley of Mexico.

The ancient masters were subtle, mysterious, profound,
    responsive.
The depth of their knowledge is unfathomable.
Because it is unfathomable,
All we can do is describe their appearance.

Watchful, like men crossing a winter stream.
Alert, like men aware of danger.
Yielding, like ice about to melt.
Simple, like uncarved blocks of wood.
Hollow, like caves.
Opaque, like muddy pools.

Who can wait quietly while the mud settles?

Lao Tsu, *Tao Te Ching*

Introduction

... men build their cultures by huddling together, nervously loquacious, at the
edge of the abyss.
> Kenneth Burke, *Permanence and Change: an Anatomy of Purpose*[1]

In August 1521 the city of Tenochtitlan–Tlatelolco,[2] once the magnificent centre of a great system of tribute exaction, but reduced in the course
of its long and desperate defence to a place of desolation, fell to a body of
Spaniards led by Hernando Cortés and a shifting coalition of Indian
'allies'. So ended the public political existence of the Aztecs, as we have
come to call them. The word 'Aztec' has been used to mean a number of
things, from the 'empire' which sprawled across much of modern Mexico,
to the people of the magnificent lake city who were its masters. It is the
people of the city in their last unthreatened years who are the subjects of
this study. While the 'Tlatelolca' and the 'Tenocha' of the twin city stren-
uously maintained their separateness between themselves, they collectively called themselves the 'Mexica', as I will do, not least to avoid the
heavy freight that 'Aztec' has come to bear. That word I will reserve for
the tribute empire that the Mexica, in confederacy with other Valley of
Mexico peoples, had constructed by the close of the fifteenth century.

This is a study built out of the attempt to catch attitudes and characteristic styles and emotions from scattered, fragmentary and defective
texts. I want to discover something of the distinctive tonalities of life as it
was lived in the city of Tenochtitlan in the early sixteenth century on the
eve of the Spanish conquest. My interest is not primarily with the doings

1

of the great and powerful or with the wisdom and aspirations of the élite, who unsurprisingly have generated most of the sources, but with some of the multiple ways in which ordinary Mexica men and women-in-the-city-street made sense of their world. By this I do not mean anything as self-conscious as 'ideology' nor as passive as 'world view', but rather those characteristic ways of apprehending, evaluating, enjoying, and managing the world in greeting, eating, trading, fighting, producing and reproducing that we obscurely but comfortably label as 'culture'.

There is one activity for which the 'Aztecs' were notorious: the large-scale killing of humans in ritual sacrifices. The killings were not remote top-of-the pyramid affairs. If only high priests and rulers killed, they carried out most of their butchers' work *en plein air,* and not only in the main temple precinct, but in the neighbourhood temples and on the streets. The people were implicated in the care and preparation of the victims, their delivery to the place of death, and then in the elaborate processing of the bodies: the dismemberment and distribution of heads and limbs, flesh and blood and flayed skins. On high occasions warriors carrying gourds of human blood or wearing the dripping skins of their captives ran through the streets, to be ceremoniously welcomed into the dwellings; the flesh of their victims seethed in domestic cooking pots; human thighbones, scraped and dried, were set up in the courtyards of the households – and all this among a people notable for a precisely ordered polity, a grave formality of manner, and a developed regard for beauty.

Europeans, from the first Spanish conquerors who saw Mexica society in action to those of us who wistfully strive to, have been baffled by that unnerving discrepancy between the high decorum and fastidious social and aesthetic sensibility of the Mexica world, and the massive carnality of the killings and dismemberings: between social grace and monstrous ritual. The Spanish friars who followed close on the heels of the conquerors saw the Mexica *ecclesia* as admirably stately in the formality of its institutions and practices – a distinct priesthood, a complex of temples, a liturgy, a religious calendar, a most devoted commitment to 'penances' – yet drenched in human blood. It was that intolerable paradox which led some of the first missionaries to the view that one of Christ's apostles had somehow contrived to preach to the Indians, who in the long interregnum had come to get parts of the message horribly wrong; and others to identify the brutal, sickening practices as demonic, the Devil's parody and perversion of the mysteries of the true Church: an intervention arising out of his endless malevolence towards humanity in general, and towards Christian missionaries in particular. W. H. Prescott, writing in the early eighteen forties what is still possibly the most widely read history of the conquest of Mexico in English, was sufficiently baffled by the contradiction to postulate two distinct sources for Mexica culture, seeing practices of what he took to be refined sensibility as inherited from the Toltecs of Tula or 'Tollan', one-time rulers of the valley, being juxtaposed with the 'sanguinary rites' of 'unmitigated ferocity' born of the Mexica's own rough beginnings. Prescott's bewildered distaste found its prime focus not in the killings, but in his (erroneous) view of the Mexica manner of consuming the flesh of their victims. It was presented, he said, not as 'the coarse repast of famished cannibals, but [as] a banquet teeming with delicious beverages and delicate viands, prepared with art, and attended by both sexes, who . . . conducted themselves with all the decorum of civilized life'. His unease was manifest: 'Surely, never were refinement and the extreme of barbarism brought so closely into contact with each other!'[3]

The shadow of the division which cost Prescott such perturbation can still be discerned in recent scholarship, although the line is differently drawn. During the rapid balkanization in the early days of the young discipline of 'Aztec studies', the detail of the human sacrifice issue, and initially the whole matter of religion, tended to be set aside in favour of other matters – state formation, economic arrangements – taken to be somehow closer to the hard surfaces of life. Accordingly a few grandly simple explanations for the mass killings were aired: human sacrifice as a device to enrich a protein-poor diet; human sacrifice as the invention of a sinister and cynical élite, a sort of amphetamines-for-the-people account; human sacrifice as technology, the Mexica response to the second law of thermodynamics, with the taking of the hot and pulsing human heart their despairing effort to replace energy lost by entropic waste.[4] Over the last decade scholarly interest has spiralled back to the meanings of the activity which consumed so much Mexica time and energy, but recent studies have remained pitched at an ideological or a theological level of abstraction, which in my view too often assumes that which most needs to be demonstrated. They have also tended to focus (naturally enough, given the tilt of the sources) on the highly visible 'official' religious performances staged in the main temple precinct of Tenochtitlan, rather than those at a local or household level: performances financed by an expanding state, and correctly if not comprehensively characterized as a theatre of terror designed to proclaim, indeed to express and to constitute, the glory and power of the state. Thus a clear distinction has come to be drawn between what is seen as the bloodthirsty imperial cult of the warriors, and those gentler agricultural rituals cherished by the common folk.[5]

Most reconstructions of Nahuatl thought rest on the semantic and etymological analysis of sixteenth-century texts in Latin and Nahuatl. The method has its limitations, which have been sensitively set out by one of its most distinguished practitioners, Alfredo López Austin. López Austin candidly acknowledges that the image retrievable from such sources 'largely reflects the thoughts of the dominant ideology, and may be attributed only very abstractly to the Nahua people'. Further, he bases his account of the Nahua world on a simple Marxist analysis, and so assumes a necessary opposition 'between members of the community and those of the privileged group'.[6]

There is nothing remarkable about this. Social distinctions and categories are routinely taken as the frame for the analysis of what has come to be called 'mentalités'.[7] But while such a distinction might well have existed in the subjugated territories, I am not persuaded of its reality in Tenochtitlan. Some distinctions were heavily marked in Nahuatl writings: the abyss between lords and commoners, with its few perilous bridges across; between the man of wealth distributing largesse and the poor who could only receive it; between the woman as heart of the home and the man as destined for battle. It is also true that in Tenochtitlan particular groups bore particular responsibility towards particular deities, and that the warriors owed a special duty to the war god Huitzilopochtli, and conquered in his name. But temporal and cultural distance can lend a spurious simplicity and clarity which denies the rich muddle of a more local view. It is possible that the carrier squatting back on his heels in the marketplace waiting for hire, and watching the great lord and his entourage stalk by, sustained a very different view of the workings of the world they both inhabited. I do not intend to assume so. My concern is to discover how ordinary people understood 'human sacrifice': their inescapable intimacy with victims' bodies, living and dead; how that intimacy was rendered tolerable; what meanings were attached to it. Mexica 'beliefs' have been discussed confidently enough, but again, academics being natural theologians, usually at an unnaturally abstract pitch. My interest is not in belief at this formal level, but in sensibility: the emotional, moral and aesthetic nexus through which thought comes to be expressed in action, and so made public, visible, and accessible to our observation. Therefore my focus will be less on words than actions, and especially ritual actions, not only because they are the best documented, but because of their revelatory potential.

The enterprise is inescapably quixotic.[8] Even in face-to-face situations emotions are fugitive for the subject, and partially veiled from the most acute observer. Given our temporal and cultural distance from the Mexica, we can hope to glimpse mood and emotion only in public circumstances, and where they are writ large or repetitively. Victor Turner has written of the 'root paradigms', the 'irreducible life stances', of a culture. These are to be sought, he says, 'not in theological treatises or explicit codes of conduct and morality, but in the stress of vital action [where] firm definitional outlines become blurred by the encounter of emotionally charged wills.'[9] 'Vital action' is therefore one quarry; not, as Turner had found it, in particular 'social dramas', those individual processes in Mexica life being largely lost to us, but wherever there are signs of general abrasions and tensions in the mundane world; and also, as I will argue, in ritual.[10]

The Mexica, latecomers to the valley and to glory, had to create themselves as an imperial people in tandem with their creation of their imperial city. A major tool in that double making was ritual, which for the Mexica was a highly elastic and dynamic expressive mode, more street theatre than museum piece. A great warrior sedately turns in the dance, the detail of his military biography inscribed in his glittering insignia; his wealth, his prestige and his power manifested in the respectful space left around him. A novice warrior dances. His years and inexperience exclude him from his elder's glory. But his youth – the exuberance of his leapings and turnings, the toss of the heavy hair, the play of light on smooth skin – carries its own message of an alternative aesthetic and an alternative source for the lustre of prestige. For both, battlefield combat was only one component of the complex experience of 'being a warrior', which was possibly most distilled in moments of formal display. These, at least, are my convictions, and my justification for the orientation of this study. The exploration of Mexica ritual, its collective concoction, and the many facets and uses of its enchantments, will occupy many of the following pages.

The distinction between 'high' and 'local' ritual in Tenochtitlan is difficult to sustain. Even in the high ceremonial at the great temple precinct there was so much involvement of 'popular' groups, so much that was minimally scripted, so much space for comment, that it is impossible to insist that only the original organizers' vision was being realized. Those extended performances, recruiting different groups of participants from different social levels in complex sequence, were themselves sculpted successions of choreographed emotions loosely organized around a theme, and made the more potent for being repeatable, public, and (perhaps, although this must be demonstrated) shared. One task will be to identify those themes and emotions, to understand their orchestration and to discover how, and how far, they caught up the themes and emotions of key experiences of individual social lives for distillation and dramatization through the ritual aesthetic. My zone of analysis will therefore include the whole span of the work of the gods in Tenochtitlan, from high ritual through to domestic, local and neighbourhood observances and involvements, and to identify the routines and institutions through which Mexica men and women, at different social levels, in different social roles, at different points in the life cycle, were brought to understand the city and the world in which they lived, and to identify its necessities.

The strategy of focussing on observable action as revelatory of thought is less self-denying than it might seem; the texts are, like all texts, contingent, with what little exegesis they offer coming from the élite. Nor is it merely a negative necessity. The Mexica, like Clifford Geertz's Balinese (and like, as I suspect, many peoples) 'cast their most comprehensive ideas of the way things ultimately are, and the way men should therefore act, into immediately apprehended sensuous symbols . . . rather than into a discursively apprehended, ordered set of explicit "beliefs".'[11] My interest is in that trafficking in symbols. My most pressing epistemological problem will therefore not be in sorting false from putatively authentic consciousness, but in estimating the alarmingly mutable gap between thought and its expression in action. These problems and doubts burden all human interaction, but they weigh particularly heavily on our interrogation of the alien dead.

The reconstruction of the patterns of life of 'ordinary' Mexica has been more clouded than clarified by the intensive work of the last few years. Ingenious research into such key matters as the basic forms of social organization, land distribution, and the precise nature and powers of the *calpulli* or 'big house', the core territorial and social unit, has yielded greatly increased knowledge, but not as yet a coherent view. Jacques Soustelle would be more hesitant now to write his *Daily Life of the Aztecs on the Eve of the Spanish Conquest* than he was thirty years ago.[12] Such is the nature of progress. Nonetheless I want to retrieve, in David Cohen's marvellous phrase, the 'interior architecture' of Mexica society: those most local institutions and patterned experiences, those clusters of sociabilities, through which individuals are made participant in cultural knowledge.[13] I will need to map the experiential landscape of household, neighbourhood, ward, and city; to track both the habitual and holiday engagement of individuals with persons and places through those zones; to be attentive to the conventional wisdom enshrined in the traditional displays of eloquence, as to unregarded asides, to the local customs offered as appropriate frames for the crises and joys of individual and group life, to the doings of delinquents, to 'superstitions', as the Spanish friars sourly labelled those practical notions for managing the sacred when it intruded into daily life; while keeping in mind the more formal performances at the main temple precinct. The procedure depends on an eclectic array and a promiscuous exploitation of sources.[14] It also entails commitment to a view of 'customs' as habituated but not mechanical action, and to the notion that beliefs do not float, pure bright shapes, somewhere above the murk of actual conduct, but inform it.

The account will unhappily, but by necessity, lack historical depth. While material for the last decades of the city's life is relatively abundant, the texts for all earlier periods are fragmentary, scattered, and in that agonistic polity typically written from positions of furious partisanship, and so are not amenable to the kind of sustained interrogation I have in mind. There will be no individuals in the story: at this distance any aspiration to individuation must be illusory. Velleities, however strongly felt, being unexpressed, will go unregarded, while 'deviants' will be glimpsed only at the ravelling edges of prescribed behaviour. Nor will I offer any systematic descriptions of Mexica society and political organization, others having written extensively and effectively from these perspectives. Tenochtitlan was a beautiful parasite, feeding on the lives and labour of other peoples and casting its shadow over all their arrangements, but I will not attempt to portray that wider economy.

Theoretical and methodological issues will be considered as they occur along the way, the epistemological status of the texts being discussed in a brief essay, 'A Question of Sources', preceding the notes. To locate the Mexica on the map of our outsiders' understanding, comparisons with North American warrior peoples will occasionally be drawn. The North American comparison has become unfashionable in post-Bandelieran days,[15] but I have found its resonances and refractions too rewarding to be resisted. The Mexica's own sense of distinctiveness will be sought through their characterizations of the otherness of the peoples they encountered, and against their own earlier selves.[16]

This being a study written for the general as much as the specialist reader, scholarly disputes will be largely relegated to the notes. The more accessible source will be preferred over the less, and the expert translation over the original form. The same few rituals will be subjected to analysis from various perspectives, in part to ease the reader's way through dauntingly unfamiliar names; in part to indicate just how complex, how 'multivocal', and multi-level, those great performances were. I have given little attention to the 'movable feasts' of the 260 day calendar, again to deepen the reader's familiarity with some of the month-long and more accessible festivals of the seasonal calendar.

I also intend a celebration of what can seem the inexhaustible riches of the twelve books of the great *General History of the Things of New Spain*, the record of the recollections of native nobles of the world they once knew, compiled and transcribed thirty and more years after the conquest, under the direction of the remarkable Franciscan Bernardino de Sahagún. (The Nahuatl version is now accessible to the reader in a fine English translation.[17]) Sahagún, arriving in New Spain in 1529, when he was thirty, had sixty years of missionary life before him. Early in those years he acquired a deep familiarity with Nahuatl, and amassed an incomparable amount of material relating to the pre-contact life of the Indians, most of it gathered by mission-trained Indian scribes from ageing Indian nobles who considered the matters laid before them, arrived at a collective report, and then dictated their findings to Sahagún's assistants, who wrote in Nahuatl what the nobles had to say. The material so collected was later edited and organized by Sahagún. On some issues narrowly focussed questions constrained Indian response,[18] but on other matters (for example, in ritual descriptions) the informants were given free rein. Much of the material was accumulated over the years in Tlatelolco and Tenochtitlan. Sahagún's marshalling, editing and writing the Nahuatl version of the *History*, begun in 1547, was completed perhaps by 1568, with an abbreviated Spanish translation or commentary added later. By 1569 a fair copy of all twelve books had been made in Nahuatl, and Sahagún's scribes had made their final corrections.[19] The resulting manuscript has come to be called the 'Florentine Codex', after the city in which it is now housed.

Sahagún's works have fallen out of favour with scholars (though one notes they continue to use them extensively) on the grounds that they are too highly mediated, too distanced from Indian actuality. The Florentine Codex is, of course, a colonial document, as its mode of production makes clear.[20] Nonetheless, it allows us to hear Indian voices, however faintly, and glimpse Indian actions, however dimly. As the largest and most coherent body of material we have deriving largely from the target area of Tenochtitlan-Tlatelolco, it has been a major source for what follows.[21] (The study is also intended to be something of a methodological exercise: to discover what can be done through the close analysis of a single, if remarkably rich, text.)

There was another friar who wrote extensively on the Indians' old way of life, and whose work has been largely translated. The Dominican Diego Durán's familiarity with Indians, as with Nahuatl, was comparable with Sahagún's: arrived in New Spain as a young child, he came to speak the tongue 'like a native'. On the story of the Mexica's rise to power his writings are indispensable.[22] For the intellectual anguish attending the missionary endeavour they are incomparable.[23] But for native ways of life and worship in Tenochtitlan they are less than satisfactory, given that his was a composite picture of 'the Indian', lacking Sahagún's geographical focus. And, unlike Sahagún's great montage of Indian recollections, Durán's is essentially a Spanish voice. His 'translations' were notably free, and his 'interview techniques' were rough and ready, moving easily into intimidation. Even more troublingly, he was capable of casually inserting his own interpretations to make Spanish sense of Indian actions. For these reasons I have used his work cautiously.

I can make no claim for the uniqueness of any particular action or

attitude described here. Some of the things I will have to say will apply to
all Nahuatl speakers, to all the peoples of the valley, or, sometimes, to all
Amerindians. That is simply a reflex of the varying scope of the material,
as of the restless movement of peoples and cultural forms within the valley
and beyond. Mexica ritual, as perhaps Mexica life, was hybrid: unique in
its elaboration and extravagance rather than in its basic vocabulary of
image and action. Like other fast-rising powers, the Mexica were deeply
engrossed by the problematics of their own remarkable ascendancy. With
their first leap to prominence in the savagely contested politics of the
valley, where determinedly autonomous units jostled for dominance, the
leaders of the Mexica had destroyed many of their old 'histories'. They
were ready to rethink and reorder an account of the past which had not,
or not obviously, presaged the magnificent fact of their dominance nor the
inference they came to draw from it: their self-recognition as heirs to the
last semi-legendary imperial power of the region, Tollan. That identification required the construction of a past commensurate with their present
hopes and imagined future. It also required that their neighbours be
brought, by persuasion or fear, into overt agreement with that identification. Therefore the Mexica were ardent archaizers, eager to emphasize
their claims to Toltec legitimacy. They were ready borrowers, too, claiming dances and ritual forms, even formulations of sacred powers, from
other and lesser peoples; pouring wealth and invention into their increasingly flamboyant ceremonial. That their own powerful glamour led
to reciprocal borrowings further complicates matters. No part of their
world was *sui generis*. What distinguished the mature Mexica ceremonial
performances was not the raw content – the names of 'months' and
'deities' honoured, the broad ritual script – but the distinctive elaborations and intensities they brought to their ritual performances, set in the
context of the great and growing structures which were testament to their
destiny. And if the Mexica penchant for borrowing obscures questions of
origins (in my view chronically obscure anyway) it casts into bold relief
questions of current obsessions, whether political, aesthetic, or metaphysical. Nor were early meanings necessarily stable: performances create
their own histories, and context and experience transform the meanings
of inherited or borrowed forms. An archaic hymn to the ambiguous fertility and warrior deity Xipe Totec, sung in an imperial city bowered in the
wealth won by war, yet constantly invoking the magical fertility of Tollan,

asserts with new and distinctive intensity the connections between war and agriculture. Therefore my concern is not with tracing origins and historical associations of different parts of the Mexica ritual repertoire, but rather to engage with the repertoire itself, as selected, developed, modified, and enacted in the last days of empire.

The chapters which follow will of necessity be essays – tentative, discursive explorations – in the strict sense of the word. Questing for a past and unfamiliar sensibility opens the immediate temptation to tame shadowy and shifting forms to accommodatingly familiar shapes. We are also trained to assume an unnatural clarity and tight coherence in what and how people 'believe', and so tend to excise contradictions and conceptual blurriness as indicative of inadequacies in informants or 'the record', instead of being how people (including ourselves) think. To inhibit such tendencies I have been conscientiously tolerant of a degree of ambiguity and disjunction between what the Mexica did, and what they said about it. I have also chosen to pursue the study by taking multiple, oblique and angled approaches, where possible against the grain of expectation: into the massive material solidity of the mature imperial city to investigate notions of temporality and change; into the tight-knit world of warriors to explore the bitterness of isolation; into the relatively guarded place of women to detect the disruptions of the dangerous sacred; into the ordered communal world of the priests to locate contest and the fine-drawn boundaries of self; into the world of the long-distance traders to discover a Mexica vision of romance; into the zone of art to find the nature of the real. So I hope to arrive at something of what the Mexica were seeing on their small lit stages before the shrines at the crest of the pyramids: what those scenes of mannered violence said to them of the human condition and of the terms of their own social existence, the one casting its natural light upon the other.

PART I

The City

I

Tenochtitlan: The Public Image

And when the eagle saw the Mexicans, he bowed his head low.
(They had only seen the eagles from afar.)
Its nest, its pallet, was of every kind of precious feather . . .
And they also saw strewn about the heads of sundry birds,
the heads of precious birds strung together, and some birds' feet and bones.
And the god called out to them, he said to them,
'O Mexicans, it shall be there !' . . .

And then the Mexicans wept, they said,
'O happy, O blessed are we !
We have beheld the city that shall be ours !'

This was in the year 2 House, 1325.
                    Fernando Alvarado Tezozomoc, *Crónica Mexicayotl*[1]

I

When early in November of 1519 Cortés and his Spaniards struggled through a snowy pass in the pineclad mountains, past the elegant cones of the twin volcanoes Popocatepetl, 'Smoking Mountain', and Iztaccihuatl, 'White Woman', and made their descent into the wide shallow bowl of the Valley of Mexico, they entered a landscape unlike any they had encountered in the New World. Wide shallow lakes covered much of the valley floor.[2] The marshland zones, speckled with the camp-settlements of fishermen and birdhunters and the low earth mounds which marked the activities of the salt-farmers, possibly looked much as they had looked for centuries. But there had been a great movement of peoples into the valley from the less favoured lands to the north from some time in the twelfth century, and that migration had transformed the land. By the early sixteenth century much of the lake edge was thickly fringed by a lacework of settlement and intensively cultivated small fields, giving way at intervals to the intricacies of substantial towns.

This dense belt of settlement, remarkable as it was, no more than framed the vast city of Tenochtitlan-Tlatelolco,[3] floating on the waters of the largest lake. Lightly moored to the land by three branching causeways, each two leagues and more long, it was closely packed with buildings. Some lordly houses were two-storeyed, the well-wrought walls framing internal courtyards and gardens; most were the smaller, humbler, mud dwellings of commoners, their flat roofs crested with the rich green of growing things. All the buildings shone with whitewash and were bordered by ruler-straight canals and well-swept footpaths. At intervals larger structures clustered around local temples, while the whole was dominated by a central zone which held a city in itself, marked by the shimmering bulk of pyramids and towers vivid with red and blue and ochre stucco. A little to the north more pyramids marked what had been the ceremonial precinct of once-independent Tlatelolco, flanking the great square of its thriving market.

Cortés was carefully laconic in his initial report to the Emperor Charles, maintaining a businesslike style as he described the Spaniards' entry into the city, the tense political negotiations with the ruler Moctezoma, and his own admirable coolness. But Charles had to know the lustre and the weight of the jewel Cortés was to add to his crown. (When Cortés wrote the account, he and his Spaniards had just been ignominiously expelled from the city, with great loss of life, but the telling of that story he discreetly postponed.) The pride of kings being what it is, Cortés began cautiously, noting that in his judgment some of the lords' houses were 'as good as the best in Spain' for the fineness of their workmanship, their gardens and pools, and the elegance of their galleries and rooms.[4] Then Spanish parallels multiplied: the Tlatelolcan market square was 'twice as big as Salamanca', with more than sixty thousand people a day coming to buy and sell, while the beautifully constructed 'towers', as he called the pyramids, rose higher than the cathedral at Seville.[5] The preparation is effective: we (and presumably Charles) are finally prepared to be told that 'these people live almost like those in Spain, and in as much harmony and order as there', and even to tolerate the possibility that the ruler Moctezoma was 'so feared there could be no ruler in the world more so'. Then Cortés delivered his accolade: Moctezoma lived in a palace 'so marvelous that it seems to me impossible to describe its excellence and grandeur . . . in Spain there is nothing to compare with it.'[6] (He proceeded to three pages of description of the 'excellence and the grandeur'; Cortés knew how to capture an audience.)

The footsoldier Bernal Díaz's account, written for a larger and less jealous readership, has less art but more impact. His description of what the Spaniards saw as they began their march across the first stage of the lake causeways has become famous, not least for its poignant intimation of devastation to come:

> When we saw all those cities and villages built in the water, and other great towns on dry land, and that straight and level causeway leading to Mexico, we were astounded . . . . These great towns and pyramids and buildings rising from the water, all made of stone, seemed like an enchanted vision from the tale of Amadis. Indeed, some of our soldiers asked whether it was not all a dream.

He wrote of the 'palaces' prepared for them, 'spacious and well built, of magnificent stone, cedar wood and the wood of other sweet-smelling trees, with great rooms and courts, which were a wonderful sight, and all covered with awnings of woven cotton', the walls 'shining with lime and decorated with different kinds of stonework and paintings which were a marvel to gaze upon'; about the orchards and gardens, with their flowers and ponds and tame birds. He concluded: 'I say again that I stood looking at it, and thought no land like it would ever be discovered in the world, because at that time Peru was neither known nor thought of. But today all that I then saw is overthrown and destroyed; nothing is left standing'.[7]

The Spaniards, habituated to the organic clutter and the endemic filth of Spanish cities, were much impressed by the cleanliness and order of the city and the evidence of its controlled growth. Tenochtitlan had the elegance of a crafted thing. The four processional ways which led out from the main temple precinct divided the city into four 'quarters', Tlatelolco, the sister city forcibly incorporated in 1473, being treated as a separate fifth quarter. (The public buildings which marked the social and religious centres of each calpulli or ward – local temple, priest house, and warrior house with its 'House of Youth' for the training of the local boys and girls – rose at irregular intervals: the calpullis had multiplied too quickly for fully controlled planning to be maintained.) The avenue to the east ended at the water's edge, but those to the north, west and south met the causeways linking the island city to the land and to the lesser cities rimming the lakeside. The freshwater springs of the city proving inadequate for its expanding population, water was brought in by a double stone aqueduct, two paces wide and six feet deep, running beside the southern causeway. To the northwest a long dike modified the seasonal movement of the lake waters, while the southern edges of the city were deeply fringed with the vivid green of *chinampas;* the long rectangular garden plots of dredged silt and lakeweed compost reclaimed from the lake, which the lake waters, the rich soil, and the most fastidious cultivation combined to make miracles of productivity, and which supplied the great city with most of its flowers and fruits.

The city's grandeur was also planned. The main temple precinct contained an area of perhaps five hundred metres square, dense with the immaculately worked masonry of more than eighty structures: the pools, pyramids, and houses of the gods and of the men and women who served them. The hallucinatory bulk of the Great Pyramid lifted its twin temples to Huitzilopochtli, God of War, and to Tlaloc, God of Rain, a full sixty metres in the clear air. As the Spaniards were to discover, only the pyramids lent the elevation necessary for the full apprehension of the city's majestic order, as only they offered constant orientation to the canoes threading the net of canals and to the men and women bearing their burdens through the narrow streets. The four processional ways marked out the Four Directions, and the sacred precinct the Fifth Direction of the Centre. Immediately beyond the precinct lay the patios and courtyards and gardens of the major palace of the Mexica ruler, the *tlatoani,* 'He Who Speaks' [for the Mexica], and those of his great predecessors, each palace enshrining the treasure won by its lord's valour.

At the time of the Spaniards' coming, the city sustained a population of more than two hundred thousand people, tightly packed in extended or joint family compounds in the grid of canals and footpaths to a density of perhaps thirteen thousand per square kilometre. (Seville, the largest city in Spain, and the last European town most of the Spaniards had seen, numbered about sixty to seventy thousand people in 1500, and by 1588 only one hundred and fifty thousand.[8]) The next largest city in the valley, Texcoco, with not more than thirty thousand people, and most of its households dispersed in small clusters around its central palaces, was

dwarfed by Tenochtitlan, and the bulk of the valley people lived in settlements of no more than five or ten thousand. The Mexica city was a marvel
in its size as much as in its exemplary shape, keyed to the great forms of
the sacred cosmology.[9]

2

The city was also something of an economic and (more particularly) a
social miracle. The Valley of Mexico, however rich in people, lacked
crucial commodities like cotton, as it lacked the precious metals, stones,
shells, and feathers which constituted 'wealth'. By the mid-fifteenth century, after the influx of displaced populations, it was also short of agricultural land. In close-packed Tenochtitlan the labour force comprised
'full-time occupational specialists rather than peasant farmers', with few
of the inhabitants engaged in any form of agriculture beyond the tending
of their own gardens.[10] While some labourers worked the lands of the
lords outside of the city, most of the city's commoners lived by an urban
trade: as sandal makers, fuel sellers, potters, mat weavers, carriers, or any
of the multitude of services required in a busy metropolis. Fishermen and
fowlers and hunters and the small-scale collectors of insect eggs and
amphibia worked the lake's margins, but despite the intensely exploited
environment and the steady contribution of the chinampas, the city was
dependent on imported foodstuffs, some of it from outside the valley,
brought in by trade or tribute. The exotic raw materials which supplied its
famous craftworkers with feathers or cotton or precious stones were
drawn in either as tribute, or by activating the network of the *pochteca* or
long-distance merchants, a network which increasingly found its centre in
Tenochtitlan. The tribute warehouses were stocked with the things which
most pleased the gods, and with the reserves of food, the cloaks, tobacco,
cacao (chocolatl) and items of adornment the ruler distributed to those he
judged deserving of reward.[11]
    Despite the difficulties inseparable from its setting – constrictions of
space, dangerous seasonal variations in the level of the lake waters, a
chronic shortage of wood and fuel – the lake-borne city enjoyed some
notable advantages. If many goods were carried on human backs, more
were moved by canoe, giving Tenochtitlan a crucial advantage in supply

over its neighbours. It also enjoyed the advantage of cleanliness, despite the density of settlement: small latrines built out over moored canoes allowed the collection and cartage of human ordure to enrich the chinampas, while water boats delivered fresh water from the aqueduct to the individual households.

The canoe men were possibly free-lance, like the carriers, but their activities still fell under the watchful supervision of the city and local administrators.[12] Although labour was cheap in Tenochtitlan, the poor hiring themselves out for service in the marketplace, the labour which cleaned the city and kept it working, was unpaid. Each quarter had its own administration, but the key social, religious, and administrative units were one step down at the ward level. The calpullis, mysterious though they are in the detail of their organization, appear to have resembled parishes in a singularly active system of parish government, given the centrality of their religious institutions for the imaginative and physical activity of their members.[13] Each was responsible for its own maintenance, with lads from the local warrior house charged with keeping the canals dredged and the streets swept. Each also owed specified services to the central city administration. Nobles worked their extra-urban mainland estates with resident labourers or *mayeques*, whose fully dependent status exempted them from tribute, but the commoners of each calpulli discharged their *tequitl* or tribute obligation in the form of labour: by construction work for the city, regular or rotational service in the temples or the palace, or the supply of firewood or foodstuffs or other necessities to designated officials. Specialist calpullis like those of the skilled craftsmen paid their tribute as a tax on the sale of their products, while the merchant calpullis met their obligations through levies on goods and the responsibility for the good order of the marketplace. The fulfilment of these local duties was overseen by local lords, who took their orders from the palace, but who were connected to their calpullis by traditional ties. Palaces, those crucial centres for redistribution, were usually supported directly by rotated tribute obligations: for example, the town of Tepepolco was responsible for supplying the royal court at Texcoco with the food required for seventy days of each year: no small obligation.[14]

The system ideally worked with minimal central intervention; indeed it is sometimes represented as if it functioned with a tautness which would be envied by the most ambitiously interventionist regimes today. Much of that impression comes from the laconic and idealizing style of the sources. In fact there is much we do not know about the city's workings, with even the structure of the calpullis now being admitted to be obscure.[15] Initially they were probably territorially based corporations administered by councils of elders, with marked internal divisions, but with some residual (if perhaps fictive) kinship associations. By the sixteenth century shared land and the notion of a shared past had become more a matter of sentiment than a historically based actuality, but the sentiment remained potent. There were variations on the theme: in the merchant calpullis, where land had never been an issue, the kinship note sounded strongly, while the *tecpanpouhque*, or 'palace folk', presumably an ad hoc and easily extended collection of individuals, must have found their defining sense of community in their prestigious service. Even by the last days of the empire the calpullis remained the crucial administrative units for the organization for war, internal tribute, and labour obligations to temple and city, and for the redistribution of some fraction of externally derived wealth. They must also have defined a powerful sense of home locality for the city's inhabitants. (A possible sub-unit of the calpulli, the shadowy *tlaxilacalli*, which could well designate a smaller cluster of streets with all its inhabitants personally known one to another, will be discussed in the next chapter.[16]) However, the calpullis were firmly subordinated to the central administration, their elders minor administrators of the state, and their lords Janus-faced: enjoying high local prestige, retaining local ties and local residences, yet looking towards the palace for their official position and authority.[17]

3

For all the magnificent solidity of the imperial city, and for all the sleekness of its administration, it was a recent creation – in the Mexica telling of it less than two hundred years old. In that telling two 'histories' intertwined: one which brushed actual events, the other speaking of Mexica legends, dreams, and aspirations. The first offers a skeletal account of the uncertain movements of a particular group displaced from their old territories some time in the twelfth century, part of the general migratory movement which followed the decline and fall of the military empire of the Toltecs at Tula, or 'Tollan', as the old stories named it, which had guarded the northern marches against the tough nomads of the steppes. There are intimations of frosts and famines presaging that fall, and the Mexica were only one of many peoples (although a small and belated one) drawn towards the more favoured and protected zone of the valley.

Some accounts recalled that long ago the Mexica had issued forth from Chicomoztoc, or 'Seven Caves', where they had lived among dangerous animals in a thorny wilderness. (This origin in the cavernous womb of the earth with its nomad overtones was a beginning shared by the many peoples who later entered the valley, as indeed more widely in Mesoamerica.[18]) The Mexica's distinctive history had begun at Aztlan, the 'Place of Whiteness', where they lived surrounded by water on an island in a lake. Then they took canoe to the lakeshore, and began their wanderings, faithfully following the sacred medicine bundle which was their god Huitzilopochtli, 'Hummingbird of the South', carried before them by his four priestly 'god-bearers'. In times of crisis he would speak to his priests in his fast-twittering voice, giving instructions, offering rebukes, and they directed their followers accordingly.[19]

The wanderers paused briefly at Culhuacan, 'Curved Mountain', where Huitzilopochtli spoke to his people, and then went on to the first place of temporary settlement, where (as was to be their custom) a temple to Huitzilopochtli was erected. At another place a mysteriously broken tree was taken as a sign of evil omen: the group disputed and divided, and the fraction designated the 'Mexica', as Huitzilopochtli ordained they be called, proceeded alone. They celebrated the first New Fire Ceremony of the migration at Coatepec, 'Snake Mountain', which stood for or was Earth Mother herself. There the hummingbird god was reborn out of the Earth as the Sun, triumphing over his siblings the Moon and the Innumerable Stars.

The tale of the rebirth perhaps masks the transfiguration of an actual human leader into a deity.[20] Certainly from this point the continuing story comes close to our notion of 'history', plotting the years spent in various places, recording the leaders, sketching the Mexica's political vicissitudes after their entry into the valley. When the Mexica at last saw the broad lakes and well-cultivated lands of the valley they already spoke Nahuatl, the dominant tongue of central Mexico, and somewhere along the way they had learnt to follow the same round of agricultural festivals practised by longer-settled peoples. The polity they entered is best thought of as passionately parochial: a mosaic of small city-states, each determinedly separate, each ruled by its own tlatoani to whom all its sub-units owed loyalty and service, each with its own account of its past and its own 'tribal' deity as emblem of that past and custodian of the future, each petty state jostling to exact rather than yield tribute and deference from its neighbours. Men described themselves in terms of their towns, the visible symbols of their corporate identity: as Texcocans or Xochimilcans or Chalcans or Tlatelolcans. In that land of wars and forced migrations, mixed populations were not rare, but the outsider group usually lived in a distinct section or ward of the adopting town, with their separateness acknowledged. We are tuned to see the horizontals of class or the verticals of gender as marking out the most significant because the most pro-foundly experienced social groupings. In central Mexico primordial loy-alties clustered around devotion to a particular place and past, and a deity emblematic of both. They were expressed and maintained by a most de-termined and constant marking-off of one's own group from all others.[21]

In such a competitive milieu wanderers like the Mexica found a cold welcome. But (at least retrospectively) the drum-beat of their great desti-ny was sounding ever more loudly. For a time they had a foothold at Chapultepec, the 'Hill of the Grasshopper', only to be driven out by the people called the Tepanecans, and their ruler sacrificed. The Mexica had found another 'Culhuacan' in the valley, a city claiming the legitimacy the closest genealogical and political links with the Toltecs of Tollan could give it. The Culhuans were ready to exchange their protection for Mexica services as mercenaries for a time, but once again the Mexica were driven away, this time to a swampy islet in Lake Texcoco.

At this nadir of their fortunes, Huitzilopochtli at last gave them a sign, or so they were to claim in the days of their greatness. There, once again in a place surrounded by water and thick with pale reeds, 'Aztlan' re-found, they saw a great eagle perched upon the cactus which bore the red-fleshed nopal fruit which represented the stylized human heart in the painted books they carried with them. Scattered around the eagle were the bones and precious feathers of many bright birds, as brilliant and various as those which had once abounded in Tollan. Seeing the tattered refugees, he bowed his lordly head in deference. 'And the god called out to them, he said to them, "O Mexicans, it shall be there !"'

Huitzilopochtli had led them to their new, god-destined place. The people accordingly raised his first modest temple at Tenochtitlan, the 'Place of the Fruit of the Cactus', and settled to seek the glory he had promised them. They had searched for the place of their city for more than two hundred years, four times burning the old 'Bundle of Years' in the course of their wanderings, and marking the next fifty-two year 'bundle' by the New Fire Ceremony. The fifth New Fire Ceremony of the migration would be celebrated in Tenochtitlan. So myth enclosed history in its golden order.[22]

With time the Mexica contrived to win a narrow foothold in the aggressive politics of the valley as tributaries and occasional fighters for the dominant city of Azcapotzalco, but their ambitions were closely monitored: when they took the step of choosing as their ruler a prince of Culhuacan of a lineage which could claim Toltec blood, a choice which hinted at their pretensions, the ruler of Azcapotzalco doubled their tribute. (Huitzilopochtli, equal to the challenge, is said to have invented the 'floating garden' of the chinampas to meet the overlord city's demands.)[23] A hundred years later, in 1428, the Triple Alliance was born: the Mexica, under the rule of the extraordinary tlatoani Itzcoatl, 'Obsidian Snake', and in alliance with Texcoco and Tacuba, challenged and overthrew Azcapotzalco, and distributed its spoils and imperial tributes between the victors. A generation later, with Tenochtitlan and its allies controlling most of the valley towns as tributaries, allies, or (more commonly) both, the first Moctezoma sent his forces out to conquer beyond the valley. By 1502, with the accession of his grandson Moctezoma the Younger, the Mexica, as dominant partners of the Triple Alliance, were apparently unchallengeable masters of a tribute empire which controlled the tropical riches of the Gulf Coast and stretched to the Pacific. To the northwest the Tarascan Indians of present-day Michoacan defied all attacks, but to the south Tehuantepec was theirs, and Mexica merchants had penetrated Guatemala. Along the furthest frontiers Mexica merchants, together with carefully devised tribute requirements imposed on frontier provinces, drew exotic materials and crafted objects from regions which still escaped the tributary net. The transportable wealth of all this great territory flowed into Tenochtitlan.

Much of the wealth of empire was spent to embellish the city as the centre, the symbol and the expression of empire, as the Mexica laid formal claim to be the legitimate heirs of the Toltecs of Tollan, those supremely noble, exemplary and wise craftsmen, and to their legendary and mythically abundant imperial domains, where the cotton grew coloured and bright birds flew, where tribute was given without coercion, and where there was neither hunger nor sadness.[24] There is now close to consensus among scholars that the Mexica sought to exact from towns in their immediate vicinity not so much maximum tribute as acquiescence, preferably voluntary, in that Mexica claim to Toltec legitimacy. It is true that the lake city vigorously secured what its managers defined as necessities: supplies of fresh water, timber and fuel, and foodstuffs beyond those drawn in by the thriving market. In 1473 the Mexica destroyed any potential counter-claim to greatness which might be made by their sister city Tlatelolco, extinguishing its independence, replacing its ruler (thrown down his own temple steps) by a military governor, filling its shrines with rubbish, and reducing it to a fifth ward of Tenochtitlan. (The Tlatelolcan sense of separateness survived, as is clear from the systematically pro-Tlatelolcan tilt of the native account of the final struggle against the Spaniards in 1521, nonetheless the Tlatelolcans fought shoulder to shoulder with the men of Tenochtitlan as 'Mexica' in those last desperate days.) But the definitions of 'necessity' remained relatively modest, as did the 'requests for assistance' made to targeted towns before the initiation of hostilities. Even allied cities were routinely called on to signal their submission by the supply of labour and materials for some Mexica project, be it the construction of an aqueduct, the embellishment of a temple, or the presentation of a batch of a town's own captives to enrich the human offering at a Mexica ceremony.

It is worth taking time over this oddly based polity, crucial as it is for an understanding of the city's workings, as for the process of its final destruction. Tenochtitlan was no Rome, despite the magnificence of its monuments, the steady inflow of tribute goods, and their spectacular consumption in a state-financed theatre.[25] Subjugation did not mean incorporation. There was no significant bureaucracy in the Mexica 'empire', and few garrisons either. Marriage alliances linked the leading dynasties, while lesser local rulers were typically left in place and effectively autonomous, at least for as long as their towns delivered the agreed tribute to the imperial city.[26] Even in those rare cases when the defeated ruler was killed, the dynasty was usually allowed to survive. But if local rulers spent months in the Mexica capital, they did not thereby become Mexica, and when their military contingents were called on to fight for the Triple Alliance they did so under their own leaders and banners. The 'empire' was an acrobats' pyramid, a precarious structure of the more privileged lording it over the less, with those poised on the highest level triumphant, but nervously attentive to any premonitory shift or shuffle from below.[27]

For towns beyond the valley Mexica imperial designs were typically signalled by a request for participation in a Mexica project, acquiescence implying subordination.[28] Those who felt themselves strong enough would refuse, perhaps indicating their refusal by killing or maltreating Mexica ambassadors, merchants, or tribute gatherers. Then they knew to watch the roads and arm for war, and to try to persuade neighbouring towns that the stories of the ferocity of the warriors of the Triple Alliance were exaggerated. They could hope that distance or other demands might deflect Mexica attentions, or that a coalescing of tributary towns could give them victory. They could expect a wave of warriors, bloody punishment, and a steep increase in tribute demands. But even with the most impudent recalcitrants the aim of psychological dominance seems not to be forgotten. In the reign of Moctezoma the Elder the people of Cuetlaxtla, already tribute payers but lured into defiance by the promise of aid from the independent province of Tlaxcala, killed and then gleefully mocked the bodies of Mexica emissaries sent to investigate the interruption in tribute payments. (The bodies were stuffed with straw, set up in seats of honour, and paid deliriously extravagant reverence: a most thorough-going snub to Mexica pretensions.) After their military punishment the town's tribute was doubled, which was burdensome enough. But the townsfolk were also obliged to provide a number of live snakes and other animals, including (obviously outrageously rare) white-furred ocelots.[29] 'Symbolic' is possibly the wrong word to use of this kind of punitive strategy: wriggling miserably around in a snake-infested cave clutching one's snake-catching stick must have brought the might of Moctezoma very near.

Given the atomistic nature of Mexican political culture, such a system was durable enough, at least until the Spanish intrusion. The Mexica sought dominance for the wealth it brought, but they were more intent on converting temporary control through occasional military terror to something very much more permanent, voluntary and thorough-going: the acceptance of the Mexica account of themselves and their destiny. Some of the tribute required had no instrumental value, but was rather exemplary of the scope of Toltec (and so Mexica) domination. Diego Durán reported that 'vassals even paid tribute in centipedes, scorpions and spiders. The Aztecs were the Lords of All Creation; everything belonged to them. Everything was theirs! From the coast came everything that could be found in the sea; scallop shells . . . large and small sea snails, curious fish bones . . . stones from the sea', as well as the turtle shells and pearls and amber which make more immediate economic sense to us.[30] (As usual, Durán gets it partly wrong: the Mexica did not and could not consider themselves the lords of 'Creation', but only lords of men.) The recent excavations of the offering caches sealed away in several layers of the Great Temple (the Mexica expanded their temples in onion-layers, a boon for archeologists) add their own testimony. The caches have been revealed to contain a great range of natural objects – fishes and shells from both coasts, whole cadavers of crocodiles and jaguars – as well as dazzling products of human skill drawn from all the regions of the Mexica domains: a material map of imperial power. We glimpse the same lavish inclusiveness in Díaz's account of Moctezoma's 'collection' of exotic animals and birds, and the care given to their quartering.[31] Cortés initially noted that 'all the things of which Mutezuma [sic] has ever heard, both on land or in the sea, they have modelled, very realistically, either in gold and silver or in jewels or feathers, and with such perfection that they seem almost real.' Then he refined the scope. It was the creatures of Moctezoma's domains which were replicated with such perfection: 'Can there be anything more magnificent than that this barbarian lord should have all the things to be found under heavens in his domain fashioned in gold and silver and jewels and feathers; and so realistic in gold and silver that no smith in the world could have done better?'[32] I will return to this passion for representation and what the Mexica meant by it at a later point, but all the objects, from the caches, from the tribute, from the palace collections, seem to speak in their range, diversity, and inclusiveness to one notion: the steady flow into the new imperial city of the bounty of far lands as the in-gathering of Tollan's wealth, dispersed in an act of reverse magic by the culture hero Quetzalcoatl Topiltzin before his self-exile.

Whatever the precise balance, which is disputed, the metropolis was clearly dependent on imported foodstuffs despite its sophisticated system of chinampa agriculture, while the tribute goods we would designate 'luxury' – rare feathers and furs, precious stones, gold – were essential to its growing corps of skilled craftsmen, whose products lured yet more food and raw materials into its markets. But the flow of goods was as necessary to the city's social and political functioning as to its economy: Tenochtitlan had an insatiable appetite for 'ritual consumables'. The struggle for authority in the valley and beyond deployed violence, but it was equally a struggle in competitive display, of pageant against pageant – a struggle which the Mexica, with their sumptuous spending of the wealth of empire, repeatedly, totally, and triumphantly won.

The Mexica made their double (and antithetical) claims to the legitimacy of their domination first through conquest, the gift of their god Huitzilo-pochtli (now elevated beyond his initial tribal affiliation to become the God of the Sun), and then through the grandeur of his city: a grandeur which established them as the legitimate heirs of the Toltecs.[33] Itzcoatl had destroyed the Mexica painted histories after the victory over Azcapotzalco, to replace them with others which recognized and celebrated Mexica glory. This was not the crass realpolitik it is too often represented to be.[34] Our public and professional devotion to 'history' as a factual account of past events held small interest for the Mexica or their neighbours, all of whom freely wrote and rewrote their histories with none of our unease. Those histories were not only esoteric, but exegetical. They could be reframed, rethought, repainted in accordance with the clues yielded by the progres-sive illumination of unfolding events. But the ancient genealogy the Mexica were seeking to establish was to be achieved primarily through works: through victories and the performances and material structures which were the manifestations of those victories. The magnificent city of Tenochtitlan was at once the forced fruit and the massive proof of a late-dawning greatness.

4

John Berger has written a few remarkable pages in which he contrasts the experiences and perceptions of peasant life, with its naked exposure to unsought change, with the lives of modern, or indeed any, urbanites, insulated as he presents them to be against the flux of days and seasons and the terrible randomness of fate. He writes of peasants' obdurate reliance on the wisdom of those who had gone before, following a narrow path of precept and example beaten out by generations of feet: a path which threads its way through known dangers, with the walkers ever watchful for the unknown. He explains their devout attachment to routine as their response to the furious uncertainty of lives exposed to the vagaries of nature and the exactions of overlords.[35] The Mexica, or most of them, lived in abundance most of the time. Yet they represented themselves as living on a razor's edge, or, as they put it, toiling along a windswept ridge, an abyss on either hand. If their great inaugurations and dedications of major monuments were primarily directed outwards, to impress potential rivals, it is worth noting that the major ritual cycle of this imperial urban people was dominated by observances to do with agriculture, and marked most precisely the movement of the seasons. Throughout Mesoamerica there was a general notion of man's tenuous place in the natural order: a recognition of the intimate interdependence of men and maize, and the problematical relationship of each with the givers of rain and growth. But the precariousness of the relationship was not usually insisted upon in so untempered a way. The Yucatec Maya of the early sixteenth century, for example, assumed a notably more equable and manipulable relationship between men and the deities on whom they depended.[36] Why this perception of instability in the largest, finest and most powerful city in Mesoamerica?

One of the most attractive brief books on the Mexica and their descendants in the valley has named them the 'Sons of the Shaking Earth.'[37] Mexico is an unstable land, whose smoking volcanoes are and were notable features of the landscape. The valley's weather has a histrionic quality: a hush, a sudden rage of wind, the tearing crash of thunder, and then the rain deluges down; a sun like a bronze gong. In Mexica times the wide shallow lakes which received the valley drainage retreated and shrank under the blows of that sun, but they could swirl into sudden flood with the rains, and always pulsed with their hidden springs and whirlpools. I am not suggesting that a distinctive religion arises from a collective response to the weather – although an Anglican serenity would seem to be precluded – but that the catastrophic account the Mexica gave of 'natural' forces was descriptive of their performance.

For a people who recognized their ultimate dependence on agriculture the valley had other disturbing attributes. Maize is a hardy crop, and yields abundantly under most conditions. In normal years, it cropped well in the valley. Showers in April would soften the ground for May plantings. Then, in the summer months of June to October, the great thunderheads would shawl the shoulders of the mountains for much of the day, leaving the sun on the crop, to roll in and dump their abundant water towards evening. The maize ear, well formed by September, could mature and then dry for safe storage through October and November. All this in 'normal' years. But the valley rains were erratic, and then men might see the maize wither before it sprouted, or bleach and die without the relief of rain. Only in the Rain God's tender paradise did the rains always fall and the crops always fruit.[38] If the rains came late, planting could be delayed, with no evil consequences provided the maturation period could be extended. But autumn in the high valley brought the threat of frost, and tardy rains combined with early frosts could destroy an entire planting. That disastrous combination occurred for three years in succession in the reign of the first Moctezoma. With the valley densely populated there was very little slack, and stores were quickly depleted. A tribute empire and a tribute city exist through an actual or assumed capacity to extort. With that capacity sapped by local hunger, city and empire faced extinction. As the famine worsened Moctezoma released his people from their duty, to seek their lives where they could, and lords sold their children as slaves to men from more securely abundant regions. (Local merchants took the chance to buy men and women at bargain prices, which the people did not forget.)

Tenochtitlan was saved by good rains and a full harvest, but the Great Famine of the year One Rabbit made clear to an urban people largely dependent on tribute and the market the fragility of complex human arrangements in time of dearth, and that 'natural' bounty is never unequivocal. At the yearly harvest festival and the welcoming of the maize deity as Young Lord Maize Cob, the Mexica, with their extraordinary flair for the compressed statement, set upon the maize-god's head the serrated cap of Itztlacohuihqui, 'Curved Obsidian Knife', the God of Frost.[39]

Berger has further suggested that urbanites draw security from the physical monuments of a city; that palaces, warehouses, temples, houses of record speak in their mass and ordered contents of the supremacy of men over nature, creatures and things, and of the continuity and solidity of human institutions.[40] Despite the density of its human population, much of the landscape of the Valley of Mexico remained lightly marked by human intervention; digging-stick cultivation does little to disturb natural contours and groundcover, and the wattle and mud structures of agriculturalists melt easily back into the earth. But there were great visible transformations wrought by men: to the south through Lake Chalco and Xochimilco the swamplands transformed into chinampa gardens to supply the markets of Tenochtitlan; to the east the great dike; the thick lacework of cities edging the lakeside; above all the city itself, standing where no city had stood before. Built out from its original rocky island on land reclaimed from the lake, its canals and streets running in clean parallels, with its crisp square shapes and fine causeways, its pyramids suavely mimicking the sacred mountains, and so much of its mass and splendour created in the memory of living men, Tenochtitlan could appear as a triumphant testament to human endeavour.

Nonetheless, the Mexica knew what a vulnerable construct it was. The dikes and sluice-gates holding back the western waters from Lake Texcoco provided a modest and adequate system for seasonal flood control, but it was also a long step back from a larger and failed intervention. When Moctezoma the Younger's predecessor attempted to bring the spring waters of Coyoacan to the city in great aqueducts, Chalchihuitlicue, 'Jade Skirt', the goddess of the lake waters, had risen in fury, surging out of the constricting walls to sweep through the city, while desperate men struggled to placate her anger and break down the structures they had built to tame her.

The city had survived that peril, but its great monuments, for all their solidity, for all their claims to the sublime security of the eternal, were and were known to be fragile edifices. There were other dangers, invisible but constant, corollary to the city's greatness. The Mexica appetite for the most conspicuous consumption of the riches of empire in ritual extravaganzas was fuelled by the identification of those great performances not only as representations of Mexica power, but as actualizations of Mexica authority. Or so they intended. It is no easy matter to persuade men of a different affiliation that they are permanently inferior, and not only must but ought to crack their sinews for your particular glory. Self-interest or fear could keep the tribute flowing in. When particular towns demurred they could be roughly reminded of their duty, and the substantial benefits of participation in the Triple Alliance were sufficiently well distributed within the valley to keep the proximate towns sufficiently content.[41] But city dwelling under such conditions could not provide Berger's sense of existential security. The Mexica's world ended at the seas; to come from a far and unknown place was to come from 'beyond the mists'. The known landscape was thickly encrusted with memories of conflict, betrayal, and isolation: the peoples of central Mexico acted their dramas on a very small stage. All around them the Mexica could see the locations of the last phases along their migration route: the cities which had humiliated them, the cities they had defeated, the cities brought to wary alliance. These were anxious intimacies, where proximity could only fuel rivalry and exacerbate difference. When relations between Tenochtitlan and its sister city Tlatelolco had already dangerously deteriorated, with the populations inflamed one against the other, the lords of Tlatelolco complained of their treatment: 'The [Tenocha] believe that we are of an alien lineage. They do not know we are [Mexica] like them, relatives who originated in the same place as they did. What new thing is this with which they wish to offend us?'[42] But it was the closeness which constituted the offence: as we will see, the Mexica were particularly wary of challenge from within the immediate group.

Tlatelolco had to be destroyed, precisely because it stood too close, but in the contest politics of Mexico the unreduced 'other' was a crucial player in the Mexica theatre of power: as potential victim, exquisitely attentive rival, and eternal adversary. On great occasions – the inauguration of a ruler, the dedication of a monument – when the Mexica slaughtered their enemies in their scores and hundreds, it was the presence of actually or potentially hostile rulers which made the slaughter meaningful. But it was Tlaxcala, the resolutely independent province beyond the mountains, which was given a role as much a product of the empire and Mexica pretensions as Tenochtitlan itself. Other Nahuatl-speaking cities could be recruited into the Mexica system, making their token submission, participating in the campaigns, taking their suitably modest share of the loot. Tlaxcala was firmly excluded. Tlaxcala's finest warriors as victims lent lustre to Tenochtitlan's killing festivals, while the possibility of death before a Tlaxcalan temple kept Mexica warriors at an edge for war. They were essential players in the Mexica drama, cast as the exemplary enemy, the eternal vis-à-vis for Mexica self-imaging. (Necessary products of the system, they were in the end to bring the system down, providing Cortés with his only secure because unambivalent allies.)

Even within Tenochtitlan the tension remained. If many strangers came to the city only to die, others walked its streets as pedlars or carriers or agents or ambassadors; given the inescapable cosmopolitanism of an imperial centre, they were a constant and necessary presence. All were marked as outsiders by speech, dress, and comportment. Their presence raised problems which went well beyond the policing of casual visitors (some of those 60,000 milling around in the market). Despite its strength, there was a dread that the lake city was vulnerable to secret attack. 'Informers' were especially feared: for a Mexica to be known to have given such men sanctuary meant destruction of his house and all who lived within it. Those fears were kept alive by the constant wash of people in and out of the city. The priests kept their night watches on the dark hills, and the great fire at the palace was never allowed to die. Tenochtitlan's guard could never be lowered: 'the ruler commanded that the rulers of the youths, the brave warriors, and all the youths, each day, at night, should sing and dance, so that all the cities which lay about Mexico should hear. For the ruler slept not, nor any Mexican.'[43] And all this at the peak of imperial power.

Some strangers came not to trade but to settle. The migratory group which had founded Tenochtitlan comprised about fifteen calpullis, with their councils of elders administering their internal affairs. By 1519, the year of the Spaniards' coming, there were perhaps eighty. We do not know how many of the eighty had been produced by fission of Mexica groups, but some at least were grafts from outside, and were probably ethnically distinct. The salt people, for example, who had worked the shifting margins of Lake Texcoco for generations, found themselves engulfed by the city's growth, while specialist groups like the long-distance merchants, goldworkers and featherworkers we see living in their separate wards, and largely endogamous, had probably been attracted to the Mexica city as its wealth increased. How were such disparate groups and individuals, with their disparate loyalties, to be integrated into the expanding city? How was the terrifying, essential, casual permeability of the city boundaries to be borne?

5

In part, by insistence on difference.[44] In crowded Mesoamerica local difference had always been expressed through specialized products: garb, ornaments, hair styles, dances.[45] The 'flowery wars', those formal battles arranged for the taking of warrior victims worthy of the most elevated sacrifice, were fought between the Nahuatl-speakers of the three towns of the Triple Alliance and the transmontane towns of Huejotzingo, Tlaxcala, and Cholula. There the marking-off was brusquely effected by violence. But difference was also defined through art. The Mexica constantly dramatized the otherness of others, presenting them through a spectrum of exemplary and monitory types in casual sayings ('O thou Otomí, thou blockhead!'), in songs and dances and details of costumes, even in whole rituals 'borrowed' from other peoples. A Mexica dance group about to perform a dance belonging to the Gulf Coast Huaxtecs affected a most particular style and costume: 'if the song was to be intoned in the manner of the Huaxtecs, their speech was imitated, and their head-dresses were taken, with which to imitate them in coloring their hair yellow; and the masks [had] arrow marks [painted] on the face, noses pierced like jug handles, teeth filed, and conical heads. And they [were clad] only in their capes': a most memorable caricature of Huaxtecan weirdness.[46] Those watching the performance could context the caricature: they knew the land of the Huaxtec people to be steamy but gloriously fertile, and the people to be wearers of fine woven garments, but wild for all that: the men, negligible as warriors, were headhunters, given to sorcery, notorious drunkards, and dispensed with breechclouts (their leader had thrown his away when deep in his fifth cup of pulque, the fermented juice of the maguey cactus). Both sexes, feckless in so much else, were ingenious and energetic in matters sexual.[47] The Mexica deployed emblematic Huaxtecans in their ceremonies; Toci, 'Our Grandmother', the fertile Earth, was accompanied in her harvest festival by an escort of semi-nude 'Huaxtec' males as icons of male sexuality.[48] If the Huaxtecans were not much regarded in the sterner world of war, the repertoire of otherness was drawn upon by the military hierarchy to name its own warrior ranks, as with those dubbed 'Otomi' in recognition of the simplicity of the namesake people's valour. (That the 'real' Otomi were also regarded as uncouth, vain, and improvident seems only to have enriched the association, these élite warriors being regarded as the berserkers of the army.)[49]

Set off against the whole spectrum of negatives stood the legendary Toltecs, with their sky-blue sandals and immaculate ways: the men of wisdom, all of whose works were beautiful. They were claimed as ancestors of 'all the Nahua', all those who 'speak clearly, not the speakers of a barbarous tongue'. Among their putative descendants the Mexica had marked themselves out by their early ferocity and their success in the savage game of war, but as the city grew they also, more tremulously, sought to identify themselves as the heirs of these men who had made a world through art.

To understand the darker consequences of that superficially elevating and reassuring identification, it is necessary to grasp something of how the Mexica understood time. The Mexica, like Mesoamericans generally, knew that Four 'Suns', or world-creations, had preceded the one in which we and the Mexica live, which is the Fifth and last Sun. Within each Sun, time was understood as multidimensional and eternally recurrent. Men attempted to comprehend its movements through a complex system of intermeshing time counts, the two most important being the solar or seasonal calendar, the *xiuitl*, comprised of eighteen 'months' of twenty days, ending with five days of ill omen, and the *tonalpoalli*, the ritual or sacred calendar, of twenty 'signs' in fixed sequence interacting with the numbers one to thirteen, as in 'One Lizard' or 'Twelve Death'. (It was this calendar, along with others more esoteric, which provided the basis for the *tonalamatl*, or 'sacred book of days', used by trained priestly interpreters for augury, and to plot the probable destiny of a baby named on a particular daysign. As each day-name and number was presided over by a particular deity, this was a complex business.)

The two calendars completed their permutations over a fifty-two year cycle, so constituting a 'Xiumolpilli', or a Bundle of Years. Under such a system, each 'day' is not the outcome of the days preceding it: it has its own character, indicated by its complex name derived from the time counts, and is unique within its Bundle of Years. It is also more closely connected with the similarly named days which had occurred and will occur in other Year Bundles than with those clustered about it in its own bundle. (Note how the word 'bundle' denies any specific arrangement of these unique items. In the visual representations we have, in stone or paint, the Year 'Bundles' are just that: round bundles tied with rope, like cords of wood.) Thus particular events were understood as unfolding in a dynamic process modelled by some past situation. This was no simple replication: the complex character of the controlling time was capable of manifesting itself in various ways. So events remained problematical in their experiencing, with innovation and desperate effort neither precluded nor inhibited.

Nonetheless, the great patterns, however obscured from human perceptions, were known to repeat themselves. Such an understanding carried sobering implications, and must have lent a dreamlike aspect to the city shimmering above its lake waters, for those who had built it as for those who observed it. If the survival of this Fifth world itself was of fixed if unknown duration, the period of the dominance of Tenochtitlan, also unknown, was also fixed. The claim of sacred favour grew less problematical with each new victory and with each embellishment to the city. But for how long would the city stand? And there were inner uncertainties. It is said that in about 1450, as his successes multiplied, the first Moctezoma sent out his magicians to carry the news of Mexica triumphs back to the home place of Aztlan. (The journey, involving transformations and testing adventures, was as much through time as through space.) At last in the presence of their kinsmen-ancestors – themselves as they once were – the envoys were berated for their soft and luxurious ways, which had replaced the simple virtues and physical hardihood of earlier times. Led before the ancient woman who was said to be their god's mother, they found the dazzling gifts which displayed the wealth of empire ignored: she spoke only of the inevitable eclipse of their greatness.[50] While this account has a whiff of colonial construction about it, contributing as it does to the 'auguries' of the Spanish coming which proliferated after the conquest, it also indicates Mexica ambivalence regarding the costs of their swift promotion to the seductions of wealth and the uncertainties of power.

The Toltecs had had small need of empire. In their time their high cold northern land was remembered as tropical, where cotton and cacao grew and parrots flew among brilliant flowers. Realizing the imperialists' dream of the uncoerced submission of lesser peoples, who desired only to contribute to their glory, their energies could flow directly into art.[51] They had invented medicine and featherworking. They were incomparable architects, and so wise that they could read the secrets of the earth, uncovering mines of turquoise, amber, crystal, amethyst. They understood the stars and their movements. Yet their glory had been a passing thing. Men still lived at 'Tollan', and indeed paid tribute to the Mexica, but the Toltecs had gone, leaving only their marvellous traces: the stone serpent columns, with the head resting on the ground, the tail and rattles above; the potsherds and figurines and the turquoise and jade armbands exposed wherever the earth was disturbed.[52] Greatness was a heady possibility, and that greatness had been perilously achieved, but one thing was certain: decline was inevitable. If a catastrophic view of the world was commonplace in Mesoamerica, there was existential verification for it in the valley.

6

As for the social miracle: while Tenochtitlan's sudden wealth earned the envious admiration of outsiders, it also brought internal tensions. The city had been founded in about 1325, a miserable collection of mud huts scraped together on a swampy island by a clutch of miserable refugees. A hundred years later the Mexica fought their way out of subject status in alliance with other subject towns by defeating their overlord city. Fifty years later again and they were ready to push beyond the valley in the quest for wider control and tribute. Then came fifty years of imperial splendour and the massive elaboration of the vision of the city. And then the Spaniards came, to destroy city and people and empire all together. If we think in generational terms, a man whose grandfather had fought as a hireling in another city's wars in the Mexica's early days in the valley would himself have seen the glory of their achieved empire, and his son watched its destruction. It is a brief and brilliant trajectory, entailing large shifts in experience; if not the 'tribal democracy' replaced by 'an aristocratic and imperialist monarchy', as Jacques Soustelle put it many years ago, still formidable, from the relative egalitarianism and known neighbours of the early days of settlement and struggle to the inequalities and social distances of the city in its maturity.[53]

Those inequalities were dramatized by jealously policed sumptuary laws; by differential systems of law for noble and commoner (nobles were punished more severely than commoners for the same offence, which rebukes our expectations); by a tribute obligation on commoners; most bleakly by the fact that even in years of good harvest, with the tribute warehouses full, some Mexica went hungry while others lived high. War captives and tribute slaves were not used for labour in Tenochtitlan: there were needy locals enough for the roughest work. Cortés took it as a final proof of Indian civility that the poor begged from the rich in city streets in Mexico, just as they did in Spain.[54]

There were other pressures. Given the flight of status to the warrior, declared indispensable for empire, there was increased pressure on all Mexica males to commit themselves to that strenuous ideal. A city of warriors, some of them professionals kept at a pitch for war and trained to edgy pride, could be an uncomfortable place to live, even without the inflow of strangers, the deepening social divisions, and the flux of individual fortune in the imperial milieu. How could their high edge be maintained without inciting them to civil depredations? How could large transformations of expectation and experience be contained? What devices could be invented and what sentiments invoked to hold the whole fissive conglomerate together?

That is, obviously, a complex question, with only preliminary answers to some of its aspects to be suggested here. The 'when' of the political transformation of the city is conventionally placed in 1428, at the time of the Mexica's emancipation from their condition of dependence. When the spoils of war and the tribute from other towns subject to the conquered overlord city came into the hands of the Mexica ruler, he chose to distribute them not to the collectivities of the calpullis, but to specially distinguished warriors in the form of offices and titles, with attendant privileges and worked lands, so, it is said, creating a nobility and a bureaucracy at a blow.[55] My own unheroic view is that we know too little of those early days, with the surviving records fragmented, garbled, all of them partisan and some of them wilfully misleading, ever to know the when of it. The 'how' is less problematical, given the devices we see at work in the mature city.

One was the elaboration and extension of the traditional reward system of a warrior society. We are familiar with the songs of praise for the triumphant Crow or Cheyenne warrior; the presentation of devices and sobriquets denoting achievement; the investment in a particular office by the formal presentation of a sacred garment, and all this before a most attentive local audience, with both passions and interests deeply engaged. We do not expect to encounter this sort of thing in an urban milieu sustaining an imperial bureaucracy, but that is what we find in Tenochtitlan.

Such a system requires the maintenance of the reality of the local community. J. G. Peristiany has seen honour and shame as the constant preoccupations of individuals in 'small-scale, exclusive societies where face-to-face personal as opposed to anonymous relations are of paramount importance and where the social personality of the actor is as significant as his office.'[56] Despite a rapidly growing and diversifying population, the Mexica state contrived to enlist those individual preoccupations in its own service – if that is not to imply too much deliberation – by nurturing that face-to-face quality. The ties of the advancing individual – warrior, noble, musician, ballplayer – remained with his particular calpulli, and the award and display of the marks of honour and office, a highly public and ceremonial affair, was also a highly local one. We have seen the ruling dynasty 'appointing' particular lords to supervise and control particular calpulli, but although those lords took their orders from the palace, their local attachments were long-term and real. There is a general notion that the calpulli councils of elders were otiose by the last days of empire, especially after Moctezoma the Younger reformed his administration by the expulsion of commoners from court office: relics of a simpler past, their roles become 'merely' ceremonial.[57] I suspect that their constant round of activities – welcoming the new crop of infants into the calpulli at the local temple, 'blessing' feasts, sanctioning marriages, honouring returned warriors and singing their triumphs – was crucial for the orchestration of the glamour of local identity: a key device in the business of enchantment.[58]

The integration so achieved was complex, multiple-stranded, and self-reinforcing. Promotion did not sever local connections, but rather linked calpulli to centre for all those who were or contrived to become close to rising men, constrained in their turn by ambition, custom, and inclination to be generous to clients and kin. The widest and most accommodating upward path ran through the warrior hierarchy. Each ward sustained its own warrior school, from which the most successful graduates could hope to win riches (initially occasional 'boons' for particular exploits, then a steady lien on a tribute warehouse), marriage to the girl of their choice, and perhaps an official post in the local warrior house or ward administration. Some few could advance to hold office in the city or the empire, or even vault into the lower ranks of the nobility. Whatever their elevation, such men knew their careers would be followed most devotedly and their triumphs would be celebrated most joyously in their home calpulli. (The tempting analogy is with something now passed or passing: the local sporting hero whose links with the home territory are never allowed to lapse, however illustrious the career, however far it carries him.)

Regular rotation between equal sub-units (most obviously the calpullis) appears to have been the great mechanism by which Tenochtitlan worked. Within each calpulli each individual was closely monitored, from birth and the recording of the name and daysign by the local priest, and then for the males through dedication and training at the local warrior school, or (more rarely) at priest school; the registering and fulfilment of tribute service and so on through the life career. Calpulli members were routinely recruited into 'state' enterprises, from temple service and municipal work gangs to providing dance groups for particular festivals and warrior squadrons for major campaigns. All those enterprises stressed ward affiliations, and honed parochial patriotism.[59] Warrior contingents were not only recruited but fought as a group under the leadership of local lords, and the tally of their warrior captives was jealously kept.

The 'public awards' system also countered the dangers of urban anonymity. We have an obstinate notion that town air makes free, at least for earlier periods: that close supervision of city dwellers is achievable only through modern forms of organization and, perhaps, modern ideological intensities. Within Tenochtitlan the visible signs of hierarchy which cut across the vertical system of the calpullis lay in highly precise sumptuary laws. No commoner was to wear cotton, or a cloak falling below the knee. No commoner could walk sandalled through the city's streets. Certain designs of cloaks were limited to certain ranks; permissible jewels and ornaments for different levels of society and different warrior grades were precisely designated. Sumptuary laws are usually honoured in the breach, pointing rather to the disintegration than the reinforcement of social divisions, but in Tenochtitlan too many individuals were too interested in the distinctions they drew for their easy flouting. Even outside the home calpulli individual occupation and relative status within the appropriate hierarchy was thus made very visible. Durán claimed Moctezoma the Elder's sumptuary legislation to be a direct response to the growth of Tenochtitlan, when its people included 'strangers as well as natives and citizens', the tightened prescriptions being necessary so that 'all might live in their status, as it was reasonable to live with decorum and good manners, regimen and order that pertained to so great a city . . . and also so that there might be given that respect and reverence, which was owed to the authority of his person and to the great lords of his kingdom, so that they might be known and respected as such'.[60]

7

These responses to change in the city were extensions of traditional institutions to meet novel circumstances. But one 'institution' was itself quite clearly novel, a creation of the imperial experience: the elaborate hierarchy of the Mexica priesthood, and the elaborate round of ritual observances as developed and supervised by the priests. The ceremonial cycle dominated the life of the city as its requirements dominated its spaces and structures. The Mexica had always had 'priests' of a kind: the pictorial 'history' of their earliest days of migration showed four priests, three male and one possibly female, bearing the sacred bundle of their god Huitzilopochtli before the people.[61] By the time of Moctezoma the Younger there were many priests in the city: sustained by the produce of allocated 'temple lands' and the rotational labour and tribute of the calpullis, trained in the exclusive priest schools, custodians of particular branches of sacred knowledge preserved in the sacred books, staffing the calpulli temples as parish priests, or dedicated to the service and celebration of a particular deity. There can be no doubt that in parallel with the growth of the city there was a comprehensive effort by the religious professionals to influence all levels of 'religious' activity. By the last days of empire local priests had come to play parts in what in the recent past must have been purely domestic rituals, penetrating the households to do so.[62] If childbirth remained the affair of midwives, priests had come to be needed to determine the daysign of the newborn; if marriage remained the affair of the kin, illness, the fear of death or other crises usually required priestly ministrations.

The desired relationship is neatly modelled in the relationships between the centre and the wards, the priests and the people, displayed in the New Fire Ceremony, the major ritual celebrated every fifty-two years to open the new Bundle of Years. The hiatus between the two Year Bundles, like most endings and beginnings, was considered to be deeply dangerous, with its intimations of the end of this world. The close of the seasonal calendar always saw a great sweeping and cleaning, but at the completion of a Bundle of Years all domestic images of stone or wood were 'cast into the water; the grinders and pestles and the three hearth stones thrown away', and all fires doused. Then on the appointed night the senior priests went out of the city to a distant hill close by Culhuacan, while the householders kept anxious vigil from the city's rooftops.[63] At the first heralding of the Sun by the appearance of the Pleiades a chosen priest whirled his Fire Drill on the breast of a noble warrior captive. Then, as the sun rose, the uncertain flames were tended and fed with the heart and flesh of the victim. The new fire was carried by swift runners to the brazier before the temple of Huitzilopochtli in the main temple precinct. From there it was distributed to each ward temple, thence to all of the priests' houses, and thence to every warrior house in every calpulli. Only then did the commoners come to the flame: they 'hurled themselves upon it and blistered themselves as the fire was taken. When thus the fire had been quickly distributed everywhere among them, there was the laying of many fires; there was the quieting of many hearts'.[64] All this was orchestrated by the priests: a nice model of dependence. While this was a traditional ceremony, and not exclusive to Tenochtitlan, the new distance, physical and social, between the actors and watchers, the agent-mediators and recipients, lent it peculiar significance in the urban-imperial milieu.

In this idealized model of ecclesiastical structure and lay dependence the flow was not only downwards. Every household sustained its own shrines and collection of images, from those particular to each house – like the swathed thighbones of 'god captives' taken by a resident warrior, or the memorials to particular ancestors – to more widely reverenced figures like the popular little clay maize-goddesses and the God of Fire.

The household compounds, the streets, the ward and central temple precincts were all venues for religious observances. A few of those observances were exclusive, a particular ward paying its particular devotions to its own deity, but more typically observances at the local level were replicated and magnified at the centre: during the major festivals the action moved progressively through the different levels like the long surge and recoil of a wave. As we have seen, individuals and (more important) groups from each calpulli were constantly being recruited into the action at the central temple precinct: a recurrent immersion in its special glamour. Even commonplace obligations like the maintenance of fires in the courtyard of temple or palace meant that temple and palace were actual experiences, known places of excitement, for the out-dwellers thus admitted behind the scenes. The most lowly individuals, familiar through obligatory service with the sounds and sights and the backstage workings of the temple, could have watched the spectacles with something of a proprietor's eye and an insider's concern.[65]

In that world of swiftly changing conditions – approximate egalitarianism to precarious hierarchy, agriculture to urban specialization, with women, for example, brought literally into the marketplace – what bound the neighbourhoods together was not mundane work – which is what we tend to see as most effectively affiliative, but which was necessarily diversified in the urban milieu – but the equally routine but notably more rewarding work of the gods. If the duties were sometimes onerous, they were also celebratory, and lit with local competitiveness and pride, as when a local warrior offered his captive in a major festival and celebrated his triumph, or when the local dance troupe of boys and girls were called on to perform in the great temple precinct. The cults of specialist communities found their most magnificent expression at the centre, as when the salt people saw the slave girl they had collectively purchased dance and die as Salt Lady before Tlaloc's shrine atop the great pyramid. And at all times the sacred action generated at the centre set the rhythm for all other observances, picking up and incorporating into its own pulse the rounds of feasting and fasting, and the concoction of special offerings of foods and flowers which marked out the seasons in the neighbourhoods and households. At a more elevated social level the enforced attendance at the Mexica 'court' of the princes of the subject cities operated not or not only as a hostage system or a way of keeping the restless under surveillance, but as an attempted seduction: an opportunity for such men to be subjected to and by the powerful attractions of the Mexica state.

8

There remains, of course, a question. The ordinary people attended the great central performances with obvious enthusiasm. When elaborate action was in play, 'the common folk massed together; indeed all came to watch. They were spread about verily everywhere, seating themselves in the temple courtyard. None ate: indeed everyone fasted' – and this after a day of high excitement and major processions in the city.[66] But did they also nurture a vision of the world similar to that of the organizers of these great occasions? There can be no doubt of the priests' intention to penetrate and control 'popular' religious observances, and to dramatize the people's crucial dependence on priestly powers and wisdom. We have the actions. The problem is to discover what the actions meant to those who performed them: an issue rather too often forgotten by enthusiastic 'readers of ritual'. We know that the most exuberant participation need not mean consensus as to meanings; that the same objects – the little maize-goddesses, for example, cherished in the temples and cherished in the households – might be differently understood by those who valued them. Did the commoners believe approximately what the creators of those great orchestrated performances presented for belief? Was Tenochtitlan, despite its dramatic expansion in size and social distance, still enough of a community to be able to claim the special allegiance of its members as a matter of obligation and sentiment, and not bare power? Or was it rather a conglomerate of different and opposed interests roughly knotted together by habit or fear or opportunism or the dread of punishment?

Such questions can only be approached circuitously. Thus far the *point d'appui* has been rather too elevated and distant, and overly concerned with formal institutions. Now I want to look at those less than formal arrangements which shaped the experience of living in late imperial Tenochtitlan, in order to discover what assumptions about life and its essential characteristics the townsfolk brought to their imaginings of the workings of power in the seen and in the sacred world.

2

Local Perspectives

The notion that politics is an unchanging play of natural passions, in which particular institutions of domination are but so many devices for exploiting, is wrong everywhere . . . the passions are as cultural as the devices, and the turn of mind . . . that informs one informs the other.

Clifford Geertz, *Negara: The Theatre State in Nineteenth-Century Bali*[1]

The city as imperial symbol, though real enough, cannot catch the texture of life as lived within it, nor those informal arrangements that crucially shape social life. The accounts of public institutions as presented by native lords exalting their ancestors, or Spanish clerics eager to draw the Christian moral ('consider how disciplined these pagans were even without God') can tempt us to exert a subtle censorship over much of what they casually reveal in favour of their more deliberate pronouncements. Yet a city is a complex of experiences, and we violate our own experience to pretend it is not. In what follows I want to point to those experiences, associations and activities, referred to only glancingly in the more formal record, which infused life in Tenochtitlan with its distinctive qualities. There is also the issue of the degree to which generalizations regarding a commonality of experience are legitimate within that fast-growing, socially complex place. A major concern will therefore be to discover where most Mexica found their most basic sense of community, and how widely their most compelling and defining experiences were shared. While 'community' is seated in the mind, it should be visible on the ground, in patterned interactions grounded in common understandings, or (shifting the metaphor) sharing a particular discourse or idiom. 'Popular' observances will therefore become important, not because they were popular as

45

opposed to something else, but because they were observable expressions of how the world was seen to be, and of what men and women thought they could do about it.

I

Were we to judge only from its complex modes of formal address and the rigour of its rules of decorum we would construe Tenochtitlan as a most delicately articulated society, ordered by strict protocols of deference.[2] So, I think, it was, from some perspectives. But despite the rhetoric of its sedate managers extolling the beauty of self-effacing humility and control the city was a startlingly violent place, with much of that violence neither individual nor unscheduled, but licensed and official. It was most dramatically visible in the killings of captives and slaves and the processing of their bodies within the city limits: the battlefield shambles delivered into the home place. But extravagant violence was also visited upon the townsfolk, although not (or not usually) to the point of death. When priests of the Rain God Tlaloc were returning to the city with the bundles of reeds required for a major festival they were licensed to seize the possessions of anyone unwise enough to cross their path. Should those who were plundered dare to offer any resistance they were stripped and savagely beaten: 'they kicked each of them . . . they beat them repeatedly, they beat the skin off them'. Then they left them naked and moaning in the road.[3] Young warriors and priests brawled through the streets on privileged occasions, the energetic combats easily expanding to catch up the passers-by, who could find themselves despoiled of their cloaks or at the least of their dignity as they were forced to take to their heels. House walls gave no certain refuge. In the same Tlaloc festival which sanctioned priestly violence local commoners were faced with trick-or-treat importunings, not from children, but from dancing bands of warriors and pleasure girls threatening to 'break their walls down', and had to buy them off with a scoop of an especially luxurious maize-and-bean porridge: play perhaps, but play with a bright edge of threat.[4]

Warrior arrogance always commanded a wide social space in the city. Given their reward-by-privilege expectations and their systematic elevation over lesser men, extortion was always a tempting possibility. From time to time it was discovered that warriors had levied an unofficial tribute on the town, 'perchance of chocolate (cacao), or food'. Such gross invasion of the prerogative of the state invoked the punitive violence of the state, and Mexica state justice was summary, brutal, public, and often enough lethal. Most offenders against Moctezoma's laws died most publicly, with the marketplace the favoured venue, where adulterers were stoned or strangled and habitual drunkards had their heads beaten in by Moctezoma's executioners.[5] 'Thus the ruler implanted fear'.[6] In-group discipline was also notably corporal, and not much less public. A youth under the jurisdiction of the warrior house discovered in an unsanctioned sexual relationship was set upon by his peers, beaten with staves, his hair scorched from his head with firesticks, so that his warrior lock would never again grow, and then flung out into the street.[7] Rank was no protection: even a 'leader of youth' discovered illicitly drinking was subject to the same public expulsion, and, as we will see, priests purged the unsuitable from their own ranks most brutally.[8]

Casual violence was not rare. The lords interrogated by Sahagún's assistants characterized commoners as being by their nature as cantankerous as turkeys, endlessly squabbling 'over perhaps their lands, their houses, or something.'[9] The market which impressed Cortés and Díaz with its peaceable orderliness nonetheless had the liveliness and explosive potential of any large promiscuous social gathering, and saw some notable brawls.[10] The story of the causes of war between Tenochtitlan and Tlatelolco, when the endemic rivalry between the twin cities finally flared into battle, is thick with marketplace confrontations. One of the first signs of trouble occurred there, when 'noble youths' of Tenochtitlan encountered the maiden daughters of some Tlatelolcan lords, 'directing flattering words to them, and joking with them'. The girls, thinking, in the way of trusting maidens, 'it was only a game', allowed the young men to escort them home, and suffered the usual penalty for maidenly trust. The tale, while too pat to carry much conviction as history, at least indicates the opportunities of the market as a place for untoward encounters and behaviour. Then market women from the rival cities got into a fight, hurling abuse at each other, and when Tenocha 'captains' dared to stroll through the Tlatelolcan marketplace to take the political temperature they heard many 'spiteful words' muttered, including the chilling enquiry: 'What merchandise have you brought to sell? Do you want to sell your intestines or hearts?'[11]

The possibility of such excitements had its charms; like any large and lively public gathering the market exercised a most powerful attraction over its habitués. Even the miserably shrunken affairs in the impoverishment following the conquest retained formidable appeal. The Dominican Durán tells a pleasant tale of a ninety-year-old woman who habitually declared herself to be too old and weak to totter to mass, but who nonetheless never missed any of the regional markets. The friar grimly reported the consequences: on one particular day, having walked a full two leagues to a distant market, the old woman was struggling home along the long hot road clutching her bundle of scrawny ears of maize when she fell dead. (She fetched up being buried in the marketplace, which probably would have pleased her.) A half-century after the conquest Durán was still unreconciled to what he saw as the Indians' puerile sociability, complaining that men and women wanted nothing better to do than to stroll the length of the market, mouths agape, gazing about them, with no purpose in mind: content simply to be there, happy in the hubbub.[12]

It would seem that there was a clear division between the commoners and the custodians of order over the issue of the unlicensed drinking of pulque. Pulque was, in theory, forbidden, save to specified groups on specified occasions, and to the aged. The incoming ruler conventionally made a speech to his people in which the evils of drink were specially rehearsed, and the Florentine Codex provides an abundance of apparently unequivocal statements of the 'absolutely nobody drank' type.[13] Nonetheless, drinking was clearly widespread. The Codex prohibitions are deeply fringed by qualifiers, of the 'but when the young men drank' kind: a characteristic movement in that text strung between the impulse to idealize and the tug of memory. While Diego Durán was perhaps exaggerating in his claim that in pre-Spanish times 'all' drank in private, in practice it is sufficiently clear that even in the well-policed towns of Tenochtitlan and Tlatelolco illicit collective drinking was commonplace.[14] (It is also clear that there were individual drunkards, or as we would say alcoholics, who brought themselves into penury in the time-honoured way.)[15]

Despite the vigour of the rhetoric, it appears that there was a degree of acquiescence in the practice. The calpullis appear to have done much of their own policing. If we can trust the recorded exhortations of the elders, shaming constituted the first line of defence of social proprieties: a formidable weapon in a face-to-face community, especially as shame extended to those responsible for the delinquent, as did the first obligation to punish. Continued delinquency (or the failure to punish) was difficult to conceal in a neighbourhood thick with its 'block supervisors', and there was no private space for face-saving withdrawal. Conflicts and delicts not resolved at the neighbourhood level fell under the jurisdiction of the court of the local lord, which functioned in the royal name. Should the matter remain unresolved, or a sense of injustice linger, even commoners could (at least in theory) appeal to one of Moctezoma's two high courts. (The second was restricted to dealing with the affairs of lords and nobles.)[16] But some offences, like public drunkenness, went straight before the royal judges. For notables, drunkenness appears to have been a capital offence, with the punishment being automatic. For commoners the matter was revealingly different, the 'obligatory' penalty being selectively imposed. The offenders were rounded up and imprisoned ('locked in the granary') while Moctezoma's judges privately assessed the degree of their guilt. Then on the appropriate day the people were ordered to assemble to hear the judgments, and to watch the punishments. Those selected to die were led with wrists bound to the middle of the marketplace, subjected to a long oration from the judges, and then had their skulls smashed by the cudgel-wielding executioners.

The elaboration of these very public occasions, the carefully dreadful pomp and circumstance of the whole affair, and (perhaps most significant) the fact that only a few of those guilty were actually executed, the rest being released, suggests that Moctezoma and his judges knew they were trying to net a tiger. Certainly the commoners seemed less than properly impressed by the bloodiness of the object lesson. Sahagún's noble informants acknowledged that the pious hope that 'all the commoners will be troubled' by the performance was misplaced; while 'the intelligent, the clear thinkers' were duly terrified, the 'perverse' and the 'rebellious' were moved to mirth, listening 'only mockingly', and dispersing with much flapping of capes and stirring-up of dust: discreet but gratifying signs of disrespect in decorous Tenochtitlan.[17]

Nonetheless, drinking to full inebriation outside of ritual sanctions appears to have aroused anxieties which were not restricted to those officially concerned with social control. Here social and sacred transgressions are easily confounded, and our own obstinate association of alcohol as primarily dangerous to the social fabric or the individual moral fibre must be resisted. The Mexica knew pulque's capacity to demoralize the individual and to disrupt social relations, and deplored it. But its deeper import and its deeper danger was its capacity to lay humans open to the sacred.[18] The man or woman who drank to inebriation outside the ritual frame offended very differently, for those who became fully drunk could become open channels for dangerous sacred forces. That capacity could be deliberately activated when the ritual frame was in place. Casually invoked outside of the control of ritual safeguards, it constituted a risk not only to the delinquent individual, but to human society itself.

2

All uncontrolled behaviour was infused with the same danger. The aggression and flamboyance proper to the battlefield was dangerous in the ordinary world, and the touchy display of the great warrior was rebuked by more sober men. The harlot was socially reprehensible: 'an old woman of itching buttocks; a filthy old dog who brings herself to ruin like a dog'. But she was also dangerous in her flaunted and intensified sexuality, as in her casual self-indulgence. '[Going] about with her head high – rude, drunk, shameless – eating mushrooms', she was likened to the victim destined for sacrificial death, who was kept flattered, dazed, and half drunk over the last days of life. Already vulnerable to lustful men, she was a walking incitement to a more formidable penetration.[19] A drunken woman described as 'just slumped down on her knees . . . tumbled there, with hair streaming out' was not, we might think, doing any particular harm to anyone. For the Mexica her 'self-abandonment' constituted a terrifyingly open invitation to sinister powers. A drunken man roused fear through his random aggression: he 'argued, harangued, enforced silence, and drove all people away, put them to flight, numbed them with terror . . . made them shrink with fright.'[20] We see this kind of conduct as no more than irritating or embarrassing. For the Mexica it could attract the lightning strike of the sacred.

States of exaltation, of abrogation of the self – drunkenness, the ecstasy of extreme anger or excitement, warriors in the rage of battle, women caught up in the compelling rhythm of childbirth – brought the sacred dangerously near, and so necessitated properly delicate handling through the application of ritual controls.[21] The old have often been represented as the most privileged category in Mexica society, as they and they alone were permitted to drink publicly and often, 'because [they] have had children and grandchildren'. While mature men and women were honoured as having reached the fulfilment of their individual destinies, the concession to the aged points less to increased status than to their graduation, on this issue, into irrelevance, their physical vigour and sexual force, avenues of the sacred, having been sapped by the years.[22] (They were of course still honoured as custodians of traditional wisdom and local affairs.) They could bring no harm on the world by their tippling, as they tottered home weeping or dancing and boasting 'like a brave warrior', or simply 'shouting at the people'.[23]

Comments on drunkenness as on other matters of moral economy derive largely from the *huehuetlatolli* or 'discourses of the elders', in which the proper conduct of human affairs was narrowly prescribed. These were the formal and traditional addresses, thick with conventional wisdom, which were declaimed on formal occasions to mark significant moments in the lives of individuals. Such occasions (the dedication of a child at the temples, a youth's graduation from the warrior house, the announcement of a young wife's pregnancy) abounded in speech-making Mexico. As 'discourses of the elders', they could be claimed to represent the official rather than the popular view. However, similar relationships, demeanours and attitudes appear to have animated general modes of formal address, with their obsessively nice differentiations and plays on rank. More important, popular Mexica strategies for handling intrusions of the sacred – 'superstitions', as the Spanish friars dubbed them – pivot on the same understandings as those articulated or implied in the 'discourses', reflecting the same fear of the dangers of sacred forces liberated by irresponsible individuals. Consider the interesting case of fresh-hatched turkey chicks. Should an adulterer go among them, 'all the chicks fell upon their backs so they died': impressively unequivocal evidence for a normally secret offence.[24] This was not an indicator of the chicks' moral sensitivity – canaries down a moral mineshaft – but rather of their physical vul-

nerability, being small and weak, to the whiff of the sacred unleashed by
sexuality 'out of place'. A man or woman in a state of pollution could
cause damage to all those around them, or be brought to their own death
– *tlazomiquiztli*, the 'filth-death'.[25]

The nature of the pollution is perhaps clearer when the highly contagious condition of slavery is considered. On the god Tezcatlipoca's
daysign of One Death, when slaves' wooden collars were struck off, and
they were bathed and soaped and pampered as 'images' (*ixiptlas*) of
Tezcatlipoca for the day, anyone who struck or abused a slave was visited
by misery and affliction: 'it was as if pustulate sores had covered and been

fastened on him; it seemed that, as a gift . . . it had been transferred to
and left on him'. The account continues in a Christian idiom: 'because at
one time the wretched slave was beaten, [the god] transferred his sins
upon him'.[26] But 'sin' does not catch the matter here, despite the deliberateness of the act: a condition of misfortune had been contracted. If the
Mexica sometimes used the language of offence and propitiation as they
invoked their deities, resorting to the usual shorthand of human emotions, their behaviour (and most of their language) does not suggest that
the gods were understood as outraged individuals punishing sins of 'diso-
bedience', but rather that humans had blundered into transgressing significant boundaries, and so suffered unpleasant consequences: not a
withdrawal of the divine in the Christian mode, but a surfeit of its uncomfortable presence.[27] That condition could be ameliorated only by a cautious, correct, and respectful renewal of the correct relationship, so that
the essential boundary would be back in place.

A multitude of small procedures and stratagems developed by the laity
for dealing with these undesired eruptions of the sacred echo the understandings of the privileged, while shared techniques for the maintenance
of the body in this world also indicate that understandings flowed easily
across social boundaries and social distance.[28] Submission to the sacred
and valuable accretions of sacred power could be achieved by the deliberate yielding of one's person to 'dirt', as with the prohibitions on bathing,
and most particularly the washing of the head, in periods of penance or
mourning. (Therefore the long blood-matted hair of the priests which so
horrified the Spaniards.) In the ordinary world a scrupulous, tireless
cleanliness was the best protection of fragile human arrangements against
the dangers of disordered things. Contamination could be purged by

appeal to the goddess Tlazolteotl, or 'Garbage God', but that was a once-in-a-lifetime cleansing.[29] Mundane life also required the routine management of sacred tensions and anomalies, and here the principles of the wider cosmology were brought into play: balance was most commonly restored and maintained through the invocation of the appropriate opposing force. Twins, being doubly charged with earth power, could involuntarily draw heat from fire (the sweatbath would lose its heat, the tamales – steamed maize-cakes – would sit in the pot all day without cooking) unless they deliberately negated their own influence by assisting the process, themselves sprinkling water on the heated potsherds, or placing a tamale in the pot.[30] The belief that hail could be diverted from one's maizefield by scattering the hearth ashes out of the house entrance into the courtyard draws its plausibility from the same notion, hail (and rain) being a manifestation of the earth power. The rough physicality of some of the 'punishments' meted out to children probably derived from similar understandings of contagion and negation: for example, the 'smoking' of the delinquent child over a fire of chillis caused much eye-watering and a flow of saliva, so drawing out the 'anger' and the recalcitrance.[31]

Daily life was full of gestures of respect to sacred things, with a special tenderness reserved for the handling of maize. Women breathed softly on the maize kernels before they were dropped into the cooking pot, the warm moist breath giving them courage for the fire. Spilt kernels were carefully gathered up so that famine would not come, and every eighth year the long-suffering maize was 'rested' for a period by being cooked without condiments, 'for we brought much torment to it – we ate it, we put chilli on it, we salted it, we added saltpetre to it, we added lime. And we tired it to death, so we revived it. Thus it was said maize was given new youth when this was done'.[32]

It is always difficult to glimpse the bent of an alien view of the sacred and its workings, especially as that view is in all probability itself somewhat vaporous, but for the Mexica it would seem the sacred could not be securely walled away from 'ordinary' life: it pressed in everywhere. If on occasions of high ritual men specially trained to survive its close encounter solicited its presence, ordinarily men worked to maintain the integument between its terrible power and their own small ordered worlds by constant attentiveness. Through the devoted sweeping and ordering of the houses of men and the houses of gods, through remembering the sprinkle of pulque and the pinch of food routinely offered at the hearth-stone, and the daily lacerations to draw forth one's own blood, the Great Ones' destructive manifestations might be held in check. For they were always present, and always potentially dangerous. The Oldest God who sat flickering between his stones in every hearth flamed high before each temple, and all men knew his genesis: kindled on the breast of a young warrior and fed with his flesh and heart.

They had watched as he had worked upon living flesh bubbling, blister-ing, smoking in the fire. There was nothing domesticated about the Oldest God, for all his kitchen uses. They knew the force of Tlaloc, paradoxically most cruelly manifested by the withdrawal of his favours and his presence, or by the surfeit of them in storm and flood, while, as we will see, the shadow of Tezcatlipoca, the Lord of the Here and Now, was everywhere, mocking human effort, falling across the smallest, most innocent things of the everyday. By their actions the ordinary Mexica demonstrated their accord with the principles of priestly action, as they sought to maintain, by small ritual acts and constant small adjustments, that frail membrane between the human world they had made, and the irrepressibly contingent and casually destructive sacred.

3

Such an understanding would lend significant power to those men who could claim the ability to influence the sacred. Since Keith Thomas's work on the vigorous, unofficial but highly active curers and cunning men of seventeenth- and eighteenth-century England, historians have been alert to the possibility of 'alternative' religious practitioners serving the folk outside the official ecclesiastical system, especially where that system must be considered as part of the apparatus of state, which was certainly the case in imperial Tenochtitlan.[33] I therefore sought and duly found them, lurking, as one would expect, at the fringes of the sources: curers, midwives, sorcerers. But I have come to think their apparent chronic marginality is illusory; an artefact of the sources themselves. The friars and their mission-trained helpers, professional religious themselves, readily identifying certain persons and practices as undesirable, bundled various roles into the one disreputable basket. In the Florentine Codex we see sorcerers apostrophized as 'evil old men', attracting fear and dread for their antisocial power, with female physicians being accused of bewitching their clients, killing them 'with medications', and deceiving them into false belief by reading their fortunes.[34] Given their esoteric knowledge, and their ability to induce extreme physiological and psychological reactions, they probably suffered the usual ambivalence of the 'my curer is good, and yours is bad and will harm me' kind. But women curers and midwives were honoured members of society, as their public celebration in the festival of Ochpaniztli makes clear, and worked in tandem with the priests, fulfilling their part of the birth rituals: that is, they were necessary functionaries in the staging of conventional rites which lay well within the control of the official priesthood.[35] (They also drew on the Book of Days for augury, as in estimating the severity and duration of an illness.)

The *nahualli* were a more sinister group: wizards, shape-changers, with direct contact with the sacred powers assigned them by their daysign. But, like the midwives, they too were distributed through all ranks of society. Even among nahualli caste distinctions were preserved: while a nobleman endowed with such magic powers was able to transform into a 'fierce beast, or a coyote', a commoner had to be content to be 'a turkey, a weasel or a dog'.[36] Some served evil, their powers used to paralyze whole households for pillage and rape.[37] Most dealt with individual crises, as in the construction of the ceremonial figures in the households of those who killed in war,[38] or concentrated on a particular field of magic, controlling hail or storms or other 'natural' disasters. And some served the state: Moctezoma maintained a team of sorcerers, whom he unleashed to halt Cortés and the advancing Spanish army. These were no clandestine servants of the 'folk': distributed and their skills utilized through the whole society, they worked in a different mode from that of the priests, but they were not in competition with them. So under enquiry the popular outside-the-system religious specialists largely evaporated. Like the curers, most sorcerers appear to have operated locally and for hire, with the cognizance and sometimes the co-operation of the institutionalized religious. Their existence seems to point neither to the existence of an alternative reading of the world nor (more conventionally in most analyses) to a flattened and vulgarized version of the 'pure' faith, nor even to that distinction between 'local' and 'translocal' luminously analysed by William Christian for sixteenth-century Spain, with the elevation and

etiolation into theological propositions of those tender sentiments wreathing around familiar sacred places and sacred things.[39] Institutionally, at
least at this distance, they look like the providers of part of the local
scaffolding for the larger system, supplying some of the myriad services
which allowed the people of Tenochtitlan to negotiate relations with the
powerful, essential, and dangerous sacred.

Our assumptions about the 'priesthood' and its necessary aloofness
also deserve consideration. Rarely prominent in analyses of the workings
of the Mexica economy and polity, priests must have been ubiquitous in
actuality; crucial agents at each level of the city organization. The head
priest of each cult was responsible for gathering the materials (including
the human) for his deity's festivals: an enormous task for those protracted
exercises in conspicuous consumption, involving tribute selections and
market purchases, negotiating the supply of regalia, the delivery to the
right place of the right paraphernalia, the co-ordination of supplies of
material for the ceremony itself, arranging that whatever would be needed
along the processional way – litters, canoes, feathered banners, slaves for
sacrifice – would be there: the operations of an entrepreneurial im-
presario rather than an ascetic withdrawn from the world.[40] They were
essential organizers in the complex rotations of services and supply which
kept the city running. Our distinction between 'sacred' and 'secular'
spheres has slight utility here, where the citizen might discharge his
tequitl to the ruler by supplying wood for a temple fire, or a weaver hers
by embroidering a shirt for a god. The independence, and indeed the
priority of the priestly organization in the city order, was asserted as much
by their visible prominence as by their distinctive dress, their prolonged
fasting periods, their gauntness and their blood-matted hair.

Despite their deep implication in the high affairs of the imperial city,
only the most lofty of the priests were remote from the general populace.
Most served the community by regulating the seasonal round and marking the key moments in that round by appropriate ritual. They also added
the weight of their own ceremonial to local observances. Mexica children
were named for a day on or close to the time of their birth, the daysign
being understood to contain their cryptic fortune, and that crucial matter
required the services of a priest who could read and interpret the Book of
Days. The naming priests could exercise some discretion in selecting the
most favourable daysign a few days either side of the physical birth, and

only their expertise allowed a satisfyingly complex account of the new-born's particular destiny. More importantly, the tilt of the Spanish-influenced sources and our outsiders' penchant for oppositional thinking could lead to an underestimation of the shamanistic dimensions of the priesthood. We tend to cast Quetzalcoatl as exemplar of priestly knowledge and wisdom, of formal learning, against the shaman Tezcatlipoca, named for the 'Smoking Mirror' of his scrying glass and strongly associated with the occult powers of the night, invisibility and the jaguar. But all priests wore as an identifying emblem their incense pouches of jaguarskin, which for the greatest priests were in effect the miniaturized bodies of jaguars, the jaguar's tail hanging from one corner, its hind feet from another, and from another its forepaws.[41] They knew and used the effects of the powerful native tobacco and other plants of power on fasting, fatigued bodies, and the more ambiguous elevations invoked by prolonged bloodletting. While their knowledge was a matter of rigorous training, under the aegis of Quetzalcoatl, their experience delivered them into the hands of Tezcatlipoca, the polarized deities so demonstrating their intimate connection.

4

'Community' is not (or not usefully) an analyst's concept, but a subject's value. We have an inclination to define it in the negative terms of absence of internal division ('solidarity'), and the absence of conflict, despite our awareness that in our own times most violence occurs within the smallest and to many of us the only acknowledged community of the family. But what makes communities actual is not peaceability or an easy egalitarianism but the persistence and frequency of significant interaction, which need be neither equal nor amiable, but which somehow builds and is built on the sense of being in the same boat: where a common cluster of ideas and images lends experience, at different social levels and despite different social roles, an underlying coherence derived from shared notions as to how people must and ought to behave given the way the world is.[42]

If the calpulli was the most emphasized local social unit, with its own temple and warrior-house, its own round of obligations to the city, its own sources of pride, there were other smaller arenas of significant action which in practice may have taken priority. For women the most important zone of interaction was presumably the household and the kin network of which it was the centre. It most commonly comprised an extended family, married sons usually bringing their new wives back to their father's compound for the first years after marriage. Given the endogamous tendency of the calpullis, the wives usually remained within easy visiting distance of their kin, and both families acknowledged the mutual bond established by the marriage at the rituals which marked its progress. (The 'kin' also included sacred objects and powers with special family connections, and the honoured dead, who, at least for the first years after physical death, remained very much part of the family group.) Evidence from the periphery of ancient Tenochtitlan suggests that a usual household construction comprised a row of rooms along the street boundary, with another row running off at right angles to form an 'L' shape, and a wall enclosing the other two sides to form a large courtyard.[43] There are references to shadowy 'women's quarters' somewhere in the enclosed structures, but the courtyard probably saw the bulk of women's work in the preparation of the maize, spinning and weaving, and the care of the smaller children.

The household entrance into that courtyard marked a real boundary for the stranger, but it seems to have been highly permeable for both neighbours and kin. For us, withdrawn into our guarded private domestic worlds, negotiating as to just who may cross the threshold and on what terms, the constant comings and goings between Mexica households is hard to imagine. Neighbourly visiting did not wait on particular occasions. A newborn baby's uncertain *tonalli*, the vigour and fate accorded him by the Sun through his daysign, or as we might say his temperament and destiny, was sustained and stabilized by its own small fire, which was kept burning steadily beside it for four days while the force took a secure hold, to be 'fixed' by a ritual bathing.[44] During those few days 'no fire could be lent' for fear the child would be weakened, which suggests that locals typically took the quick and neighbourly way should their domestic fires die, and points to the ease characterizing neighbourly relations.[45] But the family compound was most readily entered by neighbours and kin through the round of observances which marked the flow of ordinary life. When a baby was born, kinsfolk came en masse to welcome it with gifts, as they had welcomed the first news of its coming. So too did the neighbours, flocking in with their gifts of welcome. At the male infant's naming the small boys of the neighbourhood were recruited to shout the name of the newborn warrior at the house entrances and along the streets of the home calpulli, so alerting neighbours to bring their offerings of food to the home compound, with the junior heralds claiming payment in some of that food for their service.[46] We have occasional glimpses of the gaiety of the preparation for some festivals, with whole neighbourhoods staying up all night, stirring their stewpots and simmering with anticipation, before a general joyful celebration, while at the festival of Izcalli women were out in the streets at first light with their baskets of fresh-cooked tamales scurrying to be first to distribute them to neighbours and kin.[47]

The 'neighbourhood' dimension of city life is difficult to establish save through these casual asides, practical action and glimpses of small-scale supervisory systems.[48] However, it is notable that the endemic rituals of food-sharing normally included neighbours as well as kin. Clifford Geertz has pointed to the Javanese slametan, in its rural habitat a ritualized eating together, as a key institution in sustaining a sense of community, with every significant event in one's life marked by neighbours.[49] These were intricate intimacies, sometimes threaded by tension and conflict, but making all participate in the same sphere of social knowledge: constant visitors to one another's experience. That I think was the way of it for the customary food-gifting in the neighbourhoods of Tenochtitlan: indeed my justifications for seeing the 'neighbourhood' as actual are the indicators regarding the usual scope of participants in these small rituals.

5

The authority for these reciprocities, as for the proper conduct of all social interactions, was not the esoteric learning of priest or scribe but 'custom'; the tested routines of the ancestors, those 'beloved grandfathers and grandmothers' irretrievably gone to the domain of the Death Lord, the Place of No Exits, but leaving behind codes of conduct to structure daily life: marking its dangers, and avoiding or neutralizing them; bringing right order into social interchanges. 'Custom' ruled everywhere, in the handling and presentation of food around the hearth, in the styles of sitting for men and women, in the modes of greeting and polite address when deference was the main currency exchanged. But there was a more formal and a more dynamic mode of food-gift which not only marked but made social relationships: the feast. However blurred the precise demarcation in actuality, we need to distinguish the mutuality of neighbour and kin food-sharing, not too nicely calculated but with the expectation of ultimate reciprocity, from the rivalrous form of feasting which looked to establish inequality.

The fashion in Aztec studies was once to discuss feasting in terms of its 'redistributive function', which does not quite catch what the natives saw in these exciting occasions. Feasting was not mere commensalism. The exuberant mutual sharing of food at Izcalli, the festival of the eighteenth and last month of the seasonal cycle, in a time of the revivification of all social bonds, with the joyful distribution of tamales to friends and kin, and whole families gathered in happy circles gulping down tamales steaming hot, was not a 'feast', precisely because there was neither formal ranking in the seating nor any calculation in the giving and getting but rather uninhibited conviviality: 'there was giving in company; there was giving among themselves; there was giving to friends; there was giving to those whom they knew. There was no giving in ill-will; there was giving in gladness.'[50] At the festival of the sixth month, just as the first maize cobs were beginning to plump, and long before their harvest, householders pillaged their stores to cook up a rich stew of maize and beans to be given to all comers, in a deliberate display of confident dependence on Tlaloc, the god of rain and growth. This was no feasting either.[51]

Feasts were very much more calculated, public, and testing affairs, and a key social form for the linkage of individuals in finely articulated, explicit interdependence. The poorest could offer them not at all: 'they had nothing to use, with which to gather together and assemble people'.[52] Nor could they present themselves before others with propriety. The man without possessions was nothing and worse than nothing: he 'in no way excelled others. He was completely clothed in rags and tatters. He had no bowl or jar . . . he visited and inflicted pain, misery and suffering on one.' The majority of ordinary commoners like 'the workers of the field and the water folk', while obliged as social beings to meet this key social requirement, could manage only miserable affairs, in which much that was 'required and customary' (at least in the elevated judgment of Sahagún's noble informants) was omitted, so making the feast 'a failure and fruitless'.[53] What was needed to realize the full sweetness of the feast was wealth, and the readiness to spend it to lavish and elegant effect. Then, if all went well, the giver could experience the glowing triumph of carrying through the whole, complex, taxing thing: the food abundant, elaborately confected, and ideally including some stunning exotic product; the servers graceful; the speeches eloquent; his own addresses paroxysms of self-abasement: the guests in their most splendid garb, impressed, challenged, resentfully admiring of their gifts of fine cups and cloaks, and painfully conscious that the host had indeed 'excelled others'. There was glory in so abundantly satisfying one's guests: 'each and every one made him resplendent and admirable.'[54]

There was more than a touch of the potlatch about those grander feasts, with much 'vying and competition', and high anxiety as to possible slights and nice points of precedence. 'All persons wished that they be given recognition, fame, and distinction; that they might not . . . be shamed . . . belittled, or excluded from others.'[55] The god of the feast, Omacatl, 'Two Reed', was commonly represented as an elegantly dressed warrior. His image was brought into the house where a feast was to be offered, at once guest and supervisor of the protocols of invitation, acceptance, and banqueting for the 'assembling of relatives'. He was a querulous god, who like a difficult guest grew angry if not 'held in esteem', visiting the delinquent in dreams to threaten and complain. If still not adequately respected, he would make men choke on their food and drink.[56] At his own festival the 'bone' of the god (a cylinder of sacred dough) was made, 'killed', broken up, and eaten by his celebrants. That eating committed them, in accordance with the rules of strict and escalating reciprocity, to 'pay with their entrails', in the telling Nahuatl phrase: to bear the substantial costs of celebrating his next festival. At any significant feast there were inevitably men who, thinking themselves not given their proper precedence, would erupt in anger and exit precipitately. When the lapse in control had been duly relished, the outraged one would be pursued and calmed. On the few occasions when drunkenness was permitted to any but the aged (past the strenuous pleasures of competition, they seem to have giggled happily in their cups) the pride and malice conventionally conveyed by way of lavish food and gifts were more directly communicated by rancorous boasting, as when normally milk-tongued merchants sat 'jostling and besmearing one another . . . contending, re-

futing, bragging . . . they . . . held in no esteem the riches and prosperity
of others . . . each one alone wished to be best; each one thought himself
a lord, a superior person.'[57]

If food and tobacco and cups and cloaks were the obvious material
currencies in these feasting interchanges, sentiments and distinctive experiences were also being exchanged: chagrin 'sticking in the throat', or
the sour taste of envy, as well as admiration for another's success and
gratitude for largesse. These bitter sensations cannot be discounted as
somehow undesirable and therefore undesired by-products of the feasting. They were part of its sweetness, as they were part of the texture of
social life. Such performances offered a mix of convivial, gastronomic,
aesthetic, and political delights; affairs, to echo a famous formulation, at
once social transaction, economic redistribution, and blood sport.

The centrality of the feast in Mexica social thinking is suggested by
characteristic turns of phrase in 'high' speech. Politesse in address was
valued, and was as much required of the elevated as of the lowly: the man
who showed slight respect to 'the captain of the guard, the seasoned
warrior', and who if greeted by 'some poor old man or woman' showed his
contempt ('he only talked through his nose, addressed one through
clenched teeth, and growled and snuffled at him'), was to be despised.[58]
The elaborate protocols governing formal speech exchanges are most
accessibly preserved in a collection of dialogues, put together in the late
sixteenth century under Spanish direction as examples of polite conver-
sational style, illustrating how 'persons of different age and rank should
address each other on various occasions', as one of their analysts has put
it.[59]

The initial greeting, usually offered by the welcomer to the person
arriving, acknowledges that 'you have expended breath (you have worn
yourself out) to get here.' He who is being received, who does not name
the addressee directly or refer to the exact degree of kinship, conventionally responds by 'extending apologies for intrusion or making obeisances'. But 'far more prominent than obeisances', we are told, are 'apologies for importunity', such phrases being uttered by all speakers at the
beginning and end of speeches. The showing of appreciation, as we
would say 'thanking', has 'you have befriended us' as a pervasive formula.
And 'even more than through thanks, the speakers of the Dialogues
express appreciation by constantly referring to getting or receiving any-

thing as enjoying it, deserving it, being so lucky as to receive it'; that is, there is direct recognition of the generosity of the giver. All this points to the protocols of the feast as a primary language-shaper; its extravagant formulae reproduced and rehearsed in daily greeting routines. For the humble to attain something by entreaty from the generous was 'to be worthy of something' or 'to glorify oneself', 'to swell oneself up'. Again, the context of the feast makes sense of the use of such a phrase as an expression of thanks, as it does of the utility of leaving a superior's name, or one's own exact relationship to him, unspecified.[60] But politesse could not mask the tense actuality and its bitter psychological cost. A 'noble father' warning his son of the inescapable pains and demands of the world points to some purely man-made miseries which cluster around the struggle for status: 'there is mocking of others on earth. There is rejoicing over the misfortunes of others, there is laughing at others, there is ridicule on earth. And what they say, what they praise, what they tell one another is not true; there is only ridicule.'[61]

6

Feasting between rivalrous peers might establish exquisite hierarchies through the dominance of giving, and yield the most exquisite pleasures and pains, but these were momentary victories and transitory defeats. For unequals, feasts were of acute if not easily calculable economic importance, as wealth in the form of food and gifts moved about in the system. There were the conventional offerings to superiors, as when parents sought a mature son's release from the warrior house by petitioning and feasting the officials of the house. There were the conventional offerings to acknowledged dependants, as when the leading warriors of each calpulli, enriched by a successful campaign, duly responded to the calpulli elders' songs of praise with gifts enough 'to keep them in food for a year', as one of Sahagún's informants waspishly put it. The tlatoani Moctezoma was the model of lordly giving, his palace kitchens preparing 'two thousand kinds of various foods' daily. When Moctezoma himself had eaten, the dishes were distributed between his ambassadors, lords, royal officials, noted warriors, and all the 'palace folk' down to his sandal makers and turquoise cutters. Gifts fountained from his hand to successful warriors, and others who served his state. So lordly was his munificence that it was said he would take under his protection some poor commoner who saluted him pleasingly, or made him some humble gift – like so many other anecdotes of benevolent kingship, hard to reconcile with the sternly policed distance between ruler and ruled, but speaking of the wistful popular fantasy of adoption into the protection of a munificent lord, for those gifts to inferiors marked them as recognized dependants of the royal household.[62]

Moctezoma had the resources of the tribute warehouses at his disposal. But gift relationships were in all but the most institutionalized situations negotiable and shifting. That uncertainty, which gave the dependence-and-domination games between near equals their edge, made the business of feasting a desperate matter for the unequivocally inferior. With the changes and the uncertainties of fortune in city life the bonds of kinship and of legitimate dependence hung ever more slackly. How far, for example, did the obligations to neighbours, once readily confounded with kinship, persist when reduced to mere adjacency? The calpullis might continue to be the key units of administration, but their old homogeneity was eroding save for those few predicated on a shared craft, like the Amatlan of the featherworkers, where the bonds of kin, work and propinquity coincided. For the rest the old clarities of mutual obligation, based on shared fortunes, a shared past, and at least notional shared ancestry, must have become clouded. We glimpse a rising young warrior, able to spread among those who flattered him most ardently not only the maize and cloaks and tobacco from the imperial warehouses, but some of the lustre of his glory. Whom would he choose to recognize as kinsman or friend?

Such questions pressed painfully when men no longer grew their own sustenance and food had become a precious commodity. The poor are given scant attention in the sources as we have them: as so often, they press silently beyond the rim of the described. We glimpse figures slipping into the fields after the corn harvest, scuffling with their feet among the dry maize stalks for the forgotten or undeveloped ears, tucking their small gleanings into their cloaks.[63] We see a man still striving to find acceptance at a feast, intent despite his rags on being recognized and welcomed as a participant in the feasting community. Others had abandoned that hope. A prayer to Tezcatlipoca urging his compassion on the

misery of the common folk invokes the silent figure at one's house entrance, who thrusts forth a few withered chillis and salt cakes for sale.
'And no-where does he succeed in selling, somewhere by one's enclosure,
in a corner, by someone's wall . . . he is saddened; he is dry-mouthed; he
moisteneth his lips. . . . He just continueth looking at the people, just
looking at their mouths'.[64] (Note the cheek-by-jowl intimacy here of the
prosperous and the poor, and the despair of he who no longer impor-
tunes, but simply offers his pitiful wares.) Those scattered images speak
of habituated poverty, and of the isolation of the poverty-stricken with no
claims on the rich. Just how firmly based the social divisions, and how
eroded the notion of supra-kin fellowship, is indicated in the maintenance
of social divisions throughout the last agonizing days of Tenochtitlan's
resistance to the Spaniards. In the siege-induced famine, when 'the common people' were reduced to eating lizards, swallows, bitter grasses, even
to gnawing the adobe walls, and yet when the political order still somehow
sustained itself, there was no care to distribute equitably the little food
there was. The power of rank was preserved to the bitter last. Then over
the final days of starvation social distinctions at last began to collapse: 'We
[Mexica] had a single price; this was the standard price for a youth, a
priest, for a young girl, for a boy. The maximum price for a slave was only
two handfuls of maize . . . only twenty bundles of salt-grass was the price
of gold, turquoise, cloaks, quetzal plumes: all precious things fetched the
same price.'[65]

For the poor, acceptance or rejection of a claim to dependence could be
a matter of life and death. We hear of local occasions when generosity was
warmed by the birth of a child or some other personal triumph, and poor
men crowded into the courtyard hoping to be recognized and invited to
seat themselves. Others, more desperate, simply clustered round the
dwellings of the lords, offering their need and their anxious deference in
exchange for food. The Mexica had a word for the business of hanging
around the edges of feasts, waiting for handouts, desperate to suck up a
little of the sweetness: they called it 'horneting' or 'bumblebeeing'.[66]
Some miserable would-be 'bumblebees', pressing themselves forward,
desperate for recognition, were left neglected, ignored, and humiliated,
'anxious to go, unable to endure it', until they despaired and went on to
beg for food at another household.[67] Others driven by the lash of hunger
abandoned dignity altogether; a man arriving where 'several are eating',

yet angrily refused when he begged a mouthful, might nonetheless snatch
a maize cake, 'for looking askance at one does one no harm, but hunger
kills one'.[68] Feasting at all levels, save the most prescribed and formal,
must always have been spiced with the pure chanciness of recognition and
proper treatment, but in late imperial Tenochtitlan the familiar game had
expanded to fatal consequences for those for whom the stakes were not
status, but survival.

Clearly there was no notion of 'charity' nor any trace of the Christian
notion of the virtue of 'giving to the poor'. Nonetheless need was acknowledged in a brief recurrent period of largesse. In the two consecutive
months called the 'Little' and the 'Great' Feast Day of the Lords, the
ruler and his lords 'showed their bounty'. The terms of the distribution
for the second month, for which we happen to have a good description,
are worth analysis. The poor – men and women, old and young – arrived
at dawn at the distribution point. There great 'canoes', according to
Sahagún, being presumably the largest ad hoc containers available, had
been filled with maize gruel. The people were allowed to take as much
gruel as would fill the vessels they had brought. (Some, lacking bowls or
gourds, scooped it up as best they could in their clothing, a disturbing
glimpse of their desperation.) The gruel drunk, they were made to wait,
talking quietly ('twittering like birds') until noon, when they were arranged 'in order' to receive their midday meal of a single handful of
tamales. The 'order' was probably based on calpulli groups, as the servitors who doled out the food knew the people they served, being said to
favour friends, kin, and children with an extra handful. We can therefore
imagine long lines of the needy, the lines organized as to neighbourhood,
waiting to receive their small gift of food through the agents of their
particular lord.[69]

That food gift was not designed for maximum nourishment. 'Lordly
food' was doled out: tamales from the rich man's table, his wealth shown
in the intricacy and elaboration of the confection with the maize dough
twisted and plaited and perhaps crested with seeds, the fillings savoury.
There was commonly serious hunger at this season, not long before the
new harvest came in and with maize dear in the market, and some individuals attempted to grab more than their dole. Their punishment was to
be beaten by the servitors so as to 'raise welts', and to have what food they
had taken from them. And every year, in one or another of the anxious

lines, the food ran out. Then those suddenly deprived of hope broke and ran to where food was still being distributed, to be beaten back by their more fortunate fellows. The unlucky ones stood, we are told, and wept, for themselves, their hungry children, and their evil fortune.[70]

There was possibly some implication of augury in all this: were one a food-grower one's luck in the queue could intimate one's likely fortune for the harvest. But the affair has most interest at the social level. Connoisseurs of welfare systems will notice some interesting aspects. The food distribution continued over eight days. For eight days individuals and families could hope at best to receive for a whole day's waiting some maize gruel and a handful of tamales, and that only if they were patient, docile, and fortunate. They were given no food for those unable to participate directly in this gift-receiving; for the old or sick or those who had sought to hire themselves out to labour for the day: this was for all its rigour a personal transaction. And in the evenings of all those eight days the lords and warriors danced, displaying themselves in their most sumptuous array, and then retired to feast.

So much, we might say, for the 'largesse of the lords', which looks to us more like a scenario for a riot. Yet so it was called and so, presumably, it was seen: as a gesture of lordly generosity. This suggests an intensifying imbalance of reciprocities in the urban milieu, where dependants' poverty no longer compelled response, yet where any resort to direct action, or 'self-help', as we might see it, was punished vigorously and physically not only by the agents of the lords but by one's companions in necessity. (We are a long way from 'horizontal solidarities' here.) Distance was what was being insisted upon, in the delicate taste of 'lordly food' in the mouth, in the high contrast between the patient meekness of the lowly during the day, and the dancing and feasting of the privileged in the night. Deference and submission were still exacted, but there was no corresponding compulsion on the now-remote giver. There is also that interesting element of wanton chance built into the situation, of denial of agency, in that one could find oneself, however dutifully submissive, forced to accept one's powerlessness and submit to one's ill fortune when the food ran out.

The unabashed social ruthlessness of such a system – and its psychological implications – is hard for us to grasp, accustomed as we are to a softer or at least more convoluted rhetoric of deserts and duties. It is essential to the understanding of Mexica conceptualizations of the sacred.

Heavenly powers rarely merely mirror the formal relations of those below, the earthly light being more commonly refracted than reflected. It is the points of stress and abrasion in men's own social experiences, the hidden, obsessive themes in the dialogues they have with one another, which lend urgency and structure to their imagined engagement with the sacred.

7

On one issue at least scholarly disputes about the Mexica have nested in a larger consensus: where social divisions are dramatic, attitudes to the sacred must be necessarily divided in accordance with those divisions. There has also been fair agreement that while some aspects of local and household ritual were rooted in the exigencies of everyday life, and were carried through with minimal priestly intervention, the Mexica ceremonial extravaganzas staged in the main temples were dramatizations of a state ideology: exercises in hegemonic control which had more to do with the politics of terror than with service to the gods.[71] The imperial resources poured into rituals, most especially those to do with mass human killings, have been seen as largely directed outwards, but also as designed to meet the novel political challenges of late-imperial Tenochtitlan, where a social conglomerate traditionally defined in terms of a shared past and a shared tribal identity, respectful of age and the reciprocities of kinship, had been subjected to the strains of rapid growth, and social, ethnic, and economic diversification. Dispute has tended to focus on the efficacy of those attempts at dominance and recruitment rather than on the initial categorizations. Some analysts, impressed by the depth of social division in the city, are led to identify the cycle of state-sustained ceremonial as the expression of a narrow class ideology, and to cast the commoners as bemused or coerced contributors to the élite cult while contriving to pursue their own distinct and different sacred affairs independently at the local level. Other interpreters, impressed by the scope and inclusiveness of the ceremonies and the abundant indications of enthusiastic popular participation, move briskly to a functionalist conclusion. Taking as a postulate the remarkable capacity of ritual to dramatize social categories while simultaneously demonstrating their necessary interdependence, they assert the capacity of the Mexica state ideology to generate 'wild fanaticism' in the lesser ranks, without making clear just how the trick was done.[72]

It is a delicate problem, and one in which we are at maximum risk of falling victim to our own sentimentalities. There can be no doubt that social divisions were painfully real. If all Mexica owed duty to the state, only commoners paid their tribute in labour services. Commoners could not wear cotton; commoners could not wear cloaks longer than the knee; commoners could not go sandalled in the presence of their betters. It must also be acknowledged that one response of the ruling group to the changes in late-imperial Tenochtitlan was the very active making of ritual to render the changes graspable and intelligible.[73] Nonetheless, we cannot assume that such division divided experience so profoundly as to generate different visions of the world. At this point I want to postpone consideration of ritual, to look first at other ordering devices in the fluid and restless world of the city, beginning with the body of precepts earlier referred to: the 'discourses of the elders'.[74]

This body of precepts continued to enjoy high status. There appears to have been at least formal insistence on the homilies' complete adequacy as guides to living, and swift opprobrium for one 'who wishes not to live as did his beloved father or grandfather': that is, in accordance with the social and sacred relationships preserved in the discourses. How is it possible to 'live as one's grandfather' in a rapidly changing world which had taken the long leap from dependence to power, from poverty to wealth, from a harsh life shared to the harshness of unsharing? Presumably because the essential nature of the world, despite what we would diagnose as 'change', remains unchanging, and the wisdom of the elders timeless. In that sphere of practical knowledge and appropriate conduct as distilled in the discourses there are few elaborated statements as to the nature of reality, and no exegesis of first and last things. Such notions are assumed, the underpinnings of conventional action and conventional judgment. But while the homilies promote an ideal of humility and modest sufficiency, the pains and chagrins of the explicitly contestful world of feasting and display are bitterly noted, and its necessities admitted, with the posture of histrionic dependence before superiors always insisted upon. For the gods to be coaxed into generosity – in large matters, like the provision of abundant rain, or small, like accepting a child into their service – it was necessary to induce their liberality by the presentation of gifts, and by adopting the correct posture of desperate abasement.

'Pity' is a constant theme in Nahuatl literature, accounting for a whole genre of *tlauculcuicatl*, uneasily rendered as 'lament' or 'compassion' songs.[75] Christian and European influence in the Florentine Codex, or indeed in any and all of the written Nahuatl texts, can neither be discounted nor easily counted, given that Christian missionaries drew up the first dictionaries, and, unsurprisingly, rough-matched Mexica words to European words drenched in European notions.[76] Yet Amerindian 'pity' has little to do with the tender sentiment of 'mercy' in Christian teaching, with its 'there but for the Grace of God' invocation of the equality of men in misery. The Winnebago protagonist in Paul Radin's *Autobiography of a Winnebago Indian,* deliberately left behind by his parents as they embarked on a fishing trip, pursued them along the shore, running, weeping – until his display of desperation reached a sufficient level of intensity to cause them to turn the canoe in to land, and to take him along. This was not a single episode, but a known strategy; if his passion of longing was sufficiently strong, if he ran and wept hard enough, his parents would yield. Desperate need if sufficiently dramatically expressed worked coercively on the unwilling giver.[77]

Similar notions were abroad in Mesoamerica. In the traditional invocations to the deities there are hints of an understanding preserved in the archaic Nahuatl which cast a long shadow forward through time to the Plains Indian on his Vision Quest, reducing himself – by starvation, loss of blood, exhaustion – to so pitiable a state as to force the manifestation of his Spirit through the intensity of his suffering. (That we might perceive an induced physiological condition conducive to hallucination of course does not touch the actuality of the experience.) This has nothing to do with the passive endurance of affliction marked as a Christian virtue. It is a very much more active suffering and seeking, predicated on the notion of reciprocity, however asymmetrical. The sun-dancer leaning and twisting against the drag of ropes hooked into his flesh strives to tear the tatters of flesh from his body not so much as an 'offering' as in proof of sincerity: the wholeheartedness of his dependence on the wilfully absent spirit. The suppliant strives to extort a response from the sacred powers by the extravagance and extremity of his suffering, by calling and crying upon them, or standing mute in an anguish of desire.

Mexica weepings, fasting and self-lacerations were designed to snag the attention of inattentive gods in much the same way. After the conquest Spanish missionary friars were to be startled by the abuse Indians would heap on an unresponsive deity, but that abuse was presumably the obverse of the desperation of earlier unattended importunings: it was the deity's 'duty' to respond. This gives a glimpse of what the Mexica thought they were doing in their great collective approaches to the gods: not praising them with loud hosannas, but reminding them of their powers, and so of their obligations.[78]

The thread of wholehearted dependence, with the wholeheartedness coercing response, ran through all solicited relationships, whether human or sacred. When a noble wished to place his son at the *calmecac* or priests' school – called, with good reason, the 'House of Tears' – he activated the familiar system by first offering the priests a feast, and then begging their favours for his child: 'may your hearts be inclined; grant him gifts.' Within the priests' school the boy would attempt to initiate the same relationship with the god, performing penances 'all night, all day . . . while he calleth to, while he crieth out to our lord'. For in that house of 'ardent desiring with weeping, with sighs' the god will make his enigmatic decision: 'there he giveth one gifts, there he selecteth one.'[79] The highest human office was woven into the same skein of dependence: the ratification of the human 'election' of the ruler waited upon Tezcatlipoca's inscrutable choice. As the god sat at ease feasting among his friends, he might choose to heed or not to heed the sighs and tears of the ruler-elect, wrapped in his fasting-cloak, drawing forth the bright blood; might choose to withhold the regalia of rule from his own place of ineffable security: 'there thou livest, thou rejoicest among thy . . . true acquaintances. There thou selecteth, takest possession of, thou inspirest the weeper, the sorrower, the sigher . . . and there thou placest upon them, glorifiest them with the peaked hat, the turquoise diadem, and the ear-plug, the lip-plug, the head band, the arm band, the band for the calf of the leg, the necklace, the precious feather. . . .'[80] In such a system there was infinite play for the wistfulness of desire and the sour misery of envy.

In the great collective prayers to the gods there were constant exclama-

tions of respect ('O noble one, O precious person') and the listing of the
range of names which indicate the span of the god's powers; there were
self-abasements ('I come sidling up – I who am a commoner, unright-
eous'; 'I who am a commoner, a fieldhand'); there were statements of
need; there were the most earnest descriptions of the suffering caused by
the god's neglect or his 'castigations'.[81] (The correct posture before these
intimations of 'anger', which is to put it rather too personally, was intensified submission.) Consider the great prayer to Tezcatlipoca, 'He who
gives riches and happiness, and holds fortune in his hand':

> O master, O our lord, O master of the necessities of life, who hast sweetness,
> fragrance, riches, wealth: show mercy, have compassion for thy common folk. May
> thou honour them, show them a little of thy freshness, thy tenderness, thy sweet-
> ness, thy fragrance. . . . May they through thy grace know repose for a little
> time. . . . If perhaps they should become arrogant, if perhaps they should become
> presumptuous . . . should keep for themselves thy property, thy possessions; if
> perchance because of it they should become perverse, heedless, thou wilt give it to
> the truly tearful . . . the truly sighing one . . . the truly poverty-stricken one . . .
> the meek, those who prostrate themselves, who go saddened on earth.[82]

This is most relentless and aggressive importunity. The prayer to
Tlaloc demanding rain pursued the same strategy, with its urgent recital
of all those plants and creatures afflicted, abandoned and dying in their
trusting dependence: the infants playing with their potsherds, the maize,
'sister' of the god, lying prostrate, dust-covered, gaunt; the whole catalogue of dependants forgotten culminating in the plea to 'water the earth,
for the earth, the living creatures, the herbs, the stalks remain watching,
remain crying out, for all remain trusting.'[83] The efficacy of these images
did not have to do with the pathos of a reduced humanity appealing to an
attentive deity, with its soft gracenote of divine condescension to participation in the human. There was no flattery in the depth of the submission: the power of Tezcatlipoca, of Tlaloc, cannot be exaggerated. Distance was insisted upon. The aim was to waken pride.

Men had no independent power. Their survival pivoted on the doubtful
pull of dramatized dependence: a very contingent affair. The task was
somehow to animate the relationship and stimulate the giving impulse.
The gods, those notoriously abstracted givers, had first to be attracted by
performances which would catch their attention, and then coaxed to

munificence by the presentation of gifts, the richer the better. There were histrionic displays of confidence in the generosity of the lordly giver. Precious food resources were used extravagantly, wastefully, to demonstrate that confidence. In the month of Etzalqualiztli when the rains had well set in, and the maize and beans were growing strongly, everyone, including the poor, cooked up a rich porridge of maize and beans and shared it freely.[84] The porridge was a notably rich dish in that frugal economy, where 'in time of famine', as Durán tells us, 'the eating of a handful of beans is comparable to plucking a handful of eyelashes.'[85] Yet months before the harvest was due the porridge was not only eaten, but distributed promiscuously, in a display of confident and therefore (ideally) coercive dependence.[86]

8

There can be no doubt that the Mexica placed a special value on their human prestations as particularly pleasing to the gods. The Dominican Durán mourned that 'many times I have asked the Indians why they could not be content to offer quail, turtledoves and other birds they used to offer, and they answered as if it were a ridiculous thing of little moment that those were the offerings of poor and lowly men, and that to offer war captives and prisoners and slaves was the honourable offering appropriate to great lords and noblemen, and they make much of these things and remember them, and tell them as great deeds.'[87] As we will see, among the range of human 'gifts' the elaborate ixiptlas or 'god-representations' were particularly valuable.

There is possibly a general sense in which the public and deliberate killing of a human tends to concentrate attention, regardless of any particular cultural evaluation of human as against other forms of life, but to get past our own to something of the Mexica view presents a major problem. We are all touched by Christianity, with its extraordinary joining of the highest god to human flesh in the person of the Christ, and then the elevation of the living and dead flesh of saints as infused with the divine power. Remarkable, not to say preposterous, as that notion was at its first proposing, we have become habituated to the 'enormous symbolic weight' placed on the individual human body as a most significant locus of the mediation of the human and the divine.[88] Given that massive weight of unconsidered understandings, it is difficult indeed to entertain the possibility that Mexica might have killed humans with no particular regard for their individuality, but perhaps (as could seem the case with the ixiptlas) as representing a notably lavish investment, or merely as more effective because of more flexible and evocative theatrical properties.

Some clarification can be found in translation. The first great Nahuatl–Spanish dictionary, drafted in 1553, was completed in 1571.[89] The Spanish word for 'sacrifice' was insinuated into it by its Franciscan compiler, to the continuing profitable befuddlement of professors of comparative religion, the single Spanish word being used to cover three word clusters. The first meant literally 'all those who were to die before the gods,' and signified, I think, just that, being used as a simple category description, as in 'those who are to die for the gods enter left'. (Sometimes the word for death was modified to qualify the death, as in 'flowery death', meaning the honourable death of a warrior on the field of battle, or of death on the killing stone.) Two further and separate notions were yoked together as having to do with 'sacrifice'. The first concerned the drawing forth of blood from one's own body in the presence of the sacred images, and centered around notions of debt, levy, tribute, or obligation, probably deriving from the word 'to cut'.[90] (One who died the 'flowery death' on the battlefield or on the killing stone was said to have paid all his or her 'debt'.) The second cluster was typically invoked in relation to the festivals, and centered on the notion of arranging, of laying out in formal order, or of making a gift or presentation to someone. It lacked any specific identification with the offering of humans.

In their 'sacrifices' Mexica killed humans almost exclusively. The only other creature killed in anything like comparable numbers were quail, typically by having their heads wrenched off, so yielding a quick jet of blood. (The quail were, I think, killed as surrogate warriors, so identified for their moving in swift-running bevies, their scurry to reassemble when scattered at a whistled signal, and their flutterings and desperate earth-striking struggles in death.)[91] Despite radical inequalities between Mexica and those not Mexica, and between Nahuatl speakers and 'barbarians', the Mexica knew that all humans, unequal as they might be in human arrangements, participated in the same desperate plight: an involuntary debt to the earth deities, contracted through the ingestion of the fruits of the earth. That debt could be acknowledged by the payment of a regular token levy – those offerings of one's own blood – but it could be fully extinguished only by death, when the earth lords would feed upon the bodies of men, as men had perforce fed upon them. It is that divine hunger which appears to underly the gross feedings of undifferentiated mass killings. The central image for grasping what was going on with the very different killings of the human ixiptlas, as the Nahuatl words clustering about the offerings indicate, is not about feeding but feasting, which as we have seen was a very much more complex emotionally and socially charged affair.

The feast provided the distinctive cultural form through which the Mexica mediated and explored their understanding of the key relationships between men and between men and the sacred: at once metaphor and matter of social relations. It was strung between the poles of conviviality and the stretched euphoria of the status battle feasts of some North American Indian groups, where one staked all to coerce the admiration and break the poise of the guest-rival. I have suggested that the activity took on a peculiar poignancy in the imperial urban milieu, where rewards were great but uncertain, and where kinship ties were abrading under the growth and enforced cosmopolitanism of the city, while possible alternative bonds of clientage or co-residence were problematical. Relationships within feasting groups became increasingly bitter as access became increasingly crucial; an acknowledged claim to dependence could mean the hope of survival. Men who failed to keep the bonds of recognized dependence taut could die of starvation in the streets of Tenochtitlan.

Of all the gods it was Tezcatlipoca, the 'Lord of the Here and Now', who stood closest to men. Earth was known to be a place of exile, of danger, precisely because it was in the hand of Tezcatlipoca, who was what he was, and whose impenetrable will was most surely done. In such a world of chronic uncertainty friendship between men took lustre from the darkness of its setting. But there was no security even there, for the swarm of competitive would-be dependants were also 'friends', and friends of the most tenacious kind. Tezcatlipoca is reminded: 'Thou dost not want for friends. In all the world thy friends, thy real friends, remain awaiting thee, remain calling out to thee. And thy humble friends remain sighing unto thee.'

It is difficult to see 'religion' in a cosily integrative light when faced with this kind of thing. Participation in feasts as in ritual action could be profoundly stressful for the individual. The choreographed encounters between groups often seemed to dramatize and exacerbate tensions, as in the food distribution of the Great Feast Day of the Lords. Yet the essence of the enchantment lay in the tensions and miseries: those 'religious' conceptualizations and actions caught up, formalized and framed the darker obsessions and most painful anxieties of social life, not for easy comfort (the Mexica did not look for comfort) but so they could be contemplated, comprehended, and thus rendered tolerable. Some of the insights were bitter. The steady movement of individuals through fixed rites of passage in accordance with the cherished traditions of the elders – the naming ceremonies, with their invocation of neighbourhood, the gleeful marriage processions past dwellings no longer all familiar – must have measured, through their formal denial of it, just how much Tenochtitlan was changing, generation through generation; just how little, beyond the words and gestures of the rituals, had remained constant. On the Great Feast Day of the Lords men learnt again that no human action, no submission however extravagant, guaranteed response or reward. We find the same bleak assumption of asymmetry, the same desperate insistence on relationship, the extremes of deference coupled with insistence on response, in the feasting of the gods as in the feasting of men; the same attentiveness to the elegance and refinement of the arranging, the 'laying out in order' of the offerings placed before them, the same finely calculated richness in the prestations made by the inferior to the superior to induce his full liberality: in the conspicuous waste of incense and flowers, feathers and jades, and most especially in the beauty of the human offerings, and their significant cost.[92]

Submission to a power which is caprice embodied is a taxing enterprise, yet it is that which the most devoted Mexica appear to have striven to achieve. Wisdom belonged to those who accepted what it was to live in Tezcatlipoca's world: 'O master, O our lord, may thy heart desire whatsoever thou mayest desire. This is all. Thus I cast myself before thee, I who am a commoner, a field hand.'[93] For 'those who truly deliver their minds, their hearts to thee . . . there is received as merit the peace, the contentment . . . the moment of well-being by thy grace. And there are received as merit paralysis, blindness, the miserable cape, rags'.[94] Men learnt from ritual as from life that no human action, no submission however extravagant, could guarantee reward when the crucial nexus of relationship had attenuated, and the distance grown too great. The context of experience in which that lesson was set – the extravagance and abundance of the imperial city, the laceration of want in the midst of abundance – sharpened the formal lesson.

In this painful distance lies one explanation for the Mexica fascination with those living ixiptlas, the male or female 'god-representations' who were decked in the regalia of deities and paraded through the streets. In their persons the aloof gods were at last made palpable and available for solicitation and demand. One of the many attractions of the beautiful young man who was fêted as Tezcatlipoca for a full year was his inexhaustible courtesy and his tireless attentiveness to the sighs and importunings of his worshippers. The great orchestrated ritual performances held in the main temple precinct or pursued through the city streets could grip Mexica imagination because they were at once intensely relevant to the painful uncertainties of Mexica experience at all social levels, and capable of ordering those uncertainties to the bleak coherence of the inevitable.

9

At this point I want to examine the Mexica understanding of the relationship between sacred and secular power, and to test the reality of the conceptualizations I have been proposing, by an enquiry into a specific case: the social and sacred authority of the supreme ruler, the tlatoani or 'Great Speaker', as manifested in his installation rites. As usual, we have only fragments of the process of the installation rituals, the ceremonious making, of the Mexica tlatoani.[95] Also as usual, those rituals are differently valued by analysts, some dismissing them as little more than obfuscations of the enduring 'realities' of individual ambition.[96] There were contests for power and unexplained deaths in the Mexica system, as in most equivalent polities. But something was effected by the installation rites which went well beyond a romanticized notion of 'pragmatism';

something sufficiently formidable to inhibit, for example, the replacement of the imprisoned and impotent Moctezoma as tlatoani during his Spanish captivity until a moment of intolerable crisis.

The rituals were set in motion when on the old ruler's death his inner council, drawn from the adult male members of the ruling lineage, and so including all the likeliest contenders for the highest office, selected one of their number as ruler (in the Tenochtitlan case usually showing a preference for the lord who held the office of war commander) and chose his ruling Council of Four.[97] How bitterly these selections were contested and at what point in time they were arranged we cannot know: as with the selection of a pope these deliberations were secret. Given that it is the public assertions and so the public awareness about the nature and bases of political authority which concern us, the analysis of the public processes of the ruler-elect's transformation into tlatoani should display in slow-motion sequence the various sources of his claimed authority.

In a formal display of unreadiness (and perhaps in enactment of the coercion of divine selection) the ruler-elect was grasped by the great priests to be brought before an assembly of leading lords and warriors. There he was stripped, dressed in penitential garb and taken to the great pyramid and the shrine of Huitzilopochtli, where, faces veiled by the 'fasting capes' of the penitential state, he and his four advisers offered incense and were displayed before the assembled people and the Mexica deity. Then he and his council retired for four days of 'fasting' (in Mexica terms one meagre meal a day, prolonged vigil, and ritual bathing) and much penitential bloodletting. (It is not clear whether the requirements placed on the ruler-elect were more stringent than those of his councillors.) Only after that period of strengthening and purification was the new ruler permitted to enter his palace. There he was subjected to a sequence of discourses on his duties, very much in the 'custodian of the people and guardian of traditions' mode, by senior lords and priests. He responded with proper humility, and then addressed an exhortation to the assembled people. Shortly after these ceremonies he would go to war to collect an adequate number of captives for his public installation: a glorious affair of grand-scale killings of captives and gift exchanges with enemy as well as friendly or subject rulers.[98]

The killings had to be numerous because they were a statement of the power of the Mexica war god, and of the new ruler's capacity to serve him.

That message was of high relevance to those within and without the city. The ruler's submission to the instruction offered by lords and elders, and his own address to his people, established him as the superior earthly repository of accumulated traditional wisdom, much of the rhetoric of rulership being thick with metaphors of the ruler as father, custodian, and guide to his people: the head to the commoners' wings and tail of the great bird of state, the spreading tree giving protection and shade to lesser men, and (even more insistently) the parent tenderly bearing the burden of his children in his arms. But a very different theme ran in counterpoint to the 'father of the people' emphasis. At some point in the complex process of installation the ruler-elect spent a night in prayer and vigil before the image of Tezcatlipoca, standing naked before the god.[99] Tezcatlipoca, unlike other Mesoamerican deities, did not represent a particular complex of natural forces. Nor did he provide an emblem of tribal identity. He was the deity associated with the vagaries of this world, of 'the Here and Now', as ubiquitous and ungraspable as the Night Wind: fickleness personified.[100]

He was also the source and repository of worldly power. 'Tezcatlipoca' meant 'Smoking Mirror', the opaque obsidian mirror with its riddling dark reflections, or perhaps more correctly 'the Mirror's Smoke'. He was also named Moyocoyatzin, 'Capricious Creator', Titlacahuan, 'He Whose Slaves We Are', Moquequeloa, 'The Mocker'. His hand was seen most clearly when a man rich in all good fortune, with many sons, wealth and honours, was suddenly, gratuitously, brought low. As we have seen, slaves were pampered as 'the beloved sons of Tezcatlipoca' on his daysign, not through some 'last shall be first' inversion or notion of ultimate human equality, but because their calamitous position dramatized the pure arbitrariness of individual destiny. When Tezcatlipoca chose to appear on earth he wrought havoc. Sometimes he heaped bounty on a casually chosen recipient; more often – much more often – he inveigled men to their deaths, often choosing to use the intoxication of sacred experience as the lure. In the legendary city of Tollan, appearing in his favoured guise as a young warrior, he beat his drum and intoned a song of such power that others took it from his lips, and sang. Then those seduced into song began, helplessly, to dance. And then, 'when there was dancing, [when] there was the greatest intensity of movement, very many threw themselves from the crags into the canyon . . . they were as if besotted. And as many

times as there was song and dance, so many times was there death.' The
laughter of Tezcatlipoca signalled destruction. Of Tezcatlipoca it was
said: 'He only mocketh. Of no-one can he be a friend, to no-one true.'
One of his many soubriquets was the 'Enemy on Both Sides'.[101]

It was this principle of subversion, of wanton, casual, antisocial power
which was peculiarly implicated in Mexica notions of rule, and was embodied (at least on occasion) in the Mexica ruler.[102] In those hours of
standing naked before the image of the god the ruler's body was open to
invasion by the sacred force, and the choice of the god confirmed. For
most of the time the tlatoani functioned in the mundane world, his authority deriving from his exalted lineage, his conquests, and his position
as head of the social hierarchy.[103] But that was merely a human authority,
which could be displaced by Tezcatlipoca's overwhelming presence, especially when men who had violated the social order were brought before
their lord. The place of royal judgment was called 'the slippery place',
because beyond it lay total destruction. If his careful judges reflected on
the niceties of their judgments, there were no judicious metaphors in the
ruler's punishment: only obliterating sacred power.

From the moment of the first formal address to the newly chosen ruler,
the transformation in his person and his being was recognized and acknowledged:

Although thou art human, as we are, although thou art our friend, although thou
art our son, our younger brother, our older brother, no more art thou human, as
are we; we do not look on thee as human. . . . Thou callest out to, thou speakest
in a strange tongue to the god, the Lord of the Near, of the Nigh. And within thee
he calleth out to thee; he is within thee; he speaketh forth from thy mouth. Thou
art his lip, thou art his jaw, thou art his tongue.[104]

'He is within thee'. The ruler was also called the 'flute' of Tezcatlipoca;
the 'Great Speaker' sometimes spoke in the voice of the god.[105] The
ambivalence of his power was well understood. Those early and anxious
exhortations to benevolent behaviour were necessary, 'for it was said when
we replaced one, when we selected someone . . . he was already our lord,
our executioner, and our enemy.'[106]

'Our lord, our executioner, and our enemy': a desolate cadence. The
transformation was manifest: 'It was said he looked nowhere; it was said
his eyes were shooting straight. He sat even as a god.' If the Mexica ruler

went into battle in the warrior garb of the Mexica deity Huitzilopochtli, he ruled as subject and vehicle of Tezcatlipoca. After his elevation commoners could not look upon his face, and even his lords approached him without sandals and divested of their rich cloaks, in the posture of acute humility. His eating, his visits to his women, were decorously concealed, and in public ceremonial he was borne, an icon of rulership, on the shoulders of his lords, with the roads swept before him.

We know something of the range of claims for the divinity of kings: the 'great chain of being' yoking the human, the royal and the sacred; the exemplary centre replicated and diffused through human rule; the ruler as god-on-earth. Kingships by blood or by right of conquest are commonplaces in European thought. Other modes, like the 'selection' made by a god and actualized by men; the transformation through preliminary humiliation and the rites of installation, have been largely forgotten in Europe, but are familiar enough from other peoples in other places. The Mexica ruler was understood to bear multiple relationships to the divine. He went into combat in the customary regalia of the warrior god Huitzilopochtli. His image was set up as a representation of Xiutecutli, the Fire God, on the god's feast of Izcalli, which saw the renovation of all great social bonds and the acknowledgment of the 'naturalness' of human hierarchy.[107] In his priestly performances Moctezoma was associated with Quetzalcoatl, the deity of priestly wisdom. But it was with Tezcatlipoca that his association (as with all Mexica rulers) was closest. It was from Tezcatlipoca that he took his power to command, reward or punish. The tlatoani's sacredness was not a state, but a condition, intermittent, yet 'personal' in the most immediate sense, in that his body, properly prepared and adorned, could on occasion become the vehicle of that divine force.[108]

I stress the intermittent nature of the power because I think it was in no sense the ruler's 'possession', but that rather it was understood to possess him, and only for the duration of the solicited presence of the deity as signalled by appropriate ritual and the wearing of the appropriate regalia. (This is compatible with what we know of the Amerindian conviction of the transforming capacities of sacred regalia and ritual garments.) Such visitations left the ruler's person and garments residually charged with sacred force, so that his body and whatever had touched it had to be handled with appropriate care, but reverence did not attach to the human person.

'Power' was not an emanation of the ruler, but of the sacred power briefly resident within him. It has sometimes been claimed that the last days of empire saw the beginning of a cult of the ruler, initiated and encouraged by Moctezoma the Younger. The main grounds for that claim are the high port adopted by Moctezoma, and that on the days of One Rain and Four Wind some captives were killed so that 'through them Moctezoma received new life'.[109] That is possibly so: on such matters and at our distance dogmatism is not a plausible stance. But it is worth noting that on those days Moctezoma was imbued with the punitive power of Tezcatlipoca, 'doers of evil' like adulterers or thieves being put to death. One Rain was also one of the five days of the year in which the 'Celestial Princesses', demonic female figures who roamed the paths and haunted the crossroads to maim and kill, descended to earth, and when sorcerers and demons were much feared. No account is given of specific rituals accompanying the killings dedicated to Moctezoma: it is simply said that 'through these who died Moctezoma received life. By them his fate was strengthened; by them his fate was exalted, and on them he placed the burden. So it was said it was as if through them once more he were rejuvenated, so that he might live many years. Through them he became famous, achieved honour, and became brave, thereby making himself terrifying'. These are the only references we have to any human killings affecting another human.[110]

This particular triangulation of humankind, nature and the sacred, with its Jekyll-and-Hyde implications for the supreme human authority, appears to be a particular Mexica variation on a familiar theme. Tezcatlipoca was a major deity for all the peoples of Central Mexico. In the handful of surviving pre-contact codices, probably deriving from the Puebla region, he was a formidable figure, and he is everywhere recognized as the arbiter of human destinies. We do not know how distinctive the Mexica emphasis on his caprice and casual malice was, largely because we know so little of other peoples and the inner workings of their societies. But in Tenochtitlan Tezcatlipoca loomed very large.[111] The Mexica had grounds for being sensitive to the contingencies of human existence. It is therefore unsurprising that Tezcatlipoca should have impressed them as a deity of peculiar interest. The chronic asymmetry of relationships between inferiors and superiors extended across the visible and the sacred worlds: within the priesthood, the warrior houses, the merchant associations; between noble and commoner; between those who lived well and those who did not; between ruler and ruled, deity and ruler, gods and human-kind. Feast and festival caught up and tirelessly displayed those powerful and abrasive themes of life as it had come to be in the imperial city. The central drama of Mexica social and sacred relations pivoted on the prob-lematic of giving, and withholding; the acknowledgment or the denial of connection, with the old securities gone. Tezcatlipoca in the Mexica imagining of him was the epitome of the great lord: superb; indifferent to homage, with its implication of legitimate dependence; all bounty in his hand; and altogether too often not in the giving vein.

PART II

Roles

3

Victims

Let no soldier fly.
He that is truly dedicate to war
Hath no self-love; nor he that loves himself
Hath not essentially, but by circumstance,
The name of valour.

William Shakespeare, *Henry VI, Part II*, v: 2

I

A Jesuit observer has left a painfully detailed description of the doing to death by the Huron of a captured Seneca warrior in 1637. The Seneca, a man about fifty, still suffering the wounds of his capture, had been briefly adopted into a chief's family, but then rejected because of those wounds and consigned to die by fire. Soon after dark on the appointed night, after the prescribed sequence of feastings, eleven fires were lit down the length of the council house. The people came crowding tightly in, the young men, yelling and joyful, armed with firebrands. (They were warned to temper their enthusiasm so that the victim would last through the night.) The prisoner, singing his warrior's song, was brought in as the chief made the announcement as to how the body would be divided when death finally came. The description continues:

Now he began to run a circuit around the fires, again and again, while everyone tried to burn him as he passed; he shrieked like a lost soul; the whole cabin resounded with cries and yells. Some burned him, some seized his hands and snapped bones, others thrust sticks through his ears, still others bound his wrists with cords, pulling at each end with all their might, so as to cut flesh and crush bone.

87

And so, horribly, on throughout the long night. When the victim fainted he was gently revived. He was given food at intervals; was addressed, and addressed his tormentors, in kinship terms, and gasped out his warrior songs as best he could. At dawn, close to death but still conscious, he was taken outside, tied to a post and burned without restriction with heated axe heads until at last he hung silent and motionless. Then his hands, his feet and at the last his head were cut off and given to those to whom they had been promised.[1]

Obviously our sensibilities are shocked by such a performance. But it is made at least potentially graspable because we can, without too much effort, construct plausible psychological hypotheses about those brutal face-to-face, fire-to-flesh involvements: the desperate hilarity and the competitive cruelty of the young men, watching a fellow warrior endure what could so easily become their own fate; the zest of the women, able at last to tear and rend an enemy too often invisible; the resistance of the tormented warrior himself, singing his songs of defiance, maintaining the grim joke of kinship for as long as breath and control should last. Identifying possible human emotions, violent and cruel though they may be, we join victim to torturer, and each to ourselves.

As with the Huron, the Mexica attached no shame to such matters. It is Mexica picturings which dwell on the slow tides of blood down the steps of the pyramids, on skull-faced deities chewing on human limbs, on human hearts pulped into stone mouths. Three and four decades after the Spanish conquest old men were still ready to talk in lingering detail about the old festivals to scribes trained under the new order. They told of the great warrior festivals with the lines of victims dragged or driven up the wide steps of the pyramids to meet the waiting priests. At other festivals few died, but those few most ceremoniously. Some selected individuals were transformed into ambulant images of the Sacred Ones. They were fêted through the streets, to dance and die before the deities they represented – and then sometimes danced again, their flayed skins stretched over the living bodies of priest or warrior celebrants. The killings, whether large or small, were frequent: part of the pulse of living.

The Mexica laity were not physically involved in the acts of killing: at that point they were watchers only. But their engagement was nonetheless close, and all were complicit in it, either by way of the customary rotation through the calpullis of duties at a particular major temple, or more directly by personal involvement in a group festivity, as when the salt-workers or the fisher people purchased, prepared, and presented a special victim, or through the excitements in the household of a local warrior who had taken a prisoner for sacrifice. All participated in the care of victims in life, and in their dismemberment and processing in death. Warrior captives who were to die in major ceremonies were kept close by the local temples, probably in the cages the Spaniards insisted on seeing as fattening coops, and their care was a charge on the local people.[2] They were a source of pride and diversion, being fed, paraded, probably taunted, over the weeks and possibly months of their captivity. As the time of death drew near they were ritually prepared: forced to keep vigil; decked in appropriate regalia; processed through the streets, often to the place where they were to die. Finally they were prodded through the elaborate routines which were a prelude to their ascent of Huizilopochtli's pyramid. There they would be seized, forced back over the killing stone, a priest pressing down each limb to keep the chest tautly arched, while a fifth drove the wide flint blade of the sacrificial knife into the chest and dragged out the still-pulsing heart.[3] The heart was raised to the Sun and the plundered body let to fall aside. It was then sent soddenly rolling down the pyramid steps, to be collected at the base by old men from the appropriate calpulli temple, who would carry it away through the streets for dismemberment and distribution. So we have a careful, calculated shepherding of men, women, and children to their deaths. (One is reminded of Hemingway's mannered correction of the ignorant notion that the bullfight is 'cruel': 'there is no maneuver in the bullfight which has, as object, to inflict pain on the bull. The pain that is inflicted is incidental, not an end.')[4]

In sixteenth-century Europe, public executions – and the whole 'spectacle of suffering' of judicious tortures and exemplary maimings – reliably drew their crowds.[5] But such events were relatively infrequent, and certainly peripheral to the dailiness of life, while their victims, however pitiable, could be seen as culpable to some degree, and so contributing to their own misfortune. Mexica victims were purely victims. We gulp at Roman circuses, but think we recognize something of the desperate excitement of violent lethal contest: an excitement which can infect actors and audience alike. It is the combination of violence with apparent impersonality, the bureaucratic calculation of these elaborated Mexica brutalities, together with their habituated and apparently casual incorporation into the world of the everyday, which chills. Faced with that terrible matter-of-factness we are given neither a secure footing for judgement nor a threshold for fantasy, so that curiosity sickens. And we in this century are haunted by the shadows of those other victims who filed to their deaths, incredulous still, even as the tacit signs multiplied, that men could so coldly design the death of their fellows.

That sense of incredulity carries beyond narrowly intellectual matters to darker zones, threatening the vision, crucial to human studies as to a lot of other things, of an ultimately common humanity. It is not, therefore, something in which we can afford to acquiesce. How to get past that terrifying flatness? We need to know something of the range and textures of the Mexica imaginative world to grasp the place of human killings within it. But first it is necessary to establish the external circumstances of the practice: who the victims were, and how they were variously managed through to their deaths; what distinctions and categorizations the Mexica made within that large category of 'victim', and how they understood each group in terms of its relationship to themselves, to humankind, and to the gods.

2

The killing performances which most distinguished the Mexica from their neighbours were the great ceremonies which celebrated major moments in Mexica imperial rule: the installation of a new ruler, the dedication of a great temple or work of engineering. The victims who died in such ceremonies were foreigners, probably distant ones, and marked by garment, custom, and language as exotics: victims of a major war, or captives taken by subject or allied peoples, delivered as tribute to be consumed in a Mexica triumph. Although allocated between the wards for maintenance, they probably developed few connections with the local people throughout their period of captivity. Given the daunting size and unfamiliarity of the Mexica city, their social and physical isolation, and the high visibility of their own tribal affiliations in speech and dress, escape was not a plausible notion.

The Mexica made no attempt to exploit ignorance as a technique for keeping such prisoners docile. We have a description of what was done with the Huaxtecs of the northern gulf coast after an unsuccessful revolt against the rule of the Triple Alliance. The triumphant army herded the prisoners back to Tenochtitlan, the men linked by cords through the warrior perforations in their septums, the 'maidens', and the little boys still too young to have had their noses pierced, secured by yokes around their necks, all wailing a pitiful lament.[6] Priests greeted them as they approached the great city to tell them of their privilege: to die in the inauguration of the newly completed Temple of Huitzilopochtli (the same pyramid recently excavated in the square of the Cathedral of Mexico). Possibly twenty thousand victims died for that dedication: four patient lines stretching the full length of the processional ways and marshalled along the causeways, slowly moving towards the pyramid.[7]

Those massive killings marked particular and rare occasions, but the four seasonal festivals which marked the four periods for major tribute payments – Tlacaxipeualiztli, Etzalqualiztli, Ochpaniztli, and Panquetzaliztli – were also distinguished by numbers of killings, although opinions vary as to how many died. Surprisingly, the mode of the disposal of the bodies remains mysterious. We are usually told that skulls were spitted on the skull racks, limbs apportioned for ritual cannibalism, and the trunks fed to the flesh-eating birds and beasts in Moctezoma's menagerie, but such disposal techniques would clearly be inadequate. The bodies were perhaps burnt, although during their stay in the city Cortés and his men make no mention of any pyres or corpse-laden canoes, the detritus of human killings being confined, in their accounts, to the temple precincts. The land-locked lakes, precious sources of water and aquatic foods, offered no solution, so this large empirical matter remains unresolved. The provenance of the festival victims is less mysterious. They were probably drawn from tribute paid in slaves, and from the 'bank' of warriors captured during the season of war, which ran for the half-year of nine twenty-day months between the festival Ochpaniztli, presaging the harvest, and Tlacaxipeualiztli, which saw the first hopeful plantings.[8] Calpulli pride was actively engaged in these events: in the great warrior festival of Tlacaxipeualiztli, the 'Feast of the Flaying of Men', it is said that for every four hundred captives taken by the warriors of a particular calpulli came the privilege of offering one notable victim for death on the gladiatorial stone.[9] The Mexica seasonal killings of captives and warriors spoke most urgently in words and actions about feeding the earth powers and the sun, and gross feeding at that: warriors described as 'drinking cups of the gods', hearts offered hot like tortillas straight from the griddle to the Sun, the flesh and the cascades of blood – 'most precious water', as the Mexica named it – soaking into Earth Lord, Lord of Our Flesh. That much is relatively unmysterious, though the implications of so bleak a view of the relationship between humankind and the sacred powers will require some unravelling. The killings were also explicitly about the dominance of the Mexica and of their tutelary deity: public displays to overawe the watcher, Mexica or stranger, in a state theatre of power, at which the rulers of other and lesser cities, allies and enemies alike, were routinely present.

There is a strange docility in the behaviour of the non-warrior victims of the mass killings which suggests the depth of their social and psychological dislocation. If some faltered on the long climb, most apparently trudged up the pyramid steps with minimal prodding. While the acquiescence of these doomed creatures was possibly induced by demoralization, bewilderment, and fear – we have no reason to think their guardians were tender – their resignation might well have been assisted by drugs. The Mexica specified only the administering of 'obsidian-knife-water' and of *yauhtli* (thought to be powdered *Tagetes lucida*, with a mild sedating effect) to the victims. Diego Durán, with his disquieting knack for inventing plausible explanations, insisted that 'obsidian-knife-water' consisted of the washings of bloodied sacrificial knives mixed with chocolatl, which 'heathen spell' bewitched the victim into cheerfulness,[10] but it appears rather to have been a variant of the fermented milk of the agave cactus, now called pulque, in which plants of inebriating sacred power had been included. It was offered to victims from whom some sort of extravagance in performance was required.

The nomination of so few drugs used in rituals and the silence of the sources on the administering of powerful sedatives does not preclude the possibility of their extensive use. Mind-altering drugs were important to the Mexica, as to all Amerindians, who out of a relatively unpromising flora have developed an incomparably rich pharmacopoeia, especially in hallucinogens: a pharmacopoeia which could have been developed only through the most determined and intrepid experimentation.[11] The final preparation of the victims was a matter for the priests, who were presumably close-mouthed about how they achieved their effects. Nonetheless, the chapter in the 'Book of Earthly Things' of the Florentine Codex which tells of the different herbs, begins with the names of 'the many different herbs which perturb one, madden one'. The first is *ololiuqui*, the morning glory, whose seeds 'derange one'; the second is *peyotl*, which 'grows only . . . in Mictlan', the Place of the Dead to the Mexica, to us the far desert lands of northern Mexico; the *tlapatl*, or jimson weed, probably *Datura stramonium*, which takes away all hunger;[12] and *nanacatl* or *teonanacatl*, the 'flesh of the gods', the bitter little mushrooms which gave visions to their eaters. Particular kinds of performance could have been elicited by the judicious administration of pulque with specific additives. Datura with 'wine' has long been used in China as an anaesthetic for minor surgical operations, while in India it is said that dancing girls up to no good would give a man wine drugged with the datura seed, so rendering him helpless: while the victim might appear in full possession of his senses, he 'had no control of his will, was ignorant of whom he was addressing, and lost all memory of what he did when the intoxication wore off'. Whatever the exaggerations, the usefulness of such a concoction in delivering suitably co-operative victims to the sacrificial stone is clear. The herbalist Li Shih-chen also discovered that laughing or dancing movements could be induced in one who had drunk the drugged wine when those around him laughed or danced.[13] If this is true, a victim half-drunk on 'obsidian wine' could be brought to follow the dancing movements of his or her custodial entourage without the exercise of direct physical coercion.

The killing of selected warrior captives, usually accompanied by torture, was unremarkable among Amerindians, as the Huron 'burning' of the Seneca warrior indicates, but the process presumably varied in accord with different understandings of war and the consequent relationship between captor and captive. In Tenochtitlan notable captives, or those taken in a major campaign, were presented before the idol of Huitzilopochtli and then displayed at the royal palace before Moctezoma, while speeches were made on the death they would die.[14] The warrior from a Nahua city participant in Mexica understandings of war was particularly cherished, being tended by stewards in the local temple and constantly visited, adorned, and admired by his captor and the captor's devoted entourage of local youths. Such a man presented for death before

Huitzilopochtli's shrine crowning the great temple pyramid ideally leapt up the steps shouting the praises of his city. (That act of courage might have been made easier by the great bulk of the pyramid, which loomed so huge that a man at the base or on the long climb upwards could not see what awaited him.) Some, we are told, faltered on the stairs, and wept or fainted. They were dragged up by the priests. But, for most, pulque, anger, pride, or the narrowing existential focus of their days somehow got them through.

Mexica combat at its best was a one-to-one contest of preferably close-matched combatants, with one predestined to triumph, one to die. Given the fated outcome, and given the warrior obligation to seek and embrace the 'flowery death' on the field of battle or the killing stone, no shame need attach to defeat. The captive was in a deep sense the reflex of his captor, who accordingly took a tense and proprietary interest in that final performance. The quality of his own courage would be on public trial there.

Such prized captives were preferably offered at the festival of Tlacaxi-peualiztli, the 'Feast of the Flaying of Men', on what the Spaniards thought of as the 'gladiatorial stone', to die after having engaged in combat with a sequence of selected Mexica warriors. The victim was tethered by the waist to a rope fastened to the centre of a round stone, about waist high, a metre and a half wide, and elevated in its turn on a platform about the height of a man. The 'display' element was made explicit by the procession of 'gods' (high priests in the regalia of their deities) who formally took their places around the small round stage. The tethered victim was given a long draught of pulque, and most cere-moniously presented with weapons: four pine cudgels for throwing, and a war club, the club being studded not with the usual shallow flint blades but with feathers. He then had to fight up to four leading Mexica war-riors armed with bladed clubs, who fought from the platform, so giving the captive the advantage of height – an equivocal advantage, as we will see.[15]

Despite the combat theme, the conditions so carefully constructed in the 'gladiatorial' encounter bore slight resemblance to ordinary battle. The combat with each warrior was presumably timed, so there was pres-sure on the Mexica warrior to perform at maximum. The victim, elevated above his opponent and released from the inhibition against killing which

prevailed on the battlefield, could whirl his heavy club and strike at the head of his antagonist with unfamiliar freedom. The Mexica champions were also presented with a temptingly easy target. The victim could be disabled and brought down with one good blow to the knee or ankle, as on the battlefield. But such a blow would simultaneously abort the spectacle and end their glory, so the temptation had to be resisted. Their concern under these most taxing and public circumstances was rather to give a display of the high art of weapon handling: in an exquisitely prolonged performance to cut the victim delicately, tenderly with those narrow blades, to lace the living skin with blood (this whole process was called 'the striping'). Finally, the victim, a slow-carved object lesson of Mexica supremacy, exhausted by exertion and loss of blood, would falter and fall, to be dispatched by the usual heart excision.[16]

Throughout all this the captor, who had nurtured his captive with such care and pride, watched his mirrored self on public display. His warrior at last dead, the heart burnt in the eagle vessel in homage to Huitzilopochtli, the head removed for use in a priestly dance and then skewered on the appropriate skull rack, the cadaver carried to his home calpulli, the captor was given a gourd fringed with quetzal feathers and filled with the blood drawn from the welling chest cavity to carry through the city, daubing the blood on the mouths of the stone idols in all the temples. Then he returned to his own ward temple to flay and dismember the body, and to distribute the limbs in the conventional way. Later again, he watched while his kin, summoned to his home household, ate a small ritual meal of maize stew topped by a fragment of the dead warrior's flesh, as they wept and lamented the likely fate of their own young warrior. For that melancholy 'feast' the captor put off his glorious captor's garb, and was whitened, as his dead captive had been, with the chalk and feathers of the predestined victim.

The captor himself did not eat the flesh, saying, 'Shall I perchance eat my very self?' He had earlier, we are told, addressed his captive as his 'beloved son', and was addressed in turn as 'beloved father'. A surrogate 'uncle' had supported the captive through his last combat, offering him his draught of pulque, sacrificing quail on his behalf, and wailing for him after his death. There has been a tendency to take the invocation of kin terms as indicative of a particular emotional response, but that claim seems ill-founded: there was slight tenderness in the Huron's slow killing of the

Seneca prisoner, for all the mutual use of kin terminology. Neither do we
see any trace of grief for the victim in the Mexica ritual: the tears shed are
shed for the victor, and his putative fate. I have written elsewhere on the
ambivalence of the privileges attaching to the honour of offering one's
captive on the gladiatorial stone, and the acuteness of the psychological
manipulations which blurred the boundaries of self, as the two identities
were juxtaposed and overlaid. The offering warrior was projected into a
terrible and enduring intimacy with his victim: having proudly tended and
taunted him through the days and weeks of his captivity, and watched his
own valour measured in the captive's public display, he had seen life leave
the young body and its pillaging of heart, blood, head, limbs, and skin.
Then he had lent out the flayed skin to those who begged the privilege, and
pulled it on over his own body as it went through its slow transformations:
tightening and rotting on the living flesh; corrupting back into the earth
from which it had been made.[17] Powerful emotions must have been stirred
by these extravagant and enforced intimacies with death, and more with the
decay and dissolution of the self, but there is no indication that pity or grief
for the victim were among them.

What of the victim? It was clearly essential for reasons sacred and
secular that the warriors tethered to the stone should fight, and fight well;
the spectacle and the value of the offering would collapse should they
whimper and beg for a quick death. There must always have been an
element of risk here, but most captives seem to have performed adequately, and some magnificently. There could have been no individual
bargaining. The warrior's life had been forfeit from the moment of his
submission on the field of battle, or at least from the cutting of his warrior
scalp lock. How, then, were they persuaded to fight?

In view of the uninhibited triumphing over comrades in Mexica warrior
houses, I would guess warrior victims were often enough teased into
anger and so to high performance, especially as 'wrath' was identified as
the elevated state in which a warrior was suffused by sacred power. The
victim was also more subtly conditioned. He had been presented by his
captor to the people in a sequence of different regalia over the preceding
four days at the pyramid of Xipe Totec, 'Our Lord the Flayed One', so
coming to know the place where he was to die.[18] He had practised the
routines: on each occasion he had been forced to engage in mock combat,
and then to submit to a mock heart excision, the 'heart' being made of

unsoftened maize kernels. On his last night of life he kept vigil with his captor. His scalp lock was cut at midnight, marking his social death as warrior: he would fight not in his warrior regalia but in the whitened chalk and feathers of the sacrificial victim. It was as designated victim that he watched other men from his people, men he had known when they were alive, fight and fall on the stone, until it was his turn for his last display of maximum skill and valour. If he died well, his name would be remembered and his praises sung in the warrior houses of his home city.[19]

The 'rehearsals' – the garments changed again and again, the mock combats at the stone, the mock heart excisions – doubtless reduced the individual's psychological capacity to resist as he was led step by step down a narrowing path. We will see that same technique of conditioning by familiarization used on non-warrior victims. The pulque given the gladiator came late, and I suspect its effect was more psychological than physiological as he took the taste of the sacred drink into his mouth. But the best guarantee was the co-operation which came from common understandings. For such public deaths victims were preferably taken in a special kind of war: the 'Flowery Wars' initiated by the first Moctezoma. These were battles staged by mutual arrangement between the three cities of the Triple Alliance, and the three ultramontane provinces of Tlaxcala, Huejotzingo, and Cholula, solely for the mutual taking of prisoners worthy of sacrificial death.[20] The men who fought in the Flowery Wars were men of the highest rank, and they fought against matched opponents. Their capture was in a sense a selection by the god, and perhaps borne the more stoically for that. The finest demonstrations on the gladiatorial stone depended on agreement as to the nature and the necessity of the performance itself.

If few warrior captives died under such intense scrutiny, some suffered crueller fates, and there no co-operation was assumed. Victims destined for the singularly agonizing death required for the celebration of the Fire God were tightly bound before they were cast into the fire, to be hooked out, still living but badly burned, and dispatched by the usual heart excision. (We are told that yauhtli was blown in their faces before the ordeal, which perhaps had some slight analgesic effect.) What we see in the handling of warrior victims is a pragmatic and finely adjusted balance between direct physical control (those bound victims cast into the fire), coercion, and psychological conditioning and reward. That they would die was unproblematical; it was the manner of their deaths which required management.[21]

3

To this point discussion has focussed on stranger-victims. It is sometimes claimed that the Mexica found volunteers for sacrificial death among their own people. Jacques Soustelle, for one, has written of women who had vowed to die for the earth goddesses, dancing as they awaited decapitation, feigning ignorance of their fate while the dark-robed priests behind them waited for the moment to make their heads fall like ears of maize.[22] It is an affecting image, but I can find no evidence for it. (Nor would the decapitations have been easily effected, given Mexica equipment – rather more hacking than lopping.) There is no indication of voluntarism among victims, although some appear to have acquiesced in their fate. Among the legions of victims only one group was certainly drawn from within the Mexica polity: the small children offered to Tlaloc over the first months of the ritual calendar.[23] These children were necessarily of known origin, as it was required that they had been born on a particular daysign, and be further marked by a double cowlick.[24] They were 'purchased', we are told, 'from their mothers'.[25] These sales might well have been coerced, the priests being hard to deny. Given the clarity of the identifiers (Mexica babies were normally born well thatched, but even the finest down would betray the tell-tale contrary sweep of the cowlick), it is possible the infants were marked by the naming priests as destined for Tlaloc a very few days after birth, and perhaps that apartness inhibited the development of the usual ties. Sahagún claimed the children to be purchased while still at the breast, but it is not clear that the priests took custody of the children at that very early age. Nonetheless the friar was in no doubt as to the anguish of those who gave over their children for killing, writing of their 'many tears and . . . great sorrow in their hearts', and recognizing Satan's tireless cruelty in their suffering.[26]

The children were kept by the priests for some weeks before their deaths (those kindergartens of doomed infants are difficult to contemplate). Then, as the appropriate festivals arrived, they were magnificently dressed, paraded in litters, and, as they wept, their throats were slit: gifted to Tlaloc the

Rain God as 'bloodied flowers of maize'. (They were thought then to enter the gentle paradise of Tlaloc, which may have assuaged the parents' grief.) The pathos of their fate as they were paraded moved the watchers to tears, while their own tears were thought to augur rain. But their actual engagement with the people would be slight, being removed from their natal homes at two or three, and possibly well before that, and being very probably the children of lowly dependants.[27]

Then there was the great category of the ixiptlas, the 'god-representations' or 'god images' who danced and died in many of the feasts. These figures will be explored more fully at a later stage, but in origin the god-images offered in sacrifice were slaves who had been purchased by specialist merchants and ritually prepared (that is, purified or 'bathed') for sacrifice. The 'bathing' seems to have consisted of two parts: a preliminary purification with a special 'holy water' which cleansed the slave of the stigma and status of 'slave',[28] and then the 'face washing' by a skilled older woman during the course of the ritual which at once sedated the victims and brought them closer to the sacred state.[29]

The consensus has been that most of these slaves were natives of the city: delinquent Mexica who had sold themselves into servitude under the easy terms of Mexica enslavement, who had been thrice formally judged recalcitrant, so rendering themselves liable for ritual preparation and offering as a 'bathed slave'. My contrary view is that the god-images group, like the victims of the mass killings, were probably all, or nearly all, outsiders: slaves – most received in tribute – along with some selected war captives. This is clearly an important issue. It would make a significant difference in the likely response of watchers were they watching the doing to death of known people, perhaps a woman or a man notorious for irresponsible behaviour in the home calpulli, or, with less moral freight and personal affect, and a more distanced connoisseurship, 'innocent' strangers, drawn from distant places.[30]

We do not know with any certainty where the slave merchants secured their slaves. 'Slavery' in Mexico was a most expansive category, and a most various condition. Within Tenochtitlan slavery could be imposed as a penalty to render compensation for some offence, but more commonly it was a matter of contract: the sale of one's labour for an agreed period in return for physical maintenance. In time of hardship a family might contract to supply the labour of a young lad, the particular individual being

replaced as another child grew big enough to take his place, while the
socially vulnerable – children of concubines, secondary wives left un-
provided on the death of their protector, or other victims of misfortune –
might sell themselves to secure survival. But slavery provided a social net
not only for those suffering gratuitous misfortunes. Chronically shiftless
individuals – the man who gambled or drank compulsively, the self-
indulgent woman who 'ignored her rearing' and fell into prostitution –
sold themselves to expunge accumulating debt and to escape the difficulties of independent living. Only the most determined fecklessness could
then bring a Mexica slave to the three separate judgements of recalcitrance or 'non-fulfilment of contract' which condemned them to the
wooden yoke of the slave liable for ritual death, yet it is this category
which is commonly claimed as the source for the 'god-images' who played
their terminal parts in the festivals. Certainly such intractables might well
have died as part of the unremarkable and anonymous category of 'slaves'
for group killings, but it is unlikely that they would have been entrusted
with a starring role in one of the great ritual events. Terrible warnings of
the sacrificial fate reserved for the heedless proliferate throughout the
rhetoric of the Florentine Codex, most particularly in the homilies addressed to youth, but that earnest reiteration does not prove the point.
Proven recalcitrance does not sit easily with the physical grace, the skills
and the social docility required in a god-image – a readiness, as we would
say, to 'take direction'. All claims here must be tentative, the sources
being what they are, but it is essentially on grounds of psychological
implausibility that I reject the notion that Mexica slaves were a main or a
significant resource for the most valued 'bathed slaves' consumed in
Mexica ritual.

What, then, were the possible origins of these prestigious victims? A
substantial but unknown number of young men and women were brought
in as tribute, and it is likely that not all captives from defeated towns died
in the victory celebrations, but were reserved for other uses.[31] The Mexica did not use slaves for rough labour; there were needy locals enough
for that. I suspect a luxury traffic in foreign skilled 'prestige' slaves –
embroiderers, concubines, body servants, drawn from among the tribute
slaves or brought to the local slave markets of Azcapotzalco or Itzocan by
specialist merchants – prized as much for their display value as for actual
labour performed. We know the nobles competed to buy not only talented

but graceful slaves for domestic and other service.[32] My view is that it was from this 'exclusive' end of the slave market, supplemented by the priests' selections from among human tribute levies, that the 'bathed slaves' came.[33]

4

If these significant victims, like the warriors, came largely from outside the group, their apparent co-operation remains a problem. Some roles were compatible with coercion: for example, the men and women who died at Izcalli, the 'Sprouting', every fourth year were formally displayed in circumstances which precluded direct physical control, but where escape was impossible, and at all times they were closely guarded.[34] But in most festivals a degree, often a high degree, of co-operation was essential. How was it achieved?

The preparation for particular rituals lay in the charge of the high priest of the deity to be honoured. It was for him to assemble the necessary paraphernalia, and to co-ordinate the different participants and the stages and levels of the ritual action. It would be his task to select and initiate the men or women required for preparation for their god-image roles, well before the culminating ritual in which they were to die. He would be ultimately responsible for their 'bathing' and their training in dance, speech, deportment, or whatever their role required. (We, of course, have access only to the final performance, and have to infer from the action the kind of preparation and control entailed.)

An example: merchants were important consumers of this form of human merchandise, being permitted to offer slaves as surrogate warrior captives at the great festival of Panquetzaliztli, the 'Raising of Banners'.[35] For all their warrior parallels, the slaves appear to have been primarily regarded as items of notably conspicuous consumption: costly to buy, expensively trained to dance and to sing; then, garlanded and splendidly arrayed, being made to dance with their flowers and tobacco tubes at a series of feasts in demonstration of the merchant's wealth. Yet these slaves, purchased in the market and used so explicitly as display objects, co-operated to a very high degree, being paraded through the households of their 'relatives', and then setting off in procession to the pyramid. En

route they were waylaid and forced to fight with war captives led by
Mexica warriors. And then they climbed the pyramid steps in company
with the merchant who had owned and offered them.

I have chosen this case because I find it the most difficult to explain. It
could be argued that the account we have is idealized, which is almost
certainly true. Nonetheless, we have to assume substantial docility if the
ritual was to be played through. If I am right, these people would be
strangers, with no prior bond with their purchasers (I take the 'relatives'
here to refer to fictive ritual kinship, as with the 'uncle' who supported the
warrior captive fighting on the gladiatorial stone). Through their last
hours they were kept drunk, as we will see, but their earlier co-operation
requires explanation.

Possibly the fact (and the vanity) of their initial selection played some
part in their acquiescence, along with the habituation of the training
period, with its flattery and pampering. There were other and more subtle
techniques. At the close of the third and last feast the slaves were relinquished to the priests and their guards, and to the care of two 'face
washers': mature women gently laved their faces with warm water at
intervals, each washing being at once a benediction and a step towards
death. These women tended them until they died. There are haunting
echoes of childhood here, and the possibility of a process of infantiliza-
tion, with the old social identifiers stripped away, to be replaced by constant physical cosseting by a devoted mature woman.[36] Furthermore,
Nahuatl phrases to do with the 'washing of the face' appear to have
carried the meaning of a transformation of identity: for example, when a
youth blooded in combat had his juvenile nape lock cut, and was so
'made' a warrior, 'it was said the sun, the lord of the earth, has washed thy
face. Thou hast taken another face'.[37] Such understandings, like the
power of regalia to transform, were widely recognized among Amerindians. Bathed slaves, as with their warrior counterparts, suffered ejection
from the social world through the removal of their old identifying marks,
and then were given 'another face' – and another being – through repeated lustration and the final assumption of their ritual regalia. All this could
well effect the radical etiolation of one's old sense of self, and a readiness
to submit to a new and compelling script.

A powerful erotic component sometimes played a part. The young man
presented to the people at the festival of Izcalli Tlami as he who would die

for the Fire God at Tlacaxipeualiztli forty days later received not only adulation and gifts but a 'pleasure girl' as his constant and most loving companion. (When his time of death came, she bundled up his clothing and adornments as her payment.)[38] He was most luxuriously treated by his purchaser: 'before he died, much did the bather of slaves esteem him; he paid much attention to him. He regaled him; he gave him things; all good was the food which he gave him'.[39] In a social world so finely calculating in its gift exchange, the owner's 'gifts' – including the pleasure girl's happy availability – however unsought, possibly carried significant obligation.

The final technique was cruder, but of proven efficacy, especially for the last stages of the victims' performances when wilder behaviour was appropriate. Over their fourth and final night the bathed slaves destined to die at Panquetzaliztli were made to drink 'obsidian wine' 'in order that they would not dread death'. Plied until they were 'quite drunk', they were kept dancing and singing all night.[40] When waylaid on the way to the pyramid and made to fight the 'chieftains' – the 'men of war' who were lying in wait for them – they were probably drunk enough to put up something of a battle, especially given that death was in any case inevitable. Arrived at the foot of the pyramid, exhausted, excited, the focus of a massed audience, how could there be turning back?

In that one strand in a complex ceremony we see deployed most of the Mexica arsenal of victim management, from the potent psychological force of special selection, of habituation through rehearsal, of admiration, of the sweet weakening of autonomy through the cosseting of a surrogate mother to the narrowing, heightening of awareness through dance and battle and drink. Even expert custodians could sometimes go too far with their potions: it was said of the featherworkers' human offerings that after being given drink 'some of the bathed ones became deranged; quite of their own wills they climbed – ran – up to the top [of the pyramid] of the devil, longing for – seeking – death.'[41] Skilled handlers could normally prevent too early a breakaway, but that glimpse suggests how touch and go the problem of management could be.

The movement of the ritual itself imposed its own coercion, with the action so relentlessly taxing, with its swift transitions between furious effort and controlled formality and its painful delays, as to be intolerable physically and psychologically: we are told the victims were finally brought to be so 'anguished in spirit [that] they looked forward only to their deaths'.[42] This technique of the depletion of energies was widely used: the woman who played 'Teteo Innan', Mother of the Gods in the harvest festival of Ochpaniztli, the 'Sweeping of the Roads', was pushed and pulled by her circling escort of curing women, teased and harassed in 'play combat' over hours and days, and must have been in a delirium of exhaustion when she was adorned for the last time and swept up the pyramid stairs to the knives of the priests.[43] The very deliberateness of the preparation, the patient procedure of the 'rehearsals', then the smooth accelerating progression into the final days, would give small purchase for an individual decision for defiance, while to be one of a number of victims possibly further aided acquiescence. In one elaborate festival, when a whole group of slaves was led through elaborate preparations, to be arrayed in their paper vestments on their last dawn and taken in procession to their places of death, each was held tightly for the ascent of the pyramid 'lest they faint', but most climbed steadily upwards, and walked directly to the offering stone.[44] And always, along with the coaxing and the pampering, there was the hidden edge of coercion and the certainty of death: always '[the ritually purified victim] went knowing that there was his tribute of death at the appointed time'.[45] Perhaps potential victims went gently to their deaths because of the promise of a fine afterlife. However, that promise was not sufficiently persuasive to lead Mexica to volunteer, or indeed to represent the fate as desirable: to end on the killing stone was represented in the discourses of the elders as a most bitter fate.

5

In some few cases, where the 'god-presenter' had to perform a prolonged and intricate part, and finally to move alone to his death, all the techniques of manipulation, control and coercion could not have achieved the desired theatrical effect, so commitment (of a kind) must have played its part. Here it is worth examining the management of the star performer in one of the most famous Mexica festivals, the great celebration of Toxcatl in the fifth month of the eighteen-month seasonal cycle, dedicated to Tezcatlipoca and Huitzilopochtli.[46] Missionary friars took this festival to be the most important of Mexica ceremonies, in part because it celebrated spring (the young maize was in its first stage of growth) and so fell close to Easter, but also, we have to assume, because it generated peculiar excitement and interest.[47] The interest seems surprising, as the festival did not require much preparation, at least by Mexica standards, and participatory action was restricted to the final stages, and then to warriors and chosen women. Its excitements and significances are therefore initially elusive, at least to the outsider.

A young captive had been chosen at the end of the previous Toxcatl festival as 'Tezcatlipoca' for the full year. He was selected for his beauty and address, from among a group of ten or so captives also selected, guarded, and trained by the priests for the role. Moctezoma himself adorned him with the richest garments and jewels; a most signal honour, as to adorn another was to acknowledge subordination. The young man went crowned and caped with flowers, legs belled with gold, his sandals tufted with ocelot ears, his blackened face and hair hanging loose to his loins marking him as 'one who fasted', and who was therefore in a sacred state. At all times he was escorted, and doubtless discreetly guarded, by four 'pages' and four 'masters of youth' from the warrior houses. So he roamed through the streets with his entourage, playing his flutes. When the people heard the flute and the bells they came from their houses to greet and adore him, and to offer him yet more flowers: 'he was importuned, he was sighed for.' Then, twenty days before his death, his long hair was cut and bound into the dress of a 'seasoned warrior' – the sign of a most honoured veteran who had taken four captives. The transition to maturity thus effected, he was given four 'wives' (again specially selected and trained, and presumably tribute slaves) named for the goddesses of the young maize, of flowers and of erotic love, of salt and of fresh water. For the last five days of his festival he ruled in the city, Moctezoma secluding himself while Tezcatlipoca and his entourage danced and sang and banqueted in his most sacred places. Then on the fifth day the god and his followers quit the city, taking canoe to a small island. There his wives farewelled him, and he and his warrior servants went to a small temple. At a moment of his own choosing he mounted the steps, breaking his flutes as he climbed, to meet the knives of the waiting priests. As the old Tezcatlipoca died, his heart cut out, his head skewered on the skull rack, the flutes of the new Tezcatlipoca were heard in the streets of the city.[48]

I will return to this rich ceremony more than once, but the aspect which most concerns me now is the grounding for the complex and sustained co-operation of the Tezcatlipoca figure, and then the kind of response he called forth in those who watched him, most especially over the days of that last month. The young man did not arrive at his role by 'chance': he was chosen, selected as the ideal embodiment of young male beauty in body and manner. While the selection was made by the priests, they chose in accordance with widely agreed criteria (the details of desired and undesired physical characteristics run to a solid page of print). Therefore we may assume there was aesthetic and probably some emotional investment in the choice.

His 'beauty' appears to have been a matter of right proportion. He was to be neither too tall nor too short; firm of flesh, the skin smooth and without break or blemish. (The underlying metaphor appears to be that of a sleek fruit.) But manner was at least as important as looks. He was trained to manipulate his smoking tubes, his flutes and his flowers with easy grace, and to respond with unwearying affable courtliness to the salutations of the people. He could be trusted to conduct himself as a ruler over the last days of his life, and then, with no break in his poise, to choose the moment of its ending. All this points to the necessity of a ready, sustained and informed co-operation. In his case drugs could not be used to sustain any mood beyond the mildest euphoria: 'Tezcatlipoca' had to conduct himself with controlled elegance, not the frantic exuberance of the bathed slave.

No information is given for the provenance of the candidates, save that they were captives selected 'when captives were taken'. Given the precise detailing of the physical characteristics required, and the formulaic eloquence of Mexica styles of address, the potential players must have been Nahuatl speakers, and of an admired local physical type. They would therefore be participant in Mexica cultural understandings. The ten or so others trained for the role who were not chosen were killed by their captors, to whom ownership presumably reverted.[49] If these young men were indeed drawn from within the Nahua region, where rivalry for distinction, always powerful, was most powerful among young males, triumph in that contest of beauty, grace, and address would bring not only an extension of life, but personal gratification.

There was also, perhaps, a subtler lure. Tezcatlipoca was worshipped throughout Mesoamerica as the all-powerful but arbitrary master of human destinies; as Titlacahuan, 'He Whose Slaves We Are'. We all seek to find shapes in our lives, tirelessly ordering the flow of happenstance into a plausible story. Even in our disenchanted world the notion of yielding to an event we can plausibly represent to ourselves as 'fated' is oddly exhilarating. Deliberately to choose a role which must lead to death is beyond most of us. (That surprising numbers insouciantly undertake roles where death is the most likely outcome at very short odds is another matter.) But if the mental preparation had been sufficiently careful (remember those expert stewards) the 'selection' as the living-image Tezcatlipoca could have been experienced not so much as a selection but as the revelation of a godly choice already made. His fate manifest, he had only to follow the script, magnificently, through to the end.

6

The Tezcatlipoca impersonator was also touched by the special glamour, the special erotic poignancy, of he who must die. Here I want to make another detour northwards and forward in time, to the Plains Indians and the curious behaviour of those young men who, having suffered some great chagrin or fallen into the melancholy which can plague early manhood, took a public vow to seek death on the warpath. (I am not concerned with questions of diffusion here, but rather with exploring an adjacent sensibility which, being much more richly and recently documented, can suggest the range of ways in which men have made sense of their world.) The vow sworn, the warriors became 'Crazy Dogs Wishing To Die'. Having chosen to reject the comfortable continuities of society, they were also liberated from its restrictions. They could snatch meat from any cooking pot, a privilege open only to (pre-social) children. They could also lie with any woman who offered herself, without attracting penalty or rebuke. Such young men adorned themselves richly, danced and sang their songs in the camp to the admiring praise of the women, and their deaths were mourned with full formality.[50]

The magic here is not spectacular courage in one or two battles but the glamour of commitment to death at the peak of youth and beauty: the poignancy of the exhibitionistic narcissism of youth determined once and for all on magnificent expenditure rather than slow wasting and remorseless physical deterioration. That public display of doomed youth, self-absorbed, yet feeding on the public gaze; marking the centres by stalking the furthest margins of society, has exerted a powerful appeal in more than one culture, including our own, with its voracious appetite for figures at once sexually vivid, blessed by fame, and dramatically disaffected from the society which courts them.

Some of that sacred sexual grace must have attended the young Tezcatlipoca. Women seem to have commented freely on each Tezcatlipoca's physical charms or defects, and Mexica women were not mealy-mouthed. The giving of 'wives' to the impersonator on his symbolic maturation pointed to the sexual privileges granted only to the successful warrior, while the festivities after his death have a decidedly erotic pulse. The flawless exemplar of the perfection of youth, in body, in manners, in eloquence, magnificently adorned by Moctezoma's own hand, his enacted life followed the ideal trajectory of the young warrior.

A further characteristic of the performance, and an important source of its compulsion, was its dreamlike, radically detached quality. In that society of dense, ambivalent yet insisted-upon relationships, he was a stranger: an emblem of young manhood, and only that. He had no kin, no narrowing affections and affiliations: he looked with equal favour on all. There was also no struggle in his warriorhood; no combat, no violence: a matter of signs only. That, perhaps, was a large part of his fascination. While the Mexica were very visibly implicated in the physical management of warrior captives, I suspect their engagement with the Tezcatlipoca figure was of a more intimate kind, tangling deeper into the individual imagination. Detached from the imperfections of actuality, he provided a free zone for fantasy. 'God-images' figured not only as palpable representations of deities. They also allowed the production of self-representations, ideal images, for different groups. That the young were particularly susceptible to the glamour of these figures is indicated by the dour warnings of 'the elders', who spoke in the conventionalized rhetoric of the 'discourses' against the imitation of their headily flamboyant styles of dress and conduct: a most public counter-image to that obsessive 'carefulness' on which the elders insisted. The Tezcatlipoca figure, exemplary of different qualities as he moved along the Death Path – a lordly generosity preposterously accessible to all, the sexual power and physical perfection of the young male contained by the fasting state, then the grace of that power and perfection socially tamed to warriordom and marriage – must have been powerfully and variously responded to by those who flocked to see him. Young girls, boys, women, aspiring and actual and ageing warriors: each could find a particular emphasis in that single, changeful, compelling image. Among all the living god-representations in all of the ritual calendar only he died removed from public awareness, and with public attention deflected away to his successor.[51] The fact of his individual death was for the watchers deliberately muted; he remained a vision of physical and social perfection, of noble affability eternally renewed.

His appeal was shadowed and deepened by the parallel performance of a dark counterpart. Another young man had been chosen at the same time as the main figure, and had lived alongside him for the full year. He also had been given the name 'Titlacahuan': the same among Tezcatlipoca's many soubriquets most often applied to the central figure.[52] After the great festival day of dancing and offerings, which followed the death of Texcatlipoca, the second young man led a serpent dance of warriors. He too chose the moment of his death, but he met it publicly, climbing the steps of the Great Temple to die a warrior's death before Huitzilopochtli's shrine. Then his severed head was spitted on the skull rack alongside that of his bright twin.[53]

A number of meanings, many of them conflicting, have been ascribed to this mysterious figure. The visual signs point to the deliberate contrasting of the elegance and discretion of the main figure's address and array, and the wild, violent and dangerous character of his dark double. The second Tezcatlipoca danced with the warriors. His paper eagle-feather head-dress was 'disordered', he wore a flint knife of feathers on his forehead, and over his netted warrior jacket hung an animal skin. These elements echoed the motifs of the regalia adorning the great seed-dough figure of the war god Huitzilopochtli which had been constructed and paraded over the last day of the festival. The god wore a facsimile of a warrior's jacket, but his was woven not from maguey fibre but from nettles. A flint knife of feathers, half of it blood-red, rose from his head-dress. His underjacket was painted with representations of human limbs, and his great cape with severed head and human bones.[54] Tezcatlipoca was, as we will see, closely associated with Huitzilopochtli: one of his names was 'The Young Warrior'. The violence so carefully suppressed in the first impersonator's performance is here given free play: another aspect of male servitude to the god of human destiny.

Crucially, the Mexica identified their victims – whether warriors or captives from hostile tribes, or Mexica children not yet fully members of the group, or delinquents disqualified from it, whatever the psychological or physiological technology activated for their management – as humans indeed, but as 'other': those who we are not. We have seen Durán's unhappy awareness of the peculiar value placed on the human offerings presented in the 'feasting' of the sacred powers. That value was not only material. We will see Mexica tenderness towards the very young child – the welcome given the newborn baby, when the little naked body was gently stroked by all the kin, men and women alike, 'to show it that it was loved' – and we know the onlookers wept as the children destined for Tlaloc the Rain God were carried weeping in their litters, and wept as the terrified wailing choked and stopped. 'God-presenters' snared other groups and individuals in the bonds of identification and admiration, as with that ideally beautiful youth Tezcatlipoca, exerting what the elders saw as a dangerous fascination over the young, but also most poignantly figuring the possible fate of their own sons. It might be said we are dealing here with the crocodile tears of 'ritual' and therefore unreal emotion. If those individual emotions spontaneously arising in the mundane world are accepted as establishing the measure of reality, one must agree. But the measure is a mistaken one. Emotions experienced in a ritual context are 'real' and powerful in their fashion, not least in being not individual and unscheduled, but collective and reproducible. They are also infused with the transcendent reality of the aesthetic.

Many more strands remain to be unravelled in the Mexica attitude to ritual killings. Nonetheless, the recognition of the force of that designation of 'otherness' – that the victims were seen as strangers from beyond the city, or social outcasts from within – makes a beginning.

4

Warriors, Priests and Merchants

Regarding fortitude, which among them was esteemed more than any other virtue, wherefore they raised it to the highest level of worth: they conducted impressive training in this as appears in many parts of this work. As to the religion and the adoration of their gods, I do not believe there have been in the world idolators to such a degree venerators of their gods, nor at such great cost to themselves as these of this New Spain.

Fray Bernardino de Sahagún, Prologue to the Book of the Gods[1]

Europeans have largely forgotten the glamour which can invest the male born for battle and shadowed in the daylight world by the sacred burden of wounds and death, despite the increasing incidence of such curiously archaic warriors in the mountains, and in the cities, of the late-twentieth-century world. Mexica society was committed to war, not as an occasional heroic obligation, but chronically, and its members had to be brought to bear the social and psychological costs of that commitment. The allure of the warrior style penetrated deep into the few other desired and reputable masculine careers. Neither priests nor merchants, despite their separate professions and institutions, and despite superficially distinctive demeanours, were immune from it. Priests led the warrior march to battle, while merchants boasted of their trade expeditions in warrior idiom, and dispersed much of their hoarded wealth for the privilege of playing a warrior's ceremonial part for a day. The main ceremonial calendar was built out of the swing of the seasons, marking the transitions out of the time of agricultural growth into the season of war.[2]

In long-ago Tenochtitlan we may trace the translation of a warrior ethos developed in a small-scale community into a potentially impersonal urban milieu, to identify the social forms and performances through which it maintained its magic, and to seek what it was in Mexica history or faith or experience or ideological manipulation which rendered the costs of wounds, deaths, and chronic war tolerable. Intensely competitive and intensely individualistic as it was, the warrior ideal nonetheless functioned as a crucial social integrator in the late imperial city, while the high glamour of the triumphant warrior illuminated Mexica notions of the helplessness of man. It is the elucidation of those apparent paradoxes which will be the concern of this chapter.

I

To be born a male in Tenochtitlan was to be designated a warrior. The attending midwife met the birth of a boy child with war-cries, and lifted the baby, still slippery with the birth fluid, away from his mother's body to dedicate him to the Sun, and to the 'flowery death' of the warrior in battle or on the killing stone. The umbilical cord would be entrusted to a seasoned warrior, to be buried 'in the midst of the plains where warfare was practiced'.[3] At the child's naming a few days after birth the small boys of the neighbourhood were recruited to shout the name of the tiny warrior through the streets and at the house entrances, so awarding him his first triumph. After the ceremonious dedication at birth came the first marking of warriordom into the flesh. A few days after the naming ceremony the priests drilled the male infant's lower lip in preparation for the warrior lip-plug. With each year to follow there were new markings, when at the close of the warrior festival of Toxcatl all young males down to infants on their cradleboards were cut on stomach, chest, and arms by the priests, to sign their commitment to Huitzilopochtli, god of the Sun and of War. Males also bore a line of scars burned into the skin of the left wrist to indicate their dedication to the Turquoise Prince, the Sun, through his association with the Turquoise Lord of Fire. (Girl children were not exempt from this physical signing, those dedicated at the priest house being cut on hip and chest to affirm their affiliation with the deities of the earth.) For their infant years commoner lads stayed in the care of their mothers, but by the age of three more of their instruction devolved on their fathers, as they began to learn the skills and tasks of men. At six they were allowed the freedom of the streets. From the age of ten they began to be shaped for their warrior future; while most of their hair continued to be close cropped, a single tuft was left to grow at the back of the head.[4]

All young Mexica males were exposed to warrior training; all were given the opportunity to excel; those who did excel were lavishly rewarded. At puberty most commoner boys, save for those few specifically dedicated to the calmecac or priest house, came under the full jurisdiction of the *telpochcalli*, the 'House of Youth' of the local warrior house, although they had probably spent as much time as their fathers allowed close by that magnet of male activities in their younger years. Their days were spent in work details for the ward, under the direction of a more senior lad, and in the further practice of a range of masculine skills, few commoners being so successful in battle as to emancipate themselves entirely from ordinary labour. The mass of Mexica warriors was part-time, returning from campaigns to their usual pursuits of horticulture, peddling, fishing or hunting, sandal-making, pulque-brewing, or any one of the other trades the city supported. A trade was a necessary safeguard, should fortune not be with them. 'Fortune' came through battle, in the tangibles of material goods, of sexual pleasures, a desirable Mexica girl for marriage, and – most important – prestige, honour, fame. 'Success' was measured narrowly by the number and status of enemy warriors taken alive in one-to-one combat.

The city folk knew the penalties of war: the fate of the warrior outmatched or momentarily off guard, captured, then bloodily and ceremoniously killed, was constantly enacted in the streets and temples. They knew the desolated households, the young wives suddenly bereft. They knew its lesser costs, too, in the incidence of the casual, semi-licensed violence and depredations of restless young men with small respect for the peaceable trades and those who practised them. In the most solemn ceremonials the probability, indeed the inevitability, the necessity, and the desirability of the warrior's death in battle or on the killing stone was insisted upon. But these darker notes were muted in the public display, where it was the splendour of the warrior which was most lavishly glorified.

For the boys the glamour was irresistible. Their nape locks, now grown to substantial length, would be cut only when they had taken their first captive. That time was drawing near. Their evenings were given over to learning the songs and dances which told of the glories of war and of warriors, most especially those of their own calpulli, and to practising ceremonial songs and dances along with the trainees from other calpullis at the *cuicacalli*, or 'House of Song'. (There they were also allowed to dance and discreetly flirt with the local girls, ordinarily frustratingly inaccessible, who were being prepared for ceremonial performance in the cuicacalli.)[5] Formal training in weapon handling did not usually begin until about the age of fifteen, but the boys had practised with their miniature bows and arrows and their makeshift clubs from their earliest days, and they were already trained in the lore of warriordom through those evening hours of watching, listening, dreaming. While most noble youths and other favoured groups took much of their early training in the priest houses, they too were turned over to senior warriors for intensive training in weapon handling at about fifteen.[6] Obsessive concern for their performance in war gripped young males of all social ranks.

The warrior system of training was simple, but it had its peculiarities. While physical toughness was tested and expanded in the daily work details at the Houses of Youth, and it is likely, boys presumably always being boys, that there was informal competition in those tasks, the long initial training period seems to have included no organized competition. At about eighteen the novice warriors were allowed their first venture to the field of battle, where they were required to observe the conduct of an exemplary warrior. Then, at last, came the test. On their second venture they were to take a captive, and on this occasion and this occasion only the capture could be in concert: up to six novices could combine to drag a warrior down. In concert, but not 'collectively': should the youths succeed, the body was nicely apportioned in accordance with a strict system of priority, with the torso and right thigh awarded to the major captor; left thigh to the second; right upper arm to the third; left upper arm to the fourth; right forearm to the fifth; left forearm to the sixth.[7] And then, at last, the nape locks of boyhood were clipped, and the fledgling warriors began their battlefield careers.

The ladder of promotion was marked out in a straightforward, arithmetical way: the taking of captives – in single combat, and scored as to quality – for presentation for death on the killing stone. The first captive so offered made one a 'leading youth', a 'captor', marked by appropriate face paint, the right to wear a breechclout with handsomely long ends instead of the brief boyish affairs of the novices, and a cape bearing a design in place of a plain mantle: no small reward in self-conscious and narcissistic youth. The 'leading youth' also enjoyed perfect powers and privileges within the warrior house, and could anticipate marriage, as his parents began to cast around for a suitable wife and to save against the expense of the elaborate feast which would buy his release from the full jurisdiction of the House of Youth. (It is possible that marriage could end commitment to the warrior house for some men, but it remained the locus of male social action, excitement, and reward.) Two captives presented to the gods brought further elaboration in dress and privileges. Three, and the way was opened to the office of Master of Youth, authorized instructor in the warrior way, with the privilege of wielding authority over the junior warriors, and of dancing, displaying, and even drinking at certain festivals. Four captives taken, and one entered the select ranks of the 'seasoned warriors', the 'veterans' or 'professionals' as we might say, privileged to have their own unchallenged seat within the warrior house, and to wear the most coveted warrior insignia: the long lip-plugs and the headbands with eagle-feather tassels which spoke of their great deeds.[8]

At that point the upward trajectory could falter if one were to capture mere Huaxtecs, or other unregarded barbarians. Rewards, honour, and the delights of re-animated reputation came only with the taking of captives from Nahuatl cities – tough warriors, with much the same system shaping their training and aspirations. If a man took his fifth captive from among these formidable opponents he was acknowledged a *quauchic*, and distinguished on dress occasions by his vivid red netting cape, blue lip-plug, and most dramatically by his head, naked of hair save for the single warrior lock bound with red cord floating above the shaven pate. Two such distinguished victims, and he could wear at will either the long blue or the yellow lip-plug, the breechclout with the eagle-claw or marketplace design, the red or orange leather sandals, the elaborate headdress. When so arrayed 'he filled everyone with awe'.[9] These were the greatest of warriors, 'each of whom was considered [equal to] a battle squadron, who did not hide themselves behind something in war; they who turned [the enemy] back, they who wheeled them around.'[10] From among such legendary warriors the 'general' and the 'commanding general' were selected. (But not the custodial chiefs, the administrators: they were men of a quieter temper.)

What is notable about the system, apart from its glamour, is how very little co-operative it was. The great warriors were solitary hunters. After that initial group capture the novice was in direct competition with his peers, as he searched through the dust and confusion of the battle for an enemy of equal, or ideally just higher, rank. We glimpse a version of that tense stalking in the 'Feast of the Flaying of Men', the warrior festival which closed the season of war, when four of the greatest Mexica warriors intent on displaying the full panoply of their martial skills advanced on a tethered enemy warrior. We are told they advanced snaking low to the ground, leaping up, gazing about, brandishing their weapons, in what seems to have been a stylization of battlefield searching, sighting, attacking.[11] (To stalk so effectively as to erupt before an adversary at the moment of one's own choosing was to snatch psychological dominance, that act of selection designating the other as prey.) Warrior regalia aided the important business of battlefield identification. The towering feather 'headdresses', commonly built on light wicker frames strapped to the back and therefore not impeding movement, signalled warrior status, and against known enemies it is likely that personal identifications could be made even in the wild swirl of the field.

While the Mexica had projectile weapons, their use belonged to the preliminary stages of battle, being aimed rather at demoralization than death. Their lack of penetrating power is indicated by the invading Spaniards' abandonment of their own metal armour in favour of the quilted cotton of the Indians. The matched duel with obsidian or flint-studded 'swords' was the preferred mode of combat, with the long shallow blades designed to incapacitate rather than to cut deep: Mexica warriors sought captives, not corpses. What they strove to do was to bring their opponent down, most often by a blow to the legs – cutting a hamstring, crippling a knee – so he could be grappled to the ground and subdued. It is possible the seizing of the warrior lock, the formal sign of submission in the painted screenfold books, was enough to effect submission, although there were usually men with ropes on hand to bind the captives and take them to the rear.

After that first blooding, the honour of capture was personal, and could not be shared: indeed the fine hierarchy in the apportioning of the first 'group' captive suggests that even at the novice stage ranking was more important than any notion of team spirit. Intervention to aid a companion who was being worsted was liable to be interpreted as an attempt to pirate his captive, and to be accordingly resented, while to pass one's own captive to another for his credit (a small glimpse of disaffection from 'official' values, and of the pull of private loyalties and affections) meant death for both conspirators. The men we would be tempted to call 'officers' in the Mexica forces ordered the initial disposition of the warriors and dealt out rough discipline as the men jostled for advantage, but once the attack had begun their main task was the adjudication of disputes over captives among their own men. Leadership-by-example fell to the glorious quauchic: it was they who leapt forward with fine ferocity to fire others with their courage. The 'shaven headed Otomi', an exclusive society among the seasoned warriors, vowed never to take a backward step in battle. They typically fought in pairs, which must have given some protection on the flank in the confused early stage of selection of adversaries, and perhaps once battle was joined. But should one partner fall, and the survivor, disoriented, turn to flee, it was the task of his fellow warriors to kill him.

Honours once won were not secure: their retention depended on the maintenance of high performance. Any significant lapse from exemplary courage on the battlefield was punished by the delinquent being stripped of his regalia and thrust out of the warrior group into the miserable exile of his own household, with only women and children for company.[12] There he might be left to mourn through one or two seasons of war until the ruler chose to restore him to his place, and the chance of recouping himself. (The lifting of the punishment was signalled by the presentation by the ruler of elaborate gifts of maize, chia, and capes, all negotiable in the market, and so restorative of wealth, along with the exiled one's warrior regalia, so that the spur of massive obligation was added to the lash of personal humiliation.)

The ruler concerned himself only with the highest warriors. Discipline for the lower ranks came from within the warrior houses at the hands of one's peers or immediate superiors. Some of the lesser punishments suggest an element of bravado, as when in the course of a prolonged and erotically charged dance of young warriors and pleasure girls any untoward advance by a youth was met with a public beating from the senior boys charged with policing behaviour; one guesses the livelier lads sought at least a few blows, and wore them as badges of honour. For more serious offences judgement and punishment was swift and brutally physical. Observed drunkenness among a rank not admitted to that privilege, or indulgence in an unauthorized or improperly prolonged affair with a pleasure girl meant permanent exclusion from the warrior group, the expulsion being marked by a near-lethal and very public beating and the scorching from the head of the warrior scalp lock, presumably never to grow again through the scarring. Such punishments were not limited to delinquent juveniles. At the great warrior festival of Panquetzaliztli blooded warriors of noble lineage were privileged to drink pulque, as were the highest ranks of the commoner warriors. But the 'rulers of youths', or as we would say the principals or directors of the warrior schools, stood one rung below that coveted privilege. Nonetheless, we are told, they secretly gathered to drink: 'they hid themselves well in the dark . . . in order not to be seen'. Something of an open secret, it would seem. But if that secret were breached, or their conduct were less than discreet – 'if anyone discovered them, if they made it known that indeed they drank pulque' – then they were mercilessly drubbed, even to death: beaten, dragged, and kicked, their heads shaved 'like servants', and then cast out, which is not the sort of treatment we expect to be meted out to a school principal, especially at the hands of his juniors.[13] Those 'rulers of youths' were presumably driven less by passion for pulque than by the determination to filch the privilege of those just above them, with the lower and excluded ranks of the group ardently protecting the privileges attached to the highest rungs of the hierarchy: a not unfamiliar phenomenon where the passion for the marks of rank is intense.

It is not clear how far and how many commoners advanced in the warrior hierarchy. There were the early casualties: those unhappy youths who failed to take captives over two or three opportunities, whatever the balance of bad luck or cowardice or excited misjudgement in that failure, and who therefore were expelled from their local House of Youth, to live as best they could in some mundane occupation. On expulsion their heads were shaven into the tonsure of the *tamene,* or carrier, the lowliest of Mexica occupations, the resort of the man who had nothing to sell but his strong back. Thus they were formally marked with the sign of failure at an age when humiliation bites deep. With that expulsion they lost not only the incomparable excitements of the warrior house, but also the chance of supplementing income, of social advancement, of local prestige. And always they could see the image of what they had lost in the quauchic stalking through the city streets, taking confident precedence: magnificent in the intoxicating sweep of his open-weave mantle, the glory of his scars, his hide sandals, his spectacularly embroidered and fringed breechclout, the arrogant curve of his lip-plug.

For those brave, quick, and fortunate the way to advancement was wide: Moctezoma opened his hand to his warriors. War against a selected city began with the distribution of insignia already won, with more insignia taken into the field for the immediate reward of prowess. The market-folk were alerted to provide the usual quantities of toasted maize grains, maize flour, bean flour, toasted tortillas, sun-dried tamales, chillis, and cakes of ground cacao,[14] along with the carriers necessary to transport them, although the more seasoned warriors doubtless took what rations they could conveniently carry. (In 'pacified' zones the warriors expected to be well fed, and behaved as soldiers far from home too often do if they were not.)[15] The campaign over, messengers raced to carry the news of its outcome to the home city. If the triumph had been great and 'the flesh of men taken' they bound their hair as they ran, but should they come with hair unbound, the watchers knew there had been Mexica men killed and taken, and that Huitzilopochtli had denied them victory. Then the messengers dispersed to tell some families the woeful news of a son or a husband or a father taken, and to others whose men had triumphed the details of their rewards – capes and breechclouts, chocolate and food, devices, labrets and earplugs to the commoners; wealth, office, devices of gold and quetzal feathers and princely garments to the nobles.

Those rewards were headily tangible and public. George Catlin, painting the Indians of the Upper Missouri in the 1830s, found the chiefs demanding subjects; once they submitted to having their portraits painted they sat with splendid stoicism, but he learnt their insistence that the smallest detail of paint or feather or fall of hair had to be most precisely represented, however taxing of patience or destructive of the requirements of composition, because each was cherished as a statement of specific prowess, which all who knew the conventional signs could read.[16] Equally the warriors of the Mexica, appearing on 'dress' occasions at the local or central temples, presented in their distinctive war paint, their feathered warrior suits and headdresses, their tassels and braids their own combat histories, and so the quality of their capacity to play the part of great men. The houses of those who had taken captives were centres of abundance, and their kinfolk were fat through the leanest season. Their names were celebrated in the songs and chants of the local warrior house, and, as their fame spread, in other wards, and even perhaps in other cities. And as they took yet another distinguished captive the whole neighbourhood would be caught up in the celebrations at the main temple precinct, at the neighbourhood temple, in the warrior's own household, and in the streets and households of the locality. For the warrior, fame was the immediate point of it all: the flowers, the cloaks, tobacco, and food from his lien on the tribute warehouses, won by his valour and distributed through his gift to an increasing tribe of dependants and admirers. The reward was experienced most intensely at the most local level: in the glances of the women, the adulation of the children, the careful respect of one-time peers, the overleaping of the distinctions of age and birth; such a man, honoured, envied, took constant precedence in local affairs. He moved easily amongst Moctezoma's administrators, and the elders of the calpulli would court him.

Warrior prowess could also open a narrow path into the nobility. Diego Durán borrowed the term 'Caballeros Pardos' or 'Gray Knights' from homeland Spain for such men, seeing them as similar to those commoners elevated by the Spanish Crown to special rewards and privileges, yet kept distinct from the hereditary aristocracy. A 'Gray Knight' had the right to wear cotton, not maguey fibre, garments and to walk sandalled through the city streets. He was freed from the obligation to pay tribute in goods or labour, and was given wealth from the tribute warehouses. He could drink pulque in public. He was permitted to keep concubines. He could enter the palace at will, and claim his ration at the royal table. On ritual occasions he was privileged to dance with the lords. His children were benefited: 'in sum these men began a new lineage, and their children enjoyed their privileges, calling themselves knights.' Durán was nonetheless confident that a man's origins were never forgotten, nor were meant to be. As we would expect, the point of difference was made by a characteristic in the regalia: the war shirts of the 'Gray Knights' were unfeathered, bearing only strips of the skins of appropriate animals over their cotton quilted armour, while the nobles' were all of featherwork, feathers being reserved to those noble by blood.[17]

While it is unclear how many commoners ascended to the upper ranks of the warrior hierarchy, in such matters numbers do not much matter: a commoner could prosper mightily through the pursuit of arms, so the dream if not the actuality of a career open to talent was kept alive. It was the high-burnished glamour of the local hero as much as the flow of material rewards that bound ordinary men and women to the great enterprise of war and of empire. The warriors' most significant service was performed far from the city, in the 'unproductive' milieu of war, their most immediate products the bodies of the warrior captives and tribute victims. Nonetheless, the central utility of warrior action was proclaimed socially, and ceremonially insisted upon, as we shall see. 'Ordinary' productive labour was given some respect, but it was deprived of significant social value unless it enhanced the glory of the warrior. Embroiderers, featherworkers, all the high-prestige crafts not only depended on the warriors for much of their raw materials and most of their market, but for the social lustre their products acquired as warrior adornments. The long-distance merchants, who secured for Tenochtitlan exotica which lay beyond the reach of empire, and who enriched the tribute by their supple trading, were also sensitive to that powerful allure, enacting, as we will see, an in-the-lion's-mouth performance at the warrior festival of Panquetzaliztli, when they insisted on the ceremonial statement of their own warrior status in face of warrior hostility.

Given such a system, all knew what was owed 'the man dexterous in battle':

Such honour he won that no one might be adorned [like him]; no one in his house might assume all his finery. For in truth [because] of his dart and his shield there was eating and drinking, and one was arrayed in cape and breechclout. For verily in Mexico were we, and thus persisted the reign of Mexico.[18]

2

The requirement of exemplary performance in battle, heavy enough on the commoner, lay oppressively on those of noble birth. It is likely that only nobles could seek membership in specified élite warrior societies like those of the eagle or of the jaguar knights.[19] The sons of lords were typically taken into a priest school or calmecac somewhere between ten and thirteen years old, more for the moral discipline of close supervision and steady application rather than for full priestly training. (Those boys dedicated to the priesthood began their training significantly younger, at six or seven.) At fifteen they began their military training, for their fate too depended on the outcomes of the fierce, explicit, most consequential struggle on the battlefield, their captives at once trophies of victory and warrants for social reward. And they too had to face the possibility of failure: a failure less materially damaging but more painfully and publicly humiliating than that risked by the commoner. The years brought no remission for those men who continued in the profession of arms. Some, having achieved warrior respectability – two captives, or perhaps three – might proceed to other imperial duties. While ambassadors and tribute-collectors were not secure from danger, being favourite early targets for unwilling tribute payers, they were largely freed from battlefield testing. Such elevations were increasingly restricted to those of noble birth, which Moctezoma the Younger appears to have made a prerequisite for all state service early in his reign.[20] Others were absorbed into the administration of the wards or the warrior schools. But for most warriors, whether noble or commoner, early success meant a continued commitment to the battlefield until age allowed honourable retirement. For the most elevated among them the 'Flowery Wars' constituted the greatest and most honourable of battles. They must have been costly in noble lives. And they were the affair of men: not of lads persuaded of their immortality or reckless in their anguish for notice, but men with wives, family, office, and status, regularly brought to stake all – family, status, office, life – in the ultimate gamble of one-to-one combat, and this not by individual whim but institutional necessity.[21]

Modern pragmatists find non-materialistic motives for consequential battles disquietingly unintelligible. They are equally uneasy with an extravagant devotion to a narrowly defined 'honour' and the excitements of its highly public testing. Such things have lost favour in our society, being subdued into 'sport' or pushed away to the margins of awareness and society alike in the touchy companies of the more antisocial young males. We are also perturbed by the apparent nakedness of contest in the Mexica warrior system, where success came at the direct expense of one's comrades, and through taking an enemy one triumphed over one's friends. To tell of an all-male system for dealing with juveniles, in which corporal punishments are dealt out by one's senior fellows; where morale depended on in-group discipline and reverence and emulation of local heroes in an atmosphere of pervasive contest, is to summon up the ghost of another sufficiently harsh system for training young men for the rigours of imperial duties. But unlike these aspiring Mexica, British public schoolboys were securely privileged in the outside world, though perhaps that matters little when you are eight and far from home. While for the Mexica there was pride in one's own warrior house, ward, city, as opposed to those of others, the 'team spirit' aspect so prominent in British public school life was effectively lacking. Men fought under the banners of their ward, and jealously compared ward performances, but it was personal distinction they coveted. However competitive the British system, there were always (at least formally) alternative models of reputable behaviour: the 'team player' or the 'good loser'. With the Mexica, it was winner take all.

Triumph was not modestly worn. During one of his secret descents into the world of men Tezcatlipoca had taken on his warrior guise, and aided only by a tiny body of despised followers, had won a smashing victory over Tula's enemies. The myth-story described his danced entry into the city he had saved. Tula's ranking warriors (who had inadvertently missed the entire battle) came to honour the victorious ones well outside the city, laying before them their own most magnificent regalia: quetzal feather headdresses, turquoise inlaid shields, 'all the array they had with them'. Having made his selection and adorned himself in their best, Tezcatlipoca began his triumph:

He came dancing . . . . He came showing disdain. He came vaunting himself . . . . The song came pouring out . . . they came blowing flutes for him . . . the shell trumpets came gurgling. . . . And when they went to reach the palace, then they pasted [his] head with feathers and they anointed him with yellow ochre and they colored his face red. And all his friends were so adorned.[22]

Here we have vaunting raised to an art form. While Tezcatlipoca's humble 'friends' were honoured with him, warriors from the same city who had missed the battle by chance were looted of their finery, and made to endure humiliation. There were constant expressions of collective pride, in dance as in the organizing for war. But what we glimpse in the day-to-day interactions appears determinedly abrasive, and we have seen the brutal punishments meted out to comrades. What becomes of congeniality, what becomes of friendship, under such circumstances?

Faced with a situation so unfamiliar, the temptation is to assume that the meliorating elasticities have been censored out by that idiosyncratic but most devoted censor, time. However, the evidence, scattered though it is, is consistent, and the rigour therefore probably real. An early 'origin of the world' myth briskly makes the point. With the world in darkness, the gods discussed which of their number would leap into a great fire, and so become the Sun. The contest narrowed to two, one a rich and beautiful god, the other a little god covered in boils. The great god, awarded the first opportunity, faltered. In that moment of hesitation the little god leapt, and gloriously rose as the Sun. The coward then took belated courage to make his leap into the fire, and rose equally gloriously as the Moon. Equal brilliance being intolerable, he was struck in the face (with a rabbit, the Mexica said, discerning the outline of a rabbit on the Moon's pale face) and his light forever dimmed.[23] In the Mexica world there were no equals, and no second chances.

Among the Plains Indians, where intense rivalry seems to have provided a nexus for intimacy – rivals, therefore friends – the rivalries were notably less sharply focussed, with a significantly wider range of rewarded behaviours drawing in a wider range of psychological types (the soft-footed thief who could spirit a prized horse away from deep in an enemy camp, the planner as well as the hero of a war party) and with acts of assistance to one's comrades (the brave who paused to save a comrade) acknowledged as virtuous.[24] Yet if the range of rewarded actions was comfortably wide, the rich accounts also tell us something of the high emotional pitch of life where combat was glorious; where acts of magnificent rashness – touching an armed enemy with hand or coup-stick – were those most intensely admired; and where the expectations of one's own group regularly put the individual at extreme risk. Lewis and Clark recorded the dedication of a Dakota warrior society whose members had vowed always to proceed without deflection, forswearing any evasion or concealment. The vow was observed with heroic literalmindedness: a party of Dakota, including some of these élite warriors, was crossing the Missouri River on the ice when they came upon a hole directly in their path. The hole 'might easily have been avoided by going around, [but] the foremost man went on and was lost. The others were dragged around by the party.' In a single battle with the Crow 'out of 22 of this Society 18 were killed, the remaining four being dragged off by their party'.[25]

Such men, Lewis and Clark thought, took their vow for 'life', short as that was likely to be, and enjoyed formidable status, being awarded public triumphs, many opportunities to recite their valorous deeds, the leading place in the dance (including the interesting privilege of kicking the lesser dancers) and precedence in all situations.[26] But we note that the people who honoured them for their superb indifference to death also sought to protect them from the full consequences of their vow by intervening in times of acute danger, and that such interventions were not only tolerated, but presumably expected and desired.

Most Plains warrior societies concentrated the highest risks in offices held for only one season of war. 'Staff-bearers' were always in danger, and were required to display maximum courage: to stand and face the enemy to cover the flight of friends; in battle to drive the lance through the sash of office, so the warrior was actually pinned to 'his' territory. (He could be released only by the lash of the 'whipper' of the society, so being 'driven' from his chosen position: once again the reliance on the care and risk-taking of a comrade.) Such offices were often forced on less-than-willing recipients. One such revealing moment has been recorded.

The Crow Young-Jack-Rabbit was forcibly 'elected' as an officer in the Lumpwood warrior society when the older men who made the selections came to him as he sat in the lodge, and offered him the pipe:

They brought the pipe to me, but I refused to accept it, saying I did not wish to take it. One of the pipe-offerers was my own elder brother. He seized me by the hair, hit me on the chest, and said, 'You are brave, why don't you smoke the pipe?' He wished me to die, that is why he desired me to smoke the pipe. He said, 'You are of the right age to die, you are good-looking, and if you get killed your friends will cry. All your relatives will cut their hair, they will fast and mourn; your bravery will be recognized; and your friends will feel gratified.' I took the pipe, and began to smoke.[27]

A cynic might see an advanced case of sibling rivalry here, but that would be to miss the Crow point. The brother (who had previously held the office himself) was moved by love and pride. It is a double ideal he invoked, one aesthetic, one social: the fine and tender melancholy of death in the beauty and strength of young manhood, and the single glorious stroke which, overleaping ambiguities and the trials of competition, establishes worth unequivocally and once and for all. These same hard men could be moved – coerced, more precisely – to magnificent generosity and to the most reckless personal undertakings by the lamentations and pleas of those who had lost loved ones to the enemy, and whose grief could be assuaged only by revenge. Obviously the bonds of community and sentiment among the Crow were laced in ways unfamiliar to us.

These are constructed contrasts, and it would not do to overstrain them. At this distance, and given the obstinately external nature of the Mesoamerican texts, it is impossible to be confident how far similar sentiments moved the Mexica, however suggestive some of the parallels. But the oppositions are clearer, and instructive, in the furiously guarded independence of the Mexica warrior, who (at least ideally) tolerated no intervention, and whose competitive edge was not dulled by comradely interdependence. It seems that among the Mexica we have an intensification of internal rivalries through the deliberate forcing of warrior achievement into that single and simple measure of captives taken.

That measure was then extended to all other aspects of life. On formal occasions the ranking was precise, the ordering of 'the youths, the masters of the youths, the leaders of the youths, the seasoned warriors, the "shorn ones, the Otomí" being a standard sequence.[28] When the greatest of warriors condescended to dance where the dancers were not grouped according to rank their status was still manifest, not only in their glorious array but in the careful space left around them as they revolved like suns among planets. That ubiquitous ranking also provided the unstated referent in every general male activity, functioning as a leash on camaraderie. In the month preceding the season of war, when the young men were restless, they went out in a thronging mass to find, fell, and drag back to the city a fine tall tree. Arrived at the main temple precinct, amid much shouting and instructions from the overseer, the young men 'expended their strength' to haul the tree upright. (The phallicism is manifest, but that is a later story.) So it remained, unadorned, for twenty days, and was then lowered, and on the day of the feast smoothed, strengthened and hauled upright again, braced and laced with great ropes, decorated with sacred paper, and the *Xocotl* – a little moulded seed-dough figure decked with paper regalia – placed at the top. Then, after the main business of the festival (the slow killing by fire of warrior captives in the dawn) at midday all the men and youths down to the 'small boys, those with a little tuft at the back of the head' first arranged themselves into the 'serpent dance', winding and twisting around the lines of women in a swirling mêlée, and then swept to the great tree for the assault on the Xocotl. Tough warriors, all 'masters of youths', had been set to guard it, so the wave of men had to break through their whirling pine staves, taking the blows as they fell. Then, clawing and kicking and holding each other back, they clambered up the ropes – perhaps as many as twenty men festooning each one – until the swiftest climber, feet in the faces of those below, managed to reach the little figure, seize it, break it, and send the fragments scattering to the crowd below, who in turn brawled enthusiastically for even the smallest piece. The Xocotl tree was then brought crashing to the ground. The 'captor' of the image was taken by the old men to the temple, praised, given gifts, and then, attended by a procession of priests blowing their shell trumpets, escorted through the streets to his home. He was also privileged to wear the distinctive brown mantle with a striped feather edge which marked him as the captor of the Xocotl – provided he had already taken a man in combat.[29]

Other male-centred rituals initially recalled earlier, simpler days, as in the hunting festival of the fifteenth month, Quecholli, when infants were presented to the old women at all of the neighbourhood temples, and all able-bodied males down to the youngest lads made arrows together and tested their marksmanship, honoured ancestral hunters, and then went out to the hills, to camp and to hunt together. We seem to be looking at an actualization of Victor Turner's 'communitas', as social barriers dissolved in happy mutuality. But the reminder of how little of that old egalitarianism survived came swiftly. The hunt began in tight co-operation, with the hunters linked in a great circle. Then the circle exploded as individuals scrambled to lay hands on the most prestigious animals: an exercise calculated to reward he who first abandoned the group effort for private advantage. Moctezoma distributed rewards for the animals taken in strict accord with each hunter's status as a warrior, and the captors were fêted in the warrior mode: precisely the same transformation as had followed on the joyful group selection and erection of the Xocotl tree, with initial co-operation collapsing into violent competition, and the competition resolved by individualistic victory rewarded in accordance with the battle-built warrior hierarchy.[30]

'Rivalry' is a densely textured relationship, building opposition out of similarity, and solidarity out of the intimacy of shared ambition and mutual envy. Those battlefield prohibitions against yielding one's own captive to a friend indicate a powerful sympathetic impulse to put affection or generosity to a comrade first. Loyalty to one's particular group was displayed when the warriors of Tenochtitlan paraded in their massed glory against the warriors of the sister city of Tlatelolco, or in the dance performances of one warrior house against another. It was exuberantly explicit when the young men of the warrior schools and the priest houses challenged each other over a full day of running battles and mutual raidings and ransomings in the middle of the season of war. Nonetheless, a tense competitiveness charged relationships between warrior peers, as between the members of other male groupings. The delicts which could bring such stunningly violent and immediate retribution from one's warrior peers were not necessarily remarkable within the group (that 'secret' warrior drinking, the illicit sexual joking) nor even intentional, as with the sudden breaking of courage in battle. If consequential contest was restricted to the battlefield, it was kept vivid by its constant replication in everyday life.

The focus on imposed and continuing contest accompanied the widening of empire, with office becoming at once more finely hierarchical and more fiercely desired. The 'aristocratic revolution' said to have been carried through by Moctezoma the Younger, with high office ideally reserved for the nobly born, hints at an exacerbated contest over place by the days of the late empire. But that competitiveness found its ground in the experiential intensities of the streets and warrior houses of the city, in those early, desperate, and continuing struggles for the scarce resource of individual fame.

3

In the secluded world of the priests contest was muted by collective observance. Mexica priests were athletes of self-mortification: in prolonged fasting, vigil, and the laceration of ears, thighs, shins, tongues, and penises for the drawing forth of blood. At first such discipline was externally imposed, young novices being sharply disciplined in the priest schools. But soon the novice priest routinely collected the maguey spines he would stain with his own blood, and endured near-continuous fasting as the ceremonies proceeded in their orderly round. While Mexica warriors sang and danced in their warrior houses it was the duty of the priest to go out alone into the dark of the night to patrol the rim of hills outside the city, marking the long night watches with the blast of his shell trumpet, and drawing blood from his body in offering at fixed places on his round. The night was a time of terrors for the Mexica, so that lonely circuit took its own kind of courage. How that mournful duty and the isolating marking of the narrow boundaries of the physical self in pain was understood we cannot know. But it was continuous, and inescapable. In the painted records priestly status is indicated not only by the black face paint of 'penance' and the tobacco pouch at the waist, but by the bright smear of blood below the ear.

Such men seem far removed from the showy exuberance of the warrior style. Nonetheless, they were concerned to demonstrate their own forms of physical toughness, most directly in the gleeful manhandling of 'captives' in the day of licensed battle between young priests and warriors. The priests subjected their prizes to laceration with maguey spines, gouging the skin of ears, shoulders, chest, and thighs until the victims cried out. (The warriors rubbed captured priests with a sort of itchy powder made from ground maguey, so that they squirmed and writhed and quite lost the acute decorum which was their hallmark.)[31] In those 'play' battles they also declared their warrior capacity to push encounters to a dangerous pitch. Some priests were officially warriors, although how the two hierarchies were integrated is unclear, and in major campaigns the squads of warriors, grouped by calpulli, ward, and city, were led by their priests, each bearing the image of his god upon his back. Arrived at the targeted city, with the warriors formed into edgy order, it was a priest who whirled his firestick to make new fire, and the moaning blast of a priestly shell trumpet which sounded the attack, while the first warrior captive taken was given over to the priests to be offered immediately to the gods.[32]

These activities were all part of the public sphere. We know little of priestly lives within the priest houses, and less of their thoughts. Few priests, easily identifiable as they were, survived the phobic hatred of the Spanish conquerors, and the destruction of their finely articulated ecclesiastical structure must have cast those few survivors into a social and cognitive void. Priestly doings were concealed from outsiders. In all of Sahagún's great compilation the only priestly ceremony described in any detail is one which would have been accessible to novices who failed to

proceed to priesthood. That one account has its interest for what it
reveals of values and relations between priests and laity, and, more particularly, within the priestly group.

The occasion was the ritual preparations and purifications for the
celebration of the major festival of Etzalqualiztli, or 'the eating of maize-
bean porridge' in the sixth month of the Mexica seasonal calendar, when
the Rain God Tlaloc was solicited for sustained rain. It began with the
priestly show of authority already discussed: returning to the city bearing
specially gathered reeds to furnish their priest houses, they stripped any
travellers encountered on the road of their possessions, savagely drubbing
those unwise enough to resist.

The next acts of violence were performed within the group. One of the
functions of the first days of the festival was to cull those priests unfitted
to the tasks ahead. Accordingly all priests down to the youngest novices,
who could not have been much more than six or seven years old, had to
endure five days and nights of minimal food and sleep while performing
certain prescribed tasks with unrelenting precision. The particularities
are worth getting clear. At twilight of the first day every priest, from the
most senior to the lowliest junior, had to place offerings – maize balls or
tomatoes or chilli peppers, all round objects – before the fire in the priest
house with such delicacy that they did not roll. The priests then stripped,
lacerated their ears with maguey spines, so that the blood smeared and
dripped on the naked body, and went in procession through the night to
the priests' bathing place on the lake, where they plunged into the chill
water. Returned to their priest house, naked and shivering, they huddled
in the poor warmth of their cloaks until noon, when they were served their
one meagre meal of the day. There the test was to handle their small
ration of maize cakes so neatly, despite weariness and hunger, that the
sauce did not spill or spatter. After the meal they set out with their fellows
on a long hike to the mainland to collect fir branches and reeds which
they then ran to distribute between the temples and priest houses of the
city. At twilight, returned to the priest house, they began the whole taxing
round again. So it continued over five days.[33]

Considered separately, the tasks are simple enough. Considered as an
unremitting sequence, especially for a hungry, tiring, anxious novice, they
are formidable. All had to be performed under the jealous eye of one's
fellow priests: should the smallest flaw in performance be detected – an

offering nervously placed shifting slightly, an unremarked cobweb or trace of dust on a garment picked up in the course of a desperately demanding day, a stumble in the carrying of the branches, or, more brutally, simply being the last one back to the priest house – it was any priest's duty and obligation to 'mark' the delinquent, who then had to pay a ransom to his 'captor' to expunge the fault. On the fifth day, when fatigue was at its worst, and when the younger novices must have been close to physical and emotional collapse, the lapses were inexpungeable. The punishment of the delinquents was public and brutal. A noisy procession of priests harried and bullied them down to the lake edge, the youngest offenders dragged by the hand or carried on the shoulders, the older hauled along by their loincloths. Sacred paper and rubber and incense 'gods' were burnt at the lakeside, presumably to summon Tlaloc's attention to the fate of those who had failed to serve him well, and the victims were mercilessly ducked and rolled in the water until half-drowned – punished by 'Tlaloc' himself – and then left, shaking and choking, to be rescued and tended by their kin, who had formally relinquished them in infancy to the priest house, and to whom they had been so brusquely returned. Only priests who had triumphantly survived the test went on to perform their priestly roles in Tlaloc's festival.

Our notions of justice are outraged by all this. The delicts were trivial, at least in our eyes: not matters of faith and morals, but involuntary lapses in muscular or mental control, some failure in stamina. Those lapses were defined by denunciation, the denunciation being made by one's companions, who profited from the fine they were permitted to levy: not a situation conducive to trust. (As the fines were adjusted to the wealth of the offender, the most wealthy were presumably watched with high attentiveness.) In this ruthless selection for failure one's comrades were at once fellow competitors, judges, and executioners.

The purged and perfected priesthood proceeded to four more days of fasting and ritual preparations before carrying out their public roles. Priests in the full glare of public ceremonial moved with the poise of dancers in their cumbersome regalia; made their offerings with fastidious exactitude; climbed and descended pyramids; subdued victims; performed the bloody business of sacrifice: all with the magisterial composure and unshakeable poise inculcated by the testing process. But the implication of the necessity of a strong inner composure with minimal dependence on one's 'comrades' remains. The treatment of those who had failed; their subjection to public violence and public humiliation; their reduction to coughing, vomiting, choking, pathetically bedraggled figures, points to the most deliberate public unmaking of the mystique attached to the person of the priest – or, more correctly, constituting that persona. We are tempted to assume that seniority conferred effective immunity from being marked as an offender, but such immunity was rare in the Mexica polity. Granted that public humiliation must have fallen most often on the youngest and least experienced of the priests, all priests were required to participate. And all priests, down to the novices, were accorded significant status by virtue of their office, as the violence inflicted on those hapless travellers indicates. Public physical humiliation and extreme violence is used economically in most polities, and against the prestigious rarely and as a last resort: in Tenochtitlan it was used extravagantly, publicly, and as a first resort. The muffled drum-beat of warrior contest sounds through the whole testing performance, with its seizings of 'captives', its ransoms and the deliberate and public humiliation in the dragging to the place of punishment. More profoundly, there is the familiar tense competitive watchfulness between peers, the involuntary or trivial delict designated as decisive, then the public stripping of the insignia, and the violent expulsion from the group back into social infancy: a bouleversement in the case of the priest both metaphorical and actual, as all the painful training in fastidious control ends in the choking misery of not knowing which way is up.

4

Some groups stood somewhat to the side of the warrior ethos. Those prestige craft calpullis like the goldworkers and featherworkers seem to have been very tight communities, typically endogamous, aware of their distinctive origins, pursuing their own affairs and their own observances. They pledged their sons to initial training in the priest school, the iconography of featherwork being momentous: while trained scribes drew the initial designs to guide the work, those who executed them needed some knowledge. Sons were trained to confident skill in the craft, daughters in embroidering and the exacting business of judging colour and dyeing fur and feathers to a precise match. Nonetheless the luxury craftsmen were profoundly implicated in the imperial city, their art a reflex of its glory, its warriors providers of their raw material and ardent consumers of their products.

The pochteca or long-distance merchants could be thought to stand even further outside the contest culture and display economy. They were notable servants of the state, policing the petty traders of the local markets and collecting their taxes, trading on the ruler's behalf, providing information on the outer reaches of empire. But much of their public conduct appears designed to deny their status. If Mexica warriors and lords moved in accord with a style of watchful pride, the merchants practised a thorough-going self-effacement, habitually wearing the maguey fibre cloaks of the commoner and cultivating an address of conscientious humility. They lived separately and sedately in their own calpullis, the powerful merchant associations controlling their own members, giving special worship to their own deity. Their sons were merchants, and married the daughters of merchants. The first trading venture of the novice trader was an elaborate but exclusive affair, the main public ritual being the feasting of the leaders of the merchant calpullis, and the dutiful acceptance of their exhortations regarding proper conduct and of their blessings against the dangers of the road. Then, the hired carriers assembled and the loads distributed (the smallest boys on their first apprentice journey carrying only the water gourds) there was a swift leavetaking, with no backwards step or even glance permitted, as in the dark of night the laden canoes slipped away on the first leg of the journey.[34]

That swift and secret departure from the city is compatible with all we know of merchant caution, their acute discretion in their dealings with the non-merchant Mexica, and their developed preference for secrecy regarding the movement of their goods and the extent of their wealth. Their separateness extended to matters religious. Mexica merchants' religious practices had the portability we would expect of professional travellers. Merchant youths attended the priest schools to learn to keep their painted records, but also to read the daysigns and calculate propitious times along the way: no priests were needed to open the path of trade. Those setting out on expeditions made their private offerings, within their own courtyards, to images of the Fire God and the Earth Lord they had themselves concocted out of rubber-painted paper. Their own god was always with

them: wherever the distinctive merchant travelling staves were leant together along the road Yacateuctli was present, standing guard over his
people. Unlike most Mexica deities this eminently portable god was satisfied with little. He accepted the meagre fare of the traveller, and even at
the homecoming seemed more confederate than lord, being content with
an offering of turkey heads and a private moment of gratitude beside the
home hearth.

The returning expedition again used the cover of night to enter the city,
and stored their precious cargo in the warehouses of kin members to
obscure the issue of personal ownership. Their private wealth was placed
under the protection of the elders of the merchant association, who stood
high in the ruler's favour. So-called 'disguised merchants' were said to
operate as spies for Moctezoma, 'passing' as natives in hostile territories
while they gathered intelligence: 'So that they did not look like Mexicans,
in order to disguise themselves, they took on the appearance of [the
natives]. As was the manner of cutting the hair of the people of Tzina-
cantlán, of Cimatlán, of the Otomí, of the Chontal, just so did the merchants cut their hair to imitate them. And they learnt their tongue to enter
in disguise.'[35]

It makes a pleasant tale. It also strains credulity. Possibly some merchants crossed 'enemy' or unreduced territories undetected, but as their
interest also lay in securing desirable local products it is difficult to see
how local populations could have long remained unaware of their interests and their origins. (These were also towns much smaller and therefore less permeable than Tenochtitlan.) Doubtless merchant information
was highly valuable to the ruler as he plotted new conquests, and doubtless merchants faced real hazards, one of the most expeditious ways for
subjugated peoples to signal disaffection from Mexica domination being
to maltreat Mexica merchants. But it is likely that most merchants trav-
elled easily in far lands because they were known and trusted there, and
fitted into the local scene. Cosmopolitans in an intensely parochial polity,
they moved confidently in a dozen provinces, speaking the languages,
wearing the local dress, and probably enjoyed close and stable relations
with the local merchants. Whatever their protestations of single-hearted
involvement with the expansion of the Mexica empire, other evidence,
circumstantial as it is, points to a rather different relationship between

merchants and the Mexica. They probably bore no historic allegiance to the city before Tenochtitlan's rise to prominence. Certainly there are powerful indicators of their separate, and prior, organization. Twelve cities were implicated in the merchant league, whose members could be entrusted with each other's goods. Their involvement in the steps of advancement for the individual within the Mexica merchant corporation indicates that the league framework existed well before the dominance of Tenochtitlan. The merchant corporation extended a near-equal role to merchant women, who could trade by proxy in the expeditions, and were the custodians of the goods of their absent male kin, presumably taking the responsibility for their release on the market as they judged appropriate. Their special status was recognized in the festival of Panquetzaliztli, when the merchant, privileged to escort his human offerings to the killing stone, was accompanied on this most prestigious occasion by his wife.[36] Such distinctive elements in merchant social organization suggest significant time depth in its development, while the generally beleaguered quality of merchant life in the imperial city points to their outsider status.

For Mexica warriors the wealth of merchants, secured not in open battle but in secret and inglorious ways, was not virtuously won. Their separateness was also noted: following their quiet ways in their closed calpullis, with their covert comings and goings, their conscientiously humble garb. (The tempting analogy is with Spanish Christian ambivalence towards fifteenth-century Spanish Jewry, at once essential, separate, and mistrusted by the wider society, until the withdrawal of royal protection imposed the bitter choices of forced conversion or expulsion.) There was also anger, still vivid thirty and more years after the conquest, at merchant actions in the famine year of One Rabbit (1454) when unseasonably early frosts had for three years blighted the maturing maize, and Moctezoma the Elder released his people from their duties, to survive as best they could. In those bitter days even nobles sold their children into slavery, and the merchants bought them: 'this was the time they bought people; they purchased men for themselves. The merchants were those who had plenty, who prospered; the greedy, the well-fed man, the covetous . . . the mean, the stingy, the selfish. Into the homes of such men they crowded, going into bondage.'[37] The rulers of the city – those involved in the conceptualization and the maintenance of the whole political structure – were well aware of the merchants' importance in that structure, but time and again we glimpse warrior hostility, and warrior rapacity.

Merchants recognized and responded to the threat. They provided lavish feasts for the leading warriors and lords: feasts with nothing reciprocal about them save perhaps an implied agreement by the lords to control their aggression. On occasion merchants laid out their most prized possessions and allowed the nobles to make their own selection in what looks very like a covert levy. And should the ruler relax his vigilance or withdraw his protection, 'then the chieftains, in envy, falsely, by means of false testimony, condemned the disguised merchants, in order to slay the innocent, so that by means of [their goods] the shorn ones, the Otomí warriors, the war leaders, might be sustained.'[38] Merchants knew to tread softly in the streets of Tenochtitlan.

They also made a most deliberate effort to approximate their merchant activities to the warrior ideal. They made strong claims as to the physical hazards of their trade – the fatigues and terrors of travel – and the heroic tenacity, physical toughness, coolness, and courage required to practise it.[39] Above all they insisted on their historical, and continuing, role as crypto-warriors. Vanguard merchants venturing abroad claimed they sometimes went 'girt for war' 'because they passed through the enemy's land, where they might die [and] where they took captives.'[40] During the reign of Ahuitzotl, Moctezoma the Younger's predecessor, this readiness for battle had been elevated into a claim of remarkable warrior achievement. Mexica merchants in the province of Anahuac towards the Gulf coast were besieged for four years by the warriors of eight large cities, and then attacked by the people of the whole region. Nonetheless they prevailed utterly, with each of these supreme warriors taking fifteen or twenty captives of extraordinary magnificence, with golden ear pendants hanging to their shoulders, sumptuously feathered war shirts, turquoise mosaic shields, panaches of quetzal feathers.[41] Returning triumphantly to Tenochtitlan, having brought all of Anahuac to submit to Huitzilopochtli, they were greeted by the ruler himself, who bestowed upon them the richest of warrior devices to wear at the warrior feasts of Tlacaxipeualiztli and Panquetzaliztli.[42] He further rewarded his 'reconnoitrers', the 'disguised merchants' who spied out new lands for conquest, with the golden lip-plugs which signified their special warrior status.[43]

So, at least, the merchants told it. There are two oddities here. First, the insignia were to be worn only on specified occasions; that is, they did not become part of the merchant warrior's 'face', his constant public persona. And in the intensely individualistic and unstable world of the Mexica warrior the status was awarded collectively, and in perpetuity. Those anomalies help explain the settled animosity of warriors to merchant claims of warriordom, and their malevolent watchfulness for merchant pretension. At the great feast of Panquetzaliztli at the pivot of the season of war nominated merchants were permitted to present purified slaves as surrogate warriors for ritual killing, with their offerings being accorded the place of honour, following after the presentation of actual warrior captives. The individual who bore the brunt of the huge costs and labour involved in that glorious undertaking was carefully supervised by senior merchants, the sumptuousness of his offering and the elaborateness of the requisite preliminary feasts bringing prestige to the whole merchant community. For the individual the dispersal of his painfully accumulated wealth bought advancement within the merchant hierarchy: an early (and rare) intimation of the 'cargo' system of ranked ritual obligations still practised in some twentieth-century Mexican Indian communities.[44]

The slaves the merchant offered were expensive in their initial purchase: a fine young man who was a skilled dancer could fetch up to forty large capes. Guest-gifts and provisioning for the sequence of four banquets at which the slaves were formally displayed could cost up to twelve hundred elaborate capes, four hundred breechclouts, and unnamed quantities of skirts and shifts, along with huge amounts of food: eighty or a hundred turkeys, forty dogs, forty or more jars of salt, twenty sacks of cacao beans.[45] At the first 'display of the slaves' feast a lord might choose to insist that an especially well-favoured slave be set aside for his own use: honoured guests have their privileges. So the great merchants won an uneasy acceptance through 'generosity' of a rather coerced kind: as unsympathetic informants briskly put it, 'the rich one, the prosperous one, perhaps the [merchant] bather of slaves, although not a brave warrior, only because of his property was he praised, because many times he invited others to banquet, he gave gifts to others'.[46]

It is tempting to see these merchants, with their careful humility in a contestful world and their accumulation of secret wealth in a world of display, as sustaining values very different from those of the larger society, for all their judicious obeisance to prevailing values. It was those attributes which led Jacques Soustelle to characterize the merchants as a 'nation within a nation', totally opposed to the values of the larger society: a 'rising class of traders' whose deference before the warrior cult was no more than a 'pious falsehood'.[47] But perhaps they were not, finally, so calculating. Merchant participation in the festival of Panquetzaliztli entailed the dispersal of hoarded wealth. For reward they had the admiration and recognition from their own people, and their elevation in status within their own group. They also had to endure submission to the 'real' warriors' arrogance and greed, with no guarantee of their goodwill. (Warrior resentment would find its clearest and cruellest expression in the threat of the last-minute expropriation of the pseudo-captive just before his presentation at the killing stone, as we will see.) Nonetheless, while the 'bathed slaves' so proudly displayed at Panquetzaliztli exemplified ostentatious and luxurious beauty, at the feast of their first presentation the males wore the curved labrets and leather earplugs of the warrior, with dance-rattles and ocelot-skin bands at their ankles, while at the third feast they displayed short jackets with skull and bone motifs and paper prairie-falcon wings tied to each shoulder. More tellingly, the offering merchant chose to act the 'warrior' fantasy through to the end. The hair of the surrogate captives was taken on the midnight of the day they were to die, and cast into the eagle vessel, with the victims being called upon to fight with actual warriors en route to the pyramid. And then, the offering made, the merchant had the body carried back to his house, and a meal of maize and human flesh prepared for his kin, sharing out the flesh of his 'captive' just as the real warriors did.[48] Given that all this was practised in the seclusion of their own calpulli and household, concealed from non-merchant eyes, we must assume that even merchants were not immune from the potent glamour of the warrior.

Merchant activities on the day Four Wind in the tonalpoalli calendar of 260 days nicely exemplifies the ambiguity of their situation, and of their sentiments. Four Wind was a day of dread for most Mexica, when evil forces were loose on the earth; demons and sorcerers roamed unopposed, and adulterers or thieves who had contaminated the group by their improprieties were put to death. On such days the people stayed close to home, avoiding any conduct which could attract the attention of the malign spirits; even stuffing leaves into the smokeholes of their houses to seal them against invasion. But on that day the merchants enjoyed a major feast. Secure in their own wards, the greatest merchants laid out their most prized goods for display in the calpulli temple – the splendid feathers and depthless stones and rare animal skins, which spoke of far places and exotic experience. Then they smoked and lounged and feasted, delighting in their possessions, basking in the midst of their treasures.

Then came the drinking, and with it the boasting. While others in the city were hushed, nervously suppressing discord, the merchants forgot their practised discretion to quarrel, reminisce, and to trade tales of great adventures in a world much wider than Tenochtitlan. They boasted of their wealth, their valour in seeking out far places, their battles, their discoveries. And they sneered mercilessly at those who frequented only the Tenochtitlan marketplace, 'buying, selling and deceiving' in that pitifully local arena. So painful was the jeering to the stay-at-homes that their cultivated control collapsed, 'so at the place of congregation there was dispute and discussion . . . they sat jostling and besmearing each other, disputing and quarrelling among themselves, contending, refuting, bragging'. 'Each thought of himself as the only one, the best'.[49]

To behave in so reckless a fashion on that day of dread indicates an aloofness, if not a contempt, for local notions, but the style of the behaviour points to susceptibility to warrior influence. The uninhibited blustering declared a competitiveness at odds with their habitual submission to the merchant collectivity. Even in these protected circumstances they revealed a developed inclination towards warrior notions of honour. There was no celebration of trading coups; of objects gained cheap and sold dear. On the contrary, to gain advantage by sharp practice was deplored. Praise belonged to those most daring in the quest for rare and exotic things, for their physical and mental toughness, their stamina, their fighting prowess in face of sudden ambush, their audacity in the face of the unknown. The stay-at-homes were ridiculed as frauds: 'so there they made light of, scoffed at, exposed, revealed, abused and tortured those who knew no places, who had gone nowhere . . . who only at the ashes of his fire called himself a warrior, and lived prudently and impudently only here in the marketplace.'[50]

'Called himself a warrior'. Obviously the warrior theme sounded loudly on these unbuttoned merchant occasions. The dealers in the slave markets played on the weakness: they presented their finest male slaves as facsimile seasoned warriors, with all the elaborate accoutrements of capes and breechclouts, the earplugs, the amber labrets, to tempt potential purchasers to extravagance. In the cluster of rituals surrounding trading ventures the warrior analogy was sustained. For all the days and months of the merchant's absence his immediate kin would not submerge their bodies in water, and would wash their hair only every eighty days, as befitted a time of nervous penance. Should news come of the traveller's death, his mourners built his image out of pine staves, set it up in his home place, and burnt it as the sun was sinking in the west, the period of grief lasting four days. Should he have died in battle the image was decked in paper array and seated for a day in the calpulli temple, to be burnt at midnight in the god's courtyard at the eagle vessel or the skull rack in solemn imitation of warrior rites.[51] Had the dead man offered ritually bathed slaves at one of the warrior festivals, their scalp locks and other memorabilia were burnt with his image, as were the relics of a warrior's sacrificed captives at his death.[52]

So it appears the 'merchant as warrior' mythology was not merely a politic product for non-merchant consumption. We know little of competition within the merchant group, save for that momentary indulgence in passionate boasting; the account given by Sahagún's merchant informants is of a dutiful conformity, leading easily to success in a smooth progression from novice trader to merchant leader. Yet a cargo system is more than an age-ranking device: it can function only where there are few places and more candidates. The competition within the merchant group appears to have been held under dignified control, and gracefully clad in formal protocols, but it was competition for all that. That one drunken boasting scene is the only indicator we have of explicit rivalry in the merchant ranks. Nonetheless, it seems that the lustre of the warrior style had penetrated even the merchant imagination, challenging that conscious effacement of the public self which provided the manner and licence for their existence.

5

The Masculine Self Discovered

> Our lord, the lord of the near, of the nigh, is made to laugh. He is arbitrary, he is capricious, he mocketh. . . . He is placing us in the palm of his hand; he is making us round. We roll; we become as pellets. He is casting us from side to side. We make him laugh; he is making a mockery of us.
>
> Florentine Codex[1]

I

The notion that the social being of men was made by the public recognition of an unfolding destiny was widespread among Amerindians.[2] Transformations in appearance transformed the social being. The Mexica spoke of the 'apparel' laid out by the sacred powers for the yet unborn child, which with time and fortune he would win as his own. The formulation of 'face' had to do with the public award of socially ratified signs of changes in status, and the pride taken in the new image of the public self: when the young lad's nape lock was shorn, so making him a warrior, he was said to have 'taken another face'.[3] Thus the award and adornings with specified garments and insignia could be interpreted as the actualization of an always immanent destiny.

The actualization was not irreversible. What was made could be unmade. The first markings in the flesh which declared one male or female were fixed, but all later markings, like those identifying occupation and rank, were not. We have seen the violent unmaking visited on the warrior or the priest when their peers judged them no longer worthy of their rank. 'Faces', sufficiently hard to win, were harder to maintain, and impossible to defend: if honours could be won only by individual action, the indi-

vidual was helpless to act when those honours were threatened or attacked.

There were also subtler torments. The Mexica male self was constructed in competition with, 'in face of', his fellows. Even without overt
challenge the positions so won were precarious, because they were relative. While each step of the ladder of rewards within the warrior house
system was explicit in its devices and public privileges, no individual had
security of position within his own group, and in face-to-face situations it
is relative status which counts. That position could be subverted in one
campaign, with seasoned warriors forced to swallow their chagrin and
yield precedence to some young upstart who had somehow contrived to
subdue a couple of particularly prestigious warriors. Even the brilliant
warrior's fame was not secure. It could be eclipsed at the high point of
triumph, with the whimpering collapse of the captive selected to fight on
the gladiatorial stone, or even by an awkward and inept defence. Should
the captive fight sturdily, his fame (and so his captor's) could be outshone
in an instant by some more spectacular performance. And despite the
intensity of his interest the offering warrior had no licence to intervene.
With no control over the working through of an event which concerned
him mightily, he could only watch his fate as it fell.

That same miserable reduction to powerlessness threatened the merchant who had been permitted (at the cost of his fortune and weeks of
taxing preparation) to offer his 'captives' at Huitzilopochtli's shrine at the
warrior festival of Panquetzaliztli. That most public offering would bring
honour to the giver and to the whole merchant corporation – if the
warriors, and 'fate', allowed. En route to the pyramid the purified slaves
were waylaid by a body of warrior-captives assisted by some of the leading
Mexica warriors, and forced to fight. The episode recalled a mythic
moment in Huitzilopochtli's early struggles against his murderous siblings
the Stars, but it had more immediate import as well, for this skirmish was
not 'mock', but was fought in earnest until the arrival of the running priest
of the War God put an end to it. Why the merchant's slaves put up any
kind of fight is unclear: perhaps for a more dignified death on the killing
stone, rather than at the hands of those hard-eyed arrogant men; perhaps
through drunken bravado; perhaps simply to postpone the coming of the
dark. But fight they did, and occasionally – very occasionally – well
enough to kill a warrior. Much more often a warrior was able to seize a

slave, and then the offering merchant faced either the humiliation of submission to unregulated extortion in the form of an unnegotiable ransom demand, or the immediate killing of his captive. (The lavish gift-giving and feasting of ranking warriors by the merchants before the festival day were perhaps a form of insurance against malicious intervention.) So for the merchant all that stretch for social privilege, that expensive public assertion of merchant worth, collective and individual, could be snatched away, his claims to warrior status contemptuously brought low, at the moment of his high-bought triumph.

In the ubiquity of tense competitiveness and the striving for individual dominance; in the resolution of nearly all encounters into contest and contest into hierarchy; in the hunger for public honours uncertainly held, we find a tangle of those 'root metaphors' and distinctive 'life stances' which Victor Turner saw as defining the particularity of a culture.[4] The associated patterns of action – elevations so publicly marked, reductions so decisive – imply a particular understanding of the individual as a highly vulnerable social construct, made or unmade through a series of public acts, and to a particular notion of 'fate'.

Here the most popular forms of Mexica gambling and the structuring of 'chance' are worth investigation. Spaniards, no mean gamblers themselves, characterized Indians as infatuated gamblers. What were the springs of that passion? The ballgame, played by nobles or by squads of professional players sustained by the lords, was contexted by ardent gambling, the wagered goods being laid out and displayed in counterpoise before the game began: a synchronic variation on the alternating sequence of contest gifting associated with the feast.[5] Variations between the ballcourt shapes throughout Mesoamerica suggest significant variations in the rules and the shape of the game, but by Mexica times the courts were commonly 20 or 30 feet wide and could be up to 150 feet long, with small stone rings set vertically at the centre of the side walls of the court. The game required a small solid rubber ball to be propelled from end to end of the long court, the ball to be struck only with hips and buttocks, not hand or foot. Stone markers suggest the possibility of service courts, but the main aim seems to have been to keep the ball in play, failure to do so giving a point to one's opponents. The players played naked save for loincloths, mitts to protect hands slamming against wall or floor for fast recovery and extra speed, and wide leather belts to blunt the terrible impact of the hard-driven ball, which was still sometimes sufficiently bruising to lead to internal bleeding and death. (The elaborate regalia adorning the beautiful ballplayer figurines from the Maya island of Jaina were probably 'parade' dress.)[6] Fifty years after the conquest the friar Diego Durán, curious as to the style of the Mexican game, coaxed some Indian elders into giving a demonstration. He acknowledged the experiment to have been a failure – what he saw, he said, bore no more relation to the game once played than does a picture to the living original – but he nonetheless made some interesting observations. There were opposing squads of players, but that they could be considered 'teams' in our sense is doubtful. Durán reports that while a mass of players stayed to the back of the court, the attack was sustained by a few main players at the centre, 'since the game was played in the same way they used to fight in battle or in local contest': combat pursued by other means.[7] It could also be played between individuals, as in the game between Moctezoma and the ruler of Texcoco, when Moctezoma's defeat portended the destruction of his city.

The normal method of scoring was through the slow accumulation of points. But that process could be dramatically pre-empted. To send the ball through one of the rings – a feat, given the size of the ball and the ring, presumably rarer than a hole in one in golf – gave instant victory, ownership of all the goods wagered, and the right to pillage the cloaks of the onlookers (note again that echo of the looting warrior). The scorer's most precious reward, says Durán, was fame, for 'he was honoured like a man who had vanquished many warriors in single combat'.[8]

If the ballgame was the favoured 'spectator sport' in Tenochtitlan, the most accessible and popular gambling game was *patolli*, the 'game of the mat', set up anywhere the mat could be shaken out. Played with six counters, with four beans as dice, it had its equivalent in the freakish ballgame goal: if he who was throwing the beans 'made one of them stand up, if one of the beans stood up there on its thicker end, it was taken as a great omen . . . then he won all the costly goods . . . thus all came to the end of the game' – as well they might, given the probabilities.[9] In that jangle of misapprehensions which constituted Spanish–Mexica relations during the conquest period there is a haunting moment. During his captivity the Mexica ruler Moctezoma would play with Cortés a board game called *totoloque*, of which we know little. In one engagement the tlatoani discovered Pedro de Alvarado to have been persistently mis-scoring, of course in Cortés's favour. Díaz read Moctezoma's unconcern at this discovery as evidence of lordly liberality and the untroubled acceptance of losses (they were playing for gold). Perhaps so. But perhaps it could point to a quite different locus for the meaning and excitement of the game: Moctezoma may have been intent on watching the way the counters fell.[10]

All game situations set up and order risk taking, formalizing the zone of contingencies. But how ample a space is allowed the contingent depends on wider notions about the capacity of humans to control actions and outcomes: the whole complex issue of agency. Precisely how patolli was played we don't know, but if it were indeed close to parchisi and backgammon it must have accommodated very rapid reversals of 'fortune', unlike, for example, the cumulative weight of skill of that other board game, chess. If for us the outcome of contest games depends on luck, strength and skill, the relative importance of any one of them depending on the kind of game it is, for the Mexica it seems the luck element was always dominant, however magnificent the strength, however stunning the skill. Why else leave space for that wild circumstance of the ball somehow slipping through the ring, the bean balancing on its end? It is not the nice measurement of strength or skill, but revelation which is being sniffed out here. The extravagant winner-take-all, loser-take-nothing mentality allowed in the structure of the scoring – triumph or disaster, with nothing in between – echoes that most insistent Mexica metaphor for man-to-man relations: matched combat, with its matched odds, the stakes being death or glory, with the space allowed for fortuitous but decisive reversal underscoring the final irrelevance of human endeavour.

As we have learnt from another people, belief in a determined destiny need not lead to a folded-hands quietism. Mexica men strove. Through that endless round of imposed contests – some in the 'innocent' form of games or edged with play, but endlessly prefiguring, in the riddling way of portents, what was to come – the individual came to construct, or, rather, to discover, to himself as to others, his social being. Yet he remained always aware of the fragility of that construction. The obsessive gambling connects to the same understandings as the devoted attentiveness to larger portents and auguries. Men 'played' with time: with the moving boundary between the now and the to come, trivial to the enduring sacred powers, so important to the merely human. Through that play they could enjoy a fleeting sensation of control, as they pressed the future, in one small aspect, to reveal itself. And so, perhaps, they could ease the chronic and pervasive uncertainty which was the human condition.[11]

Something of that same passion to know must have informed Mexica concern for dreams. Unhappily, Sahagún, like other Spanish recorders, had scant interest in such matters, noting only the depth of Indian concern for their meanings, and that dream interpretation was an active field for priestly expertise. But he reveals a little of the hobgoblins which haunted the Mexica midnight imagination. Most were embodied portents, playing on men's desperate desire to know something of what was to come. Should a man be sufficiently brave to pursue and grapple with the terrible phantom Night Axe – a headless torso scuttling along the ground, its split chest opening, then shutting with the dull 'chunk' of an axe blow heard in the night – he could perhaps force it to speak, and to extort from it two or three thorns as tokens of wealth and captives to come. But sometimes it remained mute, and then the desperate seeker had to seize the moment to tear out its heart, escape with it, and then bury it. Later he would return to dig it up, and to know his fate. Should he find thorns or white feathers he would be fortunate. If he found rags or a piece of charcoal, he knew he was destined to live in misery.[12] When merchants feasted noble warriors, only the warriors danced, as was fitting. But warriors and merchants alike ate the bitter mushrooms they called the 'Flesh of the Gods', which provided them with visions (clouded as such visions are) of their individual destinies.[13] It is possible that these 'dreams' too were interpreted, given the shamanistic role of the so-called priests, and their likely role in guiding the individual through ecstatic experience.

The understandings exposed here constitute a notably bleak view of human existence. Apparent good fortune was to be accepted warily. The young mother in her first pride was warned to be ready with her sighs and tears lest the Lord of the Close and Near would choose to destroy 'this tender thing', the baby. No pleasure could be unconfined, as with those bouquets of flowers to be sniffed only at the outer edges: the swooning sweetness at the centre belonged not to men but to Tezcatlipoca.[14] Willard Gingerich, wrestling with the question of the Mexica understanding of the person and the role of the will, has claimed that the discourses of the elders presented the world as 'dominated by one moral hue: evil'.[15] Yet what was elaborated upon was not 'evil', nor anything so oriented

towards mankind, but rather hardships: heat, cold, famine, fatigue, affliction. Those were most movingly rehearsed, but they were presented as
'natural' afflictions inherent in the human condition, not the 'cut-throat,
vicious reality' of man's own contrivings that Gingerich takes them to be.
On One Death, the daysign of Tezcatlipoca, that most arbitrary and fickle
of deities, slaves were pampered and made much of, 'for they were
[Tezcatlipoca's] likenesses and representatives; his beloved sons.' Were
any man to strike a slave on that day, he would come to suffer as a slave, or
would die on the killing stone.[16] We are all slaves of Tezcatlipoca, 'He
Whose Slaves We Are', victims of the giant unpredictability of the world.

That view was dramatized in the repeated spectacle of the public and
violent unmaking of the warrior-victim: his warrior regalia stripped from
him, his scalp lock shorn, his heart excised, his emptied body broken into
its parts and dispersed to be eaten. Behind the gambling, behind the
ubiquitous 'play' contests, stood the great metaphor of the fatal contest of
battle, where one's destiny as victor or victim was revealed. That looming
reality cast its shadow back over the adulation, the triumphs, to reveal the
desperate fragility of the painfully constructed (or serially revealed) 'face'
of the seasoned warrior. Endless striving, the endless, anxious, making of
the self and then the reversal: the sudden, massive, physical assault by
one's peers in punishment for some perhaps unintended, possibly involuntary delict; the merchant, all payments made, deprived of his reward;
the priest cast out; the great warrior shamed. For the elevated those
reversals may have happened only rarely, men in authority usually knowing how to protect themselves. But the threat was always there, as was the
most telling evidence for its reality, in the lines of captives – warriors
yesterday, victims today – going to their deaths on the killing stone.

Here it is worth turning the crystal of the festival of Toxcatl once more.
The young man who represented Tezcatlipoca in his aspect of 'The Young
Warrior' exemplified in the glories of his last month of life the acclaim and
rewards of warriordom. He was escorted and admired through the streets,
drenched with flowers and sighs, bathed in sexual bliss. In that dreamlike
presentation, the 'active' aspects of a warrior's life – the triumphs, the
battles, the violence, the blood – were completely suppressed. The essential preliminary selection of who would live to play the role was enacted
offstage. The young man's elevation to warriordom was intimated solely by
changing details in arrangements of hair and face paint. If Toxcatl provides

the ideal text of the ideal warrior's life, ending, as the ideal ought, in sacred death, that death and the final confrontation with the priests was secluded, its moment voluntarily chosen. Why were contest, violence and chance so firmly excluded? Not because their terrors were inadmissible, untameable even in ritual: there were rituals enough in which warrior actions and fates were most bloodily re-enacted. He who had ruled for a year as Tezcatlipoca, and who died (and was reborn) at the festival of Toxcatl, represented a more abstract level of commentary. He was at once Tezcatlipoca's exemplar, and his exemplary victim. He lived to display the god's gracious accessibility and his arbitrary, magnificent bounty; he died to demonstrate his caprice. The artificially glorious, artificially brief parabola of his ritual life displayed what it was to live in a world ruled by Tezcatlipoca, the deity of human destiny.

One passage reflecting on his fate points to his earlier riches and pride, brought low in death. If a superficial reading could seem to carry a Christian message of the sorry end to worldly vanity, what is being pointed to here is not the moral failings of an individual, but the conditions of universal subjugation to Tezcatlipoca, whose nature is perfectly realized in the destruction of his servitor at the pinnacle of honour and social bliss. Toxcatl carried a dark undertext of social prestige as fiction; of the power of men to make this perfect thing, and destroy and replicate it at will. It also spoke, more deeply, of the desperate fragility besetting experience itself; of the evanescence not only of man-made things, but of beauty, pride and desire; of the impenetrable, inexhaustible fickleness of Tezcatlipoca, with its 'I am what I am' sonorities. The god bore as his main identifying emblem the 'scrying glass' of the shaman which gave him his name: 'Tezcatlipoca', 'The Mirror which Smokes', or, even more ethereally, 'The Mirror's Smoke'.[17] Mexica mirrors were slabs of dark obsidian, yielding vague dreamlike images which rose and floated and sank in a melting darkness: obscure intimations of what was to come endlessly dissolving back into obscurity. The use of a shadowed mirror as medium between the human and the sacred suggests the ubiquity of the illusory, and the ultimate impenetrability of the sacred.

Through a multiplicity of manifestations we glimpse a shared and steady vision common to the different social groupings in Tenochtitlan, as were the experiences which validated it: the anguish of powerless dependence, the constancy of insecurity, the painful insubstantiality of status and reward in the imperial city of Tenochtitlan, and the casual, inventive, tireless malice of the only sacred force concerned with the fates of men.

2

The most practised, or at least the most approved, demeanour before these bleak realities was the maintenance of external control in face of the miserable vagaries of fortune.[18] Loud and public bragging was accepted and indeed invited, but the man who bore his honours and his burdens impassively, aloof from his own shifting fortunes, was the most admired. So one sought to maintain discipline, carefulness, watchfulness. To lose control of oneself was to court misfortune: Tezcatlipoca, like other inimical sacred powers, was attracted by extravagance. Alternatively a man could simply 'fail', yield up ambition, and live modestly on the fringes of the male drama of warriordom, although even the lowliest was not immune to the bleakness of imposed 'competition', as with the food distribution of the Great Feast Day of the Lords discussed earlier. Priests followed their own path: through mortifications and the painful mapping and remappings of the boundaries of the self; through study, and endless attentiveness to the clues as to the essential and hidden nature of things. Lesser men could graduate in time into the peaceable busywork of old age, singing for the warriors, pattering on about calpulli affairs. Probably the most common escape was absorption in the mundane routines of daily life. But if cultures must provide options for temperaments beyond the heroic and the melancholic, they also offer recognition of those who act out the most extreme and therefore the clearest cultural definitions of the nature of the world and men's place within it. What compelled the Mexica imagination were the men who were prepared to play the end game, to accept and embrace that final ritual of violent death. An imperishable glamour attended those warriors who vowed never to turn their backs in battle: a defiant shortening of the odds, as we might say; a more urgent pressing for revelation as I think they understood it. If 'the warrior ideal' animated social ambition, as the way to 'honour, flowers, tobacco', local wealth and local prestige; if it provided the justificatory nexus between wealth and poverty, noble and commoner – however great the gulf, pure courage and individual effort could bridge it – it also indissolubly linked the social and the human to the sacred in the person of the great warrior.

It was here that knowledge came into play, and a chance of resolution of the painful tension between a fate acknowledged as determined, and wistful impulses towards autonomy. Should 'possession' by the sacred power be invoked, it was by that invocation chosen, its fatal power invited and acquiesced in, so that human action was at last rendered non-trivial. (There is an aestheticism in the stoicism here: a chrysanthemum-and-sword resonance with the samurai, those other gorgeously clad, supremely laconic warriors, folded in upon themselves, then blossoming into explosive action.) When 'Huitzilopochtli overcame one' in deliberately invoked battle fury, consciousness of self was obliterated through that yielding to unknown consequences.[19]

Struggling to survive the assaults of his Mexica adversaries in the last battle for Tenochtitlan, Bernal Díaz noted and was appalled by a shift in the intensity of the attack marked by a terrible forgetfulness of self: when the great horn of Cuauhtemoc sounded, his warriors pressed forward over the swords' points in their rage to seize the enemy.[20] That sacred rage had nothing to do with the edginess or arrogance of warriors in mundane time. If the fate of the individual was usually only slowly revealed through time, combat forced the moment of revelation. Subjectivity could at last be forgotten. The warrior in mortal action was at last freed from the constraints placed on humans in this world.

The terminal courage of the Mexica warrior was deeply tinctured by this kind of understanding, as he sought out the long-feared confrontation, and leapt to embrace it. I have written elsewhere of the poignancy of the performance of the doomed warrior on the gladiatorial stone, where strength and grace, coolness and skill could be displayed precisely because the actor had passed beyond the agony of achieving the self, having been transformed by the fact of his capture into predestined victim. The last moments of the warrior who accepted his death on the field of battle had at least ideally that same transcendental quality, as the swaddling obscurities of the confusions of experience fell away to reveal at last the final shape of his destiny, and he embraced it.

The theme was always present. The young warrior who had offered a notable captive to the gods feasted his kin on the flesh of his captive, but at that mournful feast the captor wore the white feathers and chalk which marked the designated warrior victim, and his kinsfolk wept for him. When Toci, 'Our Grandmother', formidable aspect of the Earth Mother, called her warriors to her service on the pivot from the harvest to the season of war, she set her young men racing to be the first to plunge their hands into a great trough of chalk and feathers, and to toss the white dust and down into the air so that they and their companions were slowly misted and marked with the colour of sacrificial death.[21]

With death, the warrior, freed at last from the burden of knowledge, would enter on the ease in the pure being of butterfly or hummingbird: 'and there, perpetually, time without end, they rejoice, they live drunk [with joy and happiness], not knowing, no longer remembering, the affairs of the night . . . eternal is their abundance, their joy. The different flowers they suck, the choice ones, the flowers of joy, the flowers of happiness; to this end the noblemen go to death – go longing for, go desiring [death].'[22] The devoted made their plea for their final encounter with Tezcatlipoca: 'Show him the marvel. May his heart falter not in fear. . . . May he desire, may he long for the flowery death by the obsidian knife. May he savor the scent, savor the fragrance, savor the sweetness of the darkness. . . . Take his part. Be his friend.' And this to the Enemy on Both Sides.[23]

For others, too, the same note sounded. When long-distance merchants travelling their far roads heard the laughter of the white-headed hawk, they knew that danger was waiting. It was the leader's charge to steady his men, not, we are told, by denying the omen, but by yielding to its implications. He was to remind them that their kin had lamented when the merchant train departed, pouring out 'their sorrow, their weeping, that perhaps here, somewhere, on the desert, on the plain, in the gorge, in the forest, will lie scattered our bones and our hair, in many places our blood, our redness, will spread, poured out and slippery.' Should that moment come, 'let no-one feel womanish in heart. Yield completely to death; pray to our lord. Let none think of or brood over [our condition]; for only later shall we know of whatsoever things we may strike against. Then in the end we may weep for ourselves'.[24]

Men could master the terrible randomness of fate only momentarily, and only by yielding to it. Human autonomy flared to light the voluntary act of acquiescence, as the war club or flint knife came smashing down. With the moment of self-extinction came the moment of self-possession.

6

Wives

Thou wilt be in the heart of the home, thou wilt go nowhere, thou wilt nowhere become a wanderer, thou becomest the banked fire, the hearth stones. Here our lord planteth thee, burieth thee. And thou wilt become fatigued, thou wilt become tired; thou art to provide water, to grind maize, to drudge; thou art to sweat by the ashes, by the hearth. [*The umbilical cord was then buried by the hearth.*] It was said that by this she signified that the little woman would nowhere wander. Her dwelling place was only within the house; her home was only within the house.

Florentine Codex[1]

These words were spoken by the Mexica midwife, in a culture which knew the power of words, to a newborn female baby: an unpromising introduction for a girl-child into a warrior society. The address lacks both the challenges and the glittering images of value ('thou art an eagle, an ocelot; thou art a roseate spoonbill, a troupial')[2] addressed to the boy-child destined to warriorhood. Rank did not mitigate female destiny: newborn females regardless of caste were all condemned, it would seem, to a destiny of unrelieved domesticity. At the naming ceremony which followed close on the birth the male child's hand was closed around a tiny bow, arrows, and a shield, signalling his warrior destiny, and the girl's around miniature spinning and weaving implements and a tiny broom, while each were presented with miniaturized versions of their appropriate adult garb.[3] If his social duty was to be a warrior, hers was to be a wife. In what follows I want to explore the implications of that early dedication and the justice of our 'natural' response to it.

I

Sources, as is usual for the female half of the human race, are deficient. We hear no Mexica women's voices at all: the little we can discover must come indirectly. In pre-contact times public and therefore recorded matters were the business of men. The conquest, apart from the disquieting Doña Marina, interpreter to Cortés, was a male affair, at least in the male telling of it. (The women, of course, suffered it.) After the conquest those who recalled or commented on the Mexica past were males, and often celibate foreign males at that: the Franciscan Sahagún, usually so flexible in enquiry, briskly assumed women in temples to be 'like nuns' in a school for virtue, and midwives he dismissed to the household-and-family zone. Other material he simply deleted as trivial: we know that girls as well as boys were educated in the calpulli schools; we do not know what the girls were taught.[4] But sources are always inadequate for our aspirations, and records always distanced in multiple ways from the actuality we seek to retrieve.[5] Sahagún's encyclopaedic ambitions, signalled by that grandiose title the 'History of the Things of New Spain', trawled a wide net, and he was indulgent of details not readily classifiable. Mexica women (like Mexica children, like Mexica commoners) were neither the makers nor keepers of the records, but something of their circumstances of life, and even, with luck, some sense of their experience of those circumstances, can reasonably be sought for.

The 'discourses of the elders' are indispensable sources for all issues to do with collective attitudes and social values, and so for the proper rearing and conduct of women. The genre is notoriously idealized, but at least it enshrines conventional, if consciously lofty, sentiments. Sahagún also pursued a long interrogation into the qualities of different categories of persons (the 'old woman', the 'noble youth', the 'mature man') on the model of Bartolomeus Glanville's systematic mapping of social roles through their characteristic virtues and vices.[6] His local informants had to struggle with an unfamiliar cognitive set, and presumably in the struggle flushed out ideas normally left implicit. That imposed mode of analysis was in counterpoise to the natives' own classification of the characteristic fates (differentiated for men and for women) ascribed to individuals born on particular daysigns, as set down in the 'Books of Days', the signs and fates being partially recorded in the fourth book of the Florentine Codex.

There are omissions, deformations, and slippages between the systems, but deformations are revelatory in their own way, and a multitude of other less formal and focussed references should help adjust the vision. One unusual characteristic of the sentiments recorded in the Codex is worth noting. Elderly males of the authority-wielding class talking about the well-ordered days of their youth are likely to exaggerate both the clarity and the clout of social rules, and that idealizing tendency will obviously influence accounts of preferred female behaviour. But the tone of the Indian male voices we hear is casual, not hostile: they speak of women with neither stridency nor mistrust.

2

Birth celebrations were jubilant, with babies of both sexes being welcomed as valuable 'captives', and saluted as infinitely precious gifts, despite their different destinies. There was no clear difference in treatment through the first infant years. (While it is reasonable to assume that the insistence on the battlefield destiny of the male child would have subtly influenced his handling, whether that influence worked in the direction of more or less tenderness is impossible to guess.) Infants stayed close to their mothers until their final weaning, which was probably delayed for two or three years, or even longer.[7] Then their paths diverged, as the boy followed his father to learn his skills, and the girl her mother, grinding maize to smoothness, cooking, spinning, and finally learning the intricacies of weaving. Boys and girls alike were formally initiated into their social and sacred obligations at a special four-yearly festival of Izcalli, but about six commoner boys enjoyed the freedom of the streets (we have seen them pelting through the neighbourhood shouting the name of the newborn 'warrior'). Noble boys proceeded more sedately, practising the indispensable social grace of appropriate greeting. Little girls of the same age, already miniature women in ragged variants of their mother's blouse and skirt, were largely home-bound, although they were probably not as restricted as the midwife's words would lead us to expect; they certainly attended the frequent religious observances at the local temple, and maidens made regular offerings of food or flowers or maize at the calpulli temple at first light each morning, moving unescorted through the familiar streets.[8]

From puberty the daughters of nobles were more restricted than their commoner counterparts, being secluded for some years in the girls' division of one of the priests' schools, where they were specially instructed in embroidery. This could seem no more than a 'Get thee to a nunnery' technique for preserving valuable maidenheads, but weaving and embroidery were independently valued as the highest and only exclusively female arts, approaching painting in their significance, and presumably allowing for substantial individual challenge and expression of self. At puberty commoner girls began to attend their section of the local House of Youth, and also learnt songs and dances for ceremonial performance along with the local lads at the House of Song; the Mexica, like other people in other places, exploited the exuberance and narcissism of youth for the special grace they lent ritual performances. Chaperonage was close, but it was probably least effective in the excitement of mass ceremonial, where the girls, usually carefully modest in dress and demeanour, painted their faces and feathered arms and thighs to dance in the fire-lit zone before the temple, and watched as prospective husbands leaped and turned.

Marriage was the Mexica woman's ambition, and indeed her fate, save for those few who vowed their lives to temple service. Social maturity came only with marriage, for men as for women, when the couple established their new household: the noble father and mother of their 'little dove' urged her to honour her lineage by her diligence in her womanly tasks and her loyalty to her husband. Were children to come they came as a gift from Tezcatlipoca, the Lord of the Here and Now. The earliest news of pregnancy brought celebration among the kin, congratulation and cosseting and intense supervision. The young woman, 'our most precious feather, precious jade', was the custodian of an object of great worth. Her pregnancy was a local happening, generating a plethora of family feasts with attendant speeches, or rather speeches accompanied with some eating, the first being at least as important as the second in Mexica eyes. The birth was an all-female, high-drama affair, with a bevy of devoted and skilled attendants, and a successful birth brought unaffected delight, with the round of celebrations it generated going on for ten or even twenty days.

3

For all her local honours, the young mother would and could have no public role. The god-images of female deities who died on their festival day were women; the priestly god-images who directed the festival were always male. When 'priestesses' danced and sang in public ritual their song and their dance were led by male adepts. Women had no right to speak on high public occasions, and this in a polity in which the highest office was that of tlatoani, 'He Who Speaks'. (Hence the perturbation at the physical prominence and verbal dominance of Doña Marina, Cortés's native interpreter, during Spanish negotiations with native lords.) Nor was this a narrowly defined restriction, but rather one which appears to have put a general curb on women's tongues in public places, save on licensed occasions. Only men could become public musicians or poet-singers.[9] Contrast the destinies attaching to the day One Flower. The man named on that day would be 'happy, quite able, and much given to song and joy: a jester, an entertainer': that is, a lively verbal performer. The women born on One Flower would be 'great embroiderers', mutely plying their needles.[10] Women were handed about to cement alliances, like the Tlax-calan noblewomen presented to Cortés and his men, and while the primary wife enjoyed security and prestige, men took concubines and secondary wives as will and wealth allowed. (When nobles made offerings of their 'own' children for sacrifice, the children they handed over to the priests were probably the issue of these most vulnerable dependants.) 'Adultery' meant sexual relations with a married woman, fornication outside marriage being no offence for the male provided his partner were unmarried and not otherwise formally restricted, as for example by temple vows.[11] Other men's concubines were apparently fair game. Mexica prostitutes sauntered through the marketplace, and the girls in the state brothels (almost certainly tribute girls from the provinces, not local Mexica) were doled out to young warriors as part of their system of rewards. In such a system women could seem no more than feeders and breeders of warriors, and their casual toys.

It is true that on the standard tests of sexual equity the Mexica conspicuously fail. But 'standard tests' are notoriously blunt instruments. There are sufficient indicators that Mexica women could achieve fair indepen-

dence and substantial mobility in Mexica society, despite their exclusion
from the spectacular careers open to males, and that some women –
admittedly few – achieved positions of public prominence. Significantly,
no special note seems to have been taken of the onset of menstruation,
nor was there any extravagant fear or disgust of menstrual blood: that is,
no shame appears to have been attached to the simple condition of being
female.[12] If decorum was urged upon the young unmarried girl, it was
decorum of a sturdy kind. She was free to walk alone through the streets,
and in no shamefast way. She was urged to adopt a tranquil, pleasant
demeanour, calmly ignoring any improprieties addressed to her: a style
more withdrawn than the gentle affability recommended to the young
male, but one wearing its own dignity as its protection.[13] Younger girls
were permitted a more vivid public persona, a 'good' little girl of noble
rank being characterized as 'self-respecting, energetic, deliberate, reflec-
tive, enterprising': not always the qualities applauded in a girl-child.[14]

Rather a lot has been made of the implications of a particular ritualized
'game' played over one day in the month of Tititl. On that day men –
most gleefully lads – stuffed nets with shredded paper and reedflowers.
Then, the bags tucked under their cloaks, they stalked their victims
through the streets. Women were the favoured targets, the males surrounding them, and then, with a shout of 'Have a bag, lady', whacking
them with the bags. Some women – older, more cantankerous matrons,
perhaps – thought to arm themselves with thorny branches or staves when
they went into the streets on this day of licence, and energetically
thwacked back, putting their would-be assailants to flight. Others, less
resolute, stood, we are told, and wept. Was this performance a licensed
display of the deep-seated hostility felt by men towards women in a
warrior society; a naked expression of male determination to keep women
in their place and off the streets, as it has been claimed to be?[15] That
would seem altogether too strenuous a reading. The weepers are identified as young girls, 'maidens . . . yet with the long hair-dress.' While girls
were obliged to make an offering of food or flowers at the local temple in
the fresh of the morning, no necessity forced them on to the streets later
in the day. In that city latticed by canals, the canoes of the watermen
penetrated close to all the households, and Mexica women were largely
free from the daily drudgery of water-hauling. If girls were on the streets
on that particular day, I assume they chose to be there. It is possible that

the flailing bags were teaching an early and hard lesson in the necessity for maidenly modesty, which some of the more forceful older women had refused to learn or contrived to forget. It is certainly expressive of some tension in male–female relations. But I think that the tension was much more probably erotic, an expression of adolescent sexuality in a clumsy kind of courtship, with the number of her 'attackers' a public measure of a girl's attractions.[16]

Other glimpses of girl–boy interaction do not suggest Mexica girls were typically reduced to quivering passivity by male attention. When young girls carried the seed maize to the temple of the goddess of culti-vated foods, they went under the close and interested escort of lads of the equivalent age group of about sixteen, as yet unblooded and so still wearing the long nape lock which advertised their humiliating ignorance of the battlefield. The boys were, officially, forbidden to speak to the girls, but 'joking' being a standard mode of flirtation, they seem to have been ready to risk it. The response was a flood of stinging insult focussing on that shameful uncut lock and its implications. The boys could retaliate with vengeful insults directed at the girls' infuriating physical poise, their smug beauty (summing up with 'just be an old maid, then!') but the advantage lay decidedly with the women:

Although the words of us men were like this, they were verily only vain, they were only weak words. For . . . thus the women could torment young men into war . . . thus the women could prod them into battle. . . . Indeed we men said: 'Bloody, painful are the words of the women.'[17]

Physical violence was not reserved to men. Uninhibited wrangling be-tween marketwomen was a constant irritant in the exacerbated relations between Tlatelolcans and Tenochans before the war of 1473. While the male child named on the evil sign of One Eagle would be aggressive in speech, interrupting, grumbling, scoffing, belittling, a woman born under that same baleful influence, while also 'big-mouthed, of biting words', was represented as a reckless and ruthless brawler: if angered by another woman who had done no more than look at her sideways she 'scratched, clawed, tore, and hacked her face . . . she tore out, plucked, pulled and jerked out her hair . . . she struck and broke her teeth . . . she rent her clothes into pieces.'[18] Possibly the exuberant language indicates the re-markableness of such conduct, as I doubt that uninhibited physical assault between women was commonplace, but the violence so vividly evoked had presumably been seen. But it was in the violence of speech that women seem to have excelled. Excluded though they were from formal public discourse, they were uninhibited, fluent and loud in public comment: no small power in a warrior society where the most valued currency was public admiration.[19] In the last desperate days of the siege of Tenochtitlan some high-ranking Tenochan warriors were said to have taken refuge in Tlatelolco, cutting their hair to obliterate the signs of warrior rank. The Tlatelolcan women clustered around them to taunt: 'Have you no shame? No woman will ever paint her face for you again!' while the Tenochan women wailed in humiliation.[20] While this says something about women in a warrior society, it does not suggest they were its harassed victims.

4

Marriage brought social maturity and the full recognition of adulthood. Save for the few women vowed to permanent temple service, and perhaps some priests, everyone married, usually at about twenty for the male, when ideally he had already taken one or two captives and was ready to graduate from the warrior school, with the girl perhaps a year or two younger. (It sometimes happened that a couple would live together without ceremony until a child was born, but marriage in Tenochtitlan was typically more formal.)[21] The selection of the partner, like most decisions to do with offspring, was made by both the mother and the father. (The joint nature of the parental role is emphasized by the persistent celebration of the male tlatoani, the highest lord in the all-male political sphere, as 'father and mother' of his people.)[22] But these were typically very local alliances, and the young people had many ways of making their preferences clear to the negotiators, with much courting going on at the evening dance rehearsals at the House of Song.[23]

As with most things to do with the household, a much more expansive territory than our 'domestic zone', marriage was largely a women's affair. Old women of the neighbourhood acted as go-betweens. The young man's representatives, laden with gifts, then made several expeditions of solicitation to the girl's home, where her aunts and uncles joined with her parents in the potential bride's ritual denigration, lamenting her laziness, her lack of grace and beauty, her shameful indiscipline, her hopeless stupidity ('a lump of dough with eyes') as she sat demurely silent, glowing in garments of her own best weaving. Finally, after all the obligatory exchanges, the girl's parents conceded the prize. Then the older kins-women of her husband-to-be descended to carry her off in a noisy pseudo-abduction, with her own kin pressed around her, to be applauded through the streets in a rollicking procession to the house of her hus-band's people: at once a celebration of individual, family, and neigh-bourhood.

There was no rhetoric of sexual subordination in the marriage ritual: no swaddlings and leadings and handing from male to male; no affectation of the mental, moral, or physical ineptitude of the bride. What was em-phasized was the transference of care of the young man from mother to bride. The young pair sat together on a mat, a corner of the man's cloak was knotted to a corner of the girl's shift, the girl was given garments and fed four mouthfuls of tamales by her new mother-in-law, as she in turn fed her new husband, and then the celebrations of the kin could begin. The couple were sequestered over four days, during which time they were expected to refrain from sexual intercourse. Whatever the expressed rea-sons for this preliminary abstinence, it allowed a time of familiarization between the young pair: a gentle introduction for the virgin girl, and possibly also welcome to the young man, who as a new graduate from the warrior school had probably had only limited experience with the 'daugh-ters of joy', and for whom the new relationship was very much more significant.[24]

While marriage was a social, not a sacred bond, for both the man and the woman it opened a wide new territory. For the commoner woman attendance at the market became an obligation. Even a wife with no impulse or need to supplement income by peddling tortillas or fruit or pots in the market had to barter for chilli, salt, maize and other household necessities, traditionally being presented with five cotton capes by her new husband as her starting capital, and so she was immediately involved in face-to-face and independent negotiations with strangers in the city's liveliest centre.[25]

The market, with its hordes of buyers and sellers and casual lookers, was also an invitation to profit. Maize-and-bean tamales could be produced from a woman's own garden and maize-bin in a small extension of her own domestic cooking. Other richer market foods (frog with green chillis, birds with toasted maize, duck stewed in a pot, gophers with sauce) imply specialist suppliers, indicating either regular market purchasing or co-operation with a male kinsman.[26] Women were also specialist traders, although some of those apparently independent woman market traders were probably the commercial end of a family chain of production, as when the salt-seller sold the product of collective kin effort, or the fisherman's wife undertook the sale of the catch. Nonetheless, the crucial economic decision of price often lay in female hands.[27]

The Mexica passion for formal feasting invited co-operative ventures between women. It is unclear whether the women called in to cater for private feasts were distinct from the market food-sellers. They were certainly 'professionals', taking over households for whole days and nights if necessary. Even in its simplest edible form maize was a great consumer of woman-hours, requiring soaking, washings, and then the hours of labour kneeling at the grinding stone as the pulpy mass was reduced to smoothness. 'Feast' food, at least away from the unusually meat-rich cuisine of the palace, seems to have depended for its prestige on the ingenuity of its maize-based confections, and these women were adept at folding, stuffing, and spicing maize dough, twisting and plaiting it, cresting it with bean 'seashells' and other elegancies, with their expertise applauded and well rewarded at the feasts.[28] Other women worked in family manufactures, with sexual differentiation still being reflected in the division of skills; in featherworker families women dyed the coarser feathers, spun rabbit fur into thread, and supplied the required fine needlework, while men were responsible for the final cutting and placement of the feathers. That close engagement in a shared enterprise must have carried with it the increased intimacy of an expanded zone of shared values and experience.

Mutual dependence was deeply marked and ritually celebrated among the long-distance merchants, the pochteca, in their powerful merchant associations. Women did not participate directly in the trading ventures. The merchant train went out among the tears of the kin, with those departing making a special plea for tenderness towards the 'beloved mother, . . . beloved great aunt, . . . beloved elder sister, . . . beloved aunt' they were leaving behind. This was more than a formal show of affection in an endogamous calpulli. As we have seen, merchant women seem to have played something close to an equal role with their men, their exclusion from trading expeditions compensated for by the readiness of the men to trade as their proxies, and more by the women's special responsibilities as guardians of the warehoused goods, and of the rate and price of the goods' release on to the home market.

5

Despite such recognitions, public prestige and power remained a masculine preserve. Women who worked outside the control of male kin were viewed with some suspicion; the embroiderers, presumably full-time professionals working for particular cults, the court, or directly for the market, were thought to run the risk of becoming 'very great whores' by Sahagún's noble informants. But disapproval did not translate into control. It is possible the embroiderers were typically skilled slave women, indebted to their masters for some of their profits, or concubines past their sexual prime, or other social unfortunates forced to survive by their needle, yet they were sufficiently organized for many to undertake the 'long fast' of eighty days before their special festival on the day Seven Flower. Their divine patron was Xochiquetzal, 'Precious Feather Flower', the goddess of song, dance, and sexual pleasure, and on that day the embroiderers gathered to celebrate their amiable deity together.[29] The free-lance Mexica prostitute strolling in the marketplace attracted voluble disapproval. She nonetheless flaunted her wares and plied her trade most publicly, and without a male 'protector': while some procurers were apparently male, it is an older woman that Sahagún's scribes picture as coaxing women into the trade and soliciting customers.[30]

Here Mexica attitudes to sexuality must be addressed. First they need to be retrieved, obscured as they have been by the intrusion of Spanish Christian anxieties built into the first dictionaries and seminal translations of the sixteenth century. In the great dictionary Fray Alonso de Molina completed in 1571 he briskly translated the Nahuatl *auiani* or *ahuiani* as 'puta', or whore.[31] This category embraced the free-lance Mexica prostitutes who operated in the marketplace, along with the 'pleasure girls', the inmates of the state-controlled brothels or 'Houses of Joy'. Unsurprisingly, Christian assumptions regarding the dangers of all fleshly (more particularly sexual) indulgence, present in early dictionary-makers and in later commentators alike, have tended to be superimposed on Mexica understandings. There can be no doubt that excessive or improper sexual activity was seen as dangerous both to the actors and to society. Women were expected to be virgins at marriage, and some few – dedicated to the gods rather than to the social world – virgins for life, while priests refrained from sexual relations for their period of service. But there seems to have been no value placed on male or female chastity as such, but rather the impulse, as in fasting and vigil, to free oneself for sacred engagement from the distractions of fleshly desires.

The derivation of 'auiani' is from *ahuiy(a):* 'to be happy, content'. A knowledgeable analyst allows the notion to contain the somewhat divergent senses of 'contentment' and 'happiness' with 'self-indulgence, loose behaviour, waste', but that is a reasonably familiar tension in the sexual field.[32] It is often claimed that too great indulgence in sexual congress was 'punished' by Xochiquetzal, the patroness of erotic love, on the grounds that she is said to have afflicted with boils and pustules those who failed to observe her protocols. Xipe Totec had the same unhappy knack: he marred men with 'blisters, festering, pimples' and other unlovely disorders. All this slides with dangerous ease into a Christian account of things, but to translate it into the language of Christian ethics or theology is to deform Mexica understandings, which, I have argued, come closer to the notion of the dangers of breaching proper boundaries by improper, ignorant, or excessive human action (remember those swooning turkey chicks). The 'cure' for the young man afflicted by Xipe Totec was to wear a flayed skin throughout Xipe Totec's festival: 'Whoever of us men this befell – this sickness – it was said, vowed, that he would wear the skin of Totec'.[33] This was not an offence being purged but a relationship being re-established. 'Sin' was understood not as moral dereliction but as a physical or metaphysical impurity arising from the transgression of a prohibition. Violating the rules governing sexual intercourse would bring the 'castigation' of buboes, the affliction of an 'excess of Xochiquetzal'. Proper observances effected a realignment, so that the sacred was again properly bounded.

There was nothing negative in the glimpses we have of the pleasure girls on ritual occasions. 'Respectable' Mexica girls in ritual performance, wives in waiting, were typically 'masked' by their ritual regalia, with legs and arms plastered with feathers and faces formally painted, and as bearers of the seed maize were presented as custodians of continuity. The pleasure girls from the Houses of Joy were by contrast symbols of sexuality and eroticism, dancing with the young warriors, hair unbound and faces bare to men's glances: emblematic of sexual delight rather than of the business of what we call 'reproduction'. We know almost nothing of their conditions of life, save that they were under the close jurisdiction of 'matrons' responsible for their public decorum and for negotiating their private assignations, and that they were not quite cut off from ordinary Mexica female society, skilled curing women from the pleasure houses being included in the professional association of midwives and curers.[34] That there should have been curers in the Houses of Joy is not surprising, given the need to deal with venereal infections and to control fertility: if these were indeed tribute women from far places their local skills and techniques would be of high interest to the metropolitan curers. Mexica pleasure girls were also well protected. If on campaigns Mexica soldiers behaved as conquering soldiers usually do, taking women as they chose, within the city they had no such liberty; access to particular girls depended first on warrior status, and then on the lavishness of the gift bestowed on the matron of the house. (Compare this to the situation with the Yucatec Maya, where an admittedly hostile commentator claimed captured girls in the warrior houses were routinely 'harassed to death'.)[35]

More revealingly of Mexica attitudes, sexual activity attracted clusters of words to do with joy. The vagina was the 'place of joy', the tribute girls 'daughters of joy', and the structures which housed them the 'houses of joy'. The pleasure, like most pleasures in the Mexica world, was to be indulged in advisedly, and without loss of control. The most coherent and comprehensive single statement on these matters appears in the formal exhortation of a father to his son. The father urged enthusiasm be tempered by a proper decorum: 'thou art not to devour, to gulp down the carnal life like a dog.' Nor should sexual activity be indulged in too early. The young man ought to wait until he is 'ripe' (note the persistence of the vegetable metaphor) so that like the mature maguey cactus he will produce bountiful 'honey'. That early self-discipline will be rewarded. He will be effective in marriage; his children 'rugged, agile . . . polished, beautiful, clean', and he 'rugged, strong, swift in his carnal life', over many years. Should he waste his honey too young, he will not only display all the shamefully visible signs of sexual over-indulgence (stunted growth, drooling, pallor, premature ageing) but like the maguey tapped too soon he will simply cease 'to give forth liquid'. This will have doleful consequences, for women, like men, have sexual appetites. His wife will come to despise this ineffectual creature, 'for verily thou starvest her. . . . She longeth for the carnal relations which thou owest.' Her contempt, and her hunger, will drive her to betray him.[36]

The conviction of women's sexual enthusiasm and sexual gratification as the core of marriage is unmistakable. A ruler addressing his (virgin) daughter explains that in face of all the hardships of the world, and so that 'we may not go weeping forever, may not die of sorrow', mankind has been given certain gifts to sweeten life: laughter, sleep, food, vigour, and the sexual act, 'in order that there be peopling'. The young maiden so addressed by her father is still 'fresh' – 'there is still jade in your heart, turquoise. It is still fresh, it has not been spoiled . . . nothing has twisted it.' She is urged to cleave to her husband, as she is to keep her heart 'a precious green stone', as it is 'still virgin, pure, undefiled'.[37] This purity had nothing to do with sexual innocence. It referred to the unshadowed temperament rendered transparent by her inner submission to social and sacred obligations, and it was equally open to the young girl, and to a mature warrior in his prime.

The power of lust and its more playful manifestations were celebrated. The delicate (and not so delicate) sexiness of the 'Song of the Chalcan Women' so enchanted the Mexica ruler Axayacatzin that he requested it to be performed for all his nobles, so that 'thanks to it', as one of its proud lords recorded, 'the city of Amecameca which today is just a small town won renown'.[38] The force and legitimacy of female lust is demonstrated by the story of what happened when the god Tezcatlipoca stalked through the marketplace in Tollan in the guise of a naked Huaxtec green-chilli seller. (It will be recalled that the Huaxtecs had the reputation for being notably lusty.) The daughter of the ruler chanced to see him, and was so overcome by desire as to sicken nearly to death. Her understanding father had the lowly chilli seller brought in, cleaned up and taken to the princess, who rapidly regained her spirits. They later married. (That the matter finally turned out badly was not laid at the door of the dazzled princess, but ascribed to Tezcatlipoca's chronic, casual malice.)[39] The nobleman's exhortation to his son was rounded by the account of two snowy-haired old women haled before the Texcocan ruler Nezahualcoyotzin for their sexual adventuring with some young priests. Questioned as to how they could still be interested in the carnal act ('O our grandmothers, listen! . . . do ye perhaps still require the carnal act? are ye not satiated, being old as ye are?'), the disreputable pair replied: 'ye men, ye are sluggish, ye are depleted . . . it is all gone. There is no more. . . . But we who are women, we are not the sluggish ones. In us there is a cave, a gorge, whose only function is to await that which is given, whose only function is to receive'.[40]

A cautionary tale indeed. The sexual act here is represented not as a matter of women being penetrated, but of males being depleted, their 'honey' engulfed by that insatiably voracious 'cave', and, as we will see, the woman-as-cavern had particular connotations for the Mexica. It is difficult to know how far the male-depletion model had currency – perhaps most widely among anxious elders – although the insistence of the maguey metaphor does suggest the inevitable end of the honeyflow. Whores might trick a young man into drinking too much *macacoatl*, the steepings of a particular snake, with the result he would have sexual congress with four, five, or ten women, not once but several times with each. Then, unsurprisingly, he would die, 'well dried up', no more than 'little old eyes, only little locks of hair', 'nasal mucus hanging, trembling of neck; his flesh only hanging in wrinkles.'[41] But for all the minatory tales it is clear that the sexual act was assumed to bring joy to both partners. In the shadowed world of the Mexica sexual delight made a small sunlit space.

6

The distinction between the sexes so sharply marked in human role and function were allowed to blur in the sacred sphere. Analysts with a theological bent have found an irritating lack of structure in the Mexica sacred pantheon; once past the story of the lethal combat between the Sun Huitzilopochtli and his murderous siblings the Moon and Stars, relationships are equivocal, and images initially sharp and clear melt on longer looking into a shimmering mist of the sacred. More surprisingly, given the hard-edged gender roles in the mundane world, even sexual identity refuses to stay stable. Xochiquetzal was the deity of sexual love, artistry and delight, and threads 'her' way through multiple sexual relationships with deities.[42] But she was also Macuilxochitl, who is commonly taken to be male. Earth and water-related deities were androgynous, or, more precisely, could be invoked in either gender identity, as with 'Tlacatecutli', which we translate as 'Earth Lord', but who was apostrophized sometimes as male, sometimes as female. The Earth Monster, typically invoked as female, could also be regarded as male. Others were represented as gender-twinned: Xochiquetzal and Xochipilli, Chalchihuitlicue and Tlaloc. The maize, whose life parabola was so closely identified with humans, changed sex in mid-course, with Xilonen, goddess of the young maize when the cob was slender, the kernels milky and the corn-tassel long and silky, becoming Centeotl, Young Lord Maize Cob, as the cob swelled and hardened. Nonetheless Centeotl, apparently so unequivocally male, was on occasions addressed as female. The aggressively virile Huaxtec attendants of Toci in the festival of Ochpaniztli carried not only their erect penises before them, but also cotton blossoms and spindles with unspun cotton: female identifiers par excellence.[43] Female deities could be accoutred as warriors, with shields, eagle feathers and heron-feather sprays juxtaposed with their insignia as women.[44] This doubleness obscured not only sexual roles, but sexual difference. In a world so comprehended, our notions of 'opposition', or even of 'duality' and 'complementarity', are unhelpfully crude, as apparently firm divisions waver and melt one into another. Relationships were revealed not through differentiation, but through permutations and transformations, and spoke more clearly of connection than opposition. Only by way of interrelationships did each part yield its meaning, which was always relative, always locational.[45] The implication is that while the roles of man and wife were sharply differentiated from the moment of that first brisk birth classification, they were profoundly mutually bound through their shared humanity.

Attitudes to androgyny in the Mexica world are difficult to penetrate. In that initial classification by sex there appeared to have been no recognition of the anatomically ambiguous individual, and much ritual transvestism, whether solemn or comic, looks more like an obeisance to the sharpness of the gender distinction than acceptance of its blurring. Sexual preference for members of one's own sex was recognized, and deplored, female homosexuality being abused as even more base than prostitution, although its incidence is not clear. There are a few references to male homosexuality in the texts, but those few are suspect, given the Spanish obsession with 'the unnameable offence'. Sodomites were also vulnerable to enslavement, being outside the natural law, so the accusation could bring significant rewards. There are teasing hints of Mesoamerican fore-runners to the berdache: the biological male who adopted the social role, occupation and dress of the female; who usually (although not always) sought sexual partners among men; who often enjoyed high prestige for his access to the skills of both sexes, and who played his accepted part in many native North American warrior societies.[46] There may or may not have been Mexica berdaches, but certainly in the Mexica conceptualiza-tion of sacred forces, and also of particular high offices, like that of the Cihuacoatl, 'Woman Snake', chief adviser to the ruler, there was a read-iness to mix the identifying garments and accoutrements of the two sexes to create a figure that presumably drew significant power from the capaci-ty to participate in both.

Where sexual differentiation between the sacred ones was present and stable, the female deities were represented as sisters as often as wives; what mattered most was the social division of roles, rather than the sexual relationship.[47] The intimate female associates of the war god Huitzilo-pochtli were his mother Coatlicue and his sister and adversary Coyol-xauhqui. Their great battle was between siblings, not sexual antagonists. Indeed the notion of the 'war between the sexes' and the identification of the sexual act with violence or combat so pervasive in our world appears alien to Mexica thinking.[48]

Reciprocal relationships extended to matters of space. A shadowy zone called the 'women's quarters' in domestic dwellings was presumably their exclusive preserve, but as men had the local warrior house and the street for social intercourse, women probably enjoyed control over most of the home territory, with the courtyard the intermediate and mediating zone between the public and (largely) male, and the female and private, al-though our public–private distinction has slight utility in so remorselessly interventionist a society. Women had care of the household shrines, and the presentation of the little broom at birth signalled their sacred respon-sibility to keep the home zone well swept, and so free from potentially dangerous contamination. Given the complex integration of her social and sacred roles, there seems no doubt that within her own territory a respectable and energetic woman was formidable. We are tempted to dismiss the description of the 'good middle-aged woman' as one who has sons and daughters, and is 'a skilled weaver, a weaver of designs, an artisan, a good cook, a preparer of good food', as a tedious catalogue of minor domestic virtues, but in view of the high Mexica respect for weaving as a sacred art, and indeed, for the skilful treatment of foodstuffs, it signifies rather more grandly. George Grinnell, writing of the Cheyenne Indians as he knew them in the first decades of this century, tells of the strict 'warrior' organization of the women's quilling societies, women formally declaring their quilling feats just as men publicly counted coups. In earlier days all decorative art had been in the hands of certain women's societies, the 'selected ones', who 'had strict rules in their designs and . . . kept secret the meaning and arrangement of the colours, as well as the relation of the designs to each other'. Throughout Grinnell's account one is struck by the recognition of the complementarity – indeed, the parallelism – between men's and women's activities, with a particularly tight nexus between feats of war, and feats of female 'art': for example, errors in quilling had to be corrected by a warrior, who would recite his coups while cutting the misplaced threads.[49]

It is detailed information like this which forces recognition of the painful gaps in our knowledge of the Mexica. We do know that a woman skilled in market trading not only achieved economic independence, but could also develop her own network of feasting partners and dependants as a corollary of her accumulation and distribution of goods. While feasts were typically male affairs, the 'Book of Days' tells us that a woman fortunate in her daysign and made prosperous by her dealings in the marketplace could 'invite others to feast' and 'be visited by others': in that feasting economy at once an economic, political, and social interchange. She was also free to dispose of her wealth as she chose: 'much would she gather, collect and save, and justly distribute among her children'.[50] Her autonomy expanded with rank: a 'good' noblewoman had 'valour, bravery, courage'; more important, she was 'a good administrator, creating order, establishing rules. She is obeyed'. A 'bad' noblewoman displayed an autonomy of a different sort, going about 'besotted, eating mushrooms', which again suggests the absence of effective techniques of male control over female recalcitrants.[51]

There was one notable and highly visible exception to the exclusion of women from official public roles: the high status and authority of female curers and physicians, most especially the midwives. The experienced woman physician treated men as well as women, over a wide range of ailments. Like her male counterpart she was a knowledgeable herbalist and bonesetter, expert in massage, and with her seer's skills as much counsellor as doctor. But it was her role in childbirth which established the particularity and the power of her female expertise.[52] If sexuality was a pleasure and marriage a contract, the bearing of children was at once a social duty and a sacred act, and the women of the midwives and curers guild were deeply imbued with that sacredness. In the festival of the goddess Toci, 'Our Grandmother', aspect of the Earth Mother and Mother of the Gods, her curers and midwives wore the tobacco pouches of priestly status, and closely attended their divine mistress throughout her festival.

7

The language and measure of success and honour remained male; the woman who 'distributed sustenance' would be 'reckoned as a man', and acknowledged 'courageous, strong, and hardy'. She would perhaps have the masculine skill par excellence 'among all her gifts': she would 'speak well; be eloquent, give good counsel, and arrange her conversation and manner of speaking well'.[53] But her liberality, her courage, above all her eloquence could be displayed only 'in her home'. We might therefore still be tempted to claim not only division but subordination, with the male moving freely in the public world, and even the most dynamic female miserably constricted, aspiring at best to a pallid approximation of male status. Yet 'agency' is more in the mind of the actor than in the eye of the beholder, and, as we have seen, the Mexica male was unpersuaded of his ability to much affect the world. The praise of women in terms of male attributes – courage, generosity, resolution, self-control, the capacity to take rebuke calmly – and their contrast with the fretful, fearful, fluctuating behaviour characterized as 'womanish', could be read as denigratory.[54] However, while the words cannot be denied, I doubt their implications were pejorative. Males as potential warriors had to be educated to an

ideal of self-mastery, stamina and resolution; women, fulfilling their obligations in less taxing situations, were not. Those virtues, painfully inculcated and publicly tested as essential for the male, admired but not required in the female, remained ideals for human, as opposed to sexually
specific, conduct. It was not socially essential that a woman be valorous,
steady, just, and resourceful, but it was morally desirable. Personal weak-
nesses – vanity, self-indulgence, uncontrolled appetite – were despised in
both sexes. They could be tolerated in the female, given her social duty.
They were socially disastrous in the male.

Despite the clarity of the distinction between gender roles, and the
distinctive markings of each sex, women as wives were understood to be
and could function as independent social beings, with their social worth
recognized. Despite their partial exclusion from what we would call 'public affairs', they enjoyed within that rather narrow zone of Mexica life
open to personal decision a status fully comparable with their male counterparts. Contrast this with the chillingly systematic opposition of wife-
versus-fellow-warrior loyalty of some North American warrior societies.
Robert Lowie has reported that in the sixties and seventies of the last
century most Crow men were members of one of two rival clubs, where
competition revolved around striking the first coup of the war season, and
on the mutual abduction of wives who it could be plausibly claimed had
had some sort of sexual encounter in the past with the abductor. These
raidings and counter-raidings continued over a brief pre-war season, the
wives being paraded and used in the same way as captured 'outsider'
women. Their husbands, however fond, could not reclaim them without
great shame: a man caught in the act of retrieving his wife would be tied
up and smeared with dog excrement. Lowie reports that the correct
warrior demeanour was one of studied indifference, however valued the
wife; the display of any emotion, whether of anger or grief or chagrin, was
met with 'pitiless mirth'. (One husband neatly terminated his ordeal by
shooting his wife as she was being paraded.) Such a practice in so small a
community would seem gratuitously disruptive of social harmony, as well
as of a few other things. Another practice was the public naming of one's
married mistresses before one's comrades when well embarked on the
war path and vowed to truthfulness, so that a husband could have his first
knowledge of a wife's infidelity in these interesting circumstances. Such

exercises would seem to point to the strengthening of warrior-to-warrior ties by way of a systematic misogyny.[55]

There is no trace of such strategies among the Mexica. The midwife's address to the girl-child, as with her address to the male, was neither prescriptive nor descriptive of actuality, but rather diagnostic of the role of male and female in the design of human survival. To be a warrior and so discharge his social duty the male must be taught, his character shaped, and his conduct rewarded. Therefore the agency of males (and the structures necessary for their encouragement by social recognition) was emphasized as against the more passive 'being' of women. Social inequality derived from metaphysical complementarity.

The 'creation of humankind' story best known among the Mexica gives little indication of male priority. Four worlds and their peoples had been destroyed before the making of this our 'Fifth World', created through Tezcatlipoca's and Quetzalcoatl's manhandling of the androgynous Earth Monster. Then Quetzalcoatl ventured into the domains of the Lord of the Dead to gather up the human bones of an earlier creation. Initially the bones were kept separate, 'the bones of the man . . . together on one side, and the bones of the woman . . . together on the other side'. But in his flight from the Death Lord's anger Quetzalcoatl stumbled and dropped the bones, which shattered. He snatched up the fragments (so presumably mingling them) and took them to Cihuacoatl, 'Woman Snake', representing Earth Lady and all her vegetable abundance, who ground them into a fine meal on her maize-grinding stone. Then it was the turn of the male gods, led by Quetzalcoatl, to make their contribution, drawing blood from their penises to moisten the ground bones. A man and a woman took form from the dough.[56]

Cihuacoatl kneels by the hearth at her grinding stone, the male gods offer their warrior blood. And so humankind – women and men together – gains its life.

7

Mothers

There is . . . some persuasive rationale for dwelling on ontogeny, for its early phases take up a goodly proportion of human life for reasons intrinsic to the nature of human evolution; and yet, that fatefulness throughout history has been ignored, repressed, and mythologized for the same reasons. As we wish to study, then, the ontogenetic origins of man's visions of himself, we must become aware of the possibility that over-all images of childhood, and age-old repressions concerning it, are and always have been important aspects of changing world views . . . the mere search for beginnings always harbours some vision of an innocence lost or a hidden curse to be dealt with – and both with some sense of inescapable predestination.

Erik Erikson, *Toys and Reasons*[1]

They give them milk for four years, and they love their infants so much and care for them with such affection and solicitude that they avoid having contact with their husbands so that they can continue giving milk to the child for all of that time, and so that no ill may come to it through their pregnancy. If they are widowed and the child is not yet weaned, they will not remarry until the child has no need of milk, so they will not get pregnant. If a mother does so, it is thought to be a treacherous action.

Fr. Bartolomé de las Casas, *Apologética historia sumaria*[2]

I

The magnificent squatting image of the Mexica goddess of childbirth, naked, solitary in the ecstasy of total effort, does not represent a woman in 'labour'. Here we look upon the face of battle. If men challenged the death anguish on the jaguar meadow of war, women confronted it on the bloody field of childbirth.

> Is this not a fatal time for us poor women?
> This is our kind of war
> There our Mother
> Cihuacoatl Quilaztli
> Takes her tribute of death.[3]

'Our kind of war'. To consider the process of parturition as mortal combat rather than as labour is to colour the experience most profoundly. If the woman 'labours' in childbed, the metaphor assumes she remains responsible and in control of a familiar, if intensified, activity, to which she must apply discipline, energy and effort. That account minimizes what is in experience the extraordinary sensation of the body being invaded and shaken by a quite unfamiliar force, as normally quiescent muscles clench and relax. During the process of birth women were and were seen to be abducted from their usual gentle domesticities, and (given the Mexica sense of battle as being overwhelmed by the force of Huitzilopochtli) to be 'possessed' by some great presence beyond the self.[4]

For those who emerged victorious from the struggle, the warrior metaphor was still insisted upon, the midwife greeting the newly delivered child, the little 'captive', with war-cries, while praising the panting mother for her warrior's courage. But the woman would receive none of the material rewards of the successful warrior, and there was a bitter undertaste to the midwife's praises. As the physical bond between mother and child was severed, the new mother heard the midwife address the child:

My precious son, my youngest one . . . heed, harken: thy home is not here, for thou art an eagle, thou art an ocelotl . . . here is only the place of thy nest, thy cradle, thy cradle blanket, the resting place of thy head. . . . Thou belongest out there: out there thou hast been consecrated. Thou hast been sent into warfare. War is thy desert, thy task. Thou shalt give drink, nourishment, food to the sun, the lord of the earth. Thy real home, thy lot is the home of the sun there in the heavens. Perhaps thou wilt receive the gift, perhaps thou wilt merit death by the obsidian knife.[5]

'Death by the obsidian knife': the child, if fortunate, would die a warrior's death in combat, or on the killing stone in an enemy city. The umbilical cord was entrusted to a warrior and laid in the midst of the field of battle, pledging the infant life to its violent end.[6]

Few societies think to challenge the bond between mother and neonate, the image of the mother with the babe at her breast providing the eternal rebuke to the pretensions of overweening men and of the state.[7] There was no such inhibition among the Mexica. The mother, physically and emotionally vulnerable after the shaking experience of childbirth, was unequivocally informed that the small downy creature she had borne was not hers; that he was destined to die young, violently, and in a distant place. Each time she relinquished the baby to its cradle she was meant to practise a small act of renunciation, saying as she laid the child down,

'Thou who are the Mother of us all, thou who art its mother, receive the baby.' That systematic alienation did not temper affection. In the joyful round of household ceremonies which followed the birth of a child there was one of particular tenderness, when the baby was presented naked to its kinfolk, and the men as well as the women took turns to hold it, petting and stroking it all over 'to show they loved the child'; a practical exercise in bonding worth emulating.[8] Their pleasure must have been touched with poignancy when the child was male, as the little body was stroked and cuddled, and the rhetoric of warriordom and the celebration of warrior death rolled on.

The high social value of the wife was not forgotten during parturition: Toci, 'Our Grandmother', mistress of birth, was also patron of female social and domestic activities. Women were assisted through the birth-struggle, a noblewoman having as many as three midwives, with a cluster of attendant women, working over her, forcefully massaging and encouraging. Commoner women were almost as well served. Vigorous measures were taken to bring on a tardy birth, including the desperate remedy of the drinking of a decoction of opossum tail, which was understood to eject the child forcefully from the body. In a crisis the life of the mother was preferred over that of the child. Should she weaken to the point of danger, she was yielded into the hands of Toci, being shut away with her chief midwife in the sweathouse, Toci's curing shrine, where the sacred presence was most profoundly concentrated. Should natural delivery be despaired of the midwife would insert an obsidian knife into the vaginal passage and dismember the child, drawing it forth in pieces.[9] But if all exertions failed and the mother died, the full and sinister dimensions of the warrior metaphor were allowed to unfold.

In his classic essay 'The Collective Representation of Death', Robert Hertz points to those sinister, violent and untimely deaths which societies find it most difficult to tame and contain, nominating deaths by accident or homicide; drowning, lightning, or suicide; the deaths of women in childbirth. He suggests the bodies of those so unnaturally dead 'inspire the most intense horror and are got rid of precipitately', and that despite special rites 'their unquiet and spiteful souls' are understood 'to roam the earth forever', because, as he thinks, a sacredness invests them which no ritual can efface.[10] If Hertz is right, the Mexica distributed that universal unease most unevenly. Theirs was a society where 'violent and untimely deaths' were something of a commonplace, with the bodies disposed of most deliberately, and where suicide was little regarded. But the bodies of women dead in childbirth roused intense anxiety, and their malign spirits haunted the darkest zones of the Mexica imagination.

To understand the fear it is necessary to understand something of the process of birth in Mexica terms. In the course of her battle the woman was understood to have been possessed by the Earth Mother. That great presence could be variously invoked. 'Quilaztli', 'She Who Makes Legumes Grow', was the name most often used by midwives as they worked for an easy birth: the Earth in her benign and fertile capacity.[11] But the Earth Mother had other names and other aspects which became manifest were the process to falter:

If you know me as Quilaztli, I have four other names by which I am known. One is Coaciuatl [Cihuacoatl], which means Serpent Woman; another, Quauhciuatl, which means Eagle Woman; another, Yoaciuatl, which means Warrior Woman; the fourth, Tzitziminciuatl, which means Devil Woman. And these names reveal my qualities, and the power I possess, and the harm I can do you.[12]

Cihuacoatl, 'Serpent Woman' or 'Woman Serpent', was an aspect of Earth Mother, in H. B. Nicholson's fine phrase 'the great womb and tomb of all life'.[13] Something of her primary nature can be glimpsed in the world-creation story most often assumed in Nahuatl texts. The original and essential act which created the earth and made it fruitful was not (at least overtly) sexual. The two sky gods, Quetzalcoatl and Tezcatlipoca, are said to have seized the limbs of the great Earth Monster as she swam in the primeval waters, and wrenched her body in half, one part forming the sky and the other the earth. Other gods descended to create trees, flowers and herbs from her hair; grass and flowers from her skin; from her eyes, wells and springs; from her shoulders, mountains.[14] But the monster wailed for food, refusing to bring forth until she was saturated and satiated with blood and human hearts. Only then did she yield the fruits which provided men's sustenance. This was the great Earth Lady (her names are multiple) who stood behind the range of other sacred females. We have an oblique glimpse of her nature in the detail of the opossum-tail remedy for a slow birth: the American opossum is at once a night hunter, savage fighter, blood-drinker, yet a model of fecundity, its many children adorning its sleek body.

Cihuacoatl's presence, even residually, was known to injure mere humans. Even after a normal birth care was taken that all visitors to the household should rub their joints – ankles, elbows, knees – with ashes, as a prophylactic against her crippling power.[15] That power suffused the body of the woman dead in childbirth, making it an immediate source of danger. The laying away was attended by none of the usual mourning procedures. Swiftly washed, dressed in a new shift, the hair flowing loose, the corpse was removed from the house in darkness, not by the usual 'social' entrance, but by breaking a hole in the back wall. Carried by the husband, it was escorted by an entourage of midwives, howling and shouting, brandishing shields, to a crossroad – most sinister and most marginal of places – and there buried. (The Mexica usually burned their dead, burial being reserved for those taken by Tlaloc by lightning or drowning or water-related diseases, and for these unfortunate women.) The burial party risked attack by warriors desperate to seize a fragment of the magically charged flesh – a lock of hair, a finger – to carry into battle. Something of the awe the midwives inspired is suggested by the fact that those eager young warriors found it difficult to wrest their prize from a guard of ageing women, the fragments being as much tokens of courage as talismans for it. They were also sought for their man-injuring power, 'for it was said that the hair, that the finger of the *mociaquetzi* . . . paralyzed the feet of their foes'. Thieves too sought out such corpses, for should they be able to secure the left arm of a woman dead in first childbed they could manipulate it to cast their intended victims into a helpless paralysis, and do with them and their possessions as they chose.[16]

The husband kept vigil over the grave for four nights as the magic power slowly dispersed. Then he abandoned it, with no individual memorial.[17] The spirit of the dead woman was transformed even more completely than her gentle flesh: she would become, in her servitude to Toci, first an 'Eagle' or 'Warrior' woman, and then a 'Devil Woman'. Warrior and Eagle women were those female spirits privileged to escort the Sun in his daily passage.[18] The spirits of male warriors dead in combat or on the killing stone arrayed themselves in their most glittering regalia as they awaited the Sun's first pale dawning, and then, skirmishing and displaying, escorted him to his zenith. There the Women Warriors of the western skies, the 'Region of Women', rose to meet him, bearing him in his quetzal-feather litter down to the Earth to deliver him into the hands of the people of Mictlan, the land of the dead.

Despite the sharing of the formal privilege, the difference in role is clear: men led the Sun to his time of greatest glory, women to his nightly struggle with the Earth and with Death. The paths of the spirits of the male and female warriors were to diverge yet more widely. After four years of joyful service the male warrior spirits returned to earth in the glorious (and innocent) form of butterflies and hummingbirds, to dance endlessly in the sun, sipping the nectar of the flowers. Female spirits also descended, but in very different guise. They came to earth on five spec-ified days of notorious ill-fortune as 'Ilhuica Cihuapipiltin', the Celestial Princesses, or 'Cihuateteo', the Goddesses, malevolence incarnate, haunting the crossroads, seeking out those they would afflict.

These creatures did not resemble the human women whose spirits they had engrossed, nor were they the sweet murderers of men of more famil-iar and seductive fantasies. They were typically represented with hair flowing wild and breasts bared, but there was nothing of the erotic nor of nurturance about them: they were images of death, anger and aggression; skull-faced, fleshless jaws agape, clawed hands raised in imprecation.[19] Echoes and agents of the Earth Mother or the Earth Monster, they were typically represented with fanged faces or claws at elbow and knee, indi-cating her power to cripple movement. That sinister power, fatally potent in the hair and flesh of the woman dead in childbed, invested women's things: the warrior who stumbled against a cooking stone, woman's un-disputed territory, would be leaden-footed and so at risk in war.[20] The Celestial Princesses brought that power to killing pitch, but their malice was to choose to afflict rather than to kill outright. Their preferred victims were children, whom they struck down with paralysis or convulsions or sudden deformities, twisting faces and limbs, marring and mangling, but leaving them, barely, alive. We glimpse here the classic lineaments of the witch, the inverted image of social woman, implacably malevolent, inex-haustibly envious, inimical to life, who destroys rather than nurtures children.[21]

It was they who as the Tzitzime, the 'Devil Women', were the monsters destined to destroy this Fifth World, when the Sun would at last fail to rise and the earth powers would burst forth to devour the people. At the New Fire Ceremony of every fifty-two years, when the world was poised on the rim of destruction and the Fire Priest whirled his Fire Drill to mark the Sun in his rising, children were nudged and pinched to be kept awake: should they sleep they could turn into mice. Pregnant women were masked with the thick leaves of the maguey cactus and shut away in the granaries to subdue their dangerous, involuntary power: should the terrible moment come it was they, helpless agents of destruction, who would devour their husbands and children.[22]

2

This is by any measure a chilling fantasy, especially given the normally easy social relations between Mexica men and women. The strands twisted into this particular web, or rather snarl, of meaning are multiple, tangled, and most of them obscure. But some, with patience, may be teased out.

One strand derived from Mexica attempts to penetrate the hidden processes of human procreation. Mesoamericans knew that sexuality played a general role in fertility, but while sexual intercourse clearly had to do with pregnancy, it was evidently not a sufficient cause. (These are mysterious matters. The Maasai still have their young warriors lie with their pre-pubescent girls, intercourse being understood as necessary to effect women's physical maturation: a view always empirically vindicated.)[23] The Mexica knew intercourse was needed to help the baby grow and indeed to start the growth process. But intercourse did not bring the baby into being. Rather the child was placed or 'seated' in the womb by Tezcatlipoca, whose possession it remained, and who would provide its individual 'fate' and life vigour, or tonalli, at the time of its physical birth.[24] That children were simultaneously seen as part of the lineage is puzzling only if we deny the comfortable elasticity of human thinking. Semen, the 'hot fine-textured seed of man', was called the 'essence of lineage', and the midwife might choose to give a male child as his 'earthly' name the name of his grandfather, to 'enhance his lot'. Yet there seems to have been no commitment to the idea of direct physical continuity. Physical resemblances across generations were recognized and valued, but were explained, at least in rhetoric, as due to the whimsical favour of Tezcatlipoca, the Lord of the Here and Now.[25]

The growing once begun, the mystery reduced. The mingling of two fluids, one from the father and one from the mother, and each delivered through the sexual act, was seen as necessary for the child's increase, and therefore continued sexual activity over perhaps three or four months was a duty until the child was assumed to be fully formed.[26] From that point on the baby's sustenance was understood to come from what the mother ate and drank. Were intercourse continued beyond the child's forming the surplus matter produced would at best make birth long and difficult, the baby being born 'as if bathed in a white atole [maize gruel] . . . something like pine resin would form when, at an improper time, she accepted, she received seed.'[27] When the tell-tale stuff was revealed (which must have been often, if it was the waxy coating so often seen on the new-born) the parents would be shamed for their lack of control. At worst, the substance would make the baby adhere to the womb, so that it could not be born: 'it was said she died in childbed because the baby no longer tolerated the seed; it was as if it turned into matter which glued [the baby] to the sound body of the woman.'[28] After the birth the midwife washed the baby clean of these traces of parental self-indulgence.

At the naming ceremony, after the presentation of life-equipment gifts to the child, and after the midwife had welcomed it as a gift from the high gods, from 'the place of duality above the nine heavens', the child was given water to drink: 'Take it, receive it. Here is wherewith thou wilt endure, wherewith thou wilt live on earth, wherewith thou wilt grow, wherewith thou wilt develop.'[29]

The analogy running through all Mexica descriptions of human growth is with the growth of plants; threading through various commentaries, informing language choices, and moulding the man–maize analogy to a most precise isomorphism: the baby grows in the womb in the same way and by the same processes as a plant grows in the earth. Unlike the child growing secretly in the womb, the stages of plant growth are eminently observable: the swelling of the seed, the sprouting of leaves and rootlets, the flowering, the fruiting, the withering. The how of it also seems clear – to us, instructed by plant physiologists in the invisible processes underlying all these transformations. The Mexica, with only the eye and experience to go on, identified water as the crucial element in growth, as is clear both from their rhetoric and their practice.[30] Tlaloc, god of the rains, was apostrophized as 'He who caused the trees, the grasses, the maize to

blossom, to sprout, to leaf out, to bloom, to grow'.[31] In the great invocation to Tlaloc made in times of heat and drought, Chicomecoatl, 'Seven
Snake' or 'Sustenance Woman', sister to the Rain God, was represented
as the famished, desiccated maize itself: 'the sustenance lieth suffering,
the older sister of the gods lieth outstretched, the sustenance already lieth
covered with dust, already it lieth enclosed in a spider's web.'[32] Only with
rain would she live and grow again.

Earth was no mere context for all this activity. In the same prayer to
Tlaloc the plight of the Earth was described: 'Here our mother, our
father, Tlaltecutli, is already dried up . . . there is nothing with which to
suckle that which germinateth, which lieth germinating'. The fear was of
the end of all things: 'the end of the earth . . . when the seed of the earth
hath ended, when it hath become [as] an old man, as an old woman, when
it is worthless, when it will no longer provide one with drink, with food.'[33]

It is only recently that we have begun to realize the power, always
insidious, sometimes explosive, of 'metaphors': particular ways of con-
ceiving the world and humanity's place within it.[34] Mexica imaginings
were thick with human–vegetable analogies, enacted in a thousand rituals, from the constant small proprieties and cooking protocols of the
household to the great performances at the main temple precinct. The
ritual marking of the growth of children moved in lockstep with that of
plants, as with the festival of Izcalli, with the pruning and tending of the
maguey and other cultivated perennials and the equivalent tending of
children, 'so that they would grow'. More sonorously, the whole maize
cycle was ceremonially represented as episodes in human biography, humans of the appropriate age and gender representing the maize at each
particular stage of growth, and dying to mark (and perhaps to effect) its
transition to the next stage.

Sometimes thunderous, sometimes no more than a haunting, delicate
phrase, the theme is always there: mankind is not only fully dependent on
vegetable growth, but is fully implicated in its processes. The visible
model for all this was the agricultural process most accessibly observed in
the shallow-water garden plots of the chinampas fringing the city, where a
careful alchemy of sun, earth, seeds, and water yielded vegetable abundance. The flesh-and-earth identifications are clear in the early account
of the composition of the human body inscribed in the Florentine Codex.
Blood vessels are likened to reeds, moving the blood through the flesh as

water moves through the earth. The description of the heart relates it closely to the sun: it is 'round, hot . . . it makes one live'.[35] Quetzalcoatl's theft of human bones from the Lord of the Underworld, along with other indicators, suggests that bone was understood as seed.[36] And blood is described as 'our redness, our liquid, our freshness, our growth, our life blood . . . it wets the surface, it moistens it like clay, it refreshes it, it reaches the surface . . . it strengthens one'.

For the Mexica human blood, especially human blood deliberately shed, was 'most precious water'. They understood it to be a non-renewable resource, infused with extravagant fertilizing power.[37] The creation myths, confused as they might be in detail, pivot on the creative efficacy of blood voluntarily or involuntarily shed, as when the Earth Monster, wrenched into the shape of the earth by Quetzalcoatl and Tezcatlipoca, wailed in the darkness and refused to yield her fruits until she was soaked in human blood and fed with human hearts. It is she who is obsessively represented on the underside of vessels designed to receive the blood and hearts of human victims. Whatever icons they bear on their upper surfaces, underneath she is there, her insatiable maw wide open, great fangs at knee and elbow, her head bent back, in the squatting position Mexica women adopted to give birth.[38] The great figure identified as Coatlicue, or 'Serpent Skirt' (whose looming form dominates the Aztec hall in the Mexican Museum of Anthropology), and another manifestation of Earth Lady, has old and withered breasts: it is not by her milk that she feeds mankind. Her sustaining capacity is symbolized by the blood jetting from her decapitated neck, and her necklace of human hearts and hands: it is human blood and human flesh which makes her flesh fruitful. Sexual activity is not the dynamic of production, but hunger: the engulfing, insatiable mouth of the earth powers, the desperately open mouths of humankind.[39]

A key concept which ordered political relations between rulers and ruled in the human sphere, as between humankind and the divine, was tequitl, which can be roughly translated as 'debt', 'levy' or 'tribute'. The term also carries some connotation of 'vocation', being applied to whole-hearted fulfilment of one's obligations in the world. It was used most insistently, however, to describe the offerings made of one's own blood, from the small daily token gifts to death on the battlefield or the killing stone. Only in death could the individual fully discharge the involuntary

debt by returning earth-fed flesh and blood to the earth. The identification of the human womb as participant in the enigmatic capability of the
earth to 'bring forth' surrendered the fertile woman for the period of
parturition into the field of force of the ever-hungering earth powers.
Possessed by those powers, she was open to instant transformation into a
creature implacably, inhumanly, eternally malevolent towards her husband
and her children.

We will see the celebration of the tenderness of the ideal human mother,
whose breasts nurtured with unfailing generosity, with no implication of
indebtedness. What was it in Mexica recollection or imagining which
made that indulgent being capable of so terrifying a transformation?

3

No one who has watched an eager baby take the breast can doubt that
something profoundly important in world-shaping is going on. The first
frantic rapture gives way to a slow immersion in an increasingly lan-
guorous delight as the sweet tide mounts, until the infant is floating in the
bliss of repletion and the luxury of play and confident possession of a
nipple still mouthed, still softly relished. But while the period of suckling
and weaning is thick with significant experiences, which is incontroverti-
ble, those experiences are not directly recoverable.[40] Experiences we
know to be real and important in life must sometimes escape historians,
sliding quietly through the coarse mesh of the consultable record. But I
suspect we also discreetly avert our eyes from their traces. We are deeply
wary of 'psychologizing', conventionally because adequate materials are
lacking: a sufficiently respectable reason were it not that mere lack of
material rarely inhibits the most exuberant hypothesizing about other
problematics. My concern in what follows is not with the world of the
Mexica infant, which is lost to us, nor the hidden inner life of the Mexica,
unknown even to themselves, but with expressed adult attitudes and those
more oblique preoccupations which clustered around the potent image of
the mother and the suckling child, and the fatal seriousness of the transition from mother's breast to vegetable foods.

How was that transition understood, and what were its acknowledged and less-than-acknowledged consequences? At our distance these are not easy matters to discover, especially as potentially relevant material has survived only by happenstance. One possible source, the content and interpretations of Mexica dreams, has been largely lost.[41] Dreams mattered to the Mexica, not as solitary voyages into individual interiority, but rather as intimations, in a language more or less clear, from the normally hidden world of the sacred. Books of dreams were among the Mexica's most valued possessions, and dream-readers among their most honoured experts, but Spanish clerics had small tolerance for or curiosity about either, and they are mentioned only in passing.[42] Those few indicators of dream content we have connect most closely with the Mexica concern with personal and collective augury: the nightmare figure 'Night Axe', the headless torso, plundered of its heart, which roamed the night, its gashed chest slowly opening, then thudding shut (a most vivid indicator that the Mexica did not survive their sacrificial practices without psychic cost) has the man of exemplary courage thrusting his hand into the gaping, munching aperture to pluck out the signs of his individual fate.[43]

That is almost all we know of Mexica dreams, at least directly. Here it is worth taking a sideways glance at other more accessible Amerindians, not as a model of what might have been but as a stimulus to thought. Through Anthony Wallace's researches we have some access to (male) Seneca dream life, their own sense of its high importance being so publicly acted out as to be accessible to observers. These warrior dreamers dreamt of feasts, and of sexual encounters. They also dreamt of death and of torture; of being dragged naked, bound and helpless through the streets to be dealt with by all-powerful, remote figures: a preview of their likely fate were they to fall captive to enemies.

Alongside these predictable voyages into the known terrors of the warrior condition were others less predictable: dreams about a wanting so intense as to make men sicken and die. Wallace tells us that a man tormented by this unassuageable, undefinable need would be treated by the 'dream-guessing rite', during which he would lie ringed by anxious friends desperate to divine his desire. He could come to be surrounded by 'literally thousands of objects – anything he fancies, or his friends can think of. If he dies [he does so] because he could not get a particular pair of leggings or a particular hatchet.'[44] The oddity is that the sufferer was not permitted to name the object of his desire. (My suspicion is that the sufferer did not himself 'know' what he wanted, but came to 'recognize' it when the intensity of public concern had reached a therapeutically effective level.) Wallace infers that 'the typical Iroquois male, who as a matter of fact in his daily life was an exceedingly brave, generous, active, and independent spirit, nevertheless typically cherished some strong, if unconscious, wishes to be passive, to beg, to be cared for', with 'this [normally] unallowable passive tendency' being publicly manifested in the dream-guessing ritual, which dramatized dependency 'to an exquisite degree'. 'The dreamer could not even *ask* [author's italics] for his wish; like a baby, he must content himself with cryptic signs and symbols, until someone guessed what he wanted and gave it to him'.[45]

'Like a baby'. That would indeed seem to be the controlling condition. Powerless, lacking speech; mournfully, perhaps fatally, dependent on others; saved only by the restorative effect of a passionately desired 'something' freely and abundantly given, and that gratification coming not through effort, but as a reward for total passivity. Wallace has surprisingly little to say on the child-rearing practice of the Seneca, noting only that the mother was typically 'solicitous for the child's comfort, [and] nursed it whenever it cried', and that for most of their first nine months infants were strapped to the cradleboard, tending to cry when released from it: 'their tranquillity could often be restored only by putting them back'.[46] The 'bound and naked captive' dreams mimicked that same dependent passivity, but elaborated its terrors and its ambiguities: the captive manhandled through the streets might find himself either adopted into the tribe, or subjected to a cruelly slow and inventive death. The Seneca set a social world, placing a high value on control, endurance, independence and the aspiration to hold others in the subjugation of debt, against a dream-world pivoted on the terror of helpless dependence, of vulnerability and desperate need before ambiguous all-powerful beings and ambivalent givers.

By now the strategy behind the detour into Seneca country will be apparent. We cannot properly understand the public and observable performances of the Seneca without reference to the (socially recognized) terrors and obsessions of the individual. Men are rarely voluble about primary experiences: we can hope at best for symptomatic indicators. In such an exploration there must be the usual caveat that all interpretations are tentative and contestable: there are, of course, larger dangers in pressing the long dead to speak of matters on which they spoke little in life. That said, there are distributed through a wide range of Mexica sources and areas of life some intriguing clues indicative of important themes in Mexica emotional life. The concern that dependence be recognized has already been noted, with the strategies of its soliciting through intensifyingly desperate importunings and exaggerated submission. There is evidence enough to propose that the pre-weaning period was in adult observation and recollection a time of bliss, and that the bitterness of its leaving threaded deep into adult experience. And there is evidence enough of a peculiar fascination for, gratification in, and anxiety about things of the mouth: a fascination I believe to be grounded in that particular view of the blissful state of the nursling, compounded by a particular confusion between the emotional and the erotic which was its corollary. If some readers are still uneasy with this sort of enquiry, I remind them that on a matter like the organizing principle of the calpulli the evidence is and is acknowledged to be slight and contradictory, while on the issue of the lost paradise of the suckling babe and its emotional and psychological consequences it is both more substantial, and more coherent.

The physical pampering of the new mother, together with the insistence on her complete commitment and undivided attentiveness to the child, implies a devoted introduction to breastfeeding, with unregulated access and at least an early abundance. It is clear that Mexica infants were cherished and indulged, with the newborn baby enjoying a great deal of physical fondling, as suggested by that first delighted stroking by the gathered kin, while the invocation of the ideal ruler as 'the mother and father' of his people pictures him as holding them lovingly 'on his thigh' (in his lap, as we would say), 'fondling them as children'.[47] If babies began their lives confined to the cradleboard, they were later free to explore the floor, 'spending their time piling up earth and potsherds', or indulging in other deplorable baby pleasures, as a rebuke directed to a feckless adult indicates: 'even as if thou wert a baby, a child, who playeth with the dung, the excrement, so . . . thou hast bathed thyself, rolled thyself in filth'.[48] But the most tender sentiments curled around the joys of intimacy with the mother, who 'with thee . . . hath nodded half-asleep; she had been soiled by [thy] excretions; and with her milk she hath given thee strength'.[49] That warm milk was described as 'the incomparable of her breasts'. In Mexica thinking warmth was a balm, and cold was the great enemy to human feeling, with the land of the Dead marked by its bitter cold. Through the chill nights of the high valley the baby lay close against the warmth of its mother's body.

Weaning was regarded as a difficult and potentially dangerous time. Physiologically it probably was: to replace human milk, with no transition by way of the milk of other mammals, with a maize-based diet must have raised major problems in gastro-intestinal adjustment.[50] There was also the possibility of protein deficiency, the maize gruel which in texture if not digestibility most resembled milk being seriously deficient in protein. However, Mexica cuisine typically combined maize with beans, which provides adequate vegetable protein, and the custom of touching a little dab of any new food on the baby's forehead so that when he came to eat it 'he would not choke' suggests an early introduction to a fair range of adult food.[51]

Whatever the practicalities, weaning was recognized as a time of emotional stress, with the babies at risk from *tzipitl,* or *chipilez,* the illness caused a nursing infant by its mother's pregnancy, which suggests the nursing infant only ceased to suckle when the mother's milk slackened. The infant was said to weep, to suffer from diarrhoea and to grow thin, and to seem to know it was to be displaced.[52] (A child 'too much attached to its mother' was also expected to have difficulty pronouncing its words.) Certainly the new pregnancy and the consequent cessation of breastfeeding were assumed to cause acute and perhaps fatal misery. Why was that misery seen as so profound? The loss of primary intimacy with the mother and free access to her breast was clearly part of it, as the 'displacement' theme suggests: even before its birth, the child to come had damaged and supplanted its rival. But there appear to be other associated understandings. Early weaning was thought to prevent stuttering. We easily assume some physiological connection: that too prolonged sucking inhibits the development of labial mobility, perhaps. I suspect the connection to be more metaphysical than physical. If well-controlled speech was an essential social grace, indeed the social grace par excellence (which, given Mexica notions of speech affecting, even effecting, the world is putting it rather too mildly), it could rather imply that being too long suckled – too long held in the 'natural world' – postponed the inevitable initiation, through those mouthfuls of maize, into the social world and its complex techniques of communication and control.

Certainly with weaning the child's life changed. The native artists who painted the Codex Mendoza two decades after the conquest carefully limned the events clustered around a child's birth: the bathing, with the objects emblematic of each sex laid out above and below the water bowl; the presentation of the infant to its future directors in the person of a priest or an official from the warrior school. They quite omitted the next period: we leap to the three-year-old child, the boy naked save for his short cloak, the girl in her abbreviated version of her mother's blouse and shift, and each represented with a half tortilla, the flat maize cake which was the basis of the Mexica diet, beside them. At five the children were allotted a whole maize cake, at six a careful one-and-a-half.[53]

We could be tempted to take these maize cakes as no more than a quaint shorthand measure of growth. To do so would be to miss the Mexica point. Social life, the significant human round, began with weaning and one's initiation into the maize cycle and its attendant obligations. The allocated maize was much closer to a 'ration': a ration, and a pledge. For the Mexica it was not the physiological transition which most marked weaning as decisive, nor (or not consciously) its psychological reverberations, powerful as they were. Its most immediate significance was metaphysical: it altered, permanently and destructively, the child's relationship with the gods. That transformation was marked by the formal presentation every fourth year of the most recent crop of Mexica children at the major temple, and their initiation into their religious service. The participating children had to be able to walk, and to make some attempt at dancing, which (remembering that this festival was held only every four years) suggest they would be aged between about two or three and six or seven years: that is, they would all have been weaned. I think it was that fact which established their eligibility.

The presentation was made at the festival of Izcalli, the last month of the seasonal calendar. The emotions stimulated by that first obligatory engagement with sacred ceremonial are worth investigation. On the appointed day the little ones were kept awake until midnight, and then hurried off to the temple in the care of honorary 'aunts' and 'uncles', strangers to them and possibly not well known to the parents, being ideally of higher status. At the temple priests bored holes in their ears with a bone awl, and drew through the hole a thread of unspun cotton, before pasting soft yellow parrot-down on their heads. (The children squirmed and wailed through all this, 'raising a cry of weeping'.) Then the old men of the temple held each child in turn over a fire dense with the smoke of the native incense. They were then taken back to their houses by their unfamiliar custodians, to be kept awake until the dawn, 'when the barn swallow would sing', and the feasting began.

Throughout the morning hours there was dancing and singing in the home courtyard, with the children made to dance too, being held by the hands or (for the smallest) on the backs of their pseudo-kin. It was a celebratory occasion, at least for the adults, and even for the children there may have been some gratification, despite the fatigue and the shaking tensions of the night, as they displayed their bloodied wisps of cotton and their first awarded feathers. But they were allowed no rest. After that long night and day of no sleep and new experiences, they were taken to the great temple and immersed in a huge assembly of strangers, where they heard for the first time the surge and thunder of full Mexica ceremonial, the chants 'crashing like waves' around them.

Then the ceremony moved into its last phase. As we have seen, the drinking of pulque was controlled in pre-contact Mexico, with severe penalties for unlicensed drinking, but on this day of Izcalli, as with some other specified festivals, drinking to drunkenness was universal and obligatory.[54] Pulque ran like water through all of that long night. The children down to the babies on their cradleboards were made to swallow mouthfuls of the strange, sour milk, with the new initiates being given enough of the stuff to make them drunk.[55] Then the adults settled to the serious drinking. The children, exhausted, frantic for want of sleep, and after a night of fear and pain at the hands of strangers, watched as parents and familiar adults drank to strangeness. 'There was reddening of faces . . . glazing of eyes, quarrelling, tramping, elbowing', as men and women squabbled and boasted, or grabbed at each other in anger or sodden affection: all the normally disapproved conducts on drunken display. Then they staggered back to their houses for yet more drinking, and at last sleep.

The next days did not provide the balm of a return to the security of normal household routines. The 'presentation of the children' ceremony immediately preceded the five unnamed days at the end of the calendar

round, a sinister period out of 'time' and thus beyond ritual protection, and therefore a period when the human social world was most acutely vulnerable to the eruption of dangerous uncontrolled forces. For those five days behaviour was accordingly cautious: no fires were lit, no work was done, wrangling and disputing were most earnestly forbidden, as all awaited the return of normal time. (Babies born during this period were so ill-omened as to be unlikely to survive.) Those hushed days gave a fine opportunity for men and women nursing broken heads and bruised relationships to meditate on the wisdom of self-control, the undervalued beauty of order, and the dark and demonstrably anti-social forces unleashed by the sacred pulque. The children, with familiar patterns disrupted and adult conduct strangely muted, could also reflect on their encounter with the power of the sacred. It is of course impossible to be confident of the details of this kind of reconstruction, but the broad terms of the psychological engineering involved are sufficiently clear. The temple had been presented as a place of excitement, glamour, and terror. It was also a place of isolation, where familiar protectors had first failed to protect, and had then ceased to be familiar. It was a place where the initiated children had been the focus of attention, and mysteriously elevated; where their bodies and selves had been invaded by the awls of the priests, by the choking smoke of the fire, by the sacred milk of the pulque; helpless in the grip of the sacred, and transformed by it, their status irretrievably altered.

The children would be gratefully slow to realize the implications of that transformation, but the conduct of the adults around them indicates full awareness. A child who died before being weaned remained free from involvement in the human condition, and retained its attachment to the world of the gods. The body was simply buried by the maize bins at the house entry, and the spirit was understood to return to the place from which it had been sent, the warm garden of Tonacatecutli, there to suck happily at one of the innumerable breasts of the Tree of Sustenance, the 'Wet-Nurse Tree', until it would be called again to be born into this world.[56] The living child deprived of the breast was ejected by that deprivation from an innocent paradise of warmth, of tenderness, of sweet nourishment freely and joyfully given. By taking the fruits of the earth into the mouth, the children entered into their involuntary but total obligation ('contract' has altogether too voluntarist and equitable a ring to it) to the deities from which they would perforce draw their sustenance, with all its costs.

The recognition of the significance of the transition is indicated by the abrupt shift from the indulgence and security of children's infant years to a notable harshness in their later treatment. We have seen at Izcalli the deliberate destruction of their confidence in the security of the home place and people, and the terror attending their introduction to the public, and to the world of the gods. With that entry into the hardships, the responsibilities, and the beginning knowledge of the human condition came the necessity for discipline. The rigour of Mexica punishments for children as represented, for example, in the Codex Mendoza has been dismissed as exaggerated, and it is true that child-rearing manuals (especially those concocted for outsiders' edification) have a tendency to idealize.[57] How seriously ought we take drawings of boys bristling with maguey spines, or lying bound and naked in an icy puddle in the dark, or coughing and choking and weeping as they are held, bound, over a fire of chillis; of little girls roused from bed in the middle of the night and set to sweep out the house, or small fingers lacerated for botched handwork? I think they are accurate enough. It was a dour world for which the children were being prepared, where discipline, especially for males, would be tough, physical and immediate. With the transition to dependence on the fruits of the earth the children had entered precipitately upon their social and cosmic obligation: they, their kin, and humankind would be sustained by the plants of the earth only if the gods were properly fed and properly served. Human tenderness could not temper that bleak reality, but only strengthen the individual to bear it. The young boy of six or seven years old sent to walk alone to enter the calmecac or priests' training school with its cold, its fastings, its penances, was exhorted not to look back:

O my son, O my grandson. See to it that thou lookest not longingly to thy home, to something within thy home. Do not say: 'My mother is there, my father is there. My neighbours, my protectors, exist, flourish. . . . I have drink, I have food. I came to life, I was born, at the place of abundance, a place of riches.' It is ended; thou goest knowing it.[58]

Again, we have that extraordinary Mexica determination to transcend painful emotion not by suppression, but by its acknowledgment.

4

All humans suffer exile from the paradise of the mother, in fact or in later wistful imaginings. The special poignancy for the Mexica was their concomitant enforced entry into their compact with the earth powers, at once an exile from paradise and an irrevocable recruitment into the miseries of labour, attended by the implied acceptance of the triviality of the individual's life, and the necessity of his death: a Fall indeed.

There were other, less explicit responses. Embedded in a little Aztec riddle-me-ree is a quietly horrific image. The question runs: 'What is that which grinds with flint knives, in which a piece of leather lies, enclosed in flesh?' The answer – guaranteed to alienate one from an intimate part of oneself rather decisively – is 'Our mouth'.[59] Mexica women and girls painted their faces with dry yellow ochre, darkened their feet with burnt copal and dye, and traced delicate painted designs on hands and neck. (Stomach and breasts were also painted, but those would be seen only by intimates.) Thick and abundant hair carried much appeal, being washed in costly indigo to give it a deeper glow, but at puberty the little girls who had worn their hair loose had to subdue its growing erotic appeal by binding and dressing it with increasing elaboration. (Pleasure girls dancing on ritual occasions where their role was to invoke and enhance eroticism left their hair seductively flowing.) But one cosmetic was prohibited to the respectable: the reddening of the teeth with cochineal was identified with the vulgar and the sexually dissolute.[60] Prostitutes, with no such inhibitions, habitually stained their teeth.

This was a society in which men exercised close control over the mouth, acknowledging its power, and the damage it could do as an instrument of assault through disputation and abuse. Yet a freely moving mouth among women seems to have carried a strong erotic charge. While little girls could chew chicle (ancestor to our chewing gum) in public, and married women indulge in private, men did so only 'very secretly', for such a habit marked them as effeminate. The prostitute sauntering in the marketplace, hair provocatively only half-bound, made full use of this female lure. She presented as a hallmark of her trade her energetically chewing mouth, lips and tongue in uninhibited movement, and reddened teeth clacking 'like castanets'; a vision of freely indulged oral pleasure, dangerous, enticing, and powerfully stimulating.[61] (Recall that female breasts, while usually modestly covered, seem to have had little erotic force, perhaps because they were too securely identified with nurturance.)

Tenuous filaments tease awareness here. Amerindian cultures – probably most cultures – place high importance on generous feasting, food being a most powerful symbol and currency in all societies. But eating, or more correctly swallowing solid substances, appears to have presented difficulties for the Mexica, and not only under the tension of ritual ingestion. The god of feasting punished any lack of respect by causing the offender to choke on his food, and choking was a major social delict.[62] In a feasting culture, with intense affect centering on reciprocal food-giving, decorum and poise in eating was a social necessity, but heavy obligation certainly pressed upon the act of swallowing. In mundane feasts the act of eating placed one under precise obligations to him who offered the feast; to 'eat the flesh of the god' was to give oneself to the deity as his possession. The young warriors who 'ate the flesh of Huitzilopochtli' (a fragment of the sacred dough from which his image had been constructed) thereby became his servants for a year of such taxing obligation that some sought death on the battlefield to discharge it once and for all.[63] Saliva, that necessary lubricant for solid food, was read as a symptom of anger among the Mexica.[64] The power of the mouth survived the conquest: a sermon 'obviously of native authorship', developed in the post-conquest struggle to concoct an adequately terrifying notion of the Christian hell, populated it with gape-mouthed creatures like the Tzitzime: 'they have metal bars for teeth, they have curved teeth . . . their molars are sacrificial stones. Everywhere they eat people, everywhere they bite people, everywhere they gulp people down'.[65]

The strands still float, snaring attention, webbing the manners of the social world to the world of emotion and of primary experience, and to the imagined world of the gods. Alienated riddles about the mouth, anxieties about swallowing, the seductive power of a woman's reddened teeth and mouth in movement, does not deliver us into the nightmare coherence of the cosmological economy as imagined by the Kwakiutl: a world constituted of eaters and the eaten, 'with all beings subject to the principle of being hungry and the food of other beings who are themselves hungry'.[66] The Kwakiutl recognized that in such desperate circumstances all were subject to the moral imperative of restraint. The Mexica world was more terrible, for their sacred eaters knew no moderation. The most notable feature of the goddess Cihuacoatl was her gaping mouth and ferocious teeth. Diego Durán recorded that Cihuacoatl's priests solicited a captive from the ruler every eight days to feed their famished mistress, one torn thigh being returned to the captor as what remained when the goddess was temporarily sated. So notorious was her hunger that a sacrificial knife was called 'the son of Cihuacoatl', and the maize cakes daily offered the goddess and eaten by her priests were made in the shape of feet, hands, and faces. Durán was carefully explicit: 'I have explained that in pictures the goddess was always shown with her mouth opened wide, because she was always famished, and thus in this temple and in honour of this goddess more men were slain than in any other.'[67] The open mouth, salivating, impersonally chewing, its terror misted by the drifting veils of erotic associations, was a sign of engulfment, extinction, and death:

For our tribute is death; [it is] awarded us in common as merited. And on earth there prevaileth the coming to pay the tribute of death. For there will be the following after, the approaching to thy progenitor Mictlan tecutli [Death Lord] . . . who remains unsatiated, who remaineth coveting. He remaineth thirsting there for us, hungering there for us, panting there for us.[68]

5

Pulque, the fermented milk of the maguey cactus, was a coveted beverage in Tenochtitlan, hedged by rules and restrictions. But the beverage most coveted by the Mexica lords was not the intoxicant pulque, but chocolatl: the ground beans of the cacao tree beaten to a sweet foamy froth with honey and maize gruel, then gently warmed. Consider too the notable eccentricities of the Mexica imagined warrior paradise. There was no feasting or deep drinking: this was no Valhalla. There was no violence: no echoes of war, no vying, no contest at all, save in the competition of display. Nor were there houris: these young men did not require the diversion of sexual pleasure. After four years of feastings, and joyful leapings and shoutings as they escorted the Sun to his zenith, the spirits of the dead warriors were understood to return to the earth as hummingbirds or butterflies: creatures of the sun, endlessly basking in its warmth, endlessly sipping the sweet nectar of the flowers. 'There, always, forever, perpetually, time without end, they rejoice, they live in abundance, where they suck the different flowers. . . . It is as if they live drunk [with joy and happiness], not knowing, no longer remembering the affairs of the day, the affairs of the night. . . . Eternal is their abundance, their joy.'[69]

They return to that most perfect paradise of warmth and milky bliss: of secure dependence, passivity, and endless, effortless gratification, mouths full of sweetness, without memory, without knowledge, without desire. These noble warrior spirits in their final paradise were, experientially, suckling babes once more.

Why should this milk-dripping paradise be reserved for the males? Girl-children too had to make the rough passage from the breast to the exile of the knee-baby, and to enter at weaning upon their human servitude. There can be no firm answer to that question, but it is possible that attitudes towards and so within a girl-child were indeed distinctive, and the sense and remembrance of exile less cruel. From the first moments of life the male baby was in formal rhetoric a warrior-to-be, with the parents' role correspondingly reduced. The girl-child too had her duties, but she would discharge them in the household at 'the heart of the home', exposed only to the ordinary dangers of mortality; at once the recipient, emblem, and provider of warmth and security. In adult (male) understanding the male exile from maternal and female nurturance was severe, explicit, and permanent. And given male control of public life and formal thought, we have to suppose it was their fantasies which most shaped the received account of the cosmos and its workings.

Bitterness and anger as well as regret must have attended that exclusion. Christina Stead has somewhere described the mother as 'a magic woman from whom we obtain the cure of night-terrors and the milk of paradise . . . sheltering this small creature, ourselves, obliged to live in the country of the giants'. That is true. But as we stumble on through the land of the giants we come to realize 'Mother' is a giant too, and perhaps the most powerful, certainly the most ambivalent, of them all. So we enter upon our exile.

There is a curious episode reported in one chronicle, presumably legendary, and the more interesting for that. When the struggle for primacy between the twin cities of Tenochtitlan–Tlatelolco finally erupted, the Tlatelolcans were facing defeat when they staged a last desperate defence. The tough warriors from the dominant city were unnerved when they were confronted by a dual squadron of little naked boys, wailing, with their faces blackened, and of lactating naked women, who slapped their bellies and squirted milk from their breasts as they advanced: psychological warfare *á l'outrance.* (Faced with this battalion of mothers and the multiple images of their own small selves, the Tenochans, to their credit, although 'dismayed by such crudity', stood firm.)[70]

Not only mothers and babies populated the human world, but fathers and siblings too. There is no supreme lawgiver in the Mexica cosmology, and 'fathers' are remote or trivial in creation stories, being economically reduced to a ball of feathers, generic sign of a warrior soul, in the most famous case of Coatlicue's impregnation with Huitzilopochtli.[71] The Mexica family romance turns not on the struggle between powerful father and challenging son, but on the contest between siblings. (So, of course, did the political romance in that valley crowded with related but consciously separate and highly competitive peoples.)[72] The supreme generatrix, the god–goddess of Duality, resided serene, remote, in the highest heaven: the issue of this bisexual being, the four world-creating Tezcatlipocas, coexisted in uneasy and most dynamic tension.

The compacted psychodrama of the account of the creation of this Fifth World or 'Sun' to which I have made an earlier brief reference distils and displays these concerns.[73] After the collapse of the fourth cosmic order the gods had gathered in the darkness at Teotihuacan to create the Sun and the Moon to bring light to the universe. A great fire was set ablaze, and a splendid deity was accorded the first opportunity to leap into the fire, to take on the burden and the glory of becoming the sun. A lesser and ugly little god was also allowed to ready himself, very much as a second string. The favoured one four times gathered himself to leap, and four times balked, unable to brave the flames. Then the other seized his chance, leapt, and rose gloriously as the Sun. Belatedly he whose faltering had cost him the priority cast himself into the fire, to rise as the Moon. (The jaguar and the eagle, the noblest of animals, one of the earth and one of the sky, also chose to leap into the sacred fire, and thereafter bore the signs of courage in their sooted and smutted pelts.) At first Moon was as bright as Sun: 'Exactly equal had they become in their appearance, as they shone'. But such equality could not be tolerated. Moon was struck in the face, and its brilliance forever dimmed. The newborn Sun, for all its light, could not move, so the gods immolated themselves to give it movement, feeding it with their own flesh and blood. Then the Sun moved. Only when its glorious circuit was completed did the Moon begin to move: 'so there they passed each other and went each one their own way.'[74]

In this small dense drama we have the necessity for (and the glory attending) courageous self-abandonment; the unforgiving intensity of rivalry; the intolerability of equality; and the dark necessity, even for gods, of trading blood and death for life. In the psychological subtext we also have the supplanting of a larger and more privileged being by a smaller but more audacious one. Another myth explaining Huitzilopochtli's dominance over the heavens, told below, follows a different story line, but pivots on a similar plot: it is sibling hostility which unleashes the violence when Huitzilopochtli's elder sister and brothers come arrayed for war to slay their infant brother in their mother's womb. And again the smallest and youngest triumphs, destroying or scattering his rivals.

There are other less stormy but equally translucent representations, as played out in a feast offered to Ome Tochtzin, the god of the pulque. Vessels full of strong pulque were set up, and two hundred and sixty drinking tubes laid beside them. Then, after a dance and procession, the god's servitors rushed to the jars, and began a frantic scuffle among the two hundred and sixty for the single tube which was bored right through. With the finding of the pierced tube the fury ceased. The defeated fell back and watched as the triumphant one stood, sucking happily, until the pulque was quite finished.[75] To darken the vision to bring it closer to Mexica coloration, oppose this rather cheerful image of transient triumph to that of the androgynous 'Earth Lady, Earth Lord', always present in Mexica imaginings, endlessly wailing for food: a glimpse of the supplanted, inconsolable, insatiable child.[76]

6

Ambivalent sacred females pressed close at the heart of the most sacred places of the warrior. The shrine of Cihuacoatl, the Tlillan or 'Place of Blackness', a low, dark structure like a cave (or a sweatbath, or a womb) is said to have stood close by Huitzilopochtli's temple in the great temple precinct.[77] The pyramid which sustained Huitzilopochtli's temple was identified as Coatepec, 'Snake Mountain', but also as Earth Mother herself. Huitzilopochtli had no publicly visible representation at his shrine: his presence and powers were manifested through two spectacular icons of Coyolxauhqui, 'She with the Belled Cheeks': his warrior sister, enemy and victim. It was she who had incited her brothers the Uncounted Stars against her mother Coatlicue and her shameful child, leading them in a battle array to kill the child in the womb.[78] Huitzilopochtli, armed with his Fire Serpent, had leapt forth to confront her and destroy her, and to drive his brothers before him in the surge of his fury. Coyolxauhqui's massive head sculpted in green porphyry, the eyes closed in death, once stood on the platform of Huitzilopochtli's temple. At the foot of the stairway of the pyramid a great stone disk, carved in relief and set flat on the ground, represented her at the moment she was struck down by the glorious infant; first exemplary victim of Huitzilopochtli's obliterating power.[79] It is difficult to guess the span of impact of the public art of Tenochtitlan. I do not know how many Mexica saw the Coyolxauhqui carving set at the base of Huitzilopochtli's pyramid. Possibly only those privileged to serve the god and yet to live were familiar with it: most who saw it were en route to death. But ordinary men and women charged with special duties were permitted to penetrate the sacred zones, and warriors discharged their sacred obligations there. Those who saw it would not easily forget.

Unusually, there are no glyphs defining the carving, the meaning being presumably sufficiently explicit in its composition and iconic detailing. Coyolxauhqui is represented as a warrior in her bells, her eagle head-dress, her earplugs, and in the balls of down which mark her for ritual death. She is a warrior too in her marvellously vigorous posture: even in death the dismembered limbs stamp and dance. She is a Celestial Princess, one of the sinister female spirits associated with the Earth Monster, by virtue of the fanged faces at knee and elbow and sandal-heel. She is an earth goddess through the skull at her waist and the living snakes girding her hips.[80]

She is also, like her brothers, the outraged elder sibling, endlessly supplanted, endlessly destroyed by her infant rival. She lies as much exploded as dismembered by the force of the attack, bones jutting from torn flesh: the limbs, the severed head, the plumes and the bells caught in the terrible dynamism of the moment of that annihilating violence; the jagged rhythm of the ruptured wardance controlled in that firm oval form. But all the violence, all the furious detail, is spun to the periphery. Dominating and controlling the centre of the oval is the meadowy expanse of her upper body, smooth, naked. The lower body, twisted away from the viewer, is girdled with snakes. Above them the breasts, the centre of the whole composition, are long, flawless, sleek as lilies: the elusive, eternal objects of desire.

Caught in this psychologically burdened text we have a condensed image indeed: of fratricidal sibling, magnificent warrior adversary and victim, sacred and inimical female, and nurturing mother.[81] The disk was set in the floor before the stairway to Huitzilopochtli's shrine, so she was also the eternally abased enemy. Nudity was commonly the mark of the humiliation of a defeated foe. But Coyolxauhqui retains her warrior headdress and lip-plug, and her nakedness is no reduction. Her body lies serenely, untouched in the midst of violence. So we move from blissful centre to disrupted periphery, and back again, the childhood journey reiterated in the mature warrior's movement from the home place of his first years to the field of battle, and then the return to the warmth and unthreatened sweetness of the final warrior paradise. 'Ambivalence' is altogether too bloodless a word for such a triumphant integration of counterpoised themes, bound together by the tension of their opposition.

7

The festival of the eleventh month, Ochpaniztli, the 'Sweeping of the Roads', is the ceremonial which most clearly exhibits these preoccupations. It was devoted to Toci, 'Our Grandmother', perhaps the most inclusive of the many names given to the earth powers. The primary referent of the 'sweeping' was to the rush of the winds before the brief winter rains. The rains marked the end of the season of growth and the beginning of the agricultural harvest, and the first flowering of the season of war.[82]

The preceding month had seen the celebration of the young men's physical (and sexual) strength. The solemnity of Ochpaniztli was marked off from the earlier exuberance by a five-day lull in all ritual action. Then, late in the afternoon of the sixth day, in silence, and in carefully ordered ranks, the warriors performed a slow, formal march, their hands filled with flowering branches. The formal patterning was sustained until the sun was well set. So they continued over eight days, with that ordered silent marching in the last light of the sun.

Then the pace changed with the eruption into action of the midwives and women physicians, all the women wearing the sacred tobacco pouch as the sign of their sacerdotal status. Divided into two bands, women surged back and forth in a play-skirmish; pelting each other with flowers, reeds and mossy tree-parasites moulded into balls. The group led by the three major officebearers of the curers' association swept along with them the bedecked ixiptla of Teteo Innan, 'Mother of the Sacred Ones': patroness of midwives, curers, the marketplace traders and of things domestic, and closely allied with Chicomecoatl, or 'Sustenance Woman'.[83] The doomed woman was teased and diverted; should she weep it was thought that many stillbirths and the deaths of great warriors would follow.

For four days the normally sedate women skirmished before the House of Song in the main temple precinct, the contest swaying in the pursuit-and-attack alternation enacted in the ballgame, and which for the Mexica was inscribed in the heavens. (The victim so mercilessly played with must have been close to hysteria as exhaustion and excitement mounted.) On the fifth day towards sundown Teteo Innan was brought to the marketplace, her women still encircling her, to be greeted by the priests of Chicomecoatl, and for the last time walked through her marketplace, scattering maizemeal as she went. For the last few hours of her life she was taken back to 'her' temple, and there adorned and arrayed. In the thick of the night, in silence and darkness, she was hurried to the pyramid of the Maize Lord, and stretched on the back of a priest. They were placed 'shoulder to shoulder', we are told, so she was probably looking up into the night sky when her head was struck off.[84] Then, still in darkness, silence, and urgent haste, her body was flayed, and a naked priest, a 'very strong man, very powerful, very tall', struggled into the wet skin, with its slack breasts and pouched genitalia: a double nakedness of layered, ambiguous sexuality.[85] The skin of one thigh was reserved to be fashioned into a face-mask for the man impersonating Centeotl, Young Lord Maize Cob, the son of Toci.

From this point on the priest in his skin had become and was named

'Toci'.[86] 'She' came swiftly and silently down the steps of the pyramid, her priests pressing closely behind her, and flanked by four 'Huaxtec' attendants: young, male, near-naked, wearing rope breechclouts: emblems of male sexuality. (The Huaxtecs, a people of the warm and abundant Gulf Coast, from whence Toci was understood to come, were characterized by the Mexica as caring little for war, but whose inventive eroticism was legendary.) At the foot of the pyramid were the lords and the chief warriors of the city. These men, who scorned to turn their backs in battle, fled through the dark streets to the temple of Huitzilopochtli, the only sound the thud of their running feet, as Toci and her followers pursued them with brooms, the 'domestic' female symbol par excellence, speaking of the tireless cleansing of the human zone, but now sodden with human blood. This was no 'as if' exercise in terror: as they ran, we are told, 'there was much fear; fear spread among the people; indeed fear entered into the people'.

Arrived at the great pyramid, Toci saluted Huitzilopochtli, and gathered up Young Lord Maize Cob, the son they had made together. He wore his thigh-skin mask and the backward-sweeping serrated cap which signified the killing power of frost. As the sun rose Toci was illuminated standing silent on the platform of her temple. Below the nobles were again assembled. As the sun strengthened they ran up the steps to adorn her: to place over the tautening skin her shift and painted skirt, to apply the eagle-down of the warrior to her legs and head, to paint her face, while others offered incense and quail before her. Then her priests decked her in her paper regalia and her great bannered headdress. At last fully accoutred, she slew four captives flung down in turn on the offering stone, but she left the rest of the killings to her priests, as she took her son back to the Temple of Huitzilopochtli to initiate the season of war.

The procession was led by her Huaxtecs, carrying their 'feminine' cotton blossoms and spindles made of precious feathers, and, if we are to believe an early pictorial representation, bearing magnificent erections like banners before them.[87] Around her clustered her entourage of women physicians, singing, being led in their song by Toci's priests, and beating the little two-toned drums with their hanging water gourds particular to women.

At the skull rack in the main temple precinct the seasoned warriors were waiting to receive Lord Maize Cob, 'The Man of War', and to carry his thigh-skin mask as a challenge into enemy lands. So the path of war was opened. The challenge dispatched,[88] Toci proceeded to Atempan, where the whole military might of Tenochtitlan, now ranked and in careful order, awaited her coming. The ruler Moctezoma, in full regalia of warrior lordship, 'seated upon an eagle mat . . . reclining upon an ocelot skin with backrest', had heaped before him the devices – the feathered shields, the weapons, the lip-plugs, the capes – which distinguished the ranks of the warriors. The warriors saluted him, and then one by one came forward to receive their merited regalia from his hand.

The warriors then began a slow circling of the pyramid in the dance which had ushered in Toci's festival, but this time they paraded 'in glory', and carried weapons instead of the flowery branches of the ritual's first days. On the next day the greatest nobles were awarded their insignia, with Moctezoma himself leading them in the slow-stepping dance, and the warriors, now glorious with their quetzal-plume panaches and deeply glinting gold, moving in full magnificence: 'for a great distance did they scintillate; much did the devices gleam.'

As the warriors paraded in their war array, 'moving like flowers', the watching women, 'the beloved old women, all the beloved women', raised a great lament for the men they knew would die in the wars to come. Above the wails of the women rose the song of Toci, high as the song of the mockingbird, as she danced there with her escort of Huaxtecs and women curers.

The dancing, with its eerie counterpoint of song, continued until sundown. When it ceased the priests of Sustenance Woman, clad in the skins of others who had died when Toci was born, came forth from their temple to strew maize kernels on the 'table of Huitzilopochtli', and to cast down squash seeds and many-coloured maize upon the people below, who fought and scrabbled for them, while the sacred seed maize for the next planting was laid away within Sustenance Woman's temple.

With the maize harvest and the next planting secured, Toci was ready to gather her harvest of men. The Fire Priest of Huitzilopochtli set a wooden vessel filled with chalk and white feathers on the lower level of the war god's pyramid. As the vessel was set in place the warriors waiting at the base surged up the stairs, the fleetest bounding ahead to plunge his hands deep into the bowl and toss the feathers into the air, so that the fine down and powdery chalk sifted down over himself and his crowding fellows. Chalk and feathers were the sign of the warrior victim: he who would die in battle, or on the killing stone. With that headlong rush up the stairs, and their submission to the slow drift and settling of the whiteness, the warriors marked themselves for death.

As they raced down the steps of the temple Toci again confronted them, driving them ahead of her with war-cries. Moctezoma ran with them: no warrior was exempt from this experience and this knowledge. They were still allowed some space for protest; as they ran 'everyone spat at her; anyone whose flowers lay in his hands spat at her; he cast [the flowers] at her.'

They scattered as they ran, until finally she ran on alone, save for a few priests who attended her back to her shrine on the boundary of the city. There 'Toci' removed the regalia, and peeled off the shrivelling skin. It was stretched on a wooden frame, face forward and staring outwards, to guard the city which had once again been brought to acknowledge the range and weight of Toci's authority.

Ochpaniztli had powerful historical and mythic connotations.[89] Dramatically and experientially it was a brilliantly constructed horror event, in its abrupt changes of pace and its teasing of the imagination through the exploitation of darkness, the sudden rush of feet, the whisper of brooms sodden with human blood, as in the deliberation of the slow construction of Toci, built layer by layer upon the flayed human skin, each layer revealing more of her nature, until the benign custodian of curing and the domestic stood triumphant as the pitiless mistress of war, insatiable eater of men.

Alongside that slow exposure of the nature of the sacred was a complex play on the involvement of the human and social in these sacred affairs. Human sensuality was implicated through the luxuriant sexuality of Toci's escort of Huaxtecs, whose regalia recalled another Huaxtec deity, Mayahuel, the goddess of pulque, with her conical Huaxtec cap and crescent nose ornament, linking back to the divine dangers of drunkenness. And as Toci sent the glorious men to war while human women wailed and lamented, the double aspect of Woman, as biological and sacred entity, and as social being, was most economically displayed. Midwives, mediating between the social and the sacred, were revealed as 'priestly' through more than their tobacco pouches. They were Toci's intimates, as they were the custodians of women on their field of battle, when the sacred force was fully present. Like the priests, the midwives handled living and dead flesh charged with the dangerous sacred, and in the bloody business of birth laid knives to flesh if need be. The same sacred power engulfed the Mexica woman as she approached parturition, obliterating the self, threatening to transform the loving daughter or mother or wife into a child-crippling, world-eating monster. That contingency, with its train of corrosive ambivalences, is caught in the image of the woman's broom dipped into human blood and so become a weapon of terror, before which warriors famed for their courage were driven like leaves.

And throughout, the deep mutual implication, the simultaneity of the requirements of war and of reproduction human and vegetable, is dramatized: the intimate, inevitable interdependence between the warriors' way and the growth and cropping of maize. What is most remarkable is the explicit rendering of the psychological and social cost of that interdependence. There is no veiling of consequences. We might expect the sequencing of emotions into psychologically manageable phases – a period of unclouded celebration with the distribution of warrior devices, perhaps, to be followed by sobering reflection on possible outcomes. What we are shown is all warriors being marked for death as a reflex of their warrior glory, in that distinctive Mexica talent and taste for extremism, and for allowing the untrammelled expression of emotions while not yielding an inch on the metaphysical point.

8

The Female Being Revealed

The Mexica lived in a society pivoting on the glamour of the warrior and his capacity to tap into the wealth of the tribute warehouses. But despite the vertiginous honours accorded the warriors and their own firm exclusion from public life (an exclusion too easily taken as a decisive indicator of lack of social worth), Mexica women enjoyed effective protection, and exercised a degree of individual autonomy in the small liberties and decisions of everyday life which possibly surpassed that of men. An ideology which stressed tribal identity over gender, and the common plight of humankind over tribe, allowed them to escape definition as 'other'. They were free from the notion of the polluting power of menstrual blood which sets the female apart in so many traditions, and sexuality was accepted as a legitimate delight for both sexes. In the parabola of mundane life marriage opened benefits to men and to women alike. In marriage women appear to have been regarded, and to have regarded themselves, not merely as helpmates but as partners with men in the human enterprise.

In that enterprise the trajectories of the involvement of each sex with the social and the sacred followed a similar curve. Men had most sacred and erotic power in youth, for it was then that they came closest to exemplifying the cultural and aesthetic ideal of the young warrior. Social power came in middle age, with the moral authority accumulated through experience, and through the military record, rank, offices or expertise achieved, which indicated the fulfilment of one's tonalli. Through childbirth young women were precipitated into intimate contact with the sacred, as they were caught up in the convulsive workings of the forces of procreation. After menopause, securely social beings once more, they could arrive at 'political' and social influence in household and neigh-bourhood affairs, as custodians of custom and conventional wisdom, and as organizers of marriages and therefore of inter-familial alliances. With further ageing the gender distinction lost force, men and women together graduating first to the status of respected elders, and then into the incon-sequence of babbling old age, the sacred power of the developed tonalli deformed by the corrosion of their mental capacities; their social authority quite gone.[1]

The constant marking of sexual difference was central to Mexica man-agement of the world. If women sat thus, men sat so; if men drank this, women drank that, as public and domestic ritual continued to structure and represent Mexica imaginings of the necessary order of things. This decisive sorting was designed to share and to balance rather than to divide, and the differences were nested in equivalent ritual, each being connected to the other through the peculiar intimacy of systemic opposi-tion, as in the formally managed interactions of the rest of life. But despite the elegance of the isomorphism between male and female careers and their mutual celebration, there were different consequences for each sex. Men were 'made' warriors through a system of public rewards and tri-umphs, and so, inescapably, through the tensions of remorseless competi-tion and the constant threat of displacement. Women bore children as an attribute of their being. The 'priestesses', like all the women we see in Mexica rituals, derived their special relationship with the sacred from their femaleness, not (as in the case of the male priests) by way of training and austerities.[2] In ritual performance women could be presented more as icons than agents, displayed for their existential power rather than their achieved skills or authority. There is a partial exception here with the midwives, but again their femaleness, and so their special relationship with Toci in her various manifestations, was essential to their effective-ness.

Above all, men's individual moment of invasion by the sacred, however passionately rehearsed, lay beyond their mundane lives, in the 'jaguar meadow' of the battlefield or on the killing stone. For women, the inva-sion of the social being came with each childbirth, so penetrating deep into the core of the household, and injecting a cloud of sinister affect into male–female and parent–child relations. The woman who lived through that sacred state went on to nurture and to provide the place and taste of a

temporary paradise. She who was surprised by death remained transformed, an enemy and eater of mankind.

Those intrusions and their effects were socially adjusted through ritual
and rhetoric to re-emphasize not the 'sacred power' of the female (for she
had none) but the shared vulnerability of the human, striving for the
survival of its fragile social orderings in the face of the ambiguous and
usually inimical sacred. More consequentially, the capacity of the woman's womb to reproduce was subsumed within the most pervasive and
inclusive of Mexica metaphors: the earth's capacity to bring forth food,
and the costs of its fruitfulness. It was that understanding which controlled the presentation of sex-specific implements at birth. The gifts
were paired statements regarding divinely ordained roles and duties,
pointing to cosmic rather than to social or material arrangements. They
carried no direct reference to man as food-getter or woman as nurturer.
These were sacred dedications to sacred destinies: the boy-child to warriordom on the field of battle, the girl-child to weaving by the hearth and
to constant sweeping to secure and preserve her small corner of the social
world. Nonetheless, the programmatic statement subsumes vegetable and
human reproduction: man as warrior secures the human flesh and the
blood needful to feed the earth so that the earth will yield its products;
woman as heart of the home converts those products into consumable
food in conditions of security she labours to maintain, and in parallel
nurtures the next generation of warriors.

The identification of the woman's womb with the great womb of the
earth was the foundation of the Mexica system of thought. It was that
understanding which sustained the meanings played out through the medium of the human body in each 'human sacrifice', by a dismemberment
and analysis at once physical and conceptual. The elements the Mexica
saw being manipulated in agriculture were set out for contemplation in a
different form: human flesh equated with maize, vegetable food, and the
earth itself; human blood with rain and flowing water; the human heart
with the sun and its heat.

While the same understanding informed all accounts of the relationship between the human and the 'natural' order, the Mexica, specialists in warfare, chose to render it most explicit in dramatizing the
unobvious but crucial connections between the feats of warriors and the
food of men. It was chillingly demonstrated in the Feast of the Flaying of

Men, where the young warrior was permitted to taste his 'triumph' by wearing the stinking skin of his victim, and by experiencing its slow transformation into matter until, like the pierced casing of the maize seed, it crumbled back into earth. The explosion of relief which attended the ending of the ordeal signals the bitterness of that experience, as he had rehearsed his own death and decay. When at his feast his kinsfolk took into their mouths the morsel of human flesh resting on the stew of dried maize kernels – maize in its least modified form – the lesson he and they were being taught was that the two substances, perceptually so different, were nonetheless of the same stuff, at different points in the cycle.[3]

While we transmute bread and wine into flesh and blood, reflecting the centrality of man in our cosmology, the Mexica saw human flesh and blood as transmuted into sacred maize and sacred water. Our 'man is dust and will be dust again' focusses on the brevity of the reign of the flesh, and the imperishability of the spirit. For the Mexica, man's flesh has been, is and will be again part of the vegetable cycle, and man's spirit will only briefly survive the flesh. The common task was to sustain a social order sufficiently in harmony with the 'natural' order to exist within it, with women and men pursuing their separate and dangerous paths, to maintain humankind's precarious purchase on existence.

This great tangle of ideas netted Mexica apprehension and comprehension of the world. The expression of the poignant subthemes of childbirth and childhood, sometimes masked, always insistent, bearing their burden of memory and desire and the insidious authority of experience half-remembered or dreamt, laced through and between the high metaphysical themes of the dialectic between earth and sun, warrior man and warrior woman, between blood violently shed and the quiet sequence of plant growth, between the stories of the gods and the dark concealed dramas of family and sexual intimacies. Particular themes were sometimes muted, sometimes dominant. But they were always present, endlessly displayed in the complex reciprocating patterns of the festivals as in the small routines of everyday life, and it was the connection of each with each which the Mexica most passionately explored.

PART III

THE SACRED

9

Aesthetics

The traces of the Tolteca, their pyramids, their mounds, appear not only there at the places called Tula and Xicocotitlan, but practically everywhere . . . their potsherds, their pestles, their figurines, their arm bands appear everywhere . . . and many times Tolteca jewels – arm bands, esteemed green stones, fine turquoise – are taken from the earth. . . . In truth, [the Tolteca] invented all the precious, marvellous things which they made. . . . All which now exists was their discovery. They went to seek all the mines of amber, of rock crystal, of amethyst; they went to marvel at the pearls, the opals. And these Tolteca were very wise; they were thinkers, for they originated the year count, the day count. All their discoveries formed the book for interpreting dreams. . . . And so wise were they [that] they understood the stars which were in the heavens; they gave them names and understood their influence.

They were tall; they were larger than the people today.

Florentine Codex[1]

I

The sacred could erupt perilously into the human world, using extremes of emotion and experience as its vehicle. But it was also intimated in the enchantments of 'natural' beauty, and could be courted, pursued and revealed through the regulated procedures of 'art'.[2]

A sixteenth-century Mexica song-poem pivots on what we might be tempted to take as no more than an engaging trope: that the experienced world is a painted book, endlessly sung and painted into existence by the Giver of Life; constantly perishing, constantly renewed:

> With flowers you write,
> Giver of Life.
> With songs you give color,

With songs you shade
those who live here on the earth.

Later you will erase eagles and tigers.
We exist only in your book
while we are here on the earth.[3]

In what follows I will pursue the exercise of tracing the implications of this small text, taken not as a literary extravagance but as a simple statement about the nature of things, to see how comprehensively it orders Mexica aesthetic expressions, whether through objects, songs, or performances.

First, to dig out the embedded propositions. The experienced world is a representation composed out of representations, the original models in the mind of the divine artificer deriving from the world of the sacred. What we call 'nature' is the creation of sacred art. So too are human arrangements. In this painted world men enjoy no priority: they (like everything else) are figments, their brief lives shaped by a divine aesthetic impulse. Even the achieved magnificence of the 'eagles' and 'tigers' (the 'jaguars') of the greatest warrior orders is a fabrication, and fleeting as a flower.

Such a view is subversive of most of our complacencies. Our art–nature distinction lapses where nothing is 'natural', the objects of the seen world being themselves the highest art. Our world is not the measure for the 'real', but a fiction, a thing constantly made and remade by the divine artificer, its creatures and things called into transitory existence through the painting and the singing of an elaborate pictorial text. This might seem not far removed from a 'works of Creation' Christian sensibility, but there the crucial mediation of the painted text, with all its implications, is missing, and it is not the giant labour of creation (and the moral burden so placed on man) which is central, but rather a continuing and morally quite neutral divine aesthetic impulse.

The human artist mimics the divine activity. The Mexica born on a propitious daysign who recognized and cultivated his or her implicit talent could come to be acknowledged as 'a Toltec', a spiritual descendant of those legendary craftsmen of Tula whose works continued to astonish the artists of imperial Tenochtitlan.[4] The true 'Toltec' was one who 'converses with his heart, finds things with his mind . . . invents things, works skilfully, creates.[5] Among artists, the scribe – 'he who paints in the red and black ink' – was most honoured, as he most closely modelled the activities of the divine painter, in a sense seeking to replicate the original divine text. The scribe's wisdom preceded and defeated history: even before the building of Teotihuacan, the 'Cradle of the Gods', there had been a people who had 'carried with them the black and the red ink, the manuscripts and painted books, the wisdom. They brought everything with them, the annals, the books of songs, and their flutes'.[6] As this sequence makes clear, the poet-singers and musicians who called the painted books to life were only slightly less honoured than the scribes; indeed there is a suggestion in some poems that the processes of chant and inscription were simultaneous, the 'text' as much sung as painted. But all arts were intimately interrelated, as all were manifestations or activations or clarifications of the divine text and sustained by the sacred impulse. While human artists could not equal the divine athleticism of the god who moved with absolute freedom across the trivial boundaries within the beauty-making realm, the poet indicated their sacred elevation through metaphor, as we will see, singing of 'painting' songs, making drums 'blossom': envisioning a sense-transcending, hallucinatory expansion of the possible.

Given such an understanding, 'art' among humans becomes a collective quest for the really real, with men working in paint or song or gold or feathers or stone to approximate the images of the exemplary text, and to retrieve the original unsullied sacred vision from the blurred and shifting images before them. Despite its fragility and inherent instability this uncertain world remains a text: defective, incomplete, chronically mutable to human eyes, yet to be deciphered as a painted book is deciphered by those with the skill to ascertain something of the enduring sacred world it imperfectly mirrors. 'Mirrors' is precise here, recalling those Mexica mirrors of smoky obsidian, with their obscure images dimly figured in the darkness. There are also intriguing resonances with the account of man and his epistemological relation with the world given in the Popol Yuh, the 'Book of the Council' of the Quiché Maya, where the first four humans created by the gods 'saw all and knew all . . . their vision penetrated trees, rocks, lakes, seas, mountains, plains . . . they saw the four sides, the four corners' (that is, the entire world). Their vision, and their knowledge, was equal to that of the gods. But the gods dimmed their eyes as a mirror is breathed on, so 'now they could only look close by; just as far as what was obvious'.[7]

Aesthetic responsiveness to things of the world, which are either creations of the divine artist or made by men to approximate those creations, therefore became worship, as did devoted observation as the signs of the sacred were watched for. Beauty of 'natural' appearance (in accordance with the Mexica canon) or some special grace or authority in movement indicated a high precision in replication, the living jaguar or eagle being rendered by that understanding an ambulatory text, worthy of special contemplation, special reverence. In the Templo Mayor caches we find not only masks and figures and incense burners, stone frogs, beads – made things – but the skulls of coyotes, swordfish beaks, whole cadavers of crocodiles, leopards stretched out as if at rest. Considered together these things constitute an 'all things living in the empire' category, as I have argued. But they are also individual offerings, to be valued in their own right; the 'natural' jaguars and crocodiles the creations of the master artificer, the superb replications in stone man's attempted 'realization' of divine models.[8]

Ephemerality, too, becomes an indicator of the sacred when the divine artist 'writes with flowers' and 'colours with songs'. Fugitive beauty hints at the unseen but real world of the sacred and the enduring. Therefore frail and fleeting things are to be cherished precisely because they are evanescent, constantly melting back along that shimmering margin into the invisible and real.

2

If those are the principles, now for the application. To begin with what is usually classified as a 'minor art': featherwork. The Mexica passionately prized feathers. We do not readily think of a feather-led expansion of a trade and tribute empire, but that is the merchants' account of the growth of the empire as they told it to Sahagún's scribes: an account which moves with the steady beat of the oft-told tale.[9] Initially, 'in times of old', under the first ruler, commerce had begun with trading in 'red arara and blue and scarlet parrot feathers'. With the second ruler came access to the splendour of quetzal feathers ('but not yet the long ones') and the glory of the gold and black troupial: 'when it spreads its tail, then the yellow shows through. The black ones show splendour, radiate like a flame; like embers, like gold they show through'.[10] Along with troupial feathers came the first turquoise, jade, and cotton clothing. The reign of Moctezoma the Elder at last saw an abundance of the coveted long quetzal feathers, long troupial feathers, the blue feathers of the cotinga (the 'turquoise bird'), and the pink and chilli-red of the roseate spoonbill. The skills and the status of the merchants' close associates, the featherworkers, expanded as the rich feathers flowed in to supply their sacred art, the scribes tracing the preliminary outlines of the designs which would be realized through delicate skill.[11]

All feathers were passionately valued, but the quetzal plume held a special place in the Mexica (and the Mesoamerican) imagination. It was rare, the shy male bird which grew the two long curving tail feathers living deep in the remote rainforests to the South.[12] The feather filaments are light, long, and glossy, so that the smallest movement sets them shimmering. And the colour, a gilded emerald haunted by a deep singing violet blue, is extraordinary: one of those visual experiences quite impossible to bear in mind, so that each seeing is its own small miracle. Here is the Resplendent Trogon, the Mexica 'quetzal', as described by an (unusually poetic) ornithologist:

His whole head and upper plumage, foreneck and chest are an intense glittering green. His lower breast, belly, and under tail coverts are of the richest crimson. . . . The dark, central feathers of the tail are entirely concealed by the greatly elongated upper tail coverts, which are golden green with blue or violet iridescence, and have loose, soft barbs. The two median and longest of these coverts are longer than the entire body of the bird, and extend far beyond the tip of the tail, which is of normal length. Loose and slender, they cross each other above the end of the tail, and thence diverging gradually, form a long, gracefully curving train which hangs below the bird when he perches upright on a branch and ripples gaily behind him as he flies. The outer tail feathers are pure white and contrast with the crimson belly. . . . To complete the splendor of his attire, reflections of blue and violet play over the glittering metallic plumage of back and head, when viewed in a favorable light.[13]

The Mexica description as dictated to Sahagún's scribes is very much longer, with notably finer discriminations between categories of feathers being anatomized over several paragraphs. But the underlying analogy linking the particular descriptions is worth noting. The underbody feathers designated 'crimson' by the ornithologist were identified as 'chilired', 'resplendent, wonderful' by the Mexica. The description continues: 'The feathers which grow on the tail are called *quetzalli*. [They] are green, herb-green, very green, fresh green, turquoise-colored. They are like wide reeds: the ones which glisten, which bend. They become green, they become turquoise. They bend, they constantly bend; they glisten.'[14]

Few Mexica could have seen the majestic bannered flight of this extraordinary bird rippling across the sky, the trailing quetzal plumes sensitive to each shift and movement in the air, but even in stillness their import was clear. The chilli-red underbody, the tail-feathers' constant shift in colour between turquoise and 'herb-green', most precious because most divine colours, their lift, curve, colour, and movement like 'wide reeds' betrayed their intimate connection with vegetable growth. But they were unlike any reed in their shifting iridescence: such beauty identified this marvellous creation as mediating between the seen and the sacred unseen, so rendering the unseen visible. The Mexica called their most valued feathers and featherwork 'the Shadows of the Sacred Ones', the marvellous projections into this dimmed world of the light, colour, and exquisite delicacy of the world of the gods.[15]

The ephemerality theme was everywhere, in the high value placed on the ritual expenditure of flowers and feathers, on fire, on the snuffing out of human life and human beauty. I suspect it informed a small routinized ritual procedure, one of the conventionalized notations of ritual actions, called 'entering the sand', the actions of which remain unspecified in the sources. It was performed by particular ixiptlas at four specified sacred locations, and usually closely preceded the victim's final presentation for death. My guess (and it can be no more than that) is that it refers to the destruction of sacred sand paintings, perhaps themselves entered from the four 'directions', by the dancing feet of the destined victim, so marking another station of the ixiptla's way to death, and displaying again the timeless significance of the ephemeral.[16]

Poetry, for us one of the most individualistic of art forms, can be said to encapsulate collective understandings among Amerindians, who have a long tradition of song-poems as public, and publicly shaped, performances. While Mexica songs were 'made' by individuals, they were more arrangements of shared formulae than full inventions, the symbology and styles within the strongly marked genres (warrior songs, burgeon songs, songs of lamentation) being very much prescribed, and particular songs entering the repertoire only if they won general acceptance. Mexica nobles were especially devoted to song-making. The 'friendship' the songs invoked so ardently was less a matter of an exclusivist intimacy between individuals than a collective sympathy, closer to what we would call fellowship or comradeship: a sentiment sufficiently rare in the abraded world of male relations in late-imperial Tenochtitlan. But despite noble commitment, songcraft remained a popularly based art, commoners with talent finding an open way into Moctezoma's favour, the palace, and renown.[17] An early myth tells of the capricious god Tezcatlipoca on one of his earthly visitations as a warrior making ready to sing his triumph song. When all the youths and maidens had gathered, he intoned a song so irresistibly compelling that 'right then they answered it. From his lips they took the song'. (Unhappily for them, while they were helplessly possessed by the song he lured them to their deaths.)[18] The story offers a glimpse not only of Tezcatlipoca's casually malevolent humour, but of the way an individual's song could be publicly taken up in performance – not too difficult a feat given the genre's strong formal patterning – and so prove its power, to the gratification and profit of its original owner. Tenochtitlan must have been an especially rich area for musical invention, with the challenge and stimulus of the songs and the styles of the tributary cities always present, and with the raised and rhythmic voice a major public medium for communication and expression, from the long formal homilies of 'ancient words' which marked most rites of passage and the sonorous chantings of Mexica priests, to the broken lamentations of the files of war captives informed of their fatal destiny. Certainly the lords practised the art and vied for recognition. While it is difficult for us to attach much excitement to the notion of speech-making as art form, my suspicion is that occasions of competitive Indian eloquence smacked more of the virtuosity of the jazz convention than the longueurs of the senate chamber. The art of poetic performance sustained itself well into the decades of conquest: at least some of the songs we have appear not only to have been written down but composed in the late sixteenth century.[19] But whatever the longevity of the form, its structures, symbols, and sentiments derived from the pre-contact world: in the celebration of the 'flowery death' in the ecstasy of battle or on the sacrificial stone; in the melancholy quest for a hard surface of reality in the uncertain world of sense; in the dark setting of isolation and mistrust which lent friendship its lustre; in the plangent acquiescence in the tough wisdom of the Mexica.

The songs are also sumptuously beautiful and intended to enchant. Sung poetry was called in Nahuatl *xochi-cuicatl*, 'flower-song', and in the painted books the speech-scrolls which indicated its speaking were coloured the deep blue-green of jade, of quetzal plumes, and of the incomparably precious. In those which survive the objects of the world and of artifice are spun into the one shimmering web. Separate arts are interwoven, or more correctly identified as aspects of a single activity, melting the human skills of polishing jade, painting, featherworking, or song-making into the 'natural' blossoming of a flower.

> I polish jades,
> sparkling in the sun.
> On the paper I am putting
> feathers of the green and black bird.
> I know the origin of songs:
> I only arrange the gold-coloured feathers.
> It is a beautiful song!
> I, the singer, weave precious jades
> show how the blossoms open.
> With this I please
> The Lord of the Close and Near.[20]

The artist does no more than 'arrange' natural beauty. The emphasis falls on the poignance of the evanescent: the 'weaving' of the fugitive glow of notoriously brittle jade, shattering at a misplaced touch; the delicacy of the opening blossom; sound hanging briefly in air, then fading to silence; while that easy crossing of our divide between the humanly contrived and the natural allows a marvellous concreteness in what we would call 'metaphors'.

This is perhaps most obvious in the songs which have to do with the bloody business of war. Warrior death, whether in battle or on the killing stone in an enemy city is invoked, disquietingly, in images of swooning sensuous beauty. The battlefield is apostrophized variously as the jade house, the flower court, the eagle patio, the jaguar meadow. Warriors summoned from their warrior paradise to sing 'beside the drum' are said to come as rain, as dew, as flowers, as jadestones pure and flawless as a newborn child: radiant images of fertility, value, and beauty. Warriors falling in death 'rain down like flowers', as the songmaker seeks out the sacred 'place of flowers':

> I inhale the perfume;
> My soul becomes drunk.
> I so long for the place of beauty,
> The place of flowers, the place of my fulfilment,
> That with flowers my soul is made drunk.[21]

The flower-songs also exhibit an interesting ambiguity of agency, with the god called to be present and in a sense to participate in their making. The songs themselves are invoked as descending from the House of the Sun. More deeply, the singer's activity is presented as an act of reciprocity or, more correctly, of restitution: the song is actualized by the singer, but it existed before his actualization as the creation of the divine maker. Bestowed by its creator, it is returned in performance. There is a hint, too, that the divine singer at times invades the human vehicle. Many of the songs are antiphonal, a dialogue between singer and deity in which the god himself, summoned by the song and the singer, 'paints' in the flowery patio, singing through the human throat with the human artist become his instrument:

> I appear in this flower court.
> Pictures blossom: they're my drums.
> My words are songs.
> Flowers are the misery I create.[22]

The artist is rewarded by the sacred intoxication of the performance, and the immortality accorded his art:

> It will be spoken of when I have gone.
> I shall leave my song-image on earth . . .
> My heart shall live, it will come back,
> my memory will live and my fame . . .
> My song is heard and flourishes.
> My implanted word is sprouting,
> our flowers stand up in the rain.
> The Cocoa flower gently opens his aroma,
> the gentle Peyote falls like rain.

> My song is heard and flourishes.
> My implanted word is sprouting,
> our flowers stand up in the rain.[23]

The flower-songs bring men into reciprocating action with the sacred. They are also, in accordance with the aesthetic imperative, ephemeral, even if constantly recreated existing only in the moment of their performance: 'blazing flower words . . . [of] but a moment and a day'.[24] After that moment, the 'flowers' return to the place of the Sacred Ones. And they further reveal the pathos of the human condition, poignant in its mingling of pain and and pleasure. Men, like flowers and song, are in the world only fleetingly: 'As a song you're born, O Moctezuma: as a flower you come to bloom on earth'.[25] While the songs evoke a daze of images of sound, scent, colour, movement, touch, the world so vividly experienced has no reality. Even moments of rapture and exaltation, like all else in this veiled and shifting world, are no more than a dream.[26] The Mexica conceptualized a universe composed of heavens above and underworlds below, those heavens and underworlds being stable and enduring. This visible world, Tlatlticpactli, 'on earth', the layer manifest to the senses, they characterized as 'that which changes': for all its vivid actuality, an elaborate deception. That recognition inserts the anguish of doubt into the heart of experience:

> The Giver of Life deceives!
> Only dreams do you follow,
> You our friends!
> As truly as our hearts believe,
> As truly they are deceived.[27]

The riddling ways of Tezcatlipoca are protean. Nonetheless some knowledge, even some wisdom, is possible, because this earthly zone, insubstantial and chronically mutable though it is, yields to the attentive watcher intimations not of mortality – that was a commonplace – but of the enduring sacred.

One great poem sums up the principles of human and of aesthetic being. The flesh of the human artist is matter, made from the god-gift of maize, but his art is ordered through the painted sacred book, and through his singing he animates the world and completes his life:

As white and yellow maize I am born,
The many-coloured flower of living flesh rises up
and opens its glistening seeds before the face of our mother.
In the moisture of Tlalocan, the quetzal water-plants open their corollas.
I am the work of the only god, his creation.

Your heart lives in the painted page,
you sing the royal fibres of the book,
you make the princes dance,
there you command by the water's discourse.

He created you,
he uttered you like a flower,
he painted you like a song:
a Toltec artist.
The book has come to the end;
your heart is now complete.[28]

3

A couple of genres do not make a generalization. Are the understandings
I claim to discern in the song-poems present in other areas of Mexica 'art'
and life? To return to the most inclusive proposition: the notion of the
world as painted into existence, with men and all else in it representations, transitory expressions of an enduring, divine sensibility. In such a
view the surface appearance and the behaviour of things are 'reality', or
man's closest access to it. Given such an understanding, characteristics or
resemblances in form or marking or colour or gait which we would dismiss as 'superficial' become of maximum moment, yielding cryptic clues
as to the relationships within the sacred world. That earnest focus on
'mere' appearance cuts across our preference for establishing likeness
through unobvious, often hidden, indicators of common origin. We have
been taught to consider the 'structural' as basic, and so – not without
effort – categorize dolphins and deer, seahorses and sharks, together. Our
ancestors would have found the Mexica obsession with appearance and
semblance very much more intelligible.

This raises the important but vaporous issue of the sensory mode to which the Mexica were most highly responsive. Dennis Tedlock, in an insightful analysis of the conceptualization of the beginning of the world in the Maya 'Popol Yuh', emphasizes the primacy given the aural sense in the Maya imagining of things: in the beginning, there was a murmurous hush which slowly defined itself into the rippling of water, of softly shifting winds, of the tiny noise of insects, as the sounds of the world separated themselves and came into being.[29] In the Mexica beginning-of-the-world story the gods first made light:

It is told that when yet all was in darkness, when yet no sun had shone . . .
it is said the gods gathered together and took counsel among themselves there in Teotihuacán.
They spoke, they said among themselves; 'Come hither, O gods!
Who will carry the burden?
Who will take it upon himself to be the sun, to bring the dawn?'[30]

There followed the self-immolation of a god, so that light and sight were brought to the world, and men could look about them to fathom the meaning of things.

We have already seen how the correspondences between quetzal plumage and lush foliage excited the Mexica imagination. Recognitions of other likenesses stud the language. Andrew Wiget tells us of a cluster of Nahuatl words centred on precise ways of describing how a flower comes to blossom. Where we are content with 'to bloom, to blossom, to flower', Nahuatl distinguishes *mimilhui*, 'to bloom in a slow unfolding', *cueponi*, 'a more sudden explosion of blossom', and *itzmolinia*, 'to regain verdure or greenness after once being brown and dry'. All these terms may be applied in other contexts, so a new song sung or a bird spreading its feathers was said to be 'made to blossom', birds and flower-songs forming a 'natural' category for men who studied what they saw, and made their inferences from their observations.[31] Given the cryptic nature of the signs all clues had to be pursued. The rosette markings on a jaguar's skin, taken along with the jaguar fondness for hunting by water, recalled the formal roundness of water lilies. In view of the creature's nocturnal and solitary habits, and its superbly indifferent demeanour, those ambiguous signs also pointed to the stars which studded the night sky, and so to the secret doings of night-walking sorcerers and of their divine patron Tezcatlipoca, the 'Smoking Mirror' of the seer's scrying glass.[32] Thus the jaguar was anatomized.

This high concentration on significant appearance helps explain some apparent peculiarities of Mexica sculpture. Mexica 'naturalistic' sculptures are to any eye magnificent in their apparently effortless verisimilitude. No concessions were made to the recalcitrance of the medium or the simplicity of the technology (sharpened stone, bird bones, fibrous cords, water, sand): technique was not permitted to be an issue.[33] Stone curves and swells as malleable as clay; the skin of a stone serpent glistens; brittle jade writhes and whirls. Sculptors produced stunningly realistic representations in burnished stone of squashes and shells, gourds and grasshoppers. The vegetable representations have the fanatical attention to detail of botanical models: a squash, for example, displayed with the flower at one end and the species-specific stem immaculately modelled at the other. The 'purpose' of these representations has been something of a puzzle. They are commonly explained as ritual 'display' objects or offerings.[34] So they probably were. But why the desperate attentiveness to detail in the vegetable representations? And why were small creatures – toads, grasshoppers, frogs, flies, fleas – displayed with equal virtuosity, but commonly in a slightly more schematic, selective, form: the grasshopper missing a pair of legs, the toad huge-headed, huge-eyed?[35] And why this passionate translation into stone of so vast a range of objects – vegetables, insects, drums, bundles of reeds, shields: a translation which seems to have been a particularly Mexica obsession? Pasztory believes the preference 'is related to the late position of the Aztecs in Mesoamerican History. They associated stone with the great civilizations of the past and apparently adopted it even for modest objects because of its connotations of permanence and associations with ancient grandeur'; which is true, but does not quite get to the heart of the matter.[36]

We are familiar with the ancient drawings of, for example, Lascaux, and their aesthetic force. They appear to have been drawn in order to 'draw' the animal, to possess it in the flesh as it was possessed in the act of the drawing and in the concentrated looking which preceded it. There is something of that intensity in the Mexica representations of the more formidable animals. But they are to our eyes clumsy and unpersuasive, notably less devoted in their realism than are the vegetable images. The jaguar images are thick and unfluent, and the few surviving eagle sculptures and carvings equally non-naturalistic. But if as realistic representations they are poor, as constructs of creatures of power they are compelling.[37] While the mythic is manifest with the 'Ahuitzotl', the terrifying water creature which Moctezoma's predecessor took as his name-sign, it is immanent in these nightmare jaguars and implausibly prancing eagles.[38]

An exhortation to Mexica sculptors runs:

What is carved should be like the original, and have life, for whatever may be the subject which is to be made, the form of it should resemble the original and the life of the original. . . . Take great care to penetrate what the animal you wish to imitate is like, and how its character and appearance can best be shown.[39]

A bland recommendation to verisimilitude? Not quite. This is a matter of 'penetrating', of representing 'character', of unravelling the implications of 'appearance'. Vegetable beings offer only their appearance as clues, so appearance must be immaculately reproduced. Creatures which move and act betray their sacred affiliations by behaviour as much as by appearance: both must be studied, and the representation made to incorporate the findings. And animate and inanimate things alike reveal significant relationships by context, and by (not necessarily obvious) resemblance in some detail of appearance.

The descriptions of fauna in the book of the Florentine Codex devoted to 'earthly things' make hallucinatory reading, with their precise accounts of the coloration, feeding, and nesting behaviour of a particular bird suddenly riven by a statement of its supernatural powers.[40] All creatures were revelatory, however obscurely. The raccoon, 'small, squat, cylindrical; tangle-haired', was called 'priestess' or 'little old woman', for its human hands and feet and its busy managing ways.[41] We have noted the opossum as a model of easy fecundity, its multiple children constantly suckling, wreathing its sleek body. It wailed and wept real tears when it was caught and its children taken.[42] Creatures like the deer or the rabbit declared the dangerous futility of unrestrained movement: constantly vulnerable to attack, they had abandoned social restrictions to become restless, nervous wanderers.

If first among birds were those of the greatest beauty, like the quetzal, the raptors also compelled attention: superb hunters, flesh-eaters, moving freely close to the sun. One falcon pierced the throat of its prey to drink the blood. It fed, its human watchers thought, three times a day: 'first, before the sun has risen; second, at midday; third, when the sun has set.' Therefore, it was concluded, 'this falcon gives life to Huitzilopochtli because . . . these falcons, when they eat three times a day . . . give drink to the sun'.[43] The eagle, incomparable hunter, was 'fearless . . . it can gaze into, it can face, the sun . . . it is brave, daring, a wingbeater, a screamer'. Among land animals the jaguar was pre-eminent: 'the lord of the animals', a solitary hunter, moving easily through the night; 'cleanly, noble . . . cautious, wise, proud'. Should an arrow pierce it, 'it leaps and then sits up like a man. Its eyes remain open and looking up as it dies'. A hunter who missed his shot was dispatched with lordly ease.[44] Both eagle and jaguar revealed by their smutted coats their presence and role in the great moment of the creation of the Sun, when they had followed the self-immolating deity into the flames, and so were forever participant in his glory. Serpents, also powerful, were more ambiguous. They slid sleekly through the crevices of the earth, moving easily between its dark moist interior and the sun-warmed surface. The road trodden by the traveller, with all its lurking dangers, was a 'serpent'; it could 'bite' without warning.[45] The snake called 'Yellow Lord', yellow as gourd-blossoms, spotted like a jaguar, its rattles marking its age, was said to be the leader of the serpents. Some snakes practised and tested their strike; some shook dance rattles in fury; the jaws of others gaped massively, engulfing whole living creatures, ready to swallow the world.[46]

The vegetable world, if equally significant, was somewhat more opaque. Perfumes, those most ephemeral, evocative, invasive experiences, were so clearly the possessions (or the emanations) of gods that men knew to sniff only at the outer edges of bouquets: the deep sweet fragrance at the centre belonged to Tezcatlipoca.[47] (Rather less lyrically, the effluvium of the skunk was identified as 'the fart of Tezcatlipoca'.)[48] Other plants, scentless and visually unremarkable, signalled their powers by the dreams they induced in men. The mushrooms the Mexica called 'the flesh of the gods' grew where they chose, but held riddling visions of what was to come. The small folded buttons of the peyote cactus growing untended in bitter and arid lands enclosed extraordinary experiences in its tough flesh. Infusions of the morning-glory seed or the raw native tobacco flooded him who took them with sensations more vivid and compelling than those of the daylight world. The heart-sap of the maguey cactus thickened and clouded into the sour 'milk of the gods', drawing those who drank it to the dangerous threshold of the sacred. Everywhere there was clear experiential evidence of the power of green growing things to move men's minds without their volition, and to precipitate them into contact with the sacred. Their potency, however concealed, must somehow have been signed in the detail of their appearance, which was accordingly most laboriously and precisely recorded.[49]

It is the stone serpents – to me the jewels of Mexica art, and a distinctively Mexica genre – which best exemplify the trajectory from strict realism to intimations of the sacred implied in other animal representations. (They also gloriously bridge the distance between the animal and vegetable worlds.) Along with the magnificently sculpted and precisely observed details of overlapping scales and coils and the precise bifurcations of rattles, some Mexica serpents are grandiosely and implausibly fanged, with the heavy spiral of coils echoing the whorl of a great shell. A line of scales ruffles into feathered or vegetable exuberance, and maize cobs grow obscurely among the tail rattles. Then, still in their serpent form, they writhe upright to become visions of vegetable abundance. These stone serpents, objects-becoming-symbols, mediate between a visible world of imperfect representations and the unseen world of the unchanging. It was, I would argue, that desire to 'realize' the unchanging original form which animated the Mexica impulse to model the transitory and the significant in stone regardless of the difficulty and the labour of the task.

There is a further implication of the priority given appearance. Despite the importance of behaviour, for the Mexica – as for Amerindians more generally – it was the skin, that most external and enveloping 'appearance', which constituted a creature's essence, and so stored the most formidable symbolic power. When a vision-creature appeared to a Plains Indian as a messenger from the sacred powers, the dreamer secured the skin of the 'same' animal as an essential part of his sacred medicine bundle (North-American medicine bundles, with their withered skins and claws and beaks, look like the detritus of a failed taxidermist). Catlin recorded the costume of a Blackfoot curer as a medley of animal and vegetable, but he noted especially 'the skin of the yellow bear . . . skins of snakes, and frogs, and bats'.[50] This power of the skin extended through the secondary 'skin' of the sacred garment, to face and body paint, masks, and adornments.

Mexica conviction of the transforming capacity of a donned skin or magically charged regalia threads through all their ritual action, and much of their social action too.[51] In the text of the painted world a human being was less than impressive: a featherless biped indeed, with no precedence or privilege. He had to construct himself, to make a 'face'; borrowing power through his capacity to 'take on' an appearance: a skin, a costume, a mask, insignia, a characteristic movement, a cry.

Some of the borrowings were simple and direct. Sahagún's informants noted that 'conjurers' performed their great deeds through the power of the jaguar hide – entire with claws and head and fangs – they carried with them.[52] Eagle or jaguar warriors found powerful models for conduct, for battle styles, even for moral codes, in the behaviour of animals whose appearances they facsimilated. If warriors 'were' eagles, we (as they) must be attentive to the creature's affectless yellow stare, its lordly stiff-winged flight, the sudden cresting of head feathers in rage, the scream, the dazzling stoop. The jaguar moved silently, softly, impenetrably aloof; then erupted in a rumble of thunder to transfix his victim with dread and make his kill. I had been much troubled by the Mexica insistence that the 'souls' of dead warriors, eternal sun-dancers, returned to this earth as butterflies and bright birds. The birds presented no imaginative check – hummingbirds, vibrating gloriously in the air – but butterflies? They were, for me, fragile, pathetic creatures: solitaries fluttering their erratic path to death. And then I saw butterflies in Mexico – great drifting clouds of them, gorgeously, languidly displaying; sauntering in companies – and had a sense of being suddenly granted a glimpse of Mexica warrior behaviour.

The warrior costumes of the Mexica, one-piece, forked, gaudily feathered garments facsimilating eagles or jaguars or coyotes, with their elaborate 'animal' headpieces, can easily seem absurd in our eyes: items of Disneyesque fancy dress, a very long step from the natural creatures we take to be their models. Here I think we are looking in the wrong direction. They were most deliberate concoctions, the detail of colour and form carefully prescribed. Warrior costumes required as tribute were commonly drawn from regions close to Tenochtitlan, where the protocols would be understood, and featherworkers commonly worked from designs drawn by the scribes.[53] So I suspect the models for the warrior costumes, as for other animal-related regalia, were not the living creatures directly observed but what were deduced to be the original models for those creatures: the stylized jaguar or eagle originally 'painted' in the original divine text, and then painted again by the human scribe to guide the featherworkers' realization.[54]

4

While all artists were honoured as 'Tolteca', we have seen that it was the scribe or *tlacuilo*, 'he who paints in the red and black ink', who was acknowledged supreme, for he was professionally concerned with the mystery of signs. Yet it is with a sense of shock that we turn from the subtle rhythms of the sculpture, powerful in any canon, to the Mexican codices. Maya codices, vase paintings, and figurines offer exuberant celebrations of details of costume and jewellery, marvellously fluid contour lines, practised techniques to suggest three-dimensional space, and precisely observed and rendered human postures – and, through those same inspired brushstrokes, finely nuanced expressions of relationships in a very human 'divine' world. Central Mexican codices seem by contrast like awkward cartoons drawn by an obsessive child: the figures vestigial, obdurately two-dimensional; the fields of crude colour sealed with a ferocious black line.[55] We know the ancient Mexica specially cultivated the *cempoalli*, the stiff bright orange and golden marigolds with the vivid green stems and leaves which compete with equally stiff and bold flowers in Mexican markets today. The taste was for clear bright colours: candid reds and yellows jostling deep blues and greens. They were sensitive to the bold colours of their pictured representations, not to 'natural' pastels. There is no shading, no modelling. Proportions coherent in the seen world are triumphantly 'wrong' in the painted: heads are huge, torsos and limbs short; a solitary eye glares beside a vast nose, or is histrionically sealed by death. Arms jut abruptly from torsos, hands from arms, with a terrible energy which comes as much from unconcern for physical plausibility as from their radical simplifications. The power and control of that black 'frame line' declares we are not faced here with drafting incompetence, but with a chosen rejection of 'realism'.

And a chosen rejection of the human. The pictographic books do not present a human world. Where men and women appear they do so as emblems of (usually naked) humanity, not as individuals. The 'painted deities' are schematically human in form, with heads, torsos, limbs, but they are supernatural entities, compiled out of elemental symbols and ciphers and significant colours. Even the representations of named rulers participate in this emblematic quality. Pose, position, and gesture do not catch moments in human life, but declare eternal relationships. Garments do not curve to flesh: they stand stiff as banners, and, like banners, inform. The 'human' forms sustaining the complex regalia are mere frames, skeletal structures for the items which constitute the person through constructing the conventional icon. Meaning is stored in the bright precision of garments, paint, accoutrements, and the most simple gestural interactions: snapshots from cosmic narratives; elemental oppositions and conflicts and mergings, with particular objects flagged to trigger recollection. Each figure, like each page, is an idea or an assemblage of ideas, as much writing as picture, or perhaps, given the importance of location and colour, more map than either.

Walter Ong is one among several commentators who have had much to say about the different sensibilities shaped by primary dependence on what he calls the 'chirographic' as against the oral mode.[56] One of his key discriminations in distinguishing the sensibility of a literary from an oral culture arises from his claim that writing, by fixing thought, allows 'study': the systematic and sequential analysis of ideas. His notion that for study to be systematic 'words' need to be arranged sequentially perches on a very narrow cultural base. Mexica pictographs, with their complex iconography and careful distribution on the page, certainly aided thought, and men brooded over them.[57] Like the monumental sculptures they so much resembled, the painted books were a flexible mode, allowing the introduction of novel propositions by the insertion of an unexpected symbol or the use of an unexpected colour in the representation of a particular sacred entity, so inviting speculation on the problematics of the sacred world and its relationship to our visible and defective copy. That is, the pictographs could generate discourse, not merely record received information. The class of specialist priests who painted and expounded them were honoured not as clerkly inscribers of fixed wisdom but as guides, custodians, and exegetes of it. In their form the pictographs resemble an elaborate ritual object – a shaman's bundle, perhaps, with its careful arrangement of 'natural' objects rendered symbolic by their significant use. If the painted books could not be 'read' as we read a linear sequence of conventionalized representations of sounds, so reconstituting speech, the exegetical voice was cued by the images and their placement and colour. The painted representation was encoded: a system of ciphers, most accessible to the alert and experienced, but never transparent.[58]

Mexica pictorial technique, like Mexica 'aesthetics' more generally, seems to have operated through a kind of surrealism achieved by dislocation: the abstraction of objects from their 'natural' setting and then their framed juxtapositions and oppositions with other similarly dislocated objects, so that resemblances, differences, possible relationships, and transformations could be reflected upon.[59] In spoken Nahuatl we find a developed predilection for the linking of two words in tension to encapsulate a conventional notion. This often involves a slight but telling shift in perspective, as in the turning of a crystal: 'skirt and blouse' for woman as a sexual being; 'face and heart' for the person; 'flower and song' to mean poetry; 'water and hill' for place; 'jade and fine plumes' for value; perhaps most poignantly 'flower-death' for death in battle or on the killing stone: a habit of mind which sought meaning in the juxtaposition of the superficially unlike. Selected and formally arranged out of a store of objects-become-symbols, the pictographs function within that same mental field. Straddling the space between concrete and abstract, actual and ideal, they point, as it were, in both directions. This tension lends a quite particular potency and immediacy to Mexica symbolic forms. It also hints at a distinctive understanding of the relations and mediation between thought and the perceived world, the abstract and the actual, the sacred and the mundane.

5

Mexica selective naturalism provides an extraordinarily flexible vocabulary for a metaphysical commentary firmly grounded in the actual. Single objects (those precise representations of squashes, gourds, snakes, grasshoppers, in sumptuously burnished stone) took power by their abstraction from their natural setting and substance, and their casting in enduring form. So they were made available for sustained and systematic contemplation. Then particular features of these significant constructs were further selected and abstracted, and used to build more complex, more abstract, and more penetrating statements.[60] Mexican deity images, some interesting exceptions aside, were rarely anthropomorphic; as Weismann has put it: 'an idol does not picture the god, but represents the godhead'.[61] The face of Tlaloc, the Rain God who ruled with Huitzilopochtli in Tenochtitlan, was formed from curving snakes and impressively tusked, with nothing human about it at all. The stone 'Celestial Princesses', representing the spirits of women dead in childbed, are nightmare projections of pure malevolence. Perhaps the most famous and formidable example of the sacred female is the great stone image of Coatlicue or 'Snake Skirt'. 'She' stands massive, four-square yet with a disquieting forward lean, more architectural than human. Her bulk, wreathed in the symbols of agricultural fertility, represents Coatepec, 'Snake Mountain', the great body of the earth itself, while the twin jets of blood from her severed neck, which form the serpent heads of her face, recall the paired shrines to Huitzilopochtli and Tlaloc in which the great pyramid, Coatepec, culminated. She is compiled out of snakes, human hands and hearts, animal paws and talons, to compose so powerful an image that even the dumbly gazing outsider hears the threatening mutter of a terrible intelligibility.[62]

There is a different but related extravagance in the representations of Xipe Totec, the Flayed Lord, god of the early spring, always represented with the same terrible simplicity. We see him as a naked man enveloped in the flayed skin of a human, the stretched face skin completely masking the living face beneath. (Typically the hands of the flayed victim dangle uselessly at the wrists, still attached by strips of skin, and the skin was worn with the bloodied side outermost: Xipe, like all the maize representations, was a red god.) Faithful to our view of things, we identify the god as the living man within, regarding the enshrouding skin as an external thing. But that is not what we are being shown, again and again, in his image: Xipe Totec is presented before us immediately, as the 'dead' enveloping skin. The same point is made by the less immediately shocking but more subtly perturbing images of Quetzalcoatl, 'Precious-Feather Snake'.[63] In some representations the tendency for the naturalistic snakeskin to break into plumage intensifies until the snake-creature is a complex whirl of long feathers, the split tongue scrolled and elongated, the mouth deep and elaborately curled, and sometimes implausibly fanged. Then the body thickens and lifts, until it rears upright. And then we see the 'human' face framed in the open jaws, the 'human' hands and feet glimpsed in the shining feathered swirl. We are not looking at a man swallowed by a feathered snake, but at Quetzalcoatl, an integrated being in his own plumed skin, the lower jaws of the 'snake' his necklace.

One part of the lesson here, that the visible surface equals the real, invites a reconsideration of the plethora of Mexica 'masks'. The use and meaning of these objects, usually superbly carved, is unclear. The eyes and mouths are typically deepened for inlays, and the ears perforated for earplugs. Some at least have been firmly identified as 'masks' of particular deities from the name-signs carved into an inner surface.[64] Among them are masks of Xipe Totec, the outer skin taut, the lips, eyes and nostrils of the face visible under the stretched skin and stretched lips forming the face. But are they masks in our sense, or are they alive, at once manifestations of power, and protection from it? A number of the famous Mexica mosaic masks, like their stone counterparts, have solid eyepieces. They are not intended to be looked through. Are they representations of the 'faces' – the external visible aspect – of aspects of particular deities? Even where the mask allows the wearer vision, the transformation of appearance presumably transformed that which was within.

The 'cultural form' (or form of the culture) which ordered the organization of those 'natural' and made objects into their complex constructs was a quincunx. The linguist A. L. Becker has alerted us to what he has called 'the iconicity of the medium', the distinctive pattern 'which connects the items of learning' in any particular culture. Becker arrived at this recognition through learning how Burmese script was shaped. He came to realize 'how that kind of written figure (a center and marks above, below, before, and after it) was for many Southeast Asians a mnemonic frame: everything in the encyclopedic repertoire of terms was ordered that way: directions (the compass rose), disease, gods, colors, social roles, foods – everything. It was the natural shape of remembered knowledge, a basic icon. . . . It was a root metaphor, the stuff that holds meaning together – just as our sequential writing lines up so well with our sequential tense system or our notions of causality and history'.[65]

In Mesoamerica something of the same formal frame – of four 'quarters' and a central or fifth direction, each with its distinctive associations of colours, qualities, time-spans – was recognized as the shape of the world, and that which organized the world through time, and therefore used to order representations of serious matters. Once seen it is ubiquitous. The quincunx form underlaid the representations in the sacred books, and defined their relationships. It structured calendars, the material and administrative shape of the city, the monumental sculptures, the pyramids. It ordered song as it shaped dance, sustaining its complex choreography.[66] It informed the patterns of weaving and embroidery, and shaped the song-poems, the structures of the main temple precinct, and the images of deities men constructed on the frame of a living body or a skeleton of sacred dough.[67] And it controlled the careful orchestration of groups and formalized movement in high ceremonial, in which the priests, supreme artificers in the Mexica world, sought to realize, however briefly, the enduring world of the sacred.[68]

10

Ritual: The World Transformed, the World Revealed

A successful interpretive practice renders audible what once went without saying.
Stephen Greenblatt, 'Exorcism into Art'[1]

I

First, to clear the ground. Historians are wary of ritual, with some reason. Private rituals are private, and tend to remain so: the individual and idiosyncratic are closed to us. We know that public and therefore more observable rituals relate to the societies which produce them variously, always partially, and usually obliquely. And having been taught irony in such matters, studiously disenchanted, we tend to think most easily of 'religious' ritual activity in Malinowskian terms, as a form of 'primitive technology' in the management of persons or forces, our first and often our last question of any particular ritual being 'What was it thought to effect?'[2]

That blunt question is notoriously awkward to answer. Precisely how devotees think their acts of worship influence themselves and their gods is always difficult to unravel, especially as these are matters the worshippers typically leave vague, even to themselves. With the Mexica, the disentangling of what we label 'sympathetic' from 'contagious' magic, and their differentiation from attempts to gain the attention of the deity and to establish a particular kind of relationship, is a complicated, frustrating and finally inconclusive matter. However, an analysis of the crisis occasion of the New Fire Ceremony, already described in an earlier chapter from the perspective of a model of dependence, could shed some light on the question.[3] The ceremony, performed on a hilltop between Culhuacan and Itztlapalapan to mark the close of the old Bundle of Years, and to welcome and possibly to assist in the beginning of the new, offers a reasonably explicit sequence of actions which ought to reveal something of Mexica notions of the reach of human agency in ritual matters.[4]

The ending of the old cycle was understood to be a time of acute jeopardy, marking a moment when the world could erupt into chaos if the precarious balance of the great sustaining forces of this Fifth Sun should lurch out of control, and men, world, and gods vanish all together. Yet the thronging priests took no action through what were recognized to be the moments of greatest danger: they merely observed the night sky until the constellation of the Pleiades passed the zenith. Then 'they knew . . . that the end of the world was not then'; that 'the movement of the heavens had not ceased'.[5] Nonetheless, this world was thought to be still in jeopardy, and it was then that they acted, one priest making a fire on the breast of an illustrious captive. That ignition through the whirling of the firesticks contained an inherent degree of chance and uncertainty: even the most experienced firelighter occasionally fails. We glimpse the designated Fire Priest's nervous preliminary practice: arrived at the place, he 'bore continuously with his fire drill; he went about making trials with his drill', because it was claimed that if fire could not be drawn, '[the sun] would be destroyed forever; all would be ended; there would evermore be night . . . and the demons of darkness would descend to eat men'.[6]

Thus it seems that the flaring of the fire was understood as a determining factor in the fate of the world: without the priest's skilled actions the fire would not light. Did man's action therefore control the fate of the world, however momentarily? The matter is complex. The Fire Priest had put on the adornments of a god: had he by that adorning ceased to be human and become a puppet of the gods through which they manifested the future, or, perhaps, an instrument through which they effected it? We are told the flame was 'a signal that the world would continue'. But to whom did it signify? Did it sign to the waiting people the success of the priest's activity, or was it understood as being made by a suprahuman power – the same power which controlled the movement of the stars – with the priest no more than accessory to a predetermined event? If the New Fire 'descended' through the Fire Drill as through a conduit, as when the sky-god Mixcoatl-Camaxtli first brought fire to earth, the implication would be that while the priest's expertise facilitated the process, it did not cause it. 'Interpretation' carries large consequences here, with one account implying some human influence, and the alternative reducing the successful lighting of the fire to a divine indication that the world would indeed continue. While there can be no certainty, the balance, I think, tilts to the latter, especially as a Mexica conviction that as humans they were able to act to postpone the end of the world would be in tension with their proclaimed submission to 'destiny': that life – their own, that of the human group, and that of the world – was beyond human control.[7]

Immediately after the fire was struck the priest opened the breast and tore the heart from the captive and with it 'fed' the fire. The fire grew from the chest cavity (aided, presumably, by more combustible fuel) to eat the whole body, and when full-fed was transported to the major temples, and thence to the waiting populace. The captive's death was not the issue here, having no influence on the fate of the world: if the stars had ceased to move or the fire failed to kindle the killing would be otiose. But when the fire was lit it was man's flesh which fed it to strength. However, while the fire was essential to mankind, its waxing or waning would have no effect upon the fate of the world. I therefore take the giving of the noble captive's heart and flesh to the fire from the moment of its blooming as a gratuitous action made by men to remind the gods of their dependence, their need and their devotion. Moctezoma was perhaps seeking to increase the symbolic value of the offering by instructing that the captive's name should include the word 'Xiu', 'Turquoise', in compliment to 'Turquoise Lord', the God of Fire, and to 'Turquoise Prince', the Sun. When the watching populace saw the flames leap up they all (even the babies) had their ears cut, and spattered the fast-flowing blood repeatedly in the direction of the fire's glow, intent in their turn on initiating their own individual and household relationship with this most powerful lord. In my view a close reading of the ritual allows little direct efficacy to human action. The sacrificial acts of priests and laity alike indicate the determination to renew a relationship with the divine powers interrupted by the completion of the old Bundle of Years.

When the New Fire was distributed to the commoners from the Houses of Youth in each calpulli, there was enthusiastic brawling as men burnt themselves in the struggle to be first to seize a burning brand and bear it off to their homes. A little rough play after the nervous strain of the night, or another attempt to establish relationships of priority in the always competitive business of securing a patron's favour? Or did that action have no singular and exclusive meaning, but felicitously subsumed them all in a celebratory moment of relief at anxieties passed and joy in the re-establishment of the routine? (The Mexica were not a people who took the habitual for granted.) Perhaps, after all, the point lay not in the efficacy, but in the affect: in the uncertainties suffered, the relationships solicited, the joy at the release of tension.

The men and women of any particular culture are trained in the great reflexive, reiterative texts of that culture: in myths and stories, in games and play, in common-sense pragmatics, in aesthetic and moral preferences; their imaginations stretched and shaped to particular themes and possibilities.[8] It is these multiple prior texts in their richness and complexity which web the space between the mundane and the supramundane, lacing the world of ritual to the world of the everyday, and each to the sacred. While Mexica ritual can be usefully considered as a technique of propitiation or an attempted regularization of 'nature', the major thrust was not instrumental, but rather aesthetic, expressive, interrogative, and creative. In what follows I will review these aspects of Mexica ritual which could be regarded as manipulative and 'instrumental'. Then I will explore the metaphysical and aesthetic implications, and finally the deeper themes of the emotional, social and psychological dimensions of ritual engagement.

2

Anthropologists have sought to locate part of the addictive power of ritual representations in their capacity to isolate, clarify and dramatically present key experiences lifted out of the wearying muddle and chronic abrasions of 'ordinary' life.[9] We have seen something of those abrasions in Tenochtitlan; in the tension of the feast with its intolerance of equality; the miseries of the slippery pole of warrior ambition; the panoply of exemplary 'game' performances of utter exertion, with the prospect of total victory or total defeat; the gambler's passionate playing with time. The imagination feeds on experience, as experience is fed by the imagination. The Mexica conviction of the inescapably contestful relationship between men and the painful necessity of inequality – a conviction honed, rehearsed and sustained by the experience of central social institutions, formal and informal – also framed their vision of men's relationship with the sacred, and infused it with its peculiar poignancy. We have identified some of the contours of those obsessive themes from the mundane world in the city's most public rituals, where agonistic events and anxieties of daily life were rehearsed, reflected upon, and ultimately 'redressed' in the largest sense by their location within the infinitely expansive sphere of the sacred.[10] Ordinary experience, knowledge and actions were rendered significant by being shown in their great implications; their 'incandescent objectivity', in Victor Turner's incandescent phrase: the dross of the everyday brought to yield its hidden light of transcendental significance.

The public ritual theatre of Tenochtitlan had other, more calculated attractions, which have tended to mesmerize outsiders' attention, but the Mexica also found it mesmeric. The 'Aztec State' was, as we have seen, a conscious and recent human construct, with the great city and its public ceremonies its material reflex. In their relations with the outside world, most especially with those other towns of the valley all too familiar with their humble beginnings, the Mexica leadership was intent on a very difficult feat: the transformation of a politics of remorseless competition into one of effortless, cosmically prescribed supremacy, a sacred order focussed on and displayed in Tenochtitlan. (Just how little assent they exacted to this proposition was to be made clear by the agile opportunism of 'friends' and 'enemies' alike during the vicissitudes of the conquest period.) These external politics of ritual cannot be divorced from internal responses, given that the attempted transformation required a shift in self-perception among all the inhabitants of the city. The Mexica had somehow to create themselves as a collective entity, incorporating individuals and groups of different origins, and therefore doubtful loyalties, along the way. Consciousness of temporality lent an exquisite edge to the glamour of the construction of both city and people, given Mexica sensitivity to the fragility of human arrangements. So they elaborated their internal ritual life for the delectation of the gods, the celebration of collectivities, the making, and the unmaking, of individuals, and the intensification of a Mexica ethos consonant with their expanded role and its increasing burdens and rewards.

We tend to think of ritual, especially state-building ritual, as fixed and

Artefacts

The Spanish View of Ritual Killings. Codex Magliabechiano, mid-sixteenth century, small volume of European paper. 92 pages, 15.5 × 21.5 cm. Ms. Magl. CI XIII (Banco Raro 232), Magl. XIII, 11, 3, Biblioteca Nazionale Centrale of Florence. Reproduced in facsimile as *The Book of the Life of the Ancient Mexicans, Containing An Account of Their Rites and Superstitions,* intro., trans. and commentary by Zelia Nuttall (Berkeley: University of California Press, 1903).

While some of the details are 'right' (the bloodiness of killings, the killing stone close to the edge of the pyramid platform, the technique of depressing the victim's limbs to arch the chest) the representations are crude, and obviously Christian and colonial in their conceptualizations, as is, of course, the Spanish commentary.

'This is a pole that is set with an arm like a cross, like those used here for feathers, which among them was like a flag that was [placed] in front of the temple when they sacrificed; and it is the first of this next figure. In the rest is when they sacrificed Indians, how they carried them to the top. And they flung one on his back on top of a stone, and they pulled out his heart. And another held him by his feet so that he would not move. And this was Tlamacaz, which means greatest of these executioners; and to do this, his head and hair were tied with a white cloak. [They did this] in order to pull out the heart to anoint the lips of the demon'. (The Codex Magliabechiano, 69 verso, Spanish commentary, trans. Zelia Nuttall)

73

'This figure demonstrates the abominable thing that the Indians did on the day they sacrificed men to their idols. After [the sacrifice] they placed many large earthen cooking jars of that human meat in front of the idol they called Mictlantecutli, which means lord of the place of the dead, as is mentioned in other parts [of this book]. And they gave and distributed it to the nobles and the overseers, and to those who served in the temple of the demon, whom they called tlamacazqui [priests]. And these [persons] distributed among their friends and families that [flesh] and these [persons] which they had given [to the god as a human victim]. They say that it tasted like pork meat tastes now. And for this reason pork is very desirable among them.' (The Codex Magliabechiano, 72 verso, Spanish commentary, trans. Zelia Nuttall)

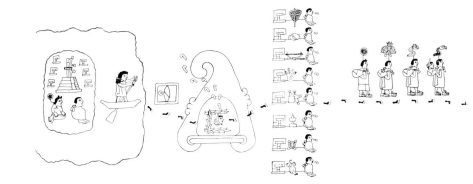

Codex Boturini, 'Tira de la peregrinación'. Amate paper roll manuscript of 549 cm. dimensions, 21-1/2 pages, 19.8 × 25.5 cm. Mexico City, early Colonial? Biblioteca Nacional de Antropología e Historia (35–8). The Codex Boturini, possibly painted in Tenochtitlan under Spanish direction, tells of the migration of the Mexica people from their island homeplace of 'Aztlan' ('The Place of Whiteness') to their early days in the Valley of Mexico. The story is drawn in black outline, without colours, and the figures are small and unimpressive, as befitted human affairs. The black footprints indicate direction and sequence.

The migration begins with the people leaving an island homeland (which has six houses and a temple: these are no rough nomads) on One Flint Knife, the daysign which marks the point where the footsteps begin. They pause at 'Curving Mountain', Culhuacan, where their god Huitzilopochtli, represented as a head emerging from a hummingbird's beak, speaks to his people from within the hill. Eight tribes, each with its leader and house, and identified by its name glyph, follow the four god-bearers, the first carrying the god in his backpack. (The last 'god-bearer' is probably a woman.) A temple to Huitzilopochtli is erected at the first place of temporary settlement, and five men eat in an egalitarian circle. The tree overlooking the temple breaks, in augury of discord and ill-fortune, and the weeping leaders consult with Huitzilopochtli, who orders the Mexica to proceed alone. They shoot an eagle, and make their first human offerings to the god, the victims being thrown back over trees and cactus plants. The story continues in terms of years spent in different places, and sketches the Mexica's political vicissitudes in the valley in a more skeletal form. It does not include the arrival at that other island in a lake which Huitzilopochtli, still leading his people, declared to be their destination, and their destiny.

The New Fire ceremony. Codex Borbonicus, section of p. 34. Screenfold manuscript, 39 × 39.5 cm. Mexico City, pre-conquest or early Colonial. Bibliothèque de l'Assemblée Nationale, Paris; complete true-colour facsimile edition, Akademische Druck-u. Verlagsanstalt: Codices Selecti (Series C, Mesoamerican Manuscript), Vol. 44. The Codex Borbonicus is a barkpaper strip 47 feet long, painted on both sides, and folded concertina-fashion into a 'book' of 38 almost square (39.5 × 39 cm) leaves. It consists of a *tonalamatl* or divinatory calendar of eighteen (originally twenty) pages, each representing a thirteen-day period; two pages picturing the Lords of the Night associated with the Year Bearers of the fifty-two-year cycle; a third section devoted to the representation of festivals of the seasonal cycle; and two final pages of the four which once recorded information relating to the fifty-two-year round.

Beginning from the top of the page represented here: Huitzilopochtli stands before his pyramid, in the year 2 Reed (the sign to the left). A pole with a blue and white banner flies from the shrine capping the temple, so connecting the ceremony with the festival of Panquetzaliztli, the 'Raising of the Banners', which celebrates Huitzilopochtli's birth. To the right a hill topped by a fire drill indicates the location of the ceremony, at Huixachtlan or Huixachtecatl (see place glyph of a tree with three leaves, beside a hill topped by a fire drill) between Culhuacan and Ixtapalapa. The dark footprints which denote sequence take the new fire past the pregnant woman enclosed in the elevated granary, closely watched by an armed warrior lest she transform into a cannibal monster, and past the men, women and children waiting in their houses. In this representation all members of the laity are wearing maguey leaf masks as protection against the destructive forces of the earth powers. The barefooted, white-clad figures may have been commoners, but not necessarily: in this greatest ritual of renewal, where all fires were doused, domestic utensils thrown away, and the houses immaculately swept, plain dress and humble bearing would be appropriate for all ranks, save, of course, for the priests. Note that the men sit in front, with the women sitting neatly back on their heels behind them. The lively child squirming in a woman's lap is being kept awake, as sleep could allow its invasion by the dangerous forces abroad, and the small, weak creature would turn into a mouse.

The flame is delivered to four Fire Priests of the main temple complex, who wear ornaments associated with the dead. They feed the new fire with the old 'Bundles of Years', the four sets (each showing four brands) probably representing the four thirteen-year segments of the fifty-two-year cycle. Seven other Fire Priests who had 'presented' their various deities in their distinctive regalia for the procession to the hill also bring their Year Bundles to be consumed. All the priests wear the black paint of penance.

Mexica feathered headdress. Quetzal plumes and other feathers, goldwork, 166 × 175 cm. Museum für Volkerkunde, Vienna, Aztec, Ausst. Nr. 103. This great headdress, almost 46 inches in height, contained over 500 quetzal tail-feathers. By 1566, its Mexica origin had been forgotten, it being referred to in an inventory as a 'Moorish hat'. It was recovered, along with two other pieces of the eight surviving examples of Mexica featherwork, in the eighteenth century, from a storage chest of a castle in the Tyrol.

The headdress was almost certainly a gift presented by Moctezoma, the Mexica ruler, to Cortés, either as one of the sumptuous objects sent via ambassadors while Cortés was on his march towards the imperial city, or while he was a 'guest' within it. The headdress was handled with sufficient care to be transported intact back to Spain, despite its size and fragility, and it was not destroyed for its goldwork, indicating its curiosity value. Both these factors imply its presentation during the early and relatively pacific period of Spanish–Mexica relations, as do the messages it conveys. The type and value of the feathers used, and the high level of skill displayed in its making, identify it as a royal object, most probably a piece of priestly regalia. It is constructed from 500 green-gold quetzal tail-plumes with some shorter quetzal plumes, blue and red feathers and golden disks. The quetzal plumes originated in Guatemala. The blue feathers came from the *xiuhtototl*, the 'Turquoise Bird', whose range is the hot lands from lowland Vera Cruz to Chiapas. The red feathers are possibly those of the Pacific parrot, or from the underwing of the *tlauhquechol*, the roseate spoonbill, found especially along the Gulf Coast, or from the scarlet macaw. So the headdress simultaneously mapped the historic growth and the scope of the Mexica tribute empire. It also conveyed not only the sumptuous presentation but something of the qualities of physical grace and control required of a luminary in the full splendour of Mexica ritual performance, while the feathers in their colours and associations – for example, the vibrant blue-green of the quetzal plumes, quintessential symbol of fertility – spoke of sacred things.

Mexica power and Mexica values were also embodied in the craftsmanship, which is extraordinary: the feathers, individually tied by maguey thread to a coarse-meshed fabric on a wicker frame, retain their freshness and delicacy after half a millenium, and the goldwork is impeccable, leaving the most fragile feather filament quite unmarred – and all this achieved with the simplest tools. (It also suggests the choices cultures make between developing a complex technology, as against remarkably high levels of human manual dexterity and precision.) As for the aesthetics: perhaps it is wrong to speak of 'ephemerality' in an object which has survived so long, but its beauty, like the technique of its making, makes clear that featherworkers were as much concerned with the play of light as with colour, attaching the feathers lightly so they were free to ripple with the lightest breath of wind. Even in the unnatural stillness of its glass case the headdress is irridescent, and seems to quiver.

All this was laid before Cortés as a statement of pride: a high card in the battle for status. It was 'read' as a gesture of submission.

Opposite: **The Eagle Man flies upwards.** Upright drum (huehuetl), wood, height 96 cm. From Malinalco, State of Mexico. Museo de Arqueología e Historia del Estado de México, Tenango del Valle, Mexico. The complex symbol with its four flanges is 'Four Movement' or 'Earthquake', signifying at once the Fifth Sun and its destined end. The central figure in the upper band is dressed in an elaborate costume with sweeping eagle-feather wings and quetzal-feather tail. He carries a stylized flower and a fan, and the elaborate song-scrolls of 'poetry' are scattered about him as he flies upwards: a warrior spirit released to the Sun. Eagle and Jaguar 'warriors' celebrating the ascending warrior flourish the paper banners of sacrifice as they dance, and their speech scrolls form the Water and Fire sign which stands for Sacred War. The eagle's tail and wing-feathers are studded with sacrificial knives. The creatures weep as they dance. Are they already victims, or do they weep in ecstatic commitment to their ultimate fate?

Malinalco, to the southwest of Tenochtitlan, where the drum was found, appears to have been particularly devoted to the cult of the Eagle and Jaguar warriors. Its temple, carved out of the rock three hundred feet above the valley floor, has as its entrance the open jaws of a serpent, and contains two crouching jaguars and carvings of eagle and jaguar ceremonial seats. An adjacent chanber shows traces of an elaborate fresco of eagle and jaguar warriors.

Warrior costumes. *Codex Mendoza, c.* 1541, p. 64, lower half. 72 pages of European paper, 32.7 × 23 cm. Bodleian Library, Oxford, MS. Arch. Selden A. 1. This page represents the changes in warrior costumes and allocated cloaks with the taking of 2, 3, 4 and 5 or 6 warrior captives. The figure on the lower right is in 'civilian' dress, but his feathered hair decorations and the design and length of his sweeping cloak mark him as a military leader.

Quetzalcoatl and Tezcatlipoca. Codex Borbonicus, section from p. 22. The two deities are in danced counterpoise. Quetzalcoatl wears his necklace of seashells, and his wind-trumpet mask as the God of Winds, while Tezcatlipoca wears his crown of stars and a great shell pendant. Locational position, gesture and each item of adornment are most precisely indicated. There is no hint of human 'interaction': these are emblems animated.

A page from a *tonalamatl*, a 'Book of Days'. Codex Borbonicus 3. This gives the count for a thirteen-day period of the 260 days of the divinatory year, from which personal destinies were predicted. The larger space is filled by the representation of the patron deity of the thirteen days, with attributes and associated objects and animals. Here the patron is Tepeyollotl-Tezcatlipoca, seizing a prisoner by the warrior lock. (The hairlock carried special potency because the *tonalli* was understood to be located in the top of the head, so the taking of the lock accordingly weakened the victim and strengthened the captor.) The days are indicated by their cyclical dates (e.g. 'Three House') within the twenty sections of thirteen days, along with two series of gods: the thirteen gods of the daylight hours, each accompanied by his or her appropriate bird, and the nine 'Lords of (the hours of) the Night'. The thirteen daysigns and their deities are arranged in a right-angled movement, the dots and bars (each bar equalling five) constituting the number. The seasonal calendar comprised eighteen months of twenty days each, with five days 'out of time', yielding 365 days. The two cycles intermeshed to repeat a particular 'day' as specified in each system only once in every 52 years, which period constituted a 'Bundle of Years'. The significances of possible permutations were multiple: for example, 260 days, the average period for human gestation, divided by the significant number five (the Fifth Sun, and the four directions plus the direction of the center) also yields fifty-two.

'The Face of Battle'. The goddess Tlazolteotl giving birth. Aplite with garnets. Height 20.2 cm. Dumbarton Oaks Research Library and Collections, Washington, D.C.

The bountiful 'Milk Tree' for children who died before they were weaned, and at whose bountiful breasts they suckled until they were returned to earth to be reborn. Vaticanus Latinus 3738 (*Codex Vaticanus* A., 'Rios'), p. 4. Manuscript, each 46 × 29 cm. See Pasztory, pp. 8, 9. Valley of Mexico, Early Colonial, *c.* 1566–89, Biblioteca Apostolica Vaticanus, Rome.

Squash. Aragonite (tecali), length 134 cm. The British Museum, London, no. 1952 Am. 18.1.

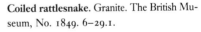

Coiled rattlesnake. Granite. The British Museum, No. 1849. 6–29.1.

Coatlicue, 'Snake Skirt'. Stone, height 3.5 m. Museo Nacional de Antropología, Mexico City. With her animal claws and feet, and the fangs at elbow and knee, Coatlicue subsumes the malignant spirits of women dead in childbed. Her shrunken breasts and her necklace of human hearts and hands declare she feeds mankind not on milk, but blood. But if she is an object of terror, she is also the eternal victim. The twin snakes emerging from her neck signify the jets of blood which sprang from the necks of the women ritually decapitated to secure its fructifying powers, as indicated by her snake-skirt of abundant vegetable growth. This is less a recognition of 'duality' than of the reciprocal action of destruction and fruition.

On the underside of the great image there is a carving not of the Earth Monster, as we might expect, but of Tlaloc the Rain God, in the squatting position associated with the Earth Monster.

Coyolxauqhui Relief. Volcanic Stone. Diameter 330 cm. Templo Mayor Project, Tenochtitlan, Phase IV, circa 1454. Museo Instituto Nacional de Antropología e Historia, Mexico City. She lies as much exploded as dismembered by the force of the attack, bones jutting from the torn flesh: the limbs, the severed head, the plumes and the bells caught in the terrible dynamism of the moment of that annihilating violence; the jagged rhythm of the ruptured wardance controlled in that firm oval form. But all the violence, all the furious detail, is spun to the periphery. Dominating and controlling the centre of the oval is the meadowy expanse of her upper body, smooth, naked. The lower body, twisted away from the viewer, is girdled with snakes. Above them the breasts, the centre of the whole composition, are long, flawless, sleek as lilies: the elusive, eternal objects of desire. See pp. 199–200.

Quetzalcoatl figure. Upright feathered serpent. Stone, Museum für Volkerkunde, Vienna, Aztec, Ausst. Nr. 103.

Quetzalcoatl. Red porphyry. Musée de l'Homme, Paris, Aztec, No. 78. 1. 59. In some representations the tendency for the naturalistic snakeskin to break into plumage intensifies until the snake-creature is a complex whirl of long feathers, the split tongue scrolled and elongated, the mouth deep and elaborately curled, and sometimes implausibly fanged. Then the body thickens and lifts, until it rears upright. And then we see the 'human' face framed in the open jaws, the 'human' hands and feet glimpsed in the shining feathered swirl. We are not looking at a man swallowed by a feathered snake, but at Quetzalcoatl, an integrated being in his own plumed skin, the lower jaws of the 'snake' his necklace. See Chapter 9, section 5.

The festival of Ochpaniztli. Codex Borbonicus, section of p. 30. In the lower section a priest in a garb similar to those of the priests on the temple platform faces the small figure of a woman in the dress of Chicomecoatl, 'Sustenance Woman', and holding a broom. Above is the next stage of the ceremony, when the priest who has become 'Toci', wearing the skin of the sacrificed ixiptla, stands on her pyramid platform. 'She' appears in Toci's full regalia, including the great bannered paper headdress of the maize goddess, and is flanked by her priests, who wear the black body-paint of penance, the Tlaloc headdress, and the blue, white, yellow or red of their appropriate directional 'quadrant'. Other priests in their godly regalia flourish their identifying accoutrements. Toci's escort of Huaxtecs, with their distinctive conical hats and their giant phalluses, process around the platform. Three dancers wearing animal masks appear at the right, while a procession of five priests moves across the top of the page. Omitted is all reference to warrior involvement in the festival. The accounts of the other seasonal festivals in the Codex Borbonicus are similarly selective. Is it possible that they were copied shortly after the conquest, and deliberately underplayed reference to the warrior cult?

Opposite, top: **Deerskin screenfold.** 17.5 × 17.5 cm. Pre-conquest. *Codex Fejéváry-Mayor,* p. 1. National Museums and Galleries on Merseyside (MI 2014). This is no mere decorative 'illustration'. Like the more famous 'Calendar Stone', it contains Central Mexican understandings of managing time and comprehending space in a precise mapping of complex information, with each item, in its colour, location and relation, conveying information: a complete text to be deciphered.

The East, the Place of Dawn, lies at the top of the page, with the North to the right and the South to the left, as if one were looking up into the sky. The page is conventionally 'read' to represent the quadrants of time and space, each with its colour, bird, and tree, and with the Nine Lords of the Night, patrons of the sequence of days in the tonalpoalli cycle, located in their appropriate segments. In the East, the direction of abundance, light, and the colour red, with its calendrical symbol the Reed, the manifestation of the Sun in his radiant youth faces Obsidian Blade. The North, a cold and sinister region, associated with death, the underworld and the colour black, and under the sign Flint Knife, represents the Lord of Death, Mictlantecutli, with Cinteotl, Young Maize Lord. The West, the region of women, with the colour white and the sign House, where the Sun is delivered to the place of the dead, pairs Xochiquetzal with 'Jade Skirt', goddess of sweet waters. In the South, the 'place of thorns, the blue region under the sign of the Rabbit, and so of unstable character, the rain god Tlaloc (identifiable by his eye volutes) faces Tepeyollotl, 'Heart of the Mountain'. At the centre is Xiutecutli, the God of Fire. The outer band of 260 dots represents the 26 positions of the Sacred Round, with the twenty signs inserted to mark each interval of thirteen days. The four 'Year Bearer' signs, Rabbit, Reed, Flint Knife and House, so named because only these four signs can begin each thirteen-year cycle of the 52-year Calendar Round, mark the furthest point of each diagonal.

The four Year Bearers simultaneously represent the four 'worlds' or Suns prior to this Fifth Sun. The Fifth Direction of the Centre belongs to the 'Oldest God', the God of Fire, and links the nine levels of the Underworlds with the Earth, while the Fire God as Xiutecutli, Turquoise Lord, connects this world to his son Xiupilli, Turquoise Prince, the Sun God, and so to the thirteen celestial levels. (The Mexica saw the central point on the Axis Mundi, the *tlalxico* or 'Navel of the World', as marked by the main temple of Tenochtitlan). Each 'direction' brings its own force to bear on the movement of Time, and on the Earth, the dynamic tension between them sustaining a precarious balance-through-movement.

Opposite, bottom: **Tlazolteotl giving birth.** Codex Borbonicus, section of p. 13. The goddess wears the flayed skin of a sacrificial victim, an elaborate Huaxtec nose-plug, and a distinctive headdress of unspun cotton, which is also worn by the newly delivered baby. The fully formed child descends to enter her womb under the auspices of Tezcatlipoca in his vulture guise, wearing his star headdress and carrying the maguey spines of penance.

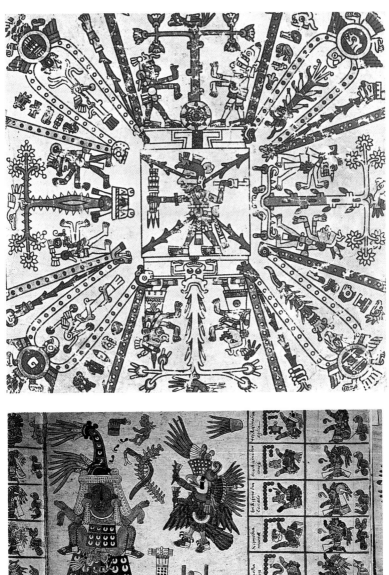

Seated Xipe Totec. Aztec, Stone. Museum für Volkerkunde und Schweizerisches Museum für Volkskunde, Basel. The figure wears the flayed skin of a warrior. Note the dangling hands and the separate 'face' mask, with the living lips just visible under the stretched lips of the mask.

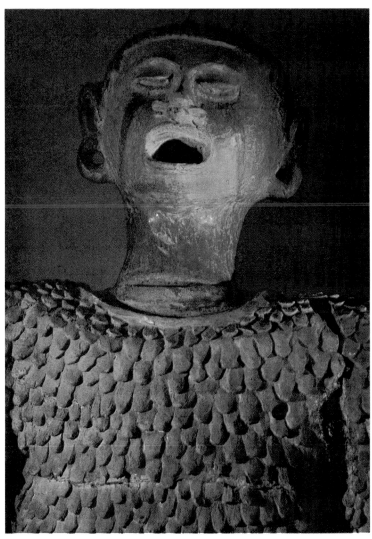

The 'red' Xipe Totec. Terra cotta, from Coatlinchan. American Museum of Natural History, New York.

Small reconstructed Mexica pyramid-temple. Santa María.

The Spaniards penetrate the main temple precinct of Tenochtitlan, June 1521. Lienzo de Tlaxcala, *Amer. a. 1, 2.* Plate 46, Lienzo de Tlaxcala, from A. Chavero's Antiguedattes Mexicanos Laminas e Text 1892. The Bodleian Library.

static, speaking to the eternal verities by way of solemn iteration. That is to misconceive the Mexica case, where ritual was more dynamic idiom than fixed text. Its improvising nature, present at every level, was most prominent at the highest, not only through the incorporation of outsiders' dances and chants and deities, but by an unabashed appropriation of popular symbols and actions from within Tenochtitlan itself, so opening the way for a most brisk circulation of social energy.[11] We have seen the involvement of the common people in maintaining the temples with their labour and products. The central precinct itself was not the monopoly of the ruling group, the stage for its exclusive dramas, the platform for its exclusive preachings. Neighbourhoods were called upon to supply teams of young singers and dancers for major festivals, which must have been a source of local pride. The great temple and its environs provided the locus for the most serious acts and crucial events of a great number of the groups constituting the city's population. In that sacred arena priests trained to the stamina of athletes and the disciplined grace of dancers moved like gods along the pyramids' precipitous flanks and between the flaring braziers. Warriors danced below the Great Temple, and saw their captives offered up in precise measure of their own valour. But salt-farmers and featherworkers and merchants, women and children, also found enthralling engagement there. The elevation and elaboration of the Great Temple and its precinct was clearly a 'state' decision, but an irresistible one, grounded as it was in local expectation and tradition as much as in political need.

3

If Mexica rituals were valued for their connections and commentaries on life and their capacity to forge a particular kind of unity out of difference, participation was itself addictive. Given that access to ritual excitements was not an occasional grace note but an enduring part of the rhythm of living, ritual-generated experience and ritual-generated knowledge among the Mexica opened zones of thought and feeling at once collective, cumulative and transformative. At least part of the attraction must have lain in the lavishness of the gifts made and the perfection of the elaborated feast, in the mighty clamour of appeal, in the calculated dramatizations of dependence; as part of those great happenings, the individual could feel himself to be more than a single pellet rolling helplessly in Tezcatlipoca's casual palm. The very order of the more formal displays – the balanced alternations of sexes or groups, the circles wheeling within circles, the complex weaving of the snake dance – modelled a patterned predictability which promised not to coerce but to tame the movements of the natural and sacred worlds, and to allow humans to move in harmony with them.[12] So the dancers sometimes mimicked the slow long step of the gods, or in their pattern reproduced the rotations of the year-bearer deities, who 'go describing circles, go whirling around', as they measure time.[13]

However socially useful or reassuring their ritual acts happened to be, the Mexica were moved, like most humans, not only to manage life, but to comprehend it. Of all Mexica artificers it was the priestly ritual-makers, impresarios of the sacred, who practised the highest art. They were intent on facsimilating, however momentarily, the masked world of the sacred, for the instruction of men as for the pleasure of those other watchers from the eternal worlds above and below.

Their attempt began from the Mexica ontological understanding that with the exception of those exquisite creatures and objects – jades, bright birds, butterflies – whose glancing beauty declared them to be fragments of the divine, the seen world blurred the reality of the sacred. Art and ritual were isomorphic. Men could glimpse the world of the gods by close observation of 'nature' in its multiplicity of examples, but they could do so much more completely when things of art and nature were displayed and arranged into the correct iconographic form: in the sacred painted books, in the monumental sculptures and structures of the great Temple, in the complex images of the ixiptlas, and in the relationships of colour, movement and sequences of action in high ceremonial.

The priests had magnificent resources on which to draw. They could freely borrow from the rituals of other peoples, and of their own laity. They could call on small, routinized, and 'named' rituals – 'the strewing of grass' or 'entering the sand' or 'the flower race' or 'the serpent dance' or the 'offering of smoke' – to provide a repertoire of procedures to link those innovations and borrowings into a sufficiently familiar whole. The wealth of empire provided an inexhaustible flow of exotic materials for ritual paraphernalia. But their richest and most resonant resource was the range of things of the daylit world which by careful framing and place-ment could be made to reveal the cryptic mark of the sacred. I have argued that Mexica aesthetics appears to have proceeded by an initial 'dis-location' of objects from their ordinary contexts, to permit reflection on their nature and known correspondences, or to search out revelatory likenesses. The ritual-makers proceeded in the same way, as evident in the recognition of the meaning of the fruit of the tunal cactus. Approx-imately the size and shape of the human heart in Mexica understanding, its green skin peeled back to reveal blood-red flesh within, so that the tunal cactus and its fruit were forever touched with sacred significance. Red human blood – the red of the youthful sun and of the east – was formally designated as blue-green, the most precious colour of jade and of vegetable growth. The selective juxtaposition of such deliberately ab-stracted and isolated phenomena accented or asserted connection; and much high ritual action, from the carefully prescribed details of regalia to the condensed dramas being enacted, turned on such pregnant juxtaposi-tions.

It has sometimes been argued that the very different costliness of the ritual paraphernalia deployed at different social levels must have signalled differences in understandings. Johanna Broda has pointed to the offerings of the 'common people' (under which heading she subsumed farmers, artisans and other professional groups) 'of quail, tortillas, maize plants, maize ears, and flowers, contrasted with the gold, the rich plumes and precious stones, the paper, the copal and cacao offered by the lords', as indicative not of shared understandings, but mere adjacency.[14] The offer-ings certainly indicated social difference, but not, I think, different imagi-native worlds. Quail for captives, tortillas for cacao, the blue-green maize for plumes, flowers for jade, caught multiple images of semblance through the different forms, the 'point' being in the counterpoint.[15] Maize stalks and maize ears, brought in from the fields and decked and adored as gods in the households, were also familiar parts of the warriors' ritual accoutrements, along with quetzal plumes and other exotica.[16] A quetzal plume was remarkably like a maize stalk in colour and 'lift'. It was very unlike in the getting, to be won only through the struggles of war or foreign trade. A maize stalk in a warrior's hand and the quetzal plume in his headdress invited the simultaneous apprehension of the connections between those different ways of getting, and beyond that the interdependence, and the dependence, common to mankind. The key articulations of the thought system and the ontological assumptions on which it rested could only be 'brought into view' by such a tireless play of references.

It is this constant traffic between the symbols of field and of empire, flesh and fertility, the familiar human and the inimical sacred, which characterized the Mexica ritual process. The warrior–plant–growth theme was reiterated in a multitude of images. The festival of the fourth month celebrating the maize was initiated by the young men drawing blood from shanks and ears and staining the white bases of sedges which they set before the household gods, receiving in return bowls of especially rich maize porridge.[17] In the great festival of Tlacaxipeualiztli, dedicated to Our Lord the Flayed One, bowls rimmed with the precious plumes of the quetzal were filled with blood drawn from the chest cavity of a warrior killed after desperate battle on the gladiatorial stone. The bright feathers were drabbled with that blood as the captor ran with his bowl through the streets to smear the lips of the stone images with the 'most precious water'. The kinsfolk of a warrior killed in battle memorialized him by building his image out of a 'nine jointed maize stalk', 'dressed' in a cape and breechclout, hung with a dead hummingbird, in recognition of its apparently marvellous yearly return to life, and the sprays of white heron-feathers which were the sign of the warrior, with the dead man's shield and arrow at the base.[18] Figures made from the 'flesh' of maize dough enriched with seeds were adored, then 'killed', broken up, and eaten, in strict conformity with the fate of human victims and human flesh. That elaborate compilation of 'naturalistic' snakes, human hands and hearts and skulls, and predators' fangs and claws which we know as Coatlicue, 'Snake Skirt', made its own massive comment: the endlessly fecund, endlessly voracious Earth actualized.[19]

The cryptic meanings clustering around a single plant or creature could be elucidated by close observation, and reflection. To consider the maguey once more: while the effects of its fermented milk unequivocally established it as a plant of power, it had other significances. It was a gracious plant to man, providing fuel, shelter, fibre for rope and twine and clothing as well as drink, so that a life, if a rough one, could be built around it. The Mexica had discovered its use for pulque during their early migration.[20] It did not depend on human cultivation: stronger with care, it could still flourish alone, with none of the dependence of the maize on human custodians. Growing on the high northern steppes as readily as in the valley, it bridged, as we would say, nature and culture, or, as the Mexica saw it, the wild life of the hunter and the settled life of the cultivator. Its thick fleshy leaves resisted drought as readily as they resisted frost. That fleshiness impressed even Spaniards, one describing the leaves as having 'the thickness of a knee and the length of an arm', with the central trunk 'as big around as a boy of six or seven'. Certainly the Mexica persistently identified the maguey with human children, as in the festival of Izcalli, when the maguey was pruned and the children 'stretched' in adjacent rituals to guarantee growth.[21]

Pulque was a gift with its ambivalences. Different stories clustered around its origins, but their most common features were of a magic woman, pursued as a deer by a hunter-hero, and finally escaping through yielding the extorted gift.[22] The maguey took eight or ten years to come to maturation, but then it gave abundantly, the sap welling from its pierced heart to yield the 'honey' so persistently associated with the sexual performance of the mature man. That honey then went through its mysterious transformation to became the sacred milk of the inexhaustible breasts of Mayahuel, goddess of the maguey, prototype of the generous mother. Mayahuel was represented as She with Four Hundred (that is to say, innumerable) Breasts. The dense cluster of associations of violence, male potency, dangerous female sexuality and the endless bounty of the 'sacred milk' theme made this a rich imaginative territory. When the sweet sap had grown sour, cloudy and potent, it became, with certain additions, 'obsidian-knife-water', the sacred fluid in which 'the obsidian knives of sacrifice were washed,' and which, drunk by those who were to die, made them careless of their fate. It was the last taste in the mouths of the captive warriors tethered to fight on the gladiatorial stone, as it was the first in the mouths of infants introduced to public ceremonial life, when pulque was drunk to full inebriation.[23] The spines were the standard implements of laceration of tongue and flesh for the drawing forth of blood to the gods. When the trickster deity Tezcatlipoca was manipulating the austere Quetzalcoatl out of his rule at Tollan, Quetzalcoatl was first persuaded into drinking deeply of the pulque, and then, adrift on its sweet tides, he incestuously lay with his sister, and in self-disgust abandoned his city and his empire.

Thus the plant shared with maize a deep implication in the sacred as in daily life. In Mexico the maguey, lying athwart the great division of the familiar and ordered social world of men, and the disordering, fructifying sacred, was, like the maize, a specially charged mediator between zones of different intensity of the sacred, its uses and transformations thick with those connections between physiology, psyche and cultural symbol that Victor Turner saw as the source of true power for symbols and substances. Fire shared that same attribute, being the key mediator between sky and earth, men and the sacred. Squatting between the stones at the centre of the hearth, it ruled the heart of the home. Yet it was also linked to the deepest core of the earth, and was closely connected with the sky: as New Fire it had descended from the heavens, and Xiutecutli, 'Turquoise Lord', claimed 'Turquoise Prince', the Sun, as his issue.

Abstractions, juxtapositions, elucidations of relationships, proliferated. Other connections, more opaque in their significance, were also presented for contemplation. Parallel transformations in substances perceptually different hinted at hidden resemblance, and so to connection. Human blood jets vivid and wet, then darkens, becomes viscous, crumbles: human skins dry and crumble to earth as they shroud the warrior dancers. Fire transforms brine into salt, water into steam, wood into charcoal. Human skin, darkened by the sun, also darkens in the fire, and then bubbles and boils like water before it blackens and peels away. (The captives thrown bound into the flames at Xocotlhuetzi were pulled clear when their flesh had blistered.)[24] The sap of the rubber tree growing in the wetlands drips white, thickens as it lies, becomes dark and elastic when exposed to the fire. More heat, and it melts to thick black droplets. Yet more and it darkens, bubbles, then burns to dense black clouds which mimic Tlaloc's thunderheads. Copal resin sweats and bubbles, and then transforms to a heavy sweet smoke.[25] In ritual action those connections and identities and relationships could be played out and puzzled over for what they revealed of relationships between the sacred forces of water, sun, and fire, and how each worked on the matter which constituted man.

The lowliest household routines and the simplest preparation of food explored the same themes, through the daily manipulations of maize, water, and heat. We find a small bridging ceremony between high ritual and domestic action in the festival of Uey Tocoztli, when the women made *atole*, a thick maize gruel, and as part of the ritual poured it into gourd bowls. We are told 'it spread shining, it spread scintillating; it was gleaming with heat . . . and when it had cooled, when it was cold, when it had thickened, when it lay in place, it spread contracting, it spread quivering.' Here we have not only close attentiveness to what heat and cold can do to maize gruel, that transformed combination of maize kernels and water, but also to the demonstration of affinity, in its density, its palpability and its quivering vitality, between the cooling gruel and living human flesh – maize gruel, as the Mexica might say, incarnate.[26] Izcalli, that celebration of continuity and the group, also contained an elaborate cooking drama. Young lads hunted small creatures – snakes, birds, lizards, frogs, fish, even dragon-fly larvae – to offer to the old men who were custodians of the Fire God, who was first represented in his glittering youth, gleaming in turquoise and quetzal plumes.[27] In return they were given wet-cooked vegetable tamales by the priests. Just what category underlay the lads' selection of animal offerings for the god is unclear, including as they did creatures of the air and of the earth, but furred and running animals were excluded. (There were plenty of small rodents which would not have been beyond the boys' hunting skills.) All the creatures, including the birds, were water-associated, which perhaps constituted the category. What was being played out might well have been a condensed history of the wandering times, a mythic 'recollection', in both senses, of the foods of those early days when the god-led Mexica, excluded from agriculture, were living as best they could by what they could glean from the marshes – but already sharing what they had with the God of Fire, the 'Old, Old God', and first companion to man.[28] In exchange for their 'wild' offerings the boys received 'tamales stuffed with amaranth greens', the food of settlement and sociability, which had become the basic currency in the settled phase for exchanges between neighbour, family and kin.[29] Then in the latter part of the month, when the ageing god, now represented in the ember colours of black and red and gold, was weary, he was allowed to consume fully most of his second round of offerings from the boys. Minimal heat was used in the preparation of the uncooked 'bracelet tortillas' consumed in this phase of the ritual, the maizemeal being no more than moistened with warm water before being patted into cakes. Thus the intricate themes of human–sacred interdependence, and the cautious, long-evolved human strategies for survival rehearsed at the domestic hearth, were enacted in the ritual theatre.

4

The insistent emphasis on the unobvious connection, together with the determined lack of definition in Mexica religious thinking, were manifest in the ritual representation of 'gods'. The 'pantheon of specialist deities' view, resting first on Seler's mighty work of tracking correlations between annotated colonial and pre-conquest pictorial manuscripts, initially appeared to be confirmed by the clear iconic identifiers of some major deities recognizable in their stone images, the painted images of the codices, and the invocations or 'prayers' in archaic Nahuatl recorded in the sixteenth century. The representations so identified were labelled and neatly installed in their special academic niches, with their special insignia, their special hymns and invocations, their special areas of responsibility. Later analysts with sharper eyes and less interest in system have found very much less conformity.[30] There is now fair consensus that the 'fixed personae' notion of Mexica deities is a misapprehension, and that the Mexica (and Mesoamericans generally) thought more in terms of sacred forces, with associated qualities and ranges of manifestations, moving in constant complex interaction: more clusters of possibilities invoked by a range of names than specific deities with specific zones of influence. Despite the firm black lines, vehement gestures and apparently balanced oppositions of deities in the screenfold books, iconographic details and colours constantly migrated and interchanged. The magnificent regalia of the ixiptla of 'Salt Lady', who died in the seventh month of the seasonal calendar, was dense with reference to her role as elder sister to the rain gods and the closeness of her association with water and fertility, from the vivid green quetzal-feather maize-tassel in her cap, and her face paint the clear yellow of maize blossoms, to her shift with its border of billowing clouds,[31] while Tezcatlipoca's capacity to sustain the possibilities of Huitzilopochtli within him could be deftly suggested by an unexpected colour or a 'borrowed' item of adornment. The inimitable insights of the ritual zone were expanded through the liberating explosion of boundaries and distinctions painfully drawn and expensively sustained in the mundane

world. (The easy androgyny of Mexica deities has been already noted.[32])
While quetzal plumes graced warrior ritual dress, female fertility deities
marked their warrior connections with eagle feathers and shields.

If we can trace the migration of characteristic iconographic details from
one aspect of the sacred to another in the codices, they were as vividly
expressed in the major monumental sculptures. Commoners saw the
sculptures only rarely, and the codices, distillations of esoteric wisdom,
not at all. But they would have seen those conceptualizations again and
again during the major rituals in the details of the actors' dress, and most
tellingly in the costly and compelling form of the human ixiptlas.

The sacred victims destined for death were peculiarly adaptable to this
kind of display, but 'ixiptla' was a marvellously elastic category.[33] Death
was not a necessary part of the definition: for example, when householders offered a feast they solicited the presence of the 'living image' of
the god of feasting to bless the occasion. A man (presumably a priest)
came to the house appropriately adorned, played his ritual part, and then
left, appropriately rewarded.[34] Other deities appear to have had human
ixiptlas, also almost certainly priests, permanently resident in their temples.[35] The high priests decked in their godly regalia who watched the
gladiatorial killings at the Festival of the Flaying of Men were ixiptlas, the
'impersonators, the proxies, the lieutenants, the delegates, of the gods.'[36]
At one festival the Mexica ruler Moctezoma was named as ixiptla of the
Fire God, and offered quail and incense.[37] Ixiptlas could be multiple, as
when the men who put on the skins of flayed warrior captives became
ixiptlas of Xipe Totec, the Flayed God.

This freedom to develop multiple representations through the range of
ixiptlas allowed the staging of most complex reflections and inversions. In
some festivals one ixiptla embodied in a priest would kill another embodied in a 'bathed slave'.[38] In all such cases the regalia were subtly different:
this was no mere reiteration, an image extinguishing its mirrored self, but
rather a complex comment on the character and potential of the thing
doubly represented. One last extravagant example: the female representation of Ilama tecuhtli, an aspect of the Earth Goddess, was led to her
death by a priest, also adorned as the goddess, who led in his turn a file of
priests representing other gods. With the woman's death the priest ixiptla
took the severed head and danced with it. His dance was distinctive: he
'kept stepping backwards', supporting himself on a trident-ended cane.

He also wore a mask, with great eyes and huge lips, which 'looked in two directions'.[39] Here we are not simply confronted by a looking-glass which is permeable and may be stepped through, but a hall-of-mirrors world of dizzying perspectives, reversed images, and retreating inverted reflections.[40] Then, after the Janus-faced priest's dance with the severed female head, the ritual movement flowed into a dense tangle of fertility and warrior imagery. A priest dressed as a young warrior set a maguey leaf upon a symbolic grain-bin, itself set in the eagle vessel which was the receptacle for warrior hearts, and the bin was set to burn as priests raced to the summit of the temple to seize 'godly flowers' and to cast them into the vessel of fire.[41] Here we glimpse again the great basic theme of the reciprocating movement between warriors and fertility, female and male, sky and earth, brought to viewable form by the elaborate cross-referencing between things normally kept apart, and invoking the imaginative expansion which attends the dis-ordering of opposites.

Ixiptlas could be vegetable. At the household level some individuals would pledge to make the 'Little Moulded Ones' for the festival of Atemoztli, in honour of Tlaloc when 'the rains . . . broke out'. They took seed-dough and formed it into the shapes of mountains, with teeth of gourd seeds and eyes of fat black beans. They also bought the maguey, the obsidian blades, the costly paper and the liquid rubber for the regalia, although its making was entrusted to the priests. Then throughout the night before their festival the little figures, propped up for their victims' vigil, were celebrated and feasted in the houses of the devotees; men sang for them, and trumpets and flutes played. At dawn the priests took weaving sticks and thrust them into the figures' hearts, and then 'twisted their heads off, wrung their necks', giving the hearts to the householders, and taking the remaining fragments of seed-dough back to the priests' houses to be eaten.[42] At the highest level a major warrior festival in the great temple precinct centred on an image of Huitzilopochtli fashioned from seed-dough. Sometimes, as at the feast of Tepeilhuitl, 'the Feast of the Mountains', human and vegetable ixiptlas echoed each other. Women representing mountains were sacrificed, while amaranth dough figures were made, 'dismembered' and eaten in the households, in commemoration of kin who had died a death associated with Tlaloc.[43]

So we see ixiptlas of one substance being coupled with or counterpoised against ixiptlas of another, as in the seed-dough and human 'mountains' parallels, or when a slave wearing the skin of a flayed captive and arrayed by the goldworkers 'to be the likeness of [Xipe] Totec' was brought to bay before a stone ixiptla of the deity, or when a slave woman ixiptla of Chalchihuitlicue, 'Jade Skirt', goddess of sweet waters, died before a frame of wood, richly dressed and decked with gold, which also bore the name of the goddess.[44] On occasion abstract ideas were given ixiptla form. A daysign could have an ixiptla, the image being set up, named, and presented with offerings.[45] Chalchihuitlicue, always present in the shining, restless waters of the lake, was 'represented as a woman': a 'natural', visible presence personified for easier intelligibility. A rather different relationship between representation and that which was represented is suggested by the usages surrounding Chicomecoatl, 'Sustenance Woman', who was herself 'the representative of maize and men's sustenance of whatever sort; what is drunk, what is eaten': that is, a rather vague conceptual category 'given body' by the name and the personification.[46] Ixiptlas could be used to personify not so much a sacred power as a sacred substance. The death of 'Salt Lady' graphically represented the work of the salt-farmers who offered her: bent sharply backwards over the stone, a swordfish blade at her throat so that her body was tensely arched, her breast struck open so that the blood jetted and boiled up like their boiling vats.[47] Then her body, wrapped in precious capes, was carried as carefully as the salt it had become, down the steps of Tlaloc's pyramid.

Maize presents a different case. On that same feast day the sacred clusters of seven maize cobs, the selected seed maize specially consecrated on that day, were simply called 'maize gods' (Centeotls), and I think were understood as 'being' the sacred substance, its very body, and therefore not 'representations'.[48] Equally the fresh green maize plants, plucked in the fields earlier in the same festival and then dressed and set up in all the houses to be worshipped, were 'maize gods', not ixiptlas.[49] We have seen the persistent emphasis in Mexica ritual (as in Mexica speech) on the isomorphism of the trajectory of the human and the maize life cycle: those weeping infants named as maize blossoms, the young girl named as the tender green ear, the young warrior named 'Lord Maize Cob' for the matured cob. A metaphorical relationship, we are tempted to say. Yet here, as so often, we are faced with the implication that the metaphor might not be metaphor at all, but simply a statement of a perceptually unobvious but unremarkable fact: that human flesh and maize kernels were seen as the same substance. My suspicion is that we have in the maize rituals demonstrations of consubstantiation: an extension of that range of ceremonies in which human and vegetable victims, human and vegetable flesh, were most deliberately juxtaposed to reveal that they were the same substance in different forms.

Ixiptlas were everywhere, the sacred powers represented in what we would call multiple media in any particular festival – in a stone image, richly dressed and accoutred for the occasion; in elaborately constructed seed-dough figures; in the living body of the high priest in his divine regalia, and in the living god-image he would kill: human, vegetable and mineral ixiptlas. Three criteria appear to constitute the category. An ixiptla was a made, constructed thing; it was formally 'named' for the particular sacred power, and adorned with some of its characteristic regalia; it was temporary, concocted for the occasion, made and unmade during the course of the action. (The great images within the shrines of the main temple precinct were not described as ixiptlas, nor were they processed or publicly displayed.)

For all their high value as costly offerings, the human ixiptlas appear to have been given no special precedence in the system of representations over the other forms, save for their dramatic potential: dancing images, and so more vivid and theatrically compelling for the watchers. At Panquetzaliztli the vast figure representing Huitzilopochtli was shaped out of the richest dough and elaborately dressed, to be 'killed' the next day by an arrow in its vegetable heart. Then the 'body' was divided, the heart falling to Moctezoma, and the 'bones' distributed to the warriors of two districts, presumably in rotation, for the ceremony of *teoqualo,* 'eating the god'.[50] If the 'human' Tezcatlipoca represented at the festival of Toxcatl lived his parabola of human glory and suffered his human fate, so displàying the nature and the power of his lord, the massive presence of Huitzilopochtli, while sometimes punily mimicked in human form, was built more powerfully and certainly in the imagination through the drama of his fabrication in the sacred seed-dough – the great bones laid out, the great loincloth unfurled.[51] We have seen the 'presenting' of Toci, 'Our Grandmother', achieved through the sequential revelation of her multiple aspects: beginning as Teteo Innan, a human, social woman, patroness of midwives and curers, scattering maizemeal in the marketplace; built layer by layer out of adornments upon the human skin flayed from her earlier self; finally revealed as Toci, mistress of vegetable growth, feeder and eater of men.

The slow assembling of an ixiptla was an act of invocation, and the completed image a potential vehicle for the sacred force. That sacredness lingered: in the person and garments of the high priest or ruler, in the living and the dead flesh of the human images, in the seed-dough 'flesh' of the vegetable figures; all remained suffused with residual sacred power. Eaten, that charged human or vegetable flesh invaded the eater. The intensity and duration of the possession varied in accordance with the rigour of the preliminary purification, and the comprehensiveness of the representation. To eat the flesh of Huitzilopochtli was to bend the neck for a grave burden. The young warriors who took the food into their mouths became his slaves for the year of their duty, with duties so onerous that some sought death to fulfil their obligation once and for all.[52] In view of the great range of observable actions, I suspect the words between which we strive to choose – 'representation', 'substitute', 'impersonator', 'image', 'representative' – are equally misleading and equally useful: sometimes appropriate, sometimes not. But given that to a modern ear the notion of 'representation' can carry the suggestion that that which represents is quite distinct from that which is represented, and given that 'impersonation' and 'representation' imply pretence rather than 'the rendering present by simulation', which is closer to the Mexica view, perhaps 'god-presenter', 'that which enables the god to present aspects of himself', best approximates the Nahuatl term. Through the idea of the ixiptla the Mexica developed a most flexible vocabulary through which they could express and explore certain propositions about the nature of the world, the characteristics and relationships between the sacred forces, and those between sacred forces and their manifestations in the seen world. And if all this makes the Mexica aficionados of metaphysical religion, so I take them to be.

5

Then there was the instilling of the distinctive moods pertaining to the sacred. James Clifford has given a luminous account of Maurice

Leenhardt's conceptualization of myth as an essentially affective mode of knowledge carved out of a distinctive emotional event: a way of 'circumscribing immediate emotional experiences that discursive language could not express', so creating 'a given experiential landscape'.[53] Mexica myths in action seem less charters for power or moral tales or ordered concepts good to think with than intense evocations of distinctive moods and experiences. We have seen enough of the enactment of the birth and first battle of Huitzilopochtli at the festival of Panquetzaliztli to acknowledge its mythic source. But we need to remember that each ritual develops its own performance history, liberating the performance from the originating moment or motive or myth for more flexible uses, and allowing its incorporation into the participants' own experiential histories. While the birth-of-Huitzilopochtli story was formidably present in the great icons of the sculptures, in the names given persons and places, in the regalia and the confrontations, what was most notable in the ritual's performance was the furious pace of the action.[54]

It began with the eruption from Huitzilopochtli's temple of a running priest who bore the image of Huitzilopochtli's lieutenant Paynal, 'He Who Hasteneth', representation of Huitzilopochtli's terrible speed. The priest paused in his forward rush only to kill four victims in the sacred ballcourt, their bodies being dragged to mark out the court with blood. He then ran a long marathon, pursued by a great press of people, who 'went howling, crying war cries. They went raising the dust, making the ground smoke.' His way was marked by more killings, and then, as he circled back to Tenochtitlan, by skirmishes between the 'bathed slaves' and the warrior captives who were to die. As he approached the main temple precinct the two 'devices for seeing', which had been carried before him, and which formed part of Huitzilopochtli's regalia, were snatched up by the first of a sequence of paired warriors, to be rushed in a breathless relay to the top of Huitzilopochtli's temple and thrown on his image. The final warrior runners, having expended their last ounce of energy leaping up the stairs, typically collapsed as they reached the summit. The tempo briefly slowed as the great 'fire serpent', a kind of Chinese dragon moved by a priest within, snaked its way down the pyramid to be burned. Then it quickened as Paynal swept down once more to scoop up the destined captives and deliver them to the shrine of his lord.[55]

During this great festival the people experienced the awesome power of

Huitzilopochtli, in the surge of feet, the desperate exertions of battle, the sudden jetting of blood, as, ferocious and invincible, he came among his people. We can recognize the force of these constructed emotional experiences, developed out of a repertoire of prescribed actions, as we can recognize their efficacy in the structuring of sensibility as well as 'belief'. At Izcalli we saw the Mexica child's initiation into ritual life, and the beauty and terror unleashed by the disruption and transformation of the familiar, with new sensations penetrating his very being: at once an experience of extreme physical and psychological disorientation, and of incomparable excitement.[56] In that same festival obligatory drunkenness had projected the whole collectivity into the realm of the sacred. They had made their perilous journey back, away from its terrifying glamour, away from its disordering of all the comforting predictabilities of human society. But no one – least of all the initiated children – would lightly forget that encounter.

The intensities of the rituals developed an appetite for a certain kind of experience. The Izcalli experience *per se* would not be repeated, but its sensations, and others equally compelling, would be rehearsed through a multitude of other ceremonies.[57] But while the scripts of the various rituals were as distinctive in nuance and balance as in their names, it ought to be possible to graph at least the broad contours of the classic parabola of actions and emotions involved in worship, to retrieve something of the shapes built into flesh and mind and imagination through those particular sequences, and so to glimpse the face the Mexica accorded the sacred.

First, the character of the standard preparation for full ritual engagement.[58] At this distance the obligatory process might be taken to be no more than 'purification', but it was rather more than that. It began with 'fasting'. The fasting state allowed the eating of only one frugal and bland meal a day. It required abstinence from sexual intercourse, and the regular drawing of blood from the earlobe, tongue, or the flesh of the thigh.[59] (These offerings need to be distinguished from the routine offerings of one's own blood to the sacred powers, the token payments-on-account acknowledging the remorselessly accumulating debt which could be discharged only at death. The fasting period imposed much heavier obligations.)

We happen to have an account which sheds some refracted light on

practices in Tenochtitlan: the preparation of Tlaxcalan priests for a great
four-yearly feast honouring their major deity. After the invocation of the
god and the offering of incense, the priests had their tongues pierced by
obsidian blades, and then drew through the slit a sequence of rods of
wood, varying in thickness, we are told, from a thumb to 'the space one
can encircle with the thumb and forefinger'. Senior priests were committed to forcing four hundred and five rods through their tongues, and the
more junior two hundred. This exercise initiated an eighty-day fast, with
the forcing of the rods through the tongue repeated every twenty days. (It
is painful to imagine that deliberate breaking-open of the barely healed
flesh.) For the second eighty-day fast it was the turn of the common
people, who imitated the priestly sacrifice at a less heroic level, being
content to draw through their tongues 'little rods as thick as duck's
quill'.[60]

What was being offered here was not, or not primarily, pain. While pain
was certainly suffered, it was where practicable minimized: that first obsidian blade sliced cleanly, while the wood of the rods was carefully
smoothed. Blood appears to be the desired and measurable product, the
bloodied rods being heaped in a special enclosure to be offered before the
deity. (There were other even more strenuous exercises, as, for example,
the slitting of the penis and the passing through the slit of a rope some
fathoms long. This could suggest the use of extreme pain to induce a
vision, as with the Sun Dance, were it not that fainting was taken as a sign
of disqualifying impurity.)[61] Only those among the Tlaxcalan priests who
had endured the fast to the end were qualified to don their regalia and to
go on to celebrate the festival. Through their preliminary performance
they had presumably demonstrated their capacity and their readiness to
serve the god. They had also been brought to a proper condition to
approach him.

Strenuous fasting was a priestly obligation, but laymen who had made a
special commitment to a festival would also fast for twenty, sixty, or eighty
days. For those young warriors who had pledged themselves by eating the
flesh of Huitzilopochtli the austerities endured for a full year. We have
seen the general fear unleashed by the uncontrolled intrusion of the
sacred powers into the human world. The fasting process appears to be
one of preparation for the dangers of an invoked and deliberate encounter
with those powers: a preparation through the transformation, or transcen-

dence, of self; of at least partial separation from the social being. For priests and laity alike the end of the fasting period must normally have seen a notable degree of skeletonization: the visible self refined, the inner self tuned to the proper pitch for the intensities of festival engagement.

The lay faster's depleted body was painted by specialist painters who worked for hire in the marketplace, dressed in its appropriate clothing, and provided with the requisite accoutrements of feathers or maize stalks or flowers, while the priests were robed with even greater ceremony: a further distancing from the mundane self, especially given Mexica conviction as to the transforming power of garments. Consider the following description of the dress appropriate to men arrayed in the likeness of Xipe Totec for the Feast of the Flaying of Men:

He put on the skin of a captive when they had flayed him . . . they placed on his head his plumage of precious red spoonbill feathers; the precious red spoonbill feathers served as his headdress. And he had his gold nose crescent, and his golden earplugs. And his rattle stick rattled as he grasped it in his right hand; when he thrust it into the ground it rattled. And he had with him his shield with a gold circle. And his sandals were red and adorned with quail feathers. Thus was the quail adornment: quail feathers were strewn on the surface. And there were his three paper flags which he carried on his back, which went rustling. And his sapote skirt was made of all precious feathers, those known as precious quetzal feathers, the color of green chilli, arranged – prepared – in rows; everywhere there were precious feathers. And his [human] skin collar was beaten thin. And he had his sapote leaf seat . . .[62]

And so on to even more infatuated detail. We have seen how profoundly the compiling mode permeated Mexica sensibility, with the ixiptlas being assembled, detail by detail, into complex living icons of extraordinary beauty, each detail carrying its special meaning, modulated by its location and relationship with other items. Man was singularly suited to this process of self-creation, because unlike non-human creatures he came into the world incomplete. The Mexica, along with other Mesoamericans, told stories of how the bodies of women and men were concocted by the gods by effort and experiment, and then given movement, speech, and their appropriate food. All the rest lay in the hands of men, or more correctly, in their hidden destinies, which would be slowly made clear through the building or revelation of the self (or the 'face') as manifested in visual signs.[63] In the liminal zone of ritual that process was

inverted: the preparation of the body and the donning of appropriate
regalia moved one away from one's social being, and for some individuals
(the ixiptlas who would die, the warrior victims) eclipsed it permanently
and altogether.

After the transformations of fasting, painting and robing, the priests and
the persons or groups nominated as participants moved into the compelling rhythms of collective dance-and-chant, opened to the great sensory
assault of full Mexica ceremonial.[64] Sounds mattered: the distinctive
voices of the different drums, the hollow moaning blast of the conch-shell
trumpet, the surge and swell of the antiphonal chants. Silence could be
used to terrifying effect, as in the midnight hush as Toci sought her
habitation in the flayed skin of a slaughtered woman. Flowers and incense, sweat and paint and the flat sweet smell of blood mingled in the
distinctive scent of the sacred, which was signalled by the brush of feathers on skin, the sudden darkening and narrowing of vision as the mask
slid down over the face, the precise, repetitive movements as the lines of
dancers interwove and the drums, dance and voices intertwined.[65]

The dances were led by men trained and ritually prepared, whose
responsibilities were formidable: should they err, and so 'mar the dance',
they would be imprisoned and left to die, not in a display of kingly
absolutism or perfectionist passion, but because this poetry, *pace* Auden,
was understood to make something happen.[66] The inference is clear:
while dance was sometimes no more than a diversion, it was on formal
occasions an essential element in the invocation of the deity.[67] As the friar
Motolinía recorded, through dance they 'called on their gods, raising
their hearts and senses to their devils', serving them 'with all the talents of
the body'.[68] 'Raising their hearts and senses to their devils . . . with all
the talents of the body': here Gadamer's understanding of dance as a form
of play, 'a movement which carries away the dancer', is relevant, as it
points to yet another Mexica route towards the eclipse of subjectivity.[69]

The organizers of this calculated assault on the senses were the priests,
contriving, by very different means, the kind of delirium we associate not
with high reverence but with Carnival. Through the chants when the
priests spoke in the voice of the gods and the people replied; the swirling
movement of processions and the slow turnings of the dancers in the flare
of the pine torches; through the long preparation, the long isolation from
the routine in the fasting period, the distancing formality of the painting

and robing; through the patterns of dance and drum and song etched into the senses and graven into the muscles of throat and calf and thigh, came a shifting in awareness and of the boundaries of the self. And only then, as the self evaporated and the choreographed excitements multiplied and the sensations came flooding in, did the god draw near.

We have seen the ritualized displays of martial art in the gladiatorial combats of Tlacaxipeualiztli, or those moments of battlefield commitment which drew on a deep cultural predilection for seeking the sacred through the extinction of the self, or (as we would most inadequately translate it) through liberation of the self into ecstasy. The final ritual processing of some of those special victims the ixiptlas presents a distilled and extreme representation of that predilection. A characteristic movement shaped their performances. Initially their conduct was closely supervised. Then for their last and very public hours, through the exhaustion of dance or simulated combat, through relentless excitation, or, more economically, through drink or drugs, they were relinquished to the sacred power their slow adorning and ritual preparation had invoked. Increasingly invaded, then obliterated by that power, 'possessed' in the fullest possible sense, they had ceased to exist as persons well before they met their physical deaths. The dancing or somnambulist puppets had become fleshly mirrors of the god, the hidden face of the sacred obscurely presented to be read in their twitching or flaccid flesh and their flickering eyes.[70] Themselves the primary focus of the sacred, the men and things about them in the ritual zone were also bathed in its marvellous light. In the full grip of the sacred, reeling, delirious, the luminous figures were thrust through the shifting darkness to the brightness beyond. Then the survivors of this close encounter with the sacred, themselves and their ritual things drenched by its presence, could take their long step back to the ordinary world, and the ritual, and the experience, was complete.

6

Within the ritual frame the priests could dare to incorporate passages of licensed spontaneity, encouraging even at the most elevated level the expression of the normally concealed as well as the approved, the contested as well as the shared: to offer a wide dark mirror in which the

Mexica could watch the workings of the imagined world, and themselves within it. At once margin and medium between this unstable place of shadows and the hidden sacred, ritual revealed a world like the one Alice discovered when she stepped through the looking-glass: heightened and coloured in extraordinary ways, yet obscurely and intensely familiar, with haunting resemblances, dreamlike associations, transformations; pre-posterous possibilities at last rendered actual and authentic. The figures on the high stage of the pyramid, whether priests or victims, were de-signed to be seen at a distance; lit by fire or sun, moving in their wide trappings of paper and feathers, communicating by large gestures, more semaphored than acted: a screenfold page animated. Given that the mes-sages were writ so large and in a simple visual code, even the observer distant in time has some chance of deciphering them.[71] What I take to be their deepest implication is unexpected.

Just how fragile our social worlds are is something normally and mer-cifully masked from us, perhaps because we have been too little sensitive to the difference between societies which proceed as if the cultural terms of their existence are reasonably well fixed, and those where the 'making' aspect is evident, and where the recognition of dynamic possibilities is counterpoised by the recognition of the fragility of that which is made: the subversive insight built into the texture of that which is built.[72] We have become familiar with the Mexica's insistence on differentiation and the fine structuring of the human world with its tribal divisions, its deeply marked social hierarchies, its moral codes of careful balance, its protocols to keep the uncontrolled sacred at bay. To make the world in such a shape and style constituted human sense. But the sacred made nonsense of such pitiful caution. Sacred sense pivoted on the predicate of the casual dis-ruption of social and human order, as distilled in the wanton interventions of Tezcatlipoca. In imperial Tenochtitlan the hierarchy was privileged to watch enactments intimating its own necessary final dissolution, or at least to acknowledge its carefully crafted state to be a made thing: another precarious human construct. Beneath the immediate and superficial mes-sage of the high rituals ('the Mexica, gloriously differentiated, gloriously dominate') the darkest aspect of the human condition was dramatized through this brilliant human making.

What the rituals finally and most powerfully represented was a vision subversive of human distinctions, with all the elegancies and elaborations of the social order collapsed into the carnal indifference of death. The glamour attending the warrior performance on the gladiatorial stone would seem to be in fine accord with the 'warrior ideology' and its classification as state-sustaining, as hand-picked Mexica warriors delicately slit the skin of their tethered victims in a display of Mexica might; but an analysis sustained over the whole parabola of the action from the perspective of the captor and his kin suggests a much darker vision.[73] And most ritual warrior deaths were notably less heroic: trussed like deer to be lugged, heads lolling, up the pyramid steps; others, similarly trussed, cast writhing into the fire. The victims who died on the killing stone, like those who fought in the gladiatorial combat, had been stripped of their distinctive warrior regalia, and wore the red and white body-paint of the warrior captive destined for death. If the most courageous did indeed leap up the pyramid steps, shouting the praises of their city, their voices would not have carried far in the thin air. Others, faltering or swooning, were dragged by the hair by one of the swarm of attendant priests. The watchers must have seen an unfluent movement of men, climbing or stumbling or dragged up the steps; then seized, flung back, a priest's arm rising, falling, rising again; the flaccid bodies rolling and bouncing down the pyramid's flanks. What they would see most clearly would be those bodies, and the blood, drenching the stone, the priests, then beginning its slow tide down the stairs. A disturbing sight, for men who dreamed and women who had sung and painted their faces for the signs of warriorhood. Honours so hardly won were denied, ignored, made meaningless as men, jealous of the least indicators of rank and ordered in accordance with that rank, watched undifferentiated bipeds being done to bloody death. They watched again as each broken, emptied cadaver was taken up to be carried to the captor's home temple for dismemberment and distribution: flesh scraped from skulls and thighbones; fragments of flesh cooked and eaten; human skins, dripping with grease and blood, stretched over living flesh; clots of blood scooped up to smear the temple walls.[74]

It might be said that these battle victims were all enemies, and so distanced from any claim to shared humanity, and that the killings were triumph ceremonies built out of their humiliation. But the case was the same with most of the human ixiptlas. The bright dolls were seized, the flaglike garments and elaborate headdresses stripped or pushed aside, so that a human figure, suddenly small, lay under the knife. Neither rank nor sex nor age had relevance then. In that butchery – there was no surgical precision here – blood jetted up, heads dangled from priests' hands, violated bodies were carried away for more dismemberings and distributions.[75] And all this where large-scale butchery of animals was unknown; where humans were the creatures men most often saw slaughtered. If (as some would claim) all ceremonial works to sustain the existing social and political order, these performances did so in most devious ways. It is a perilous business to assert over close to half a millennium and vast cultural distance what the Mexica saw, and made of what they saw.[76] It is nonetheless difficult to see these enactments as directly legitimating the Mexica, or indeed any, social order.

What was being declared here? Many things. But ultimately we have yet another piece of deconstruction and so of deciphering, yet another commentary on the transformation of states, and the connections between them. Here is a body in life. Here is a body – or rather an assemblage of elements – in 'death' or, more correctly, transformed, entering a new phase. A warrior's skull and scalp lock remained as a trophy and memorial. The rest belonged to the gods. Some of the flesh and blood fed the sacred animals of Moctezoma's collection; some was fed to the sacred images; some fed the earth and the sun; some fed men to remind them of their common condition, and their common duties. What the Mexica were shown, again and again, was a hard lesson – hard because it ran counter to human passions, vanities and affections, allowing no status to individuals or peoples or castes, but speaking only to mankind: the human body, cherished as it might be, was no more than one stage in a vegetable cycle of transformations, and human society a human arrangement to help sustain that essential cycle. 'Enchantment' and 'violence' are typically presented as alternative strategies for the maintenance of social stability, but that distinction is not easily drawn in Tenochtitlan, where acts of state-approved violence were at once part of the complex rhetoric of cosmically sanctioned human power, and, more profoundly, illustrative of the ferocious constraints on the merely human.

In the high space before the pyramid shrines the human and the sacred met. Human society, with its fine demarcations of rank and age and gender, that extraordinary human engine for survival, was juxtaposed with the inimical, destructive, fructifying sacred, and mankind's heroic, desolating dependence acknowledged in the flow of human offerings. The Mexica knew they were killing their fellow men. It was that humanity which defined them as victims. The Mexica genius, deployed across the astonishing stretch of their ceremonial life, was to figure a human stance within the inhuman conditions of existence.

7

These are not implausibly exotic inventions inflicted on a distant people. Something like the same understandings (without the desperate urgency which drove the Mexica) still appears to animate the contemporary Nahua of San Miguel, in the Sierra of Puebla, who sing a song as recorded by the anthropologist Tim Knab:

> We live HERE on the earth [stamping on the mud floor]
> we are all fruits of the earth
> the earth sustains us
> we grow here, on the earth and flower
> and when we die we wither in the earth
> we are ALL FRUITS of the earth [stamping on the mud floor].
>
> We eat of the earth
> then the earth eats us.[77]

PART IV

THE CITY DESTROYED

11

Defeat

As long as the world will endure,
the fame and glory of Mexico-Tenochtitlán
will never perish.

Domingo Chimalpahín Cuauhtlehuanitzin, *Memorial breve
de la fundación de la ciudad de Culhuacán*

In 1519 the Spaniards came. In April of that year Hernando Cortés and his men made landfall on the Gulf Coast close to what was to become 'La Villa Rica de la Vera Cruz', the 'Rich City of the True Cross'. An earlier Spanish expedition had skirted those shores, and Moctezoma's local governors had been on the alert. They quickly attended the strangers, with the Indian ruler's ambassadors arriving in a matter of days. From that time on, the agents of Cortés and Moctezoma were in near-constant interaction.[1]

The received version of the story of the conquest of Mexico stresses the superiority of Spanish arms and of Spanish tenacity, valour and resourcefulness over the moral and cognitive indecision of the natives, so echoing the account by the Spanish commander to his king.[2] This is unfortunate, given the high degree of invention Cortés brought to its concoction, and his systematic exaggeration of his control over men, Spanish and Indian alike.[3] Cortés's romantic account of the Mexica ruler voluntarily abdicating his authority in favour of Charles V – a cession which, however implausible, was crucial to his strategy for political survival – ought to have been laid to rest by Anthony Pagden's incisive commentary on the Cortés letters, which exposes the tight correlation between Cortés's implausible claims, omissions, and extravagances, and his desperate political dilemma. It has nonetheless survived, the traditional tale being too much in accord with European preferences to be easily surrendered, and the story the victors told continues to pass for truth. However, a close reading of the few Indian texts (most, admittedly, written down well after the event and deeply tinctured by Spanish understandings) set in the context of the Spanish sources, allows a partial retrieval of the Mexica view and the more concealed movement of the conquest encounter. I have explored those issues elsewhere.[4] Here I can do no more than sketch something of Mexica understanding of events.

The Spaniards were anomalous from their first appearance in Mexico: men without a city, they could not be bought, seduced, or terrified into the Mexican imperial scheme. The house-of-cards arrangement of the tributary empire had begun to totter with their landing. During the three months of nervous negotiation on the beach at Vera Cruz, and then on the long march to Moctezoma's city, Cortés did what he could to destabilize it further. By the time of Spanish entry into Tenochtitlan in November of 1519 the subtle nexus of political relationships within the valley itself was seriously ruptured. Most important, the outsiders had forged an alliance with the Tlaxcalans which would survive all vicissitudes: the Mexica would pay dearly for their past arrogance.

Meanwhile Moctezoma strove to categorize these strangers from beyond the mists, to bring them under political and (perhaps more important) cognitive control. Acting on his conviction of the revelatory power of appearances, he had sent skilled painters to the Spanish encampment on the beach to record all they saw: 'the face and countenance and body and features of Cortés and all the captains and soldiers, also the ships, sails, and horses, and Doña Marina and Aguilar, and even the two greyhounds, the cannon and cannon-balls, and the whole of our army', as Díaz remembered.[5] It was recognized from the paintings that a Mexica lord, 'Quintalbor' in the Spanish rendering of it, bore an uncanny resemblance to Cortés: he was sent with the ambassadors on their return to the coast to test the resemblance and to probe its meaning. A Spaniard wore a helmet shaped like the headdress of Huitzilopochtli: the ambassadors begged it to send to their ruler. (Cortés affably agreed, requiring only that it be returned to him full of grains of gold.)

Moctezoma initiated an exchange of gifts. From what we know of Mexica and indeed of Amerindian cultures, Moctezoma's 'gifts' were statements of dominance: gestures of wealth and unmatchable liberality made the more glorious by the extravagant humility of their giving. When the Mexica ambassadors ritually denigrated their offerings, Cortés appeared to take them seriously. He interpreted the offerings as gestures of submission, or as naïve attempts at bribery. To the next flourish – a golden disk as big as a cartwheel, a silver one even bigger, golden ornaments, crests of fine plumes – the Spanish leader riposted with three Holland shirts and a Florentine cup.[6] When the Spaniards drew close to the city, Moctezoma sent out his noblemen to greet them with golden banners and necklaces, and streamers of the rare and precious feathers which spoke of the magnificent expanse of Moctezoma's domains. The Spaniards ignored the plumes, but they fell upon the gold 'like monkeys'; 'they lusted for it like pigs'. Once again, the meaning of the message had been lost in translation. 'Thus there came to nothing still another of their meetings, of their welcomings'.[7]

The Mexica had been early informed of the peculiarities of these foreign warriors, who did not paint their bodies, or display them in combat, but sheathed them in iron. When the strangers were permitted to enter the city, 'some came all in iron; they came turned into iron; they came gleaming.'[8] The Mexica saw the great dogs, saliva, the sign of anger, dripping from their jaws.[9] They observed more formidable creatures of power whose fame had run ahead of them: the horses. They had already heard of these creatures who raced into combat, screaming, white eyes rolling, plunging and turning. Now they watched while the hooves of the sweating, neighing beasts marked and wounded the earth: 'each hoof pierced holes; holes were dug in the ground there where they lifted their feet. Separately they each formed there where their hind legs, their forelegs went stamping'.[10]

The Indians were to extend a respect for the courage of the horses they were never to grant their masters. The Mexica quickly learnt that the strangers had no notion of fighting fairly. There had already been reports that they were ready to attack unarmed men without warning, to seize and mutilate Indian emissaries received into their camp, to ride into sleeping villages at dawn and slaughter the inhabitants as they stumbled into the streets.[11] The Mexica were to discover for themselves that the Spaniards had no sense of proper behaviour on the battlefield, where they were ready to use crossbows and cannon to kill at a distance, and where they fled their opponents without shame. And the Spaniards were ready to starve enemies, non-combatants and warriors alike, into submission.

The Spaniards had been allowed entry into the city so that they would learn to appreciate the extent of Moctezoma's greatness. Instead they seized him as hostage and puppet. As they clustered around him, gazing into his face, touching and prodding him, and then shackled him to teach him fear, his sacred power drained away. Then, during Cortés's enforced absence from the city to repel another Spanish force, armed Spaniards slaughtered unarmed warriors dancing in the sacred precinct (it was the time of Toxcatl), so unequivocally identifying themselves as 'enemies'. Cortés's return with reinforcements did nothing to quell Mexica rage; the Spaniards were driven from the city with terrible losses. In the course of that great 'uprising' Moctezoma was killed, but he knew before he died that he had been replaced as tlatoani: Moctezoma manhandled by strangers was Moctezoma no longer.

Given the decisiveness of the Spanish expulsion, and Mexica 'rules of war', Tenochtitlan's new leaders believed the Spanish threat was over. Then smallpox swept through Mexico. As far as is known, Meso-americans had had no experience of epidemic disease, so it must have been a peculiar horror. Skin diseases were typically understood as afflictions from Tezcatlipoca, but we do not know if the Mexica identified those terrible pustules with more familiar lesions. As always, they noted the month of its beginning – Tepeilhuitl – and the time of its diminishing: after sixty daysigns, in the month of Panquetzaliztli. They spoke of the agony of victims unable to move for the pain; of the distribution on the body of the pustules; of the blindness which ensued when they clustered on the face; of men and women surviving the disease but dying of starvation for lack of someone to tend them.[12] We do not know how they explained it to themselves.

Within the year, the Spaniards, together with local 'allies' intimidated into co-operation or hungry for loot, had fought their way back to the lake city, and placed it under close siege. The Mexica at last learnt the full costs of empire as their subject peoples withdrew their tribute and offered intermittent aid to the Spaniards; as the lakeside towns shifted allegiance according to the play of battle; as they faced the implacable hatred of the Tlaxcalans, intent on exacting full payment from Tenochtitlan and its people for their long humiliation.

The siege was to drag on for four months. While there was an imbalance of weapons – horsemen against pedestrian warriors, steel swords against wooden clubs, muskets and crossbows against bows and arrows and lances, cannon against ferocious courage – the ground favoured the Mexica. But while the Mexica met most novel challenges with flexibility and inventiveness, on one issue they could not compromise: the taking of living opponents for presentation to the gods. This was possibly decisive, given the small number of Spaniards as spearheads to the attack: time and again the strangers struggled in Indian hands, to be rescued to fight again.

So obdurate was the resistance that to bring their cannon and horses into effective play the Spaniards found it necessary to level much of the city they had sought to preserve. Cortés, increasingly frustrated and baffled, saw the glorious prize he had promised his king reduced to rubble, and its people to human wreckage. Meanwhile the Mexica, in violation of all European notions of sense, fought on. They had seen nothing in Spanish conduct, now observed at close quarters, to retrieve their reputation as warriors. Their actions remained so treacherously unpredictable, their cowardice so contemptible, their ignorance or contempt for battle protocols so profound, as to render negotiations futile.

In those last desperate days there were some signs of demoralization among the defenders. Earlier, with the Spanish expulsion from the city, a Tlatelolcan account tells of disarray within the ruling group of the Tenocha[13]; and there had been no order or control in the recovery of the loot the Spaniards lost during their flight, perhaps because those responsible for such order were engaged in the pursuit. Not only Spanish arms and armour but gold bars, gold discs, pendant necklaces were taken 'as if merited . . . he who came upon something quickly took it, took it to himself, took it home': a most serious matter if the objects were warrior insignia.[14] We have seen something of the slow erosion of social distinctions as hunger worsened during the siege, when 'we [Mexica] had a single price', and 'all precious things (quetzal plumes, cloaks, gold) fetched the same price'.[15]

Nonetheless, the Spanish intruders were impressed, and appalled, by the unanimity of resistance: by the combination of obedience to command even where the structures of authority had crumbled, and of self-motivated courage in the fulfilment of that obedience. At a point where Spaniards had long seen their own victory as inevitable, the Mexica resorted to their end-game play: testing for auguries. A great warrior, garbed in the array of Quetzal Owl, the combat regalia of a Mexica ruler, and armed with the flint-tipped darts of Huitzilopochtli, was sent against the enemy: should the darts twice strike their mark, the Mexica would prevail. Magnificent in his spreading quetzal plumes, with his four attendants, Quetzal Owl plunged into the battle. For a time they could follow his movements in the swirl of combat, reclaiming stolen gold and quetzal plumes, and taking three captives, or so they thought. Then, leaping from a terrace, he was lost to view. The Spaniards record nothing of this exemplary combat as the city died.

As if in response to that premature attempt to force the revelation of the city's fate there came, at last, a sign. In the night a great 'bloodstone', a blazing coal of light, flared over the city before plunging into the lake, and the Mexica knew their time of rule was over.[16] Nonetheless they yielded only when their new tlatoani Cuauhtemoc, 'Swooping Eagle', was captured by the Spaniards as he sought to escape from his ruined city.

A great Mexica lament survives. It runs:

> Broken spears lie in the roads;
> we have torn our hair in our grief.
> The houses are roofless now, and their walls
> are red with blood.
>
> Worms are swarming in the streets and plazas,
> and the walls are splattered with gore.
> the water has turned red, as if it were dyed,
> and when we drink it,
> it has the taste of brine.
>
> We have pounded our hands in despair
> against the adobe walls,
> for our inheritance, our city, is lost and dead.
> The shields of our warriors were its defence,
> but they could not save it.[17]

And so it continues. The poem is often cited to demonstrate the completeness of the obliteration of a way of life and a way of thought. But what is notable here (apart from the poetic power) is that the lament was for Tenochtitlan, not its people; it at once memorialized their once-great city, and located their catastrophic defeat in the movement of time. If the

Mexican vision of empire was finished, the Mexica and their sense of distinctiveness were not. The great idols had been somehow smuggled out of the city by their traditional custodians before its fall and sent north towards Tula: a retracing of their earlier migratory route. A cyclic view of history has its comforts. The survivors were ready to leave their god-designated place, and to follow their god on their wanderings once more.

They were not, of course, permitted to do so. As they filed out of the wreckage which had been Tenochtitlan, the Spaniards were waiting. They took the prettier women and the young boys, branding them on the face or lip to mark them as possessions, and set the men to raising a Spanish city on the ruins of their own. The Spaniards reserved a special death for priests, like the Keeper of the Black House in Tenochtitlan, and the wise men who came from Texcoco by their own will, bearing their painted books. They were torn apart by dogs.[18]

Cortés had promised Cuauhtemoc honour in defeat. Then he had him tortured in the Spaniards' furious, futile drive to recover some fraction of the treasure lost in their first expulsion from the city. The Mexica leader maintained his silence. Forced along with other native rulers to accompany Cortés on his expedition to Honduras, Cuauhtemoc was charged with 'conspiracy' and hanged from a pochote tree late in 1523. With him died the lord of Tlacopan, Don Pedro Cortés Tetlepanquetzatzin ('Lord Mountain of the Banners of the Most Precious Quetzal'), and the lord of Texcoco, Don Pedro Cohuanacochtzin. So ended the leadership of the Triple Alliance on which the Aztec confederacy had rested.

With such deaths and destruction the glory of the Mexica departed, and the young found new models to follow. But the old men remembered, and told their memories to the young men who had chosen to serve the new rulers and the new religion, when they found some who would listen.

Epilogue

There is a long and painful distance between the lived Mexica world and the small clutter of carved stones and painted paper, the remembered images and words, from which we seek to make that world again. Historians of remote places and peoples are the romantics of the human sciences, Ahabs pursuing our great white whale, dimly aware that the whole business is, if coolly considered, rather less than reasonable. We will never catch him, and don't much want to: it is our own limitations of thought, of understandings, of imagination we test as we quarter those strange waters. And then we think we see a darkening in the deeper water, a sudden surge, the roll of a fluke – and then the heart-lifting glimpse of the great white shape, its whiteness throwing back its own particular light, there, on the glimmering horizon.

A Question of Sources

I

The only contemporaneous descriptions we have of the living city of Tenochtitlan come from the Spaniards who went on to conquer it, and have the defects and the advantages of outsider accounts. The most complete is that offered by Bernal Díaz, a footsoldier in the Spanish expedition, who wrote his 'True History of the Conquest of New Spain' in old age. Despite the lapse of years, and some ingenuous attempts at self-promotion, Díaz was sufficiently impressed by the pure extraordinariness of what he had seen to strive to record it, without much elaboration or interpretation. His leader Hernando Cortés, writing his reports from the field to his Emperor, is notably less 'reliable', his own desperate political situation dictating too much of what he chose to report, omit, or invent. As outsiders, both often had little understanding of what they were looking at. Their accounts, like the handful of other thinner and even more skewed conquistador reports we happen to have, are at once imperfect, and invaluable.[1]

A few pre-contact painted books or 'codices' survived the conquest and its aftermath. It is one of many poignancies of Central Mexican studies that for the area for which we have the richest post-contact written sources, the Valley of Mexico, there survives possibly only one screenfold book, the Codex Borbonicus. The Borbonicus was painted either before the conquest, or very shortly afterwards, probably for a native patron, and there are indicators that it originated in Tenochtitlan.[2] It is remarkable not only for its size, but for its beauty. There are some post-conquest codices, copies of earlier pictographic books now lost, reproduced on the orders of missionary friars the better to know their enemy, or secretly commissioned by native nobles to preserve their past.[3] Others, like the Codex Mendoza, composed on the orders of the first Viceroy of Mexico twenty years after the conquest to instruct him in how the natives had once lived, were drawn afresh, to satisfy Spanish curiosity and to answer Spanish questions.

The 'Anales' of Tlatelolco, possibly transcribed into European script in 1528, a mere seven years after the conquest, is the first indigenous document written in European script that we have, and seems to have escaped Spanish influence, although who did the transcribing remains mysterious.[4] Most post-conquest Nahuatl texts were hybrid affairs. The codices drawn after the conquest derived their information from different localities, and are deeply if unevenly tinctured by Spanish Christian assumptions and expectations.[5] The two great collections of Nahuatl 'song-poems' written down (and some possibly composed) in the 1560s give some access, through their patterns of verse, their insistent metaphors, and their mournful evocation of mood, to pre-contact sensibility, despite the years of Spanish rule and the intrusion of Christian notions.[6] The last decades of the sixteenth and the first of the seventeenth centuries saw the production of 'histories' by members of the small acculturated Indian élite of generations born after the conquest, alert to their uneasy place within the Christian colonial world, and eager to demonstrate the antiquity of their lineages.[7] The hybrid quality suffuses the 'Relaciones Geográficas' of 1578–86. Responses to a wide range of questions addressed to the royal officials and prominent Spaniards of his overseas realm by Philip II of Spain, the Relaciones provide a conglomerate of material, neatly organized for comparative studies and usefully tied to specific regions, but with the accuracy and the real authorship of the information too often uncertain to allow close critical evaluation.[8]

There were early Spanish scholars, professional men of religion mostly, whose interests were at once narrower and broader. Committed to the notion of conversion, they sought to record any material they judged conducive to a better understanding of the old ways, if only to effect their destruction.[9] They were men of their times, and from all they heard and saw they recorded only what they thought mattered. But they were sensitive to the wonders of the new lands, and their curiosity was wide-ranging. As I have said in the Introduction, the most remarkable among them was the Franciscan Bernardino de Sahagún, eliciting information from noble Mexican elders on a great range of issues, having their agreed responses recorded in Nahuatl, and organizing the mass of material so accumulated into the twelve 'books' of his *General History of the Things of New Spain*. In 1979 the final and most complete version of the Nahuatl account of the History, the Florentine Codex, as it has come to be called, was published in a magnificent facsimile edition by the Archivo General de la Nación de Mexico.[10] That publication has allowed all interested scholars to see the pages of the Codex as they were prepared between 1577 and 1580. The Nahuatl text appears in the right-hand column, the few sections empty of words being filled with floral designs. The much briefer Spanish text in the left column, which leaves some passages untranslated and others no more than summarized, allowed space for many more illustrations. Despite a scatter of 'native' characteristics, the artists were clearly conversant with Spanish forms of representation, if not with Spanish technical skills. These beguiling little drawings were probably drawn by Sahagún's assistants purely as illustrations of the Spanish and Nahuatl texts, and so do not provide an additional and independent source of native practices and concepts.[11]

The Florentine Codex has remained the major source for Mexica life in the decades before the conquest. With all its defects – produced by survivors of the erstwhile ruling group; exclusively male; further distanced from the actuality we seek to glimpse by its idealizing tendency and its Spanish eliciting and editing; abducted into English – it is nonetheless the best source we have for Mexica views, and for accounts of Mexica action as described by Mexica voices. If those voices were constrained on some occasions by inappropriate Spanish demands, on others they were allowed to run free, Sahagún being sufficiently sensitive to the risk of unwitting influence to give his informants a large degree of latitude on the issues which most interested him. We have accounts of life-cycle rituals; of drunkenness licensed and unlicensed; of proverbs and improving speeches and 'superstitions' and jokes. Sahagún's special interest was with religion, most particularly religious observances. Professionally concerned to assay contemporary 'Christian' Indian observances for pagan dross, he believed it was possible to uncover more of what men thought from the minute observation of what they habitually did than from what they might occasionally be brought to say. He therefore encouraged his informants to give uninhibitedly full descriptions, in their own terms, of their ritual performances at all levels. While the accounts of rituals are singularly rich, Sahagún was also eager to record less formal actions and words which he thought embodied native understandings. The formal Mexica imperial texts, of monuments, official chronicles and tribute lists, or the magnificent song-poems through which a warrior aristocracy pursued its vision, must be contexted within this more discursive material if we are to glimpse how the Mexica might have seen their world when it still lived.

Some artefacts escaped the deliberate or casual devastations of the conquest. Cortés shipped a number of exotic objects back to Charles V, who had them exhibited in Brussels as evidence of the wealth and strangeness of his new domains. Most then seem to have been dispersed to his noble kin throughout Europe, to be salvaged from remote storerooms and forgotten cupboards over the last century with the revival of interest in such exotica. Other objects entombed in the process of the destruction have been haphazardly retrieved during the digging of drains, sewers and subways in Mexico City, which Cortés with his developed flair for the telling gesture built on and out of the ruins of Tenochtitlan. The Templo Mayor project in the Cathedral square of Mexico City, only recently completed, has been one of the few controlled excavations within the city.[12]

So much for the remains. How can they best be exploited? They present the problems familiar to any practising historian, especially historians of the more distant past and of more remote peoples. They are fragmentary, few, skewed by special interest, and their relationship to the world which made them is mysterious, at least to us. That last issue raises some practical and epistemological issues I would like to pursue, to indicate my general strategies for their use.

2

Historians have to seek the past through any and all objects made by man's hands or marked by man's mind – 'natural' stones or rivers or hills, creatures or caves, as well as buildings and books; all of them 'made' by virtue of having been given meaning. (Consider attempting to grasp the imaginative world of Australian aborigines, or of Australian farmers or miners for that matter, without being attentive to their reading of the landscape and to what they identified as its significant features.) Some objects will have been deliberately, and some inadvertently, preserved, while some are virtually indestructible, like the vague markings left on the earth by past cultivation, or those even more ambiguous traces of the past in present lives. All constitute Nabokov's great category of 'those transparent things through which the past shines.'[13]

Nabokov had in mind the dizzying temporal perspective opened by the contemplation of 'timeless' objects and apparently timeless activities: 'you are thinking, and quite rightly so, of a hillside stone over which a multitude of small animals have scurried in the course of incalculable seasons.'[14] But among the plethora of 'things through which the past shines' it shines most brightly, at least for historians, through written texts, with which we work most confidently, most easily, and (most of us) exclusively. We are professionally text-orientated people in a text-orientated society. That can severely limit our capacity to grasp the possible meaning of texts, and more particularly of other kinds of sources, produced by other kinds of societies. How are we to discover the moods and meanings of peoples who, like the Mexica, expressed themselves most readily in song, dance and formal speech, and in 'writing' as we know it not at all? Our intellectual and imaginative parochialism renders us epistemologically naïve: skilled at locating the text in its context, alert for forgeries, we easily fall into taking the relationship between the text and its producing consciousness as unproblematical.

Against that complacency I pose Paul Veyne's bracingly straightforward comment: 'Historical criticism has only one function: to answer the question asked of it by the historian: "I believe that this document teaches me this: may I trust it to do that?"'[15] This deceptively artless question unleashes some very large theoretical dragons. For example, while most of us have no experience at first or even second hand of a less than thoroughly literate culture, we know that vast numbers of people in the past – women, children, slaves, workers, indeed almost everybody – while talkative enough in their own worlds, were retrospectively struck dumb, rendered 'inarticulate', by the selectivity of the written record, and that ninety-nine percent of our own interactions will vanish the same way. We 'know' it, but it is rather more difficult to track its devastating implications for our professional practice. If anthropologists are now suffering from epistemological angst as they strive to understand 'the other' as he stands befeathered or bejeaned before them, historians, too, face the same problems, in a form at once more rarified, and more acute. We cannot attend the speech and actions of our subjects; we question only the dead, those unnaturally docile informants, and then most commonly through their words on paper: blurred hieroglyphs of the actualities which led to their inscription.

Consider the range of anxieties roused by reflection on the Nahuatl text of Sahagún's Florentine Codex, that indispensable text. It was put together a full generation after the conquest. Sahagún was unusual in his determination to use knowledgeable Indian informants, to realize that their statements would be collective, and to check those collective statements against similar statements of other equally knowledgeable elders from adjacent settlements. The statements were elicited in part by presenting traditional pictographic material for elucidation, and in part by questions asked by his hand-picked and mission-trained Indian aides, who then wrote down the collectively agreed replies in European script.

Historians are immediately alert to the conditions of the production of such texts: they were exacted in a coercive colonial setting; what was said was shaped by what was or was not asked; that which the scribes wrote down was a further selection from what was said. The Florentine Codex was then selected from that material, and categorized and organized in accordance with Sahagún's own aims and understandings. And what of the material itself? While the native elders were trustworthy in Sahagún's view, no informant, whether native or stranger, can be securely 'reliable' on all or most matters. Consider our own biographies: memories melt and metamorphose, and shifting experience demands constant revision, as we struggle to construct a reasonably plausible account out of the exigent. For Sahagún's ageing nobles the past was lit by the brilliant but notoriously uneven retrospective light of catastrophe. They had lost the bright world of their youth not through the slow dimming of years and memory, but through the brutal intervention of foreign conquerors. It must have shown the more golden for that.

The inscription of the spoken words carries its own difficulties and deficiencies. Some are sufficiently obvious. The scribes – young men, close to the new authorities, with little respect for a far-away world in ruins before they were born – occasionally made ideological insertions: for example, the Spanish *demonios* (for 'gods'), which would not have been spoken by the informants, appears in the Nahuatl text. The consequences of the mechanical difficulties of representing the spoken word on the page are less manageable. Nahuatl was a language of compound words, and highly inflected, with prefixes, suffixes, infixes. The scribes wrote as they heard, often failing to separate words, and so leaving the 'blocks' from which the words were composed unclear. Such dubious orthographies present painful problems. In a particularly valuable colonial manuscript from 1558 a 'small ambiguity in the linguistic structure of the original' permits equally devoted translators to present the male hero either as deflowering and/or devouring the mythic female, or being himself assaulted and eaten: no small discrepancy.[16]

These much-processed and often problematical Nahuatl texts have since been translated into English. Here again we know something of the difficulties of translation, about the clouds of connotation surrounding words, and the great diversity of language games different peoples play. Where a native speaker would have been responsive to the delicacy of construction of the compound words and their nuanced subtleties, we are sometimes unable to establish even an undisputed text, much less an agreed translation. Experienced translators of mid-sixteenth-century written Nahuatl, which is often highly elaborate given the allusive nature of Nahua discourse, acknowledge that 'with the expenditure of a little ingenuity one can arrive at an indefinite number of plausible interpretations of [a] single passage'.[17] An example: the seasoned translators Dibble and Anderson accept the Franciscan Sahagún's translation of *neyolmelahualiztli* – a verbal statement made to the goddess Tlazolteotl, 'Filth Goddess' or 'Garbage God' – as a 'confession'. Miguel León-Portilla disagrees, pointing out that if the word is reviewed philologically, and the contexts of its component parts analysed, the meaning arrived at is 'an act or rite of straightening someone's heart'. Here is a case where a seductively available Spanish Christian concept lies ready to hand, perhaps obscuring a different Mexica understanding. Another less immediately dramatic but ultimately more perturbing case concerns the nature of certain mirrors known to be important in the sacred paraphernalia of the pre-contact period. Sahagún translated a phrase descriptive of the ideally wise man, *tezcatl necoc xapo*, as 'a mirror polished on both sides', presumably referring to the smoky slab of obsidian which could be used as a scrying glass, as with Tezcatlipoca. A later scholar reads it as 'a mirror punctured on both sides', taking it as a reference to a type of sceptre included in the regalia of certain deities: a 'seeing instrument' through which they could view the affairs of men. A seeing instrument punctured on both sides, presumably a kind of celestial spyglass, indicates a very different understanding of human–sacred relations than that implied by the use of a shadowed mirror polished on both sides, which suggests the ubiquity of the illusory, the ultimate impenetrability of a sacred zone which throws back only dark and clouded images.[18] Thus we are tempted to plunge into 'the abyss between the ways two languages mean', as A. L. Becker has memorably put it. Such acute problems might be infrequent, but they serve to keep complacency at bay.[19]

Historians work with those painfully retrieved words pinned like so many butterflies to the page, remote from their animate existence. It is hard to keep in mind their flickering variability, their strenuous context-dependence, in life. Words do not always mean what they seem to say. When in a speech of the most exquisite courtesy the lords of Tenochtitlan invited the lords of Tlatelolco to bring their wives and daughters to sing and dance at a Tenochan feast, we know from subsequent action what the two groups of Mexica knew instantly: an insult expungeable only by war had been delivered. When we watch the Mexica ruler Moctezoma presenting rich gifts to Cortés and making his famous speech of 'welcome', we need the reminder from other more accessible cultures of just how conventional speeches of welcome, and just how aggressive gift-giving, can be.

Then there is the question of what is not said; as José Ortega y Gasset has observed:

The stupendous reality that is language cannot be understood unless we begin by observing that speech consists above all in silences. . . . And each language represents a different equation between manifestations and silences. Each people leave some things unsaid *in order to* be able to say others.[20]

The span of the appropriate use of speech does not easily reveal itself in the historical record, especially to historians, who are not trained to be sensitive to the multiple uses of speech and silences in other societies, or even in their own.[21] Here anthropologists can alert us to unfamiliar manners. Annette Weiner describes a people who avoid words in the structuring of key social and political relationships as too ominous and too powerful for such delicate matters:

> Villagers read exchange events by treating the objects and styles of exchange as evidences of attitudes and expectations. In this way, objects communicate what words cannot. Objects change hands in formal settings, publicly announcing one's expectations but keeping the calculations verbally silent.[22]

A different balance is struck by the northern Guatemalan Maya people described by Manning Nash. They use speech frugally at all times, relying largely on glance and gesture to guide them through daily interaction. Even in novel situations there is little recourse to speech. When the technical skills of handling complex weaving machines had to be communicated to technologically unsophisticated girls, there was no verbal instruction, nor even slow-motion demonstration: the girls simply watched weavers at work over several weeks, until they declared themselves ready to take over.[23] Reading that, I am reminded of the constant exhortations to keep a tight curb on the tongue in the 'advice to the young' homilies of the Florentine Codex, and the contrast between the mannered silences of Mexica lords in their public capacity as judges, speaking few words and those softly, and their superb formal eloquence in the public setting of feasts. I am also alerted to the possibility that when mundane speech is so conscientiously curbed there might well be an equivalent expansion of a vocabulary of demeanour and gesture, where understanding must be sought through the analysis of observed action.

Fortunately for the historian, words were valued by the Mexica. If ordinary speech was restricted, formal eloquence was nurtured in the Mexica world: part of the essential training of noble youth were exercises in elegant speech, which, while constrained by convention, went beyond the formulaic to art.[24] It is a sad paradox that we have the magnificent speech of the Mexica elders only because their own way of recording the world was broken. Reading their words, we note the poise of the cadences and the practised balance of the repetitions and parallelisms: a poise and balance which somehow survive translation. The speech is always skilled: most when dictating conventional homilies or the archaic Nahuatl of the sacred chants, least when unexpected questions forced the respondents into innovation; but always skilled.

The Mexica identified the key attribute and agency of human authority in the authority to speak, calling their ruler, the tlatoani, 'He Who Speaks'. Poetic speech they called 'flower-song', representing it in their painted books as a flowered scroll issuing from the mouth, coloured the blue-green of the most precious and the most sacred. Words chanted in a framed setting were likened to 'the unshadowed, the precious perfect green stone, the precious turquoise', which for the Mexica represented the unsullied perfection of the divine in a sullied world.[25] Remembering witchcraft imprecations and curses in our own tradition, we can allow that words uttered with malice can effect physical damage, or can be believed to do so. We know something of the power of sacred words, and the darker power of their deliberate inversion. It is harder to grasp the notion of song as compulsive, or to think of sung words as world-creating. Yet the Navajo still sing mundane songs to maintain harmony in the world, and ritual songs to refresh it. To understand the lustre of the sung words of the ancient Mexica is to sense their vision of the world.

When understanding of the meaning and effect of words depends on the subtle grasp of context, which, *pace* Saussure, is always, 'being there' has incomparable advantages. Remote as we are in time, experience and understanding from the Mexica, many of their meanings must and will be lost. Faced with the disguised or double speech of wit or irony or insult, or the casual nuances of deep local knowledge, the historian will be fortunate to catch enough of the drift even to identify the kind of occasion she is dealing with. In Geertz's famous winks-and-twitches formulation, we can hope to pick the winks from the twitches (especially as twitches do not commonly find their way into the record) and some winks from other winks, but only rarely and by rare good fortune winks from nudges, or the untroubled innocent glance from the insulting refusal to wink back.[26]

Anthropologists are trained to look hungrily to myths for the masterkey to native sensibilities. Indigenous myths are not easy to find in the surviving Mexican material, not least because Sahagún and his fellow friars were not particularly interested in the foul fictions of the Devil, while Christian stories (a favoured mode of teaching) quickly overlaid and moulded recorded native tales to exemplify Christian concerns. The few myths which have survived are, as usual, skeletal, and therefore dangerously amenable to ingenious interpretation. Even where a ritual transparently dramatizes a myth, as with the festival of Panquetzaliztli, the

'Raising of Banners' ceremony which celebrated the heroic birth and first triumph of Huitzilopochtli, we cannot assume the 'story' supplied the dominant attraction and meaning for the participants.

This brushes what is perhaps the most intractable, troubling, and engaging problem of all. Nahuatl was and is a language rich in metaphor, and the Mexica took delight in exploring veiled resemblances. The puzzle is to know when they were speaking, as we would say, 'merely' metaphorically, and when they were speaking literally, simply describing the world as they knew it to be. In certain tropes, as when maize is invoked as human flesh, we casually take the linked concepts to be so widely separated that we assume we are dealing with metaphor and the cognitive *frisson* of overleaping difference. Then comes the jolting recognition that the Mexica might well have been stating a perceptually unobvious but unremarkable truth: maize was flesh. On other occasions, when the gap appears to us to be narrow, they might well have been 'speaking metaphorically'. In a differently conceptualized world concepts are differently distributed. If we want to know the metaphors our subjects lived by, we need first to know how language scanned actuality. Linguistic messages in foreign (or in familiar) tongues require not only decoding, but interpretation.[27]

Trained to be inquisitive about the distribution of 'literacy' and its social meaning, historians are less attentive to variations in cultural forms of inscription of knowledge, and to the implications the different forms might hold for social differentiation, the distribution of social power, and for those other more aery but equally real zones, the hierarchy of modes of perception, and the shape and coherence of the imagined universe. Amerindian societies have a long tradition of record-keeping through systems of conventionalized abstract representations.[28] (The phonetic content in these systems varied: in the Mexica case it was slight.) Sahagún's old men spoke their knowledge guided by traditional pictographic 'writings'. Had they the requisite training, the young scribes to whom they communicated that knowledge could have recreated the traditional mode of its representation through images of particular content and shape, distributed in particular relationships over the page. The pictographic codices have properly been judged the 'purest' sources we have, but our understanding of them is at best partial: if the pictographic mode provided a fine and flexible medium for its practitioners, it remains sadly gnomic for uninstructed outsiders struggling to decipher meanings for the patterned images alone. (The written-in Spanish glosses are largely guesses sanctified by time, while the later heavily annotated post-conquest compilations are suffused with Spanish Christian understandings.)

As has been seen in an earlier discussion, the same underlying pattern sustained different modes of recording consciousness – in buildings and their spatial distribution, carvings, and the choreography of rituals, as well as in the painted texts they mimicked.[29] The Mexica were noted even among their neighbours for the complexity and intensity of their public ceremonial, although there is little trace of all that swirling activity. Some ritual objects and structures in stone or clay survive, lit and labelled on the walls of museums, or roped away on dusty streets. Even in those unpromising surroundings they have extraordinary presence. We are a long way from the elegant elongations and the reassuringly 'human' gods of the Maya. The squat, blunt pyramids rest heavily on the earth; the heavy, blunt-bodied statues tilt blank faces upwards. The sumptuously carved fruits and squashes, the thick-coiled serpents, are oppressively weighty and earth-bound. They have the formidable completeness of archaic things. Behind these obdurate stony forms we see the shadows of grim implacable killers of men, and those horror stories of human sacrifice take on a sudden subliminal sense.[30]

The impression, for all its coherence, is mistaken. The objects displayed for our contemplation bear about as much relationship to those same objects in use as the bleaching bones of a dolphin to the bright creature in the sea. The stone-grey pyramids (like the Greek temples we now admire for their 'classical' austerity) were once vivid with coloured stucco: the Mexica palette has never been subdued. Even so they were mere empty stages until, crested with plumed banners and lit by slow-smoking fires, brilliantly clad priests and votaries moved upon them. The bleak stone figures came to ritual life only when swaddled in rich fabrics and decked with jewels, their empty hands filled with flowers or feathers or the springing green of the maize. And given the Mexica passion for the ephemeral, the skeletal quality of the few surviving objects springs from more than the carelessness of conquerors and the passage of time: the perishability of so much of the sacred paraphernalia (including the human victims) was an essential part of their meaning. So, unhappily, what most mattered to the Mexica has left no remains, and what does now remain is mute; the dance, drum, and chant which formed so central a part of Mexica ritual as lost as the wreathing flowers.

So we return to ritual action. I have already indicated the grounds for my relatively tranquil dependence on Sahagún's record. With other products of the Spanish recording impulse I am less sanguine. The Dominican Diego Durán, who arrived in Mexico 'before he shed his milk teeth', learned Nahuatl to casual fluency. But while the exuberance of Durán's 'descriptions' of ritual performances is seductive, his is very much an outsider's view. What we glimpse of his research and writing techniques – intimidation lightly mitigated by condescension; his casual and confident 'translations' where inference masquerades as description; his sense of the ludicrousness of native observances, and his readiness in that most localist polity to draw on a wide geographical zone for his statements about 'Indians' – is not conducive to confidence. The Franciscan Toribio de Motolinía, one of the original 'Twelve Apostles to the Indies', arriving in 1524, was perhaps a more careful reporter but a less shrewd observer than Durán, but he too drew on a wide locality for his generalizations.[31] The great advantage of the Sahagún corpus in the Nahuatl version is that we know the circumstances and the places of its creation, and know it to offer a reasonably dense account of ritual life in Tenochtitlan.

The narratives of ritual action as collected into the second book of the Florentine Codex, or studded through the other volumes, have a peculiar poignancy, as they must have been fully artefacts of the conquest situation. I can imagine no circumstance before the conquest in which a detailed overview of ritual action could have had utility. Responsibility for the multiple activities, from individual household through the ward to the main temple precinct, lay in many different hands, and some, the most 'customary', in no particular hands at all. Perhaps the high priest of a cult may have traced the whole complex action of his festival, at all its various levels, in his mind, as he examined the appropriate pictographic representations, rehearsed the bridging action, and considered the taxing problems of timing and supply of the necessary paraphernalia.[32] But priestly concern would have been with public and official action. Nowhere would the complex integration of action at different levels have been fully inscribed. Much of the Sahagún material has the resonance of confident memory: the chants to the gods, in their archaic Nahuatl; the formal exhortations of parents to children; even the midwife's prayer for the newborn child, spoken where no male was present – all these lay easily in the old men's memories, and rolled easily from their tongues. But the narratives of the rituals had no precedents. Their novelty is suggested by their confusions and opacities: giving a lucid account of complex and multi-level action takes practice.

Nonetheless, as nonce-narratives the Codex descriptions have their own value. They tell us that these men, little more than youths at the time of the conquest, and none of them on the evidence priests, were engrossed and knowledgeable participants in ritual life. They also tell us, by revealing the aspects of that action which lived most vividly in old men's minds, what had most compelled their imaginations when young. Were we somehow privileged to be present at one of those ceremonies, we would see a confusion of undifferentiated action, and would be bewildered to know what parts of that action were 'in' the ritual, and what were not. The Mexica voices not only set the boundaries but instruct us as to what we should mark, as they linger and elaborate on moments and objects of particular import. They are mute as to explicit statements of emotions and meanings, but their moments of sharp focus highlight significance, and so indicate the associations and processes the Mexica were seeking to display. There were particular somatic and kinetic experiences the Mexica identified with the encounter with the sacred. It has been one of the major challenges of this study to reconstruct, from fragile clues, something of the context and content of those experiences.[33]

If the listing of the multitude of impediments sounds too dismal a note, there has been a recent astonishing bonus. In 1978 a chance discovery of the magnificent carved stone disk representing Huitzilopochtli's warrior sister Coyolxauhqui renewed interest in the possibility of a controlled excavation within the precinct of the Cathedral of Mexico. The political conditions being right, the Templo Mayor project was initiated, the excavation of the great pyramid being completed in 1982.[34] Thus we have extraordinary undisturbed caches of offerings revealed *in situ*. The organizing theme of a particular assemblage is sometimes clear enough: for example, an earlier excavation, in 1900, in front of the Great Temple, had exposed clusters of things which we can easily enough identify as to do with music and its making: a seated 'idol', miniature clay pots and drums and rattles, flutes, stone drums and drumsticks, a clay turtleshell drum, and a stone turtle. Sometimes the principle of association is discernible, but not the organizing theme: what ought we make of two vessels of parrot and goose bones, or the remains of forty-five parakeets, an unspecified number of parrots and ducks, and three cranes, all carefully laid away with some maguey spines? In another Templo Mayor cache human skulls were set to face west, along with obsidian knives, flint knives, copper bells and ear ornaments. Here is a beginning intelligibility: the west is the region of the dead, flint and obsidian knives are associated with human sacrifice. But why should three flint knives be jammed between the jaws of some, and only some, of the skulls?[35] Then there are the extraordinary accumulations of natural things drawn from the sea: coral, fish bones, bird bones, drifts of shells carved and real, whole crocodiles, delicately placed on beds of different kinds of sand: what did they signify to the men who laid them out so tenderly?[36] Some clusters yield up their possible meaning only when supplemented by other kinds of sources. Considered alone, it is difficult to make much of a vessel with traces of rubber, a brazier with ashes, the remains of a sawfish snout, maguey thorns, four cakes of copal (the native incense), flint knives, and a stone frog with blue paint. Considered together, the collection silently signals 'rain and fertility ritual apparatus' to anyone familiar with Mexica ritual.

These assemblages are more rewarding than their more obviously spectacular individual parts of masks and images and jewels, for given their range and variety they promise some retrieval of Mexica categories of thought. Even where the principle of association is quite unclear, there is the heady prospect of suddenly recognizing the category elsewhere in some casual description of Mexica life. Documented Mexica behaviour of the immediate post-conquest period offers possibilities, remarkable work having been done to clarify the arrangements of pre-contact institutions and most basic assumptions through the analysis of post-conquest responses to the new regime: the modifications in language and address which point to the intensification of engagement with things and persons Spanish; the enduring patterns of organization and of ideas about the right order of things, masked but far from obliterated by imposed Spanish forms. While the procedure has some of the necessary imperfections of reconstructing shipboard life on the Titanic from social relations in the lifeboats, it has proved notably fruitful.[37] The documentation is, however, scattered, which is a particular problem for Tenochtitlan, distinctive as it was in its claimed supremacy, its size, and its ethnic and social complexity.

I have therefore drawn cautiously on findings relating to what are claimed to be persisting social and sacred understandings identified through analyses derived from other milieux, at most using them for the reinforcement of probabilities which find their essential ground within the city.

Over all there hovers the issue of appropriate strategies of contextualization. The 'ethnographic present' offers constant temptation to project present meanings backwards through time. In my view that temptation must be resisted: an impression of continuity might rest on no more than our ignorance of change.[38] The North American comparison finds its utility in pointing to possibilities, or as a reminder of just how fragmentary and piecemeal our knowledge of the Mexica is. For example: we know something of the marvellous complexity of a few North American native rituals, as with the 'smoke offering' in the Pawnee Ghost Dance hand games, which Lesser required thirty pages to describe, or the complex 'stepped' development of a ritual song.[39] By contrast we have for the Mexica no more than shorthand references to 'offering smoke', and only slight indications of a song's elaboration.

3

To reconstruct mood from written descriptions of external action, supplemented by esoteric, highly simplified and essentially mnemonic drawings and artefacts of an alien sensibility, is clearly risky. We build pictures in the mind out of the fragments we have, while crucial nuances might well escape us. I am haunted by Gregory Bateson's cautionary tale about his reconstruction of the *naven* ceremony of the Iatmul of New Guinea. Despite having had the ceremony described to him by several participants, it was only when he saw it himself that he realized the mental picture he had composed of the ritual had been wrong: no one had thought to mention that a key figure, a transvestite, was a figure of fun.[40]

A glance at any actual society, with its multiple and cross-cutting networks and its ambivalences, teaches us how unreal the most complex reconstructions must be in their unnatural simplicity. We can sometimes glimpse the ragged edges of what time, chance or prejudice has torn away from the fabric of the realized past, as through the fleeting but frequent references to the 'books of dreams' of the Mexica, none of which survive, and of which we have no developed description. But always we have to be ready to acknowledge that whole areas of life of high significance to our subjects might simply escape our awareness altogether: a demoralizing recognition, but a necessary one. For Tenochtitlan, with its people defeated and dispersed, the city itself destroyed, and its past and its present appropriated by its conquerors, much must have slipped unremarked from the record. A thumbnail sketch, a rough *semblance,* is the best to be hoped for. It is within these constraints and out of these materials that I have sought to recover something of the texture of Mexica life on the eve of the Spanish conquest.

Monthly Ceremonies of the Seasonal (Solar) Calendar: *Xiuitl*

Key: Festival: translation: probable dates: most important powers honoured: episodes discussed in text.

1. *Atl Caualo.* 'Ceasing of Water'. 13 Feb.–4 Mar. Tlaloc, Chalchihuitlicue. Infants and small children paraded in litters, sacrificed (weeping) at specified places.

2. *Tlacaxipeualiztli.* 'The Flaying of Men'. 5 Mar.–24 Mar. Xipe Totec. Pyramid killings, gladiatorial sacrifices; the taunting of the warrior *xipe totecs;* 'feasting' of the kin on victim's flesh; the wearing of the skins by offering warriors and their associates. Other warriors dance, feast. The dance of the leaders of the Triple Alliance.

3. *Tocoztontli.* 'Little Vigil'. 25 Mar.–13 Apr. Tlaloc, Centeotl (Cinteotl), Chalchihuitlicue, Chicomecoatl. The casting away of the skins; planting rituals in fields.

4. *Uey Tocoztli.* 'Great Vigil'. 14 Apr.–3 May. Centeotl (Young Lord Maize Cob), Chicomecoatl, Tlaloc. Young men stain reeds with their blood; maize stalks brought from the fields to be set up as maize-gods and worshipped in the houses. Women make atole, pouring it into gourds, where it contracts and quivers. 'Blessing' of the seed corn, carried by Mexica girls. Youths' advances rejected. Offerings to Chicomecoatl of all her bounty.

5. *Toxcatl.* 'Dryness'(?) 4 May–23 May. Tezcatlipoca, Huitzilopochtli. Performance and death of Tezcatlipoca impersonator and his dark alter ego; construction of great seed-dough Huitzilopochtli image, and the mass offering of quail; warrior dancing and the dances of Mexica

295

women and maidens, 'embracing' Huitzilopochtli. Cudgelling of young warriors who 'joke' with the maidens.

6. *Etzalqualiztli.* 'Eating of Maize-bean Porridge'. 24 May–12 June. Tlaloc, Chalchihuitlicue. Major preliminary fasting; priests' violence along the road; priests' testing, and punishment for delinquencies. Etzalli freely shared at a time when food reserves depleted; warriors and 'Daughters of Joy' demand the porridge from commoners. Offerings of jewels, hearts, to Tlaloc and the lake waters.

7. *Tecuilhuitontli.* 'Little Feast Day of the Lords'. 13 June–2 July. Xochipilli, Uixtocihuatl. Death of 'Salt Lady'. Obligatory pulque-drinking by salt-farmers.

8. *Uey Tecuilhuitl.* 'Great Feast Day of the Lords'. 3 July–22 July. Xilonen, Cihuacoatl. Nobles feed poor commoners; singing, dancing and feasting of warriors and lords; erotic dancing of warriors with pleasure girls, and assignations arranged (punishment of warriors who 'joked' with the girls). Dance of all Mexica women. Xilonen, personifying the young ear of corn, and escorted by women, sacrificed, so the green maize could be eaten. Drunkards executed?

9. *Tlaxochimaco* (Miccailhuitontli). 'Offerings of Flowers' ('Little Feast Day of the Dead'). 23 July–11 Aug. Ancestors, Huitzilopochtli, Tezcatlipoca; all the gods in general. Field flowers offered to sacred images; dead honoured. Dancing of warriors and pleasure girls.

10. *Xocotlhuetzi* (Ueymiccailhuitl). 'The Xocotl (fruit?) Falls' ('Great Feast Day of the Dead'). 12 Aug.–31 Aug. Xiuhtecutli, Xocotl, Yacatecuhtli. Fire sacrifice; raising and climbing of the Xocotl pole by the young men; the 'capture' of the Xocotl and the reward of the captor.

11. *Ochpaniztli.* 'The Sweeping (of the Roads)'. 1 Sept.–20 Sept. Teteo Innan–Toci, Centeotl, Chicomecoatl. Women skirmish; the Teteo Innan impersonator sacrificed at midnight; the construction of the Toci ixiptla; harvest of corn (Young Lord Maize Cob) symbolically gathered as the season of war is initiated; Moctezoma distributes warrior insignia.

12. *Teotleco.* 'The Gods Arrive'. 21 Sept.–10 Oct. All the gods. General merrymaking; fire sacrifices.

13. *Tepeilhuitl.* 'The Feast of the Mountains'. 11 Oct.–30 Oct. Tlaloc,

Xochiquetzal, pulque gods. Seed-dough 'mountains' sacrificed, as are five human victims named as 'mountains'. The eating of the seed-dough and the victims' flesh.

14. *Quecholli* (Roseate Spoonbill). 'Precious Feather'. 31 Oct.–19 Nov. Mixcoatl, honouring the dead. Making of hunting gear; males of all ages camp out; the communal hunt, the successful rewarded as 'captors', with animal heads as sacred trophies; sacrifice of humans trussed like deer.

15. *Panquetzaliztli.* 'The Raising of Banners'. 20 Nov.–9 Dec. Huitzilopochtli, Tezcatlipoca. The marathon race by Paynal; large-scale warrior killings; processions, merchants offer pseudo-captives, who must fight along the way to the pyramid. The drinking of pulque by the old people and by warriors of high status. (Physical punishment of those warriors who drank illicitly.) Construction, 'killing' and eating of giant seed-dough image of Huitzilopochtli ('Eating the God', with its attendant obligations enduring for a year.)

16. *Atemoztli.* 'The Descent of Water'. 10 Dec.–29 Dec. Tlaloc. Commoners undertake to make and offer seed-dough images of mountains. The images feasted (offered tiny tamales, etc.), then 'killed' by the priests (with a weaving instrument) and eaten. Exchange of grain for food and drink. Skirmishes and mutual raidings and lootings between young priests and warrior youths.

17. *Tititl.* 'The Stretching'. 30 Dec.–18 Jan. Cihuacoatl, all the gods. The sacrifice of the Ilama Tecutli ixiptla; the 'reverse' image presented by the leading priest. The 'casting of bags' in the ritual harassment of women.

18. *Izcalli.* 'Growth, Rebirth'. 19 Jan.–7 Feb. Women offer tamales to family and kin; the 'stretching' of the children, and the pruning of the maguey. Young boys exchange 'wild' (water-related?) game for tamales; the feeding of the 'young' and 'old' Fire God. The presentation of the most recent crop of (weaned?) children at the local temple every fourth year, with the unrestrained drinking of pulque. The lords dance in 'natural' symbols of authority.

Nemontemi. The 'barren' or 'useless' days, outside the day-count. 8 Feb.–12 Feb. Fasting, penance, avoidance of conflict, as evil forces are abroad, unharnessed by ritual. Danger that the world will end.

The Mexica Pantheon

This is a simplified list. For a much more complex account see H. B. Nicholson, 'Religion in Pre-Hispanic Central Mexico'.

Centeotl. 'Young Lord Maize Cob'.

Chalchihuitlicue. 'Jade Skirt'. Goddess of fresh waters; kinswoman (sister? wife?) of Tlaloc.

Cihuacoatl. 'Woman Snake'. An aspect of Earth Mother, demanding war and sacrificial victims. Patroness of Cihuateteo.

Cihuateteo. 'Celestial Princesses'. The malevolent spirits of women dead in childbirth, represented by the five Cihuapipitlin, the 'Women Warrior' goddesses.

Coatlicue. 'Snake Skirt'. An aspect of the Earth Mother, especially for the Mexica. Mother of the Sun, Moon and Stars.

Coyolxauhqui. 'She with the Belled Cheeks'. Huitzilopochtli's malevolent warrior sister, associated with the Moon, who led her brothers the Stars against their infant sibling.

Huitzilopochtli. 'Hummingbird on the Left' ('from the South'). Usually an aspect of Tezcatlipoca: for the Mexica their tribal deity, God of War, and Sun God.

Macuilxochitl. 'Five Flower'. Patron of gambling, feasting, music and dance.

Mayahuel. 'She with Four Hundred Breasts'. Female personification of pulque.

Mictlantecutli. 'Lord of Mictlan'. Ruler of the place of the dead.

Mixcoatl(-Camaxtli). 'Cloud Snake'. God of Hunting. Patron of the Chichimecs.

Ometochtli. 'Two Rabbit'. God of pulque.

Ometeotl. 'Two God'. A bisexual unit, or more frequently a male (Ometecuhtli)–female (Omecihuatl) pair. Generators of the gods, inhabiting the highest heaven (the thirteenth). No active cult.

Quetzalcoatl. As Ehecatl, God of the Wind. Associated with priestly knowledge, and identified with the evil Evening Star and the benign Morning Star. Sometimes represented as an aspect of Tezcatlipoca, but more often in dynamic tension with the great god. (See the myth relating the self-exile of the perhaps historical figure of Quetzalcoatl Topiltzin, ruler of the Toltecs, as a result of the machinations of the sorcerer figure Tezcatlipoca.)

Teteo Innan–Toci. 'Mother of the Gods', 'Our Grandmother'. An inclusive conceptualization of the Earth Mother.

Tezcatlipoca. 'Smoking Mirror', or 'The Mirror's Smoke'. The supreme power, omnipresent and omnipotent. Patron of sorcerers, master of humans' destinies. Associated with Tepeyollotl, 'Heart of the Mountain', the jaguar god of the interior of the earth.

Tlaloc. 'He Who Lies on the Earth'. Rain God and master of agricultural fertility.

Tlaloque or *Tepictoton.* Tlaloc's dwarfish attendants, resident in the mountains, where the rain and clouds are made.

Tlazolteotl. 'Filth God' or 'Garbage God'. Sometimes female.

Uixtocihuatl. 'Salt Lady'; *Chicomecoatl,* 'Seven Snake'. Goddess of cultivated foods.

Xilonen. Goddess of the young corn. ('Xilotl' is the tender young maize ear.)

Xipe Totec. 'The Flayed Lord'. God of spring, fertility, and success in war.

Xiutecutli. 'Turquoise Lord' (*Huehueteotl,* 'The Old, Old God'). The sacred fire, the oldest god, connecting the household at once with the heavens, by way of the Fire Drill Stars and the Sun, and with the deepest layers of the earth.

Xochipilli/Xochiquetzal. 'Flower Prince' and 'Precious Feather Flower'. Male and female aspects of the dance, spring and pleasure; of weaving and craftsmanship.

Yacatecuhtli. 'The Long-Nosed God'. The Merchants' God.

Notes

INTRODUCTION

1 Kenneth Burke, *Permanence and Change: An Anatomy of Purpose*, p. 294.

2 The city was also sometimes called 'Mexico–Tenochtitlan'. Henceforth I will usually use the simple form 'Tenochtitlan'.

3 W. H. Prescott, *History of the Conquest of Mexico*, book 1, chapter 3, *passim*. For the feast, see p. 48; for the Toltec inheritance, p. 51.

4 For the protein-deprivation theory, see Michael Harner, 'The Ecological Basis for Aztec Sacrifice', and 'The Enigma of Aztec Sacrifice'; Marvin Harris, *Cannibals and Kings: The Origins of Cultures*. For the responses, see Bernard R. Ortiz de Montellano, 'Aztec Cannibalism: An Ecological Necessity?' and 'Counting Skulls: Comment on the Aztec Cannibalism Theory of Harner–Harris'; Barbara Price, 'Demystification, Enriddlement, and Aztec Cannibalism: A Materialist Rejoinder to Harner'; Marshall D. Sahlins, 'Culture as Protein and Profit'. For entropic waste, Christian Duverger, *La fleur létale: économie du sacrifice aztèque;* for the sinister élite account Robert C. Padden, *The Hummingbird and the Hawk*. For a penetrating enquiry, see Thelma Sullivan, 'Tlatoani and Tlatocayotl in the Sahagún Manuscripts'.

5 For example, Johanna Broda, 'Relaciones políticas ritualizadas: el ritual como expresión de una ideología', pp. 15–76, and 'Consideraciones sobre histo-riografía e ideología mexicas; las crónicas indígenas y el estudio de los ritos y sacrificios'; for the recruiting of the general populace, Cecelia Klein, 'The Ideology of Autosacrifice at the Templo Mayor', pp. 350–60.

6 Alfredo López Austin, *The Human Body and Ideology: Concepts of the Ancient Nahuas*, pp. 6, 1–2.

7 As Roger Chartier comments, 'the great assumption has been that intellectual divisions run along social boundaries, however those boundaries are drawn.' Roger Chartier, *Cultural History: Between Practices and Representations*, p. 30. Cf.

Chartier's useful recommendation that we think of 'popular culture' as 'at the same time both acculturated and acculturating. . . . We must replace the study of cultural sets that were considered as socially pure with another point of view that recognizes each cultural form as a mixture, whose constitutent elements meld together indissolubly'. Roger Chartier, 'Culture as Appropriation: Popular Cultural Uses in Early Modern France', p. 223.

8 Quixotic, but made less so by the avoidance of the deeper problems regarding 'the inevitable gaps between reality, experience, and expression' discussed in Victor W. Turner and Edward M. Bruner (eds.), *The Anthropology of Experience*. See esp. Bruner's 'Introduction'. My practical model for this aspect of the enterprise is Michele Z. Rosaldo's *Knowledge and Passion: Ilongot Notions of Self and Social Life;* see especially pp. 18–30. Of course Rosaldo's method – the slow tracking of more complete understanding through prolonged observation of the gestural and verbal language of the Ilongot in changing contexts – is inapplicable to a long-dead people knowable only through a few miserable remains.

9 Victor Turner, 'Religious Paradigms and Political Action', in his *Dramas, Fields and Metaphors: Symbolic Actions in Human Society,* p. 64. See also his chapter 1, 'Social Dramas and Ritual Metaphors'.

10 Turner later expanded the social drama concept to include ritual performance, on the grounds that each social form followed the same distinctive movement between ordering, disordering and reordering anew, seeing different performance genres as constituting metacommentaries on the agonistic events of daily life. I suspect the movement to be rather more dialectical, with the distilled accounts offered in performance doing their part to mould and script daily encounters: as Turner himself has pointed out in another place, 'Life, after all, is as much an imitation of art as the reverse'. Victor Turner, 'Liminality and the Performative Genres', pp. 19–41, 26.

11 Clifford Geertz, *Negara: The Theatre State in Nineteenth-Century Bali*, p. 103.

12 Jacques Soustelle, *La vie quotidienne des Aztéques en la veille de la conquête espagnole.* As S. L. Cline has succinctly put it, 'What the calpulli was is still unclear; how it functioned in relation to land is merely part of a larger problem'; 'Land Tenure and Land Inheritance in Late Sixteenth-Century Culhuacan', p. 287. Frederick Hicks possibly offers the least contentious definition of the calpulli or tlaxilacalli as 'a group of households forming a small barrio and having common tributary obligations'; 'Rotational Labor and Urban Development in Prehispanic Tetzcoco [Texcoco]', p. 161. For land tenure in general, see H. R. Harvey, 'Aspects of Land Tenure in Ancient Mexico'. Jerome A. Offner argues against the existence of any form of descent principle

in Mexica society, 'thus ruling out the existence of calpulli-clans'; 'Household Organization in the Texcocan Heartland: The Evidence in the *Codex Vergara'*, p. 142. For a fuller discussion, see Offner's *Law and Politics in Aztec Texcoco*, esp. chapter 5. Much of the best recent work is being done on the Tlaxcala–Puebla and the Texcocan region, and therefore sheds uncertain light on Tenochtitlan, which was in many ways distinctive.

13 David Cohen, 'From PIM's Doorway'.

14 I am mistrustful of the judgments of Spaniards, as of the self- and group-conscious histories written by acculturated Indian lords who set about retrieving something of their grandfathers' worlds in the last decades of the sixteenth and the early decades of the seventeenth centuries, putting rather more trust in the collective and earlier voices of Fr. Bernardino de Sahagún's Indian informants, or in the conventional formulations of the 'Cantares' or song-poems. On the latter, see, e.g., John Bierhorst, *Cantares Mexicanos: Songs of the Aztecs*. Bierhorst's contention that the 'song-poems' were in the main Ghost Songs, composed under Spanish rule in passive resistance to that rule, on the model of the Ghost-Dance movement of the late-nineteenth-century Plains Indians, has won very little scholarly support, but the translations themselves have been judged by some scholars (in what is admittedly a deeply divided˚discipline) to be able. See Gordon Brotherston, 'Songs and Sagas of the Old New World', *Times Literary Supplement*, 18 April 1986, p. 407.

15 But see Karl Anton Nowotny's suggestion for the scanning of Pueblo rituals for Mexican parallels; *Codex Borbonicus: Bibliothèque de l'Assemblée national, Paris*, pp. 19, 22. Linguists have remained notably sensitive to the Amerindian connection: e.g. Gordon Brotherston with Ed Dorn, *Image of the New World*.

16 I am indebted to James A. Boon, *Other Tribes, Other Scribes: Symbolic Anthropology in the Comparative Study of Cultures, Histories and Texts*, for the realization of the necessity of this step.

17 Fr. Bernardino de Sahagún, *The Florentine Codex: General History of the Things of New Spain*, hereafter *Florentine Codex*. Recently a magnificent facsimile edition of the Codex has been issued under the auspices of the Mexican government, so making its beauty accessible to a wider audience: *El Códice Florentino de Fray Bernardino de Sahagún*. For recent work and a Sahaguntine bibliography see Luis Nicolau D'Olwer, *Fray Bernardino de Sahagún, 1499–1590;* Munro S. Edmonson (ed.), *Sixteenth-Century Mexico: The Work of Sahagún;* J. Jorge Klor de Alva, H. B. Nicholson, and Eloise Quiñones Keber, *The Work of Bernardino de Sahagún: Pioneer Ethnographer of Sixteenth-Century Aztec Mexico*, esp. H. B. Nicholson, 'Recent Sahaguntine Studies: A Review', pp. 13–30.

18 See, e.g., Donald Robertson, 'The Sixteenth-Century Mexican Encyclopedia of Fray Bernardino de Sahagún', *Cuadernos de Historia Mundial* 9: 3(1966), 617–28.

19 Nicolau D'Olwer, *Fray Bernardino de Sahagún*, chapter 4.

20 For my own assessment of the epistemological difficulties attending its use, see 'A Question of Sources', pp. 277–92.

21 The 'Primeros memoriales', which were compiled a few years earlier, using the same technique, relate more to Tepepolco and the Texcoco region. Fr. Bernardino de Sahagún, *'Primeros memoriales' de Fray Bernardino de Sahagún*. However, the 'Primeros memoriales' drawings of the seasonal calendar rituals are usefully detailed. See also H. B. Nicholson, 'Tepepolco, the Locale for the First Stage of Fr. Bernardino de Sahagún's Great Ethnographic Project'.

22 Fr. Diego Durán, *Historia de las Indias de Nueva España e Islas de la Tierra Firme*. Vol. 1, the 'History', with some omissions, has been translated by Doris Heyden and Fernando Horcasitas as *The Aztecs: The History of the Indies of New Spain*, with Vol. 2, *The Book of the Gods and The Ancient Calendar*, being separately published. For an extensive use of Durán, see Nigel Davies, *The Aztecs: A History*, and *The Toltec Heritage: From the Fall of Tula to the Rise of Tenochtitlan*.

23 For the anguish, see Inga Clendinnen, 'Franciscan Missionaries in Sixteenth-Century Mexico', and 'Ways to the Sacred: Reconstructing "Religion" in Sixteenth-Century Mexico'.

1. TENOCHTITLAN: THE PUBLIC IMAGE

1 Fernando Alvarado Tezozómoc, 'The Finding and Founding of Mexico-Tenochtitlan', from the *Crónica mexicáyotl*, 1609. See the translation by Thelma D. Sullivan in *Tlalocan*.

2 Arriving as the Spaniards did in November, it is likely the lakes had not yet shrivelled into their five dry-season components. The 'valley' was more correctly a 'basin', having no outlet.

3 Hereafter 'Tenochtitlan'.

4 Anthony Pagden, *Hernán Cortés: Letters from Mexico*, Second Letter, p. 82. Hereafter Pagden, with letter and page number.

5 Pagden, Second Letter, pp. 103–5.

6 Pagden, Second Letter, p. 109.

7 Bernal Díaz del Castillo, *Historia verdadera de la conquista de la Nueva España* (the many translations include *The Conquest of New Spain*, trans. J. M. Cohen, Harmondsworth: Penguin Books, 1963), chapter 87.

8 J. H. Elliott, *Imperial Spain 1469–1716* (New York: Mentor Books, 1966), pp. 183–4.

9 For the cosmological principles underlying the city's shape see, e.g., Johanna Broda, David Carrasco, and Eduardo Matos Moctezuma, *The Great Temple of Tenochtitlan: Center and Periphery in the Aztec World;* for an analysis of Mexica sacred monuments for their ideological implications, Richard Townsend, *State and Cosmos in the Art of Tenochtitlan,* and Rudolph van Zantwijk, 'The Great Temple of Tenochtitlan: Model of Aztec Cosmovision'. Van Zantwijk offers a more elaborate and perhaps more extravagant interpretation in his *The Aztec Arrangement: The Social History of Pre-Spanish Mexico.* For a lucid and solidly based account of the valley and the city, see William T. Sanders, Jeffrey R. Parsons, and Robert S. Santley, *The Basin of Mexico: Ecological Processes in the Evolution of a Civilization.* The authors estimate that the population of the whole valley had increased from about 160,000 to about one million people in the last two hundred years before the Spanish conquest (p. 155). They set the population of the urban conglomerate they called 'Greater Tenochtitlan', and which included the contiguous cities around the lake edge, at half a million people – the largest urban population achieved in the valley to that date. Charles Gibson estimates the native population of the entire valley thirty years after the conquest at 75,000, with Spaniards numbering 8,000–10,000. Charles Gibson, *The Aztecs under Spanish Rule,* p. 377. Certainly the valley population, massively reduced by the impact of the Spanish intrusion, was not to reach that density again until the early twentieth century. The authors also suggest that very few of the inhabitants of Tenochtitlan and only about 25% of the whole valley population engaged in agriculture, but that the large-scale chinampas of the late empire period could have supplied up to half a million people with basic foodstuffs (p. 177). They argue that the urbanized population of Greater Tenochtitlan (including the satellite towns of Azcapotzalco, Tlacopán, Coyoacán, Huitzilopochco, Mexicaltzingo and Ixtapalapa) accounted for about 20% of the valley's population, with a further 20% to 30% living in lesser cities of between 2,000 and 20,000, with their own resident tlatoanis or rulers, with the remaining 40% to 60% of the valley population distributed between the thousands of rural settlements with populations of 2,000 or less. Cf. Teotihuacan, which René Millon estimates as sustaining from 150,000 to 200,000 at its height; René Millon, 'Social relations in Ancient Teotihuacán', p. 212. For Texcoco, see Frederick Hicks, 'Rotational Labor and Urban Development in Prehispanic Tetzcoco'. Certainly Tenochtitlan's population must have multiplied several times over in the two hundred years of its existence; Edward Calnek, 'The Internal Structure of Tenochtitlan', p. 288. Population distribution and density

for aboriginal America is a highly vexed question, but the Sanders–Parsons–Santley estimates, like those of Calnek and Millon, are explicitly argued and solidly contexted in detailed local research.

10 Calnek, 'The Internal Structure of Tenochtitlan'.

11 The precise balance between local production, the redistribution of tribute goods, and the market in the city's economy remains unclear. See, e.g., Edward E. Calnek, 'Settlement Patterns and Chinampa Agriculture at Tenochtitlan'; 'The Internal Structure of Tenochtitlan'; 'Organización de los sistemas de abastecimiento urbano de alimentos: el caso de Tenochtitlan'; and 'El sistema de mercado en Tenochtitlan'. Cf. Pedro Carrasco, 'La economía del Mexico prehispánico', and his 'Markets and Merchants in the Aztec Economy'. For the Tlatelolco market, The Anonymous Conqueror, 'Relación de algunas cosas de la Nueva España y de la gran ciudad de Temestitan Mexico: escrita por un compañero de Hernán Cortés', Vol. 1, p. 392. Exhaustive listings of all required tribute are lacking: for example, silver does not appear as a regular tribute item in any source we have. The Matrícula de Tributos, precontact but presumably incomplete, lists only 33 tribute-paying provinces as opposed to the Codex Mendoza of 1541, which lists 38, while the Scholes and Adams 'Información' of 1554 lists 36; Frances Berdan and Jacqueline Durand-Forest (eds.), *Commentary on Matrícula de Tributos (Códice de Moctezuma); Codex Mendoza*, ed. James Cooper Clark; France V. Scholes and Eleanor B. Adams (eds.), *Información sobre los tributos que los indios pagaban a Moctezuma, Año de 1554*. For the expansion of empire, see Charles Gibson, 'The Structure of the Aztec Empire'; for its less obvious dynamics, Frances Berdan, 'The Economics of Aztec Luxury Trade and Tribute', and Johanna Broda, 'El tributo en trajes guerreros y la estructura del sistema tributario mexica'. Nigel Davies usefully exploits the Relaciones Geográficas (see *Papeles de Nueva España*, ed. Francisco Paso y Troncoso, Second Series, 6 vols, Madrid, 1905–6, vols. 4–6) in his discussion of tribute in his *The Aztec Empire: The Toltec Resurgence*, esp. chapter 8. It is necessary to distinguish between one-off special event tributes and regular tribute paid twice or four times yearly. For the special tribute occasion of Ahuitzotl's dedication of the renovated Templo Mayor in 1487, see Fr. Diego Durán, *Historia de las Indias de Nueva España e Islas de la Tierra Firme*, 2, 341.

12 For the possibility (to my mind slight, given the frequency of reference to the tump line as the fate of the feckless) that the carriers were a hereditary group, see Ross Hassig, *Trade, Tribute and Transportation: The Sixteenth-Century Political Economy of Mexico*, p. 30.

13 See the lucid overview by Susan M. Kellog, 'Kinship and Social Organization in Early Colonial Tenochtitlan', and for the case that the calpullis in Ten-

ochtitlan, while perhaps central to the city's religious organization, sustaining a local temple and its assigned lands, were not related by kinship and descent (p. 104). Kellog also utilizes an elegant analysis of native kinship terms to argue for the structural equivalence of men and women in reckoning descent in matters of inheritance and residence rights, and the equivalence of all siblings.

14 Fernando de Alva Ixtlilxóchitl, *Obras históricas*, 2, pp. 168–9. Frederick Hicks argues that rotational labor in Texcoco was preferred over a permanent labour force for its political cohesiveness. Hicks, 'Rotational Labor and Urban Development in Prehispanic Tetzcoco'; see also his 'Dependent Labor in Prehispanic Mexico'.

15 For a close discussion of valley institutions sensitive to the vagaries of the existing evidence, see Jerome A. Offner, *Law and Politics in Aztec Texcoco*. For an intrepid attempt to arrive at the essential conceptualizations controlling 'Aztec' understandings of their history and social organizations, see van Zantwijk, *The Aztec Arrangement*. Van Zantwijk has suggested (p. 86) that members of a calpulli may not necessarily have been co-resident, and that perhaps only the calpulli temples had fixed locations, with the members scattered. There is no 'hard' evidence against, or indeed for, such a view, but the emphasis on locality and neighbours in local observances would seem to work against it.

16 For the tlaxilacalli, see Alonso de Molina, *Vocabulario en lengua castellana y mexicana y mexicana y castellana;* Arturo Monzón, *El calpulli en la organización social de los Tenochas*, pp. 31, 40. See also Chapter 2, n. 41.

17 For an account of the likely distribution and bases of power, see J. Rounds, 'Dynastic Succession and the Centralization of Power in Tenochtitlan'; and his 'Lineage, Class and Power in the Aztec State'.

18 For example, Dennis Tedlock (trans.), *Popol Vuh: The Definitive Edition of the Mayan Book of the Dawn of Life and the Glories of Gods and Kings*, p. 360, and, for Central Mexican peoples, e.g., *Codex Boturini* (also called the *Tira de la Peregrinación*), p. 9; *Codex Aubin: Historia de la nación mexicana; reproducción a todo color del códice de 1576*, p. 3; *Historia tolteca–chichimeca*, p. 28; Fr. Diego Durán, *Historia*, vol. 2, p. 21; *Anales de Tlatelolco: Unos annales* [sic] *históricos de la nación mexicana*, pp. 31–2.

19 The best accounts for this early period are those provided by Durán, *Historia*, and Fernando Alvarado Tezozómoc, *Crónica mexicáyotl*. For a fluent secondary account, see Nigel Davies, *The Aztecs: A History*, chapter 1. For an evaluation of the 'mythic' material, Michel Graulich, 'Aspects mythiques des peregrinations Mexicas'. See also *Florentine Codex*, 10: 29, esp. 189–97.

20 See, e.g., Alfredo López Austin, *Hombre–Dios: religión y política en el mundo náhuatl, passim*.

21 For the chronological depth of such autonomous city-states, see Edward Calnek, 'Patterns of Empire Formation in the Valley of Mexico, Late Postclassic Period, 1200–1521; for the longevity of the loyalty they inspired, James Lockhart, 'Views of Corporate Self and History in Some Valley of Mexico Towns: Late Seventeenth and Eighteenth Centuries'.

22 Here I am stepping around a large and lively scholarly debate on the question of the early history of the Mexica and the other valley groups. The lost 'Crónica X' in its several variants appears to be the original source for the early history of the Mexica, providing the basis for Durán's account (see his *Historia*) as for Nigel Davies's accessible account in his *The Aztecs*. The temple was raised perhaps in 1325, with the sister city of Tlatelolco being established on an adjacent island soon afterwards. Or so the standard story goes, despite archeological indications that Tlatelolco was founded significantly earlier; Nigel Davies, *The Toltec Heritage: From the Fall of Tula to the Rise of Tenochtitlan*, pp. 194–5. For a sensitive exploration of how prehispanic historical texts ought to be 'read', see Calnek, 'The Analysis of Prehispanic Historical Texts'.

23 Durán, *Historia*, 2, pp. 57–8.

24 For discussions of the importance of the Toltec heritage, Davíd Carrasco, *Quetzalcoatl and the Irony of Empire*, esp. chapter 4; for the shadowy historical events, Nigel Davies, *The Toltec Heritage*, and *The Aztecs*. For an alternative view see Edward Calnek, 'The City-State in the Basin of Mexico'. For the city as icon of empire, see Townsend, *State and Cosmos in the Art of Tenochtitlán*.

25 It now appears Rome was no Rome either, with 'astonishingly few élite administrators' running the empire, which should be thought of as 'an aggregate of autonomous city-states under the hegemony of the supreme city-state, which was Rome', Jasper Griffin, *London Review of Books*, 15 October, 1987, p. 15.

26 For a useful discussion of the prior problem of the relationship between towns and their supplying hinterlands, see Hassig, *Trade, Tribute and Transportation*.

27 For an attractive account of the organization of empire Nigel Davies, *The Aztec Empire: The Toltec Resurgence*, esp. chapter 8.

28 For an intriguing account of the war declaration procedure, based on the Mapa Quinatzin leaf 3 and Ixtlilxóchitl, Offner, *Law and Politics in Aztec Texcoco*, pp. 71–5. See also Alva Ixtlilxóchitl, *Obras históricas* 2, 187–93. Ixtlilxóchitl gives an account of the three warnings delivered to a rebellious people by officials of the Triple Alliance, including the formal presentation of shields and arms.

29 Durán, *Historia*, 2, chapter 24.

30 Durán, *Historia*, 2, chapter 25.

31 Díaz, *Historia*, chapter 91.

32 Pagden, Second Letter, pp. 100, 108.

33 See especially Richard Townsend's fine analysis of the Dedication Stone commemorating the completion of the Great Pyramid in 1487, and of the Stone of Tizoc. Townsend, *State and Cosmos in the Art of Tenochtitlan*, pp. 40–9.

34 'Historical' dates were most significant for the Mexica when they could be made to coincide with cosmic dates, dates being 'adjusted', or actions scheduled, for significant cosmic dates. Their particular concern for 'history' is suggested by the fact that Mexica monuments, unlike those of the earlier dominant civilizations in the valley, bear identifying glyphs. Emily G. Umberger, 'Aztec Sculptures, Hieroglyphs and History'.

35 John Berger, 'Historical Afterword', esp. pp. 202–3, 206–8.

36 Inga Clendinnen, *Ambivalent Conquests: Maya and Spaniard in Yucatan, 1517–1570*, esp. pp. 176–82.

37 Eric R. Wolf, *Sons of the Shaking Earth*.

38 *Florentine Codex*, 3: appendix, chapter 2.

39 *Florentine Codex*, 2: 30: 121.

40 Berger, 'Historical Afterword', p. 206.

41 For the view that the empire had reached its 'natural' limits before the Spanish coming, see Geoffrey W. Conrad and Arthur A. Demarest, *Religion and Empire: The Dynamics of Aztec and Inca Expansionism*, esp. chapter 2. While I would agree with Conrad and Demarest that the empire was largely a result of Mexica beliefs and values, or 'ideology', and its unstable structure a reflex of Mexican political culture, not an immature phase, I am less confident than they that the contradictions generated by 'ideologically driven expansion' were dangerously acute in Moctezoma's time, and that 'ultimate social crisis was inevitable'. Their account rests on a rather too energetic reading of the few clues we have as to the state of the late empire and the late imperial city, and is underpinned by the notion that any polity has 'inevitable limits' (p. 70), which is to underestimate the flexibility of human arrangements and invention.

42 Durán, *Historia*, 2, chapter 32.

43 *Florentine Codex*, 8: 17: 56–8.

44 Full recognition of the importance of Mexica self-identification through opposition came only with the reading of James A. Boon, *Other Tribes, Other Scribes*. Boon makes clear that we too define ourselves in terms of what we are not – as in enterprises of this kind, where we make our subjects play our vis-à-vis.

45 For the range of song and dance styles at the command of the Mexica tlatoani, see, e.g., *Florentine Codex*, 4: 7: 25–6.

46 *Florentine Codex*, 8: 14: 45.

47 *Florentine Codex*, 10: 29: 185–6, 194. This whole section is heavily colonized by Spanish notions, but in its jangle of ambivalences it remains a rich source

for Mexica discriminations regarding their own virtues and defects, and the dangerous charms of otherness.

48 *Codex Borbonicus: Bibliothèque de l'Assemblée national, Paris (Y120),* fol. 30; *Florentine Codex,* 2: 30: 122.

49 *Florentine Codex,* 10: 29: 176–81.

50 Durán, *Historia,* 2, pp. 222–4.

51 The masonry remains at Tula tell a different story, with their friezes of squat warriors, and eagles and ocelots munching on human hearts. Post-conquest influence probably explains the claim that Quetzalcoatl Topiltzin, the legendary god–ruler forced out by the machinations of 'wizards' and Tezcatlipoca, had no appetite for human victims, being content with offerings of birds and butterflies; *Anales de Cuauhtitlán,* in *Códice Chimalpopoca; Florentine Codex,* 3: 12–14: 33–8.

52 *Florentine Codex,* 10: 29: 165–70.

53 Jacques Soustelle, *La vie quotidienne des Aztéques en la veille de la conquête espagnole,* p. 58. Translated as *The Daily Life of the Aztecs on the Eve of the Spanish Conquest.*

54 Pagden, Second Letter, p. 75.

55 There is dispute as to the precise timing and nature of the changes. Some of the difficulties are elegantly rehearsed in Davies, *The Toltec Heritage, passim* but esp. chapter 1. Davies believes the process was well advanced by 1428, with little power left to the calpullis.

56 J. G. Peristiany, *Honour and Shame; The Values of Mediterranean Society,* p. 11.

57 For the 'aristocratic revolution', if so it was, see Hernando de Alvarado Tezozómoc, *Crónica Mexicana,* pp. 199–200. Durán, *Historia,* 2, p. 407, claims the reforms included even the minor officers in the calpullis: 'los prepositos y mandocillos de los barrios'.

58 For the elders making the rounds of the local warriors, see Durán, *Historia,* 2, chapter 19.

59 Ingenious analysis of extensive post-conquest legal and other documentation, produced within the Spanish system but drawn up by Indian communities for Indian purposes, sheds retrospective light on more shadowy pre-contact institutions and their workings in their revelation of abiding social and political attitudes and preferences. James Lockhart has discerned a ubiquitous preference for what he calls a 'cellular' as opposed to a linear or hierarchical type of organization, in matters as various as land allocation to the structure of verse. A full generation after the conquest, the Tlaxcalan *cabildo,* or municipal government, made its Spanish-imposed structure work through a complex rotation of office and obligation between individuals and between localities. James

Lockhart, 'Some Nahua Concepts in Postconquest Guise'; James Lockhart, Frances Berdan, and Arthur J. O. Anderson, *The Tlaxcalan Actas*.

60 Durán, *Historia*, 2, pp. 209–10.

61 *Codex Boturini*, 4.

62 In the 'Primeros Memoriales' of Sahagún drawn from Tepepulco, the household women 'kill' the little dough figures of the mountain gods in the festival of Atemoztli, the sixteenth month. In Tenochtitlan the 'killing' is done by a visiting priest, although his weapon remains a woman's weaving stick. *Florentine Codex*, 2: 35: 153.

63 *Florentine Codex*, 4: appendix, pp. 143–4; 7: 9: 25–30; 7: 9–12: 25–32. See also Fr. Toribio Motolinía, *Memoriales e historia de los indios de la Nueva España*, chapter 16, p. 23.

64 *Florentine Codex*, 7: 11: 29.

65 For an ingenious reconstruction of Texcocan service, see Offner, *Law and Politics in Aztec Texcoco*, p. 102.

66 *Florentine Codex*, 9: 14: 65.

2. LOCAL PERSPECTIVES

1 Clifford Geertz, *Negara: The Theatre State in Nineteenth-Century Bali*, p. 124.

2 For example: honorific terms like 'my progenitor' were applied to all members of a generation, or to people with high-level skills. A superior might choose to call his inferiors 'fathers' or 'progenitors', presumably in graceful and flattering submission to their pretended superiority, which reversal was also applied, more surprisingly, in the address of the lower to the higher, as when a subject would address a lord with an affectionate diminisher as 'my grandchild'. *The Art of Nahuatl Speech: The Bancroft Dialogues*, edited and with a preliminary study by Frances Karttunen and James Lockhart, esp. pp. 43–51. These were admittedly post-conquest exercises in conscientiously elegant Nahuatl speech, and so probably exaggerated the niceties of the ordinary protocols.

3 *Florentine Codex*, 2: 25: 79.

4 *Florentine Codex*, 2: 25: 84.

5 *Florentine Codex*, 2: 27: 106–7.

6 *Florentine Codex*, 8: 14: 43–4.

7 *Florentine Codex*, 2: 27: 102–3.

8 *Florentine Codex*, 2: 34: 148, 149; 2: 25: 85–6. For a fuller discussion, see Chapter 4, 'Warriors', *passim*.

9 'The leaders do not stir them up; the commoners of their own accord contend among themselves'. *Florentine Codex*, 6: 41: 227; 5: 23.

10 *Hernán Cortés: Letters from Mexico*, trans. and ed. Anthony Pagden, pp. 103–5; Bernal Díaz del Castillo, *Historia verdadera de la conquista de la Nueva España*, chapter 42.

11 Fr. Diego Durán, *Historia de las Indias de Nueva España e Islas de la Tierra Firme*, 2, chapters 32-3.

12 Durán, *Historia*, 1, chapter 20.

13 *Florentine Codex*, 6: 14: 67–77.

14 For example, as when warrior groups not yet permitted to drink, but only one short step away from the privilege, took it as a mark of competitive honour to drink secretly but collectively at the festival of Panquetzaliztli. *Florentine Codex*, 2: 34: 148.

15 For example, *Florentine Codex*, 4: 4, 5: 11–17.

16 *Florentine Codex*, 8: 17: 55.

17 *Florentine Codex*, 2: 27: 106-7.

18 Anthropologists have begun to make useful sorties into different modes of drinking, and the ways in which drinking even to apparent irresponsibility can be culturally controlled. See especially Craig MacAndrew and Robert Edgerton, *Drunken Comportment: A Social Explanation*. For a penetrating study on the demoralization attending changes in drinking patterns, Elizabeth Colson and Thayer Soudder, *For Prayer and Profit: The Ritual, Economic and Social Importance of Beer in Gwembe District, Zambia, 1950–1982*. See also the mixed bag of the rather too hopefully titled *Constructive Drinking: Perspectives on Drink from Anthropology*, ed. Mary Douglas. For a classic analysis of developments in colonial Mexico, see William B. Taylor, *Drinking, Homicide, and Rebellion in Colonial Mexican Villages*.

19 *Florentine Codex*, 10: 15: 55–6.

20 *Florentine Codex*, 4: 4–5: 11–16.

21 The friar Durán was well aware that pre-conquest controls on drunkenness were because 'these people held the maguey to be something divine, celestial . . . it was not only an inebriating drink but also a god to be revered, because of its effects and power to inebriate'. Durán, *Historia* 1, chapter 13.

22 *Codex Mendoza*, part 3, 70–1.

23 *Florentine Codex*, 1: 21: 48.

24 *Florentine Codex*, 5: 24: 191–2.

25 For a discussion of tlazomiquiztli, see Louise M. Burkhart, *The Slippery Earth: Nahua–Christian Moral Dialogue in Sixteenth-Century Mexico*, chapter 4, esp. pp. 93–7. While I find much to agree with in Burkhart's impressive account, I

am troubled by her tendency to equate pollution with 'immoral behavior' (e.g. p. 97).

26 *Florentine Codex*, 4: 9: 34–5.

27 For an extended 'confession' grounded in these notions, and an indication of the seductive ease with which it takes a Christian reading, see *Florentine Codex*, 6: 7: 29–34.

28 For example, a cluster of practices (the high concern for the warrior lock, the destruction of a sorcerer's dangerous power by cutting his hair, avoidance of stepping over a child for fear that the action would injure his growth, a special concern for the disposal of hair clippings) point to the belief that the head and the hair were the locus of individual power (the tonalli) and so of vulnerability. Otherwise there was no great general nervousness over the intactness of personal boundaries, although sensible precautions were taken to avoid the malicious use of detached fragments of the person such as nail clippings and milk teeth. If warriors burnt their excrement on the battlefield, within Tenochtitlan it was promiscuously collected from the public latrines. (Somewhat surprisingly in that bloodstained universe, menstrual blood seems to have aroused no particular interest or alarm.) On these and related issues the indispensable reference is Alfredo López Austin, *The Human Body and Ideology: Concepts of the Ancient Nahuas*. While not all its findings are compelling, it is at once imaginatively daring and rigorous in scholarship.

29 Here the insights of Mary Douglas, *Purity and Danger: An Analysis of the Concepts of Pollution and Taboo*, are relevant.

30 *Florentine Codex*, 5: 36: 195.

31 López Austin, *The Human Body and Ideology*, 1, pp. 178–9.

32 *Florentine Codex*, 2: appendix, 178.

33 Keith Thomas, *Religion and the Decline of Magic*.

34 See, for example, *Florentine Codex*, 4: 11: 42–4; 31: 101–4; 10: 14: 53.

35 See, for example, *Florentine Codex*, 6: 7: 30–4, *passim*. Our clearest view of a practising sorcerer comes after the conquest, with the extraordinary Ocelotl. He deserves extended treatment, as he has received from a number of authors, but the difficulty in using his surprisingly well-documented exploits to shed light on the pre-conquest period is that it appears his range, clientele, and very likely his own notion of his role expanded vastly after the conquest: that is, we know something of the man, but not enough of the context. For Ocelotl, see *Procesos de indios idólatras y hechiceros*, pp. 17–51; Jacques Lafaye, *Quetzalcoatl and Guadalupe;* J. Jorge Klor de Alva, 'Martín Ocelotl: Clandestine Cult Leader'; for the phenomenon, Serge Gruzinski, *Man-Gods in the Mexican Highlands: Indian Power and Colonial Society 1520–1800,* and Alfredo López Austin,

Hombre–Dios: religión y política en el mundo náhuatl. For the transforming wizard, L. Marie Musgrave-Portilla, 'The Nahualli or Transforming Wizard in Pre- and Postconquest Mesoamerica'. Conrad and Demarest have suggested there was a late imperial state-organized thrust against 'the independent priest and the self-proclaimed shaman' to discredit the authority of orally transmitted traditions in favour of the new written 'ideology', in the keeping of the officially trained priesthood: 'Having reworked written history and myth, the state needed to control and alter the oral literature as well'. Geoffrey W. Conrad and Arthur A. Demarest, *Religion and Empire: The Dynamics of Aztec and Inca Expansionism,* p. 43. Theirs is a highly vigorous reading of equivocal sources.

36 *Florentine Codex,* 4: 31: 101; 11: 42.

37 *Florentine Codex,* 4: 31: 104; 32: 105–6.

38 *Florentine Codex,* 4: 19: 43.

39 William A. Christian, *Local Religion in Sixteenth-Century Spain.* For the longevity of the assumed tension between the religion of the few and of the many, see Peter Brown, 'Learning and Imagination', and his *The Cult of the Saints: Its Rise and Function in Latin Christianity.* For a compact and insightful overview of changing representations of 'popular' culture and its associated cluster of terms, David Hall, 'Introduction', *Understanding Popular Culture. Europe from the Middle Ages to the Nineteenth Century.* Hildred Geertz has urged historians to seek to comprehend 'the unarticulated view of reality', the 'hidden conceptual foundation' underpinning 'popular' practice and observances, so claiming, as Clive Holmes neatly puts it, 'equal time for the popular cosmology'. H. Geertz, 'An Anthropology of Religion and Magic'; Clive Holmes, 'Popular Culture? Witches, Magistrates and Divines', p. 86. The difficulty for the historian is implied by the adjectives 'hidden' and 'unarticulated': 'sympathetic' inference has its temptations, especially as it is always possible that there is no (distinctively) popular cosmology to be inferred.

40 For the duties, see *Florentine Codex,* 2: 206–15 (appendix).

41 For the incense pouches, see *Florentine Codex,* 2: 25: 87; for the miniature jaguars, Fr. Bernardino de Sahagún, *Historia general de las cosas de la Nueva España,* 1, pp. 166–7.

42 This is a simpler (and inelegant) form of David Sabean's 'shared discourse'; David Sabean, *Power in the Blood: Popular Culture and Village Discourse in Early Modern Germany.*

43 Calnek, 'The Internal Structure of Tenochtitlan'.

44 *Florentine Codex,* 4: 34: 111. The tonalli, like other Nahuatl conceptualizations of the body and its animistic centres, is a difficult notion to pin down, but that the conceptualizations were generally understood is indicated by ordinary

practices. The best discussion of the tonalli, focussed on the head, the *teyolia*, the spirit centred on the heart, which leaves the body at death, and the ambivalent *ihiyotl*, the 'breath' which finds its source in the liver, remains that of López Austin, *The Human Body and Ideology*, chapter 6, 'The Animistic Entities', esp. pp. 210–12.

45 *Florentine Codex*, 4: 34: 111.

46 *Florentine Codex*, 4: 35: 113–14.

47 For example, Tlaxochimaco, the festival of the ninth month, *Florentine Codex*, 2: 28: 108–10. For Izcalli, 2: 38: 167–8.

48 Diego Durán observed: 'As soon as a child is born he is registered with the heads and captains of the wards. One man had in his charge twenty households, another forty, another fifty, others had a hundred, and thus the city and its wards were divided. He who had a hundred houses in his charge could appoint five or six of his subjects and divide them among the hundred homes. If he received fifteen or perhaps twenty households, he was obliged to govern them, collecting tribute and men for public works. And so the officials of the Republic were innumerable.' Diego Durán, *The Aztecs: The History of the Indies of New Spain*, p. 183. See also Frederick Hicks (working from more abundant material from Texcoco), 'Rotational Labor and Urban Development in Prehispanic Tetzcoco', *Explorations in Ethnohistory: Indian Mexico in the Sixteenth Century*, esp. 160–1. While Hicks primarily identifies the tlaxilacalli with the calpulli ('a group of households forming a small barrio and having common tributary obligations'), he allows possible confusion between the terms, with 'tlaxilacalli' sometimes meaning a subdivision of a calpulli; 'Rotational Labor', pp. 161, 169n. 10. Chimalpahín records that when Moctezoma gave his daughter in marriage to a Chalcan ruler, two tlaxilacalli of Otomies went with her. Chimalpahín, 7th. Relación, 4 calli 1509, quoted in Jerome A. Offner, 'Household Organization in the Texcocan Heartland: The Evidence in the *Codex Vergara*', p. 142.

49 Clifford Geertz, *The Religion of Java*. For the slametan's failure to integrate in too diversified conditions, see his 'Ritual and Social Change: A Javanese Example'.

50 *Florentine Codex*, 2: 38: 167–8.

51 *Florentine Codex*, 2: 25: 84–5.

52 *Florentine Codex*, 4: 35: 113–14.

53 *Florentine Codex*, 4: 37: 124.

54 For the glory, see *Florentine Codex*, 4: 37: 121–4; for the self-abasement, 6: 43: 250; for the formal elegance of the serving, 4: 36: 117–19.

55 *Florentine Codex*, 4: 37: 122.

56 *Florentine Codex*, 1: 15: 33–4. There is an echo here of the painful sensations

attending the production of saliva, seen as a sign of anger. López Austin, *The Human Body and Ideology*, 1, p. 178–9.

57 *Florentine Codex*, 4: 12: 47–8.

58 *Florentine Codex*, 4: 23.

59 Frances Karttunen, 'Nahuatl Literacy', p. xix.

60 Karttunen and Lockhart, *The Art of Nahuatl Speech*, pp. 22–36.

61 *Florentine Codex*, 6: 20: 105.

62 *Florentine Codex*, 8: 13, 17. For the model of the feast, see *Florentine Codex*, 4: 36–7: 117–25.

63 *Florentine Codex*, 4: 38: 129.

64 *Florentine Codex*, 6: 2: 7.

65 *Anales de Tlatelolco: Unos annales* [sic] *históricos de la nación mexicana*, para. 351, p. 71; *Florentine Codex*, 12: 35: 104. Cf. conditions during the 'great famine' of 1452–4, when nobles sold their children to the ubiquitous slave-merchants.

66 'Horneting, bumblebeeing. This is said of those who eat and drink at the expense of the nobles of the city. They either ask for sustenance or are simply given it'. Bernardino de Sahagún, quoted in Miguel León-Portilla, 'Translating Amerindian Texts', p. 117. Cf. *Florentine Codex*, 6: 43: 247. See also Thelma Sullivan, 'Náhuatl Proverbs, Conundrums and Metaphors Collected by Sahagún'. Even the distribution of the leftovers of feasting was carefully designated. He who had somehow transgressed the power of Tlaloc and who therefore suffered a Tlaloc-related illness would accordingly offer a feast in propitiation. The remains of the feast were carefully gathered up to be shared out between 'the people of the household – his family, they of the same parentage, of the same womb'. *Florentine Codex*, 1: 21: 49.

67 *Florentine Codex*, 4: 37: 124.

68 *Florentine Codex*, 6: 41: 230.

69 Cf. *Florentine Codex*, 8: 13. See also *Codex Borbonicus: Bibliothèque de l'Assemblée national, Paris (Y120)*, p. 27, where Centeotl, the Maize God, is represented as seated in his litter, with four commoners (two males and two females) holding out empty bowls and Xipe Totec, the Flayed Lord of fertility, facing them; and the *Florentine Codex* illustration, 2: 27: 102, no. 27, in which well-dressed individuals, presumably lords, eat while commoners point at their own empty mouths: a neat depiction of haves and have-nots.

70 *Florentine Codex*, 2: 27: 98.

71 See, e.g., Johanna Broda, 'Los estamentos en el ceremonial mexica'; 'Consideraciones sobre historiografía e ideología mexicas: las crónicas indígenas y el estudio de los ritos y sacrificios', and her 'Conclusions' to 'The Provenience of the Offerings: Tribute and *Cosmovisión*'.

72 For deeply marked class division, see Johanna Broda, 'Relaciones políticas

ritualizadas: El ritual como expresión de una ideología'; for the recruiting of the general populace, Cecelia Klein, 'The Ideology of Autosacrifice at the Templo Mayor', esp. 350–60; for the induced 'wild fanaticism', Arthur Demarest, 'Overview: Mesoamerican Human Sacrifice in Evolutionary Perspective', pp. 227–47 esp. 234–7.

73 The accounts of ritualized action (clustered most densely in the second 'book' of the Codex, on the ceremonies, but with supplementary material scattered throughout the twelve 'books') have not been much exploited by analysts, save by Johanna Broda and Michel Graulich, whose concerns have been more with their political and cosmological implications than with their emotional nexus; see, e.g., Johanna Broda, 'La fiesta azteca del Fuego Nuevo y el culto de las Pléyades', and her articles as noted in notes 71 and 72 above; and Michel Graulich, 'Quecholli et Panquetzaliztli: une nouvelle interprétation'.

74 For a clarification of the status of the discourses see Willard Gingerich, '*Chipahuacanemiliztli*, "The Purified Life", in the Discourses of Book VI, Florentine Codex'.

75 Fr. Alonso de Molina, *Vocabulario en lengua castellana y mexicana y mexicana y castellana*, 1070, 129v. gives *tlaocolcuicatl* as 'sad and plaintive chant', from *tlaocolli*, 'pity' or 'compassion', and '*cuicatl*', 'song'.

76 For a perceptive account of Sahagún's attempt to redefine the native notion of sadness and compassion into something acceptably Christian, see Louise M. Burkhart, 'Sahagún's *Tlauculcuicatl*, a Nahuatl Lament'.

77 Paul Radin, *The Autobiography of a Winnebago Indian*, p. 4 n. 7.

78 Hassig and Andrews characterize the 'prayers' reproduced by the priest Ruiz de Alarcón as 'the communication of the speakers with a deity or a power entity, but only for the purpose of presenting a petition or issuing a command, never for that of making a confession or expressing praise or thanksgiving'; J. Richard Andrews and Ross Hassig, 'Editors' Introduction', in Hernando Ruiz de Alarcón, *Treatise on the Heathen Superstitions that Today Live Among the Indians Native to This New Spain, 1629*. Ruiz de Alarcón's 'New Spain' was the Taxco–Cuernavaca region and down into Guerrero, and his 'today' was 1629, but the austerity of the envisioned relationship between importuning human and forgetful or recalcitrant deity is sufficiently unlike the Christian posture of propitiation and praise to suggest a strong indigenous continuity.

79 *Florentine Codex*, 3: 7: 62.

80 *Florentine Codex*, 6: 9: 44.

81 *Florentine Codex*, 6: 1: 1; 6: 2: 9.

82 *Florentine Codex*, 6: 2: 8.

83 *Florentine Codex*, 6: 8: 40.

84 Durán believed indulgence to do this was granted only 'in a fertile

year . . . thus indicating abundance'. Durán, *Historia*, 1, chapter 9. At that
point the crops were still not secure, and I suspect Durán is pursuing his usual
'commonsense' interpretations here. He understood the intention ('everything
[in the festivals] was done in order to obtain food and to beg food from their
false gods': *Historia*, 1, chapter 21) but not always the strategy.

85 Durán, *Historia*, 1, chapter 9.

86 It is possible an element of bargaining may sometimes have been present. A
few of the finest jades destined for Tlaloc in that same festival of Etzalqualiztli
were not tossed into the lake waters along with the other offerings, but were
tied above the water level on upright poles at the most sacred spot in the lake,
marked by a small whirlpool. Given that the lake received the surplus rain-
waters, with the water level rising significantly in a good year, I assume the
placement of the jades indicated the priests' hopeful expectations of the watery
'reach' of the raingod. The notion of the essential justice of reciprocity where
familial or dependency bonds are established appears to have been widespread. Patrick Geary comments on the enthusiasm with which peasants berated and beat the altar of St. Calais, to whom they had long prayed and made
offerings to no effect. Patrick Geary, 'Humiliation of Saints', p. 135. Geary
sums up: 'Thus the peasants beat their saints, just as they would beat a
reluctant beast of burden, to awaken him and force him to do his job' (p. 136).
By the thirteenth century such displays were being officially discouraged as too
direct in their denial of clerical mediation and in their assumption of a close
human–sacred reciprocity (p. 138).

87 Durán, *Historia*, 1, chapters 13 and 14. Durán believed that human victims
were offered only on important festivals, or rather that the fact of their offering
was a measure of importance, for only ceremonies involving humans being
killed saw the priests in full regalia.

88 For a luminous discussion which reveals to us what we have somehow always
obscurely thought, see Peter Brown, 'The Notion of Virginity in the Early
Church'.

89 Molina, *Vocabulario en lengua castellana y mexicana y mexicana y castellana*.

90 Dennis Tedlock points out that the Maya word *puz*, from its Mixe-Zoque (and
possibly Olmec) sources down to the modern Quiché, refers literally to the
cutting of flesh with a knife, and is the primary term for sacrifice. Dennis
Tedlock, *The Spoken Word and the Work of Interpretation*, p. 265.

91 When quail were decapitated 'before the hearth, they kept fluttering and
beating their wings. Their blood was scattered by their flutterings, so that the
earth before the hearth was struck in various places. They spattered and
poured forth their blood . . .' ; *Florentine Codex*, 4: 25: 87. See also *Florentine
Codex*, 2: 24: 74; 11: 2: 49. Quail were also killed for augury, outcomes being

indicated by the direction of the deathflight; *Florentine Codex*, 9: 8: 38. Sullivan points to a further set of more sinister associations of quail with the night. See Thelma D. Sullivan, 'Tlazolteotl–Ixcuina: The Great Spinner and Weaver', p. 11.

92 There was also intense pride taken in the magnificence of the regalia which decked the human figures. See the loving account of the garments the featherworkers made for the victims presented on the feast day of their divine patron, with their perfected art valued at least as much as the human body glorified by it; *Florentine Codex*, 9: 18: 83–5.

93 *Florentine Codex*, 6: 2: 9.

94 *Florentine Codex*, 6: 9: 44.

95 Cf. the detailed, at once symbolically complex yet magnificently explicit account of the making of a Ghanaian king as described by Michelle Gilbert, 'The Person of the King: Ritual and Power in a Ghanaian State'.

96 See, e.g., Cecelia Klein, 'The Ideology of Autosacrifice at the Templo Mayor', esp. pp. 350–60. For a description of the rites of Mexica kingship, see Richard F. Townsend, 'Coronation at Tenochtitlan'.

97 The composition of the Council of Four is not clear, but it seems to have comprised the two ranking military commanders, the *tlacateccatl* and the *tlacochcalcatl*, these offices usually providing the next tlatoani; perhaps the *tlillanquilqui*, head of the priest school in which the princes of the blood were trained, with the powerful cihuacoatl perhaps being the fifth member; *Florentine Codex*, 6: 14: 75–6; 6: 20: 110; 8: 20: 74; J. Rounds, 'Dynastic Succession and the Centralization of Power in Tenochtitlan'.

98 For the speeches, see *Florentine Codex*, 6: 10–16: 47–85; for the ruler's prayer to Tezcatlipoca, 6: 9: 41–5; for the installation procedures, 8: 18: 61–5. See also Durán, *Historia*, esp. 2, chapters 39–41. See also López Austin, 'The Body and Social Stratification', in *The Human Body and Ideology*, esp. pp. 396–400.

99 'The very devout stood naked, and when someone stood, cape tied on, he placed his knot in front. And when someone squatted – placed himself as a man – he placed his knot over his shoulder'; *Florentine Codex*, 6: 9: 45. Contrast these two last arrangements, which presumably exposed the genitals, with the conventional modesty of the cape knotted at the shoulder when standing, and at the back of the neck when squatting.

100 *Florentine Codex*, 1: 3: 5. For Tezcatlipoca's identification with the 'Lord of the Here and Now', or of 'The Close Vicinity', see Chapter 9, 'Aesthetics', n. 20.

101 *Florentine Codex*, 1: 3: 5; 4: 9: 34–5.

102 While Tezcatlipoca was honoured throughout Mesoamerica, his special sig-

nificance to the ruling group of Tenochtitlan is signalled by the 'installation' speeches of Book 6, as the Nahuatl version of the Florentine Codex largely reflects the practices of Tlatelolco–Tenochtitlan. While Sahagún's first round of enquiries were conducted at Tepepolco (spelt variously as 'Tepepulco') in the Texcoco district, we have H. B. Nicholson's assurance that 'very little of the ethnographic material collected by Sahagún in Tepepolco at the outset of his ambitious project actually ended up, as such, in the final twelve books of the H(istoria) G(eneral)' H. B. Nicholson, 'Tepepolco, the Locale for the First Stage of Fr. Bernardino de Sahagún's Great Ethnographic Project: Historical and Cultural Notes', p. 217. For visual evidence of the persistent association of Moctezoma II with Tezcatlipoca, see Klein, 'The Ideology of Autosacrifice', esp. pp. 329–38. For the merging of the Mexica tutelary deity Huitzilopochtli into the Tez-catlipoca–tlatoani concept, and the claim for the primacy of Huehueteotl–Xiutecutli, the 'Old God' and the 'God of Fire', see Thelma Sullivan, 'Tlatoani and Tlatocayotl in the Sahagún Manuscripts'. One dignitary's sal-utations to the new ruler identifies him with the sun: 'Our lord of the near, of the nigh [Tezcatlipoca] causeth the sun to shine, bringeth the dawn. It is thou: he pointeth the finger at thee; he indicateth thee' (*Florentine Codex*, 6: 10: 48), while another declares 'a new sun emergeth, appeareth' (*Florentine Codex*, 6: 11: 57). See also *Florentine Codex*, 1. addendum 2, for a variety of metaphors to do with the sun. One scholar has taken this to mean that the tlatoani was seen as an equivalently fundamental part of the universe along with the sun, the earth or the underworld. Broda, 'Relaciones políticas ritua-lizadas', pp. 221–5. But as Sahagún points out, the Nahuatl saying 'now the sun shineth' means 'something new comes to pass . . . the ruler is installed, is selected', and so I take the meaning in this instance to be 'merely' meta-phoric; *Florentine Codex*, 1: addendum 2: 81. For the very different view taken of Tezcatlipoca in Texcoco; see Townsend, *State and Cosmos*, pp. 34–6.

103 For an account of his duties at this level, see *Florentine Codex*, 8: 17, 19.

104 *Florentine Codex*, 6: 10: 52.

105 Sullivan, 'Tlatoani and Tlatocayotl in the Sahagún Manuscripts'. Sullivan also ventures an explanation for Mexica sacrifices of ixiptlas, the 'god imper-sonators', seeing the ritual as one of renewal, in which the human life was incorporated by the represented deity. She also argues that the ruler was deified at death.

106 *Florentine Codex*, 6: 10: 54–5.

107 In the last stages of that festival Moctezoma and his lords danced as exem-plars of archaic lordship: 'they put on their wigs of long locks of hair . . . they

covered them with many green stones. [The hair] fell verily to the rulers' waists.' *Florentine Codex*, 1: 13: 29; 2: 38: 169. See also Townsend, *State and Cosmos*, for the significances of this ceremony.

108 For the possible historical background of this conceptualization see Alfredo López Austin, *Hombre–Dios: religión y política en el mundo náhuatl.*

109 See Sullivan, 'Tlatoani and Tlatocayotl in the Sahagún Manuscripts', *passim; Florentine Codex*, 4: 11: 42.

110 The killing of slaves to accompany a lord on his journey to Mictlan, the place of the dead, clearly belongs to the familiar category of posthumous service.

111 See Emily Umberger's intriguing exegesis of the monumental sculpture, the 'Teocalli de la Guerra Sagrada [The Temple of Sacred War]', as a model of the little stone pyramids which were placed on 'all the roads and crossroads' as seats for Tezcatlipoca, and as a symbolic throne for Moctezoma for the New Fire Ceremony of 1507. Emily Umberger, 'El Trono de Moctezuma', p. 83.

3. VICTIMS

1 Quoted in Anthony F. Wallace, *The Death and Rebirth of the Seneca*, pp. 104–7. Some reported North American rituals are strongly reminiscent of Mexica rituals: e.g., the Skidi band of the Pawnee are known to have offered specially fine captives, male or female, to their god Tiwara. After a time as a pampered but closely watched prisoner, the destined victim was taken at dawn and spread-eagled crosswise on stout poles, with a fire lighted beneath. A chosen warrior shot the victim with a sacred arrow, so that the blood ran down into the fire, and then every male in the group down to the smallest child loosed their arrows. A man then climbed the frame, opened the breast, put his hand in the cavity and smeared the blood-drenched hand across his face, while the women struck the body with spears and sticks, counting 'coup' on it. The body was then slowly consumed by the fire as the people invoked Tirawa, asking him for good crops and good health, and passing handfuls of the smoke over their bodies. The captor of the victim, who had fasted for four days before the ceremony, won much prestige through this exercise; George Bird Grinnell, *Pawnee Hero Stories and Folk Tales*, pp. 362–9. See also James R. Murie's remarkably full account of the sacrifice of a young virgin to the Morning Star in 'Human Sacrifice to the Morning Star', *Ceremonies of the Pawnee*, part 1, pp. 114–36. The resemblances are not restricted to 'sacrifices'; the Cheyenne Arrow Renewal rite echoes the patterns of the Mexica hunting festival of Quecholli, with the same process of making inventory of

the group's living members, and the involvement in collective arrow making and the reverencing of hunting ancestors by all males.

2 For the fattening coops, see Bernal Díaz del Castillo, *Historia verdadera de la conquista de la Nueva España*, chapter 78.

3 Given the simplicity of Mexica cutting equipment, this, especially the separation of the heart from its attachment to the major blood vessels, is rather easier said than done. See for the related Maya zone, Francis Robicsek and Donald Hales, 'Maya Heart Sacrifice: Cultural Perspective and Surgical Technique', esp. pp. 76–85.

4 Ernest Hemingway, *Death in the Afternoon*, p. 195.

5 Pieter Spierenburg, *The Spectacle of Suffering*. See esp. 'The Particulars of Pain', pp. 66–77.

6 Fr. Diego Durán, *Historia de las Indias de Nueva España e Islas de la Tierra Firme*, 2, chapters 19, 42.

7 Hernando do Alvarado Tezózomoc, *Crónica mexicana*, chapters 67–70; Durán, *Historia*, 2, chapter 44. Durán claims the inaugural ceremony cost eighty thousand four hundred lives – men, women, and children dying over four days of marathon killings – but that figure depends on a doubtful reading of a pictographic text.

8 Juan de Torquemada placed the opening of the season of war substantially later, in the fifteenth month of Panquetzaliztli, when 'the harvesting of their maize had been completed . . . At this stage they re-established their landmarks, boundaries, and limits, and defended their borders and mountains as well as other points. Thus during all this month all the provinces were armed and on continuous alert . . . and before the harvest none of this was customary lest the maize and the fields be laid waste and destroyed'. Juan de Torquemada, *Monarquía indiana*, Vol. 2, p. 299. The emphasis here is on 'completion'.

9 *Florentine Codex*, 8: 20: 73.

10 Durán, *Historia*, 1, chapter 6.

11 Mexico is said to have 'the world's richest area in diversity and use of hallucinogens in aboriginal societies'. Richard Evans Schultes and Albert Hofmann, *Plants of the Gods: Origins of Hallucinogenic Use*, p. 27. For vividly illuminating reconstructions of Mexican indigenous use, see the work of Peter Furst, most accessible in Peter T. Furst (ed.), *Flesh of the Gods: The Ritual Use of Hallucinogens*, and his *Hallucinogens and Culture*.

12 This could be an advantage given the presumed need to avoid too many of the victims defecating in their final terror. For the accounts, see *Florentine Codex*, 11: 7: 129–30. See also *The Badianus Manuscript: An Aztec Herbal of 1552*.

13 Quoted in Schultes and Hofmann, *Plants of the Gods*, p. 109.

14 Durán, *Historia*, 2, chapter 18.

15 In his Spanish account Sahagún indicates that should the designated victim manage to defeat the four in sequence, they would then attack him collectively, with much elaborate whirling and dancing. Fray Bernardino de Sahagún, *Historia general de las cosas de la Nueva España*, 1, p. 144.

16 For an analysis of the detail and meanings of the action in the 'gladiatorial stone' ritual see Inga Clendinnen, 'The Cost of Courage in Aztec Society', esp. 68–84.

17 Clendinnen, 'The Cost of Courage', esp. pp. 76–84.

18 This preliminary familiarization with the place of death is not uncommon in Mexica ritual: see, e.g., Quecholli (12th month), Panquetzaliztli (15th month), and Izcalli (18th month) in *Florentine Codex*, Book 2.

19 The fullest account of the Tlacaxipeualiztli festival is provided by *Florentine Codex*, 2: 20, 21, 22: 45–60, and 8: appendix B: 83–6.

20 See, e.g., Durán, *Historia*, 1, chapter 3, pp. 33–4; Alvarado Tezozómoc, *Crónica mexicana*, pp. 163–4. Chimalpahín talks of the Flowery War coming to Chalco and Mexico in the year 1 Flint (1376), with the brunt being borne by the commoners; (Domingo) Francisco de San Anton Chimalpahín, *Relaciones originales de Chalco Amaquemecan*, p. 157. For an overview, see Frederick Hicks, 'Flowery War in Aztec History'.

21 The watchers and managers knew their own young men could also die as strangers in a hostile city. Here Mexica parochialism declares itself. We tend to think of all ritual deaths as equally barbarous and equally bizarre. Not so the Mexica. Some ends, if dreaded, were familiar: 'they will cook him in an olla [clay cooking pot] and eat him'. *Florentine Codex*, 4: 9: 35. Others followed Mexica practice, and so were undesirable but intelligible: the man 'carried off by the foe' would perhaps be 'offered as a striped one in gladiatorial sacrifice, or be shot full of arrows; or his head would be burst in the fire, or he would be cast into the flames'. But there were also non-Mexica and therefore terrifying and outlandish practices: 'perhaps they would twist him in a net, or smash him, or tear out his entrails – violently tear out his entrails; or just destroy him like a water rat, pushing him under the water, spearing and stabbing him; or they would just cook him [in the steam bath.]' *Florentine Codex*, 4: 27: 93. Other cultures, other customs.

22 Jacques Soustelle, *La vie quotidienne des Aztéques en la veille de la conquête espagnole (1955)*, pp. 90–1, 93.

23 An excavated cache in the Templo Mayor on the Tlaloc side of the structure suggests the 42 'immature individuals' unearthed were probably aged between three and seven years, with the lack of osteological evidence of trauma suggesting throat-cutting (or smothering?) as the most likely mode of death; Juan Alberto Román Berrelleza, 'Offering 48 of the Templo Mayor: A Case of

Child Sacrifice'. Motolinía has an intriguing passage suggesting that the children offered over the months of the rainy season were matched to the height of the growing maize: i.e., when the maize was a span high, children of three or four were killed; when it was knee-high, children of five or six; Fr. Toribio Motolinía, O.F.M., *Memoriales e historia de los indios de la Nueva España* (hereafter *Memoriales* or *Historia*, with appropriate part or book and chapter number), chapter 20, pp. 34–5. See note 25 for Sahagún's view. My own guess is that they were rarely younger than three, and had been weaned. For the arguments, see Chapter 7, 'Mothers'.

24 *Florentine Codex*, 2: 20: 42.

25 Sahagún, *Historia general*, 1, p. 114. Sahagún claims the children to be purchased while still at the breast. It is not clear, however, that the priests took delivery at that very early age.

26 Sahagún, 'Prologue to the Book of the Ceremonies', *Florentine Codex*, Intro. Vol., p. 57. For the rituals, see *Florentine Codex*, 2: 20: 42–5.

27 Motolinía claimed the children offered when the maize was 'one span high' to have been 'not slaves, but the children of nobles', while 'slave children' were offered at the next stage, which could suggest a diminution in the quality of the offerings. Motolinía, *Memoriales*, chapter 20, pp. 34–5.

28 *Florentine Codex*, 2: 34: 141; 4: 26: 91.

29 For example, *Florentine Codex*, 2: 34: 142; 38: 168; 9: 13: 61. For an elegant review of conflicting reports of bathing and its import, exploiting the work of Fray Diego Durán, see Arthur J. O. Anderson, 'The Institution of Slave Bathing', esp. p. 82. For an account of the nature of the taint and its removal, see Alfredo López Austin, *The Human Body and Ideology: Concepts of the Ancient Nahuas*, 1, pp. 400–5.

30 Durán insisted that the 'bathed slaves' offered in sacrifice were not 'foreigners taken in war' but local people, 'natives of the same pueblos'. Durán, *Historia*, 1, chapter 20. My suspicion is that he insisted on the localism of the victims on slight grounds, not the least being their co-operation, and his being persuaded that the unnatural horrors of in-group killings provided salutary insights into the depravity of the Devil.

31 Durán, *Historia*, 1, chapter 20. See also Sahagún, *Historia*, 1, chapters 43, 34. The Cempoallan chief of the Totonac Gulf Coast people complained bitterly to Cortés of Moctezoma's levies of 'youths and maidens'. Díaz, *Historia*, chapter 46. For 'tribute captives' delivered from the frontier provinces to Tenochtitlan, see *Florentine Codex*, 1: 14: 32 (the tribute lists we have are incomplete). We know there to have been 'foreign' slaves, as we are told that those descended from outsiders captured in war normally remained enslaved for three generations. Diego Muñoz Camargo, *Historia de Tlaxcalla*, p. 191.

32 *Florentine Codex*, 1: 19: 43–4. Perhaps too much should not be made of the juxtapositions on the listings of the different structures attached to the royal service, in which the paragraph describing the houses in which captive slaves destined for death were held is sandwiched between a description of 'regional' costumes and styles favoured by the dance groups, and the aviaries of birds and the workshops of craftsmen who provided much of the rest of the ritual paraphernalia. Nonetheless the temptation is to see that casual placement as indicative of a 'humans as commodities' view of things; *Florentine Codex*, 8: 14: 45. For information on the specific material requirements for particular rituals, see France V. Scholes and Eleanor B. Adams (eds.), *Información sobre los tributos que los indios pagaban a Moctezuma: año de 1554*, 4, pp. 59–60, 91–2, 127–8, 159–60, 194–5, 226–7.

33 For a contrary account see Anderson, 'Slave Bathing', pp. 81–92. Here I must thank Professor Anderson for his gracious and encouraging response to my argument regarding 'luxury' slaves, which (given the nature of the sources) must be speculative; Arthur J. O. Anderson, private communication.

34 *Florentine Codex*, 2: 37: 163.

35 Those particular slaves appear anomalous: they seem not to have been considered god-images and their destination after death was to be the commonplace, cold and miserable journey to the Death Kingdom. For the ritual and its preparations, see *Florentine Codex*, 1: 19: 43–4; 2: 34: 141–50; 9: 10–14: 45–67.

36 Women victims appeared to have been less amenable to this form of manipulation, the more 'autonomous' deaths being restricted to men. For example, the young girl decked as the young maize-goddess was kept tipsy, constantly 'enclosed' by her attendants, or physically bound: a hieratic figure, but a passive one; e.g. *Florentine Codex*, 2: 27: 103–5; Durán, *Historia* 1, chapters 13, 14.

37 *Florentine Codex*, 8: 21: 75.

38 *Florentine Codex*, 2: 38: 169. For pleasure girls, see Chapter 6, 'Wives', section 5.

39 *Florentine Codex*, 2: 38: 169.

40 *Florentine Codex*, 9: 19: 87; 14: 63.

41 *Florentine Codex*, 9: 19: 88.

42 *Florentine Codex*, 9: 14: 64.

43 This 'depletion of energies' has provided the basis for a whole theory of the meaning of Mexica human sacrifice. See Christian Duverger, *La fleur létale. Economie du sacrifice aztèque*.

44 *Florentine Codex*, 2: 33: 139.

45 *Florentine Codex*, 2: 38: 168.

46 There is dispute as to how closely the Mexica festival calendar followed the movement of the seasons, given our ignorance of how the Mexica adjusted the true length of the year to a 364-day calendar: see, e.g., Johanna Broda, 'La fiesta azteca del Fuego Nuevo y el culto de las Pléyades', and Michel Graulich, 'Quecholli et Panquetzaliztli: une nouvelle interprétation'. While Mexica rituals sometimes presaged seasonal changes, they were certainly bound to seasons in function, and often required field products at specific stages of growth ('new' maize, hardened cobs, etc.) in performance, which could not have been supplied from the chinampas, despite their being to a degree supra-seasonal.

47 See, e.g., Durán, *Historia*, 'El Calendario Antiguo', 1, chapter 8.

48 It is difficult to imagine a warrior yielding up 'his' captive, given the intimacy of the association: yet another question of fact which cannot be answered from the sources we have. The most complete account of Toxcatl is *Florentine Codex*, 2: 6: 66–77. For an intriguing additional commentary, see Arild Hvidtfeldt, *Teotl and *Ixiptlatli: Some Central Conceptions in Ancient Mexican Religion, passim*, but esp. pp. 85–9.

49 *Florentine Codex*, 2: 24: 66. Durán claims that Tezcatlipoca impersonator was a 'slave' ('indio esclavo'): *Historia* 1, chapter 4. For the confusions regarding the Tezcatlipoca impersonator's status, see Anderson, 'Slave Bathing', p. 90. The difficulties largely evaporate if we exclude the category of 'bathed slave', and identify the young man as either a war 'captive' or a tribute slave.

50 Some 'Crazy Dogs', remarkably, survived, the vow being taken for only one season of war. While some individuals chose to renew the vow until they achieved death, others returned to ordinary life after that extraordinary season. For the information in this paragraph, see Robert H. Lowie, 'Military Societies of the Crow Indians', pp. 191–6; *The Crow Indians*, pp. 327–34.

51 Although not necessarily public awareness, a point to be pursued later. On the issue of attention: others (like the children offered to Tlaloc) might die out of sight, muffled in those litters, but not at all out of mind.

52 The secondary figure was also given other names – Ixtecale, Titlacauan – which presumably recalled other related aspects of the multi-faceted god. *Florentine Codex*, 2: 24: 76.

53 *Florentine Codex*, 2: 24: 76.

54 *Florentine Codex*, 2: 24: 72.

4. WARRIORS, PRIESTS AND MERCHANTS

1 *Florentine Codex*, Introductory Vol., pp. 48–9.

2 The warrior festival of Tlacaxipeualiztli, the Feast of the Flaying of Men, is

usually taken to mark the closing of the war path as the planting was prepared and rain was awaited, while the festival of the eleventh month of Ochpaniztli at once presaged the harvest and sent young men out to war.

3 *Florentine Codex*, 6: 31: 171. For the birth and naming rituals, see chapters 30–8.

4 For childhood and warrior training and iconography, see *Codex Mendoza, passim* but especially Part 3; *Florentine Codex*, esp. 3: 4–6: 51–69; 8: 20–21, and Appendices B, C: 71–7, 83–9. Another rich source is Fr. Diego Durán, *Historia de las Indias de Nueva España e Islas de la Tierra Firme*. See also Ross Hassig, *Aztec Warfare: Imperial Expansion and Political Control*, which amasses useful information of a general kind. For my own views, see Inga Clendinnen, 'The Cost of Courage in Aztec Society'.

5 Durán, *Historia*, 1: 188–90; *Florentine Codex*, 8: 14: 43–4.

6 It is unclear just how many priest schools there were. Sahagún names seven calmecacs within the central temple precinct, and there were at least several others, including the calmecac attended by the children of the featherworkers of Amtlan, where both boys and girls were separately instructed in their (separate) skills for their trade. *Florentine Codex*, 9: 19: 88. Given that merchants also had 'their' calmecac, the likelihood is that prestige specialist crafts sustained their own calmecacs, while others were devoted to training priests, although another possibility is that separate courses of study were available to specific groups within nominated calmecacs.

7 *Florentine Codex*, 8: 21: 173.

8 Durán, *Historia*, 1, chapter 11 for the headdress awarded to the 'brave'. Cf. *Codex Mendoza*, fol. 64. Fol. 65 makes clear that warrior-priests participated in the same system.

9 Yet higher was the tlacateccatl, who had achieved greater distinction within the telpochcalli system. *Florentine Codex*, 8: 17–18, 20–1, appendices: 61–5, 71–89 for the protocols of war and warrior ranking.

10 *Florentine Codex*, 2: 28: 109.

11 *Florentine Codex*, 2: 21: 51.

12 *Florentine Codex* 8: Appendix C: 88; Durán, *Historia*, 1, chapters 10, 11.

13 *Florentine Codex* 2: 34: 148. Diego Durán was persuaded that while there were many restrictions on public drinking, 'in private, all did'. Durán, *Historia*, 1, chapter 11. This is possibly an exaggeration, but a close reading of the Florentine Codex points to widespread drinking which attracted rebuke only if it became public.

14 Durán, *Historia*, 1, chapter 46.

15 *Florentine Codex*, 8: 19: 69.

16 George Catlin, *Letters and Notes on the Manners, Customs, and Conditions of the North American Indians*, 2 vols., Vol. 1, Letter 21, pp. 145–54.

17 Durán, *Historia*, 1, chapter 11.

18 *Florentine Codex*, 8: Appendix C: 89.

19 One order of 'knights' had their house, the House of the Eagles, in the main temple precinct. Durán, *Historia*, 1, chapter 10. The House of the Eagles has now been excavated, along with its life-size guardian figures of eagle knights. See H. B. Nicholson with Eloise Quiñones Keber, *Art of Ancient Mexico: Treasures of Tenochtitlan*, esp. Plate 24 and p. 85.

20 Durán, *Historia*, 2, chapter 53; Fernando de Alva Ixtlilxóchitl, 'Historia de la Nación Chichimeca', in *Obras históricas de Don Fernando de Alva Ixtlilxóchitl*, 1, chapter 71.

21 For an attempt to penetrate 'beneath the religious cloak to the underlying material causes and issues' of these distressingly non-instrumental engagements, see Frederick Hicks, 'Flowery War in Aztec History', p. 87.

22 *Florentine Codex*, 3: 6: 22.

23 *Florentine Codex* 7: 2: 3–8. For an analysis from a different angle, see Chapter 7, 'Mothers', section 5.

24 To restrict the worst temptations of opportunistic selectivity, I will where possible favour the Crow as the comparative case, for the solidity of the early ethnographies, and the appeal of a small tribe who with the coming of the horse transformed themselves into the most flamboyant warriors of the Plains.

25 Lewis and Clark, 'Original Journals', 1: 130, quoted in Clark Wissler, 'Societies and Ceremonial Associations of the Oglala Division of the Teton-Dakota', p. 12–13.

26 For a succinct account of one such warrior society, see Wissler, 'Societies and Ceremonial Associations of the Oglala Division of the Teton-Dakota'. I have simplified the variations between the Plains tribes: for example, those peoples whose warrior societies were arranged in an age-graded hierarchical system, and those where affiliation was fixed and rivalry between competing societies more acute.

27 Robert H. Lowie, 'Military Societies of the Crow Indians', Vol. 10, p. 116.

28 For example, *Florentine Codex*, 2: 28: 109.

29 Cf. Alfredo López Austin, *Juegos rituales aztecas*, p. 36, and *Florentine Codex*, 2: 29: 116. For the festival, see ibid., 111–17.

30 Fr. Bernardino de Sahagún, *Historia general de las cosas de la Nueva España*, 1, pp. 184–90; *Florentine Codex*, 2: 29: 104.

31 *Florentine Codex*, 2: 34: 149.

32 *Florentine Codex*, 8: 17: 53.

33 *Florentine Codex*, 2: 25: 78–90; 7: 5: 17–18, for descriptions of Etzalqualiztli.

34 *Florentine Codex*, 9: 3: 15.

35 *Florentine Codex*, 9: 5: 21.

36 *Florentine Codex*, 9: 14: 65.

37 *Florentine Codex*, 7: 8: 23.

38 *Florentine Codex*, 9, esp. 6: 32. See also 10: 16: 59–60.

39 We are fortunate here to have something like the merchant voice on such matters. Unlike the priests, merchants had the sorts of skills which helped them survive in the troubled times after the conquest, their knowledge of far peoples and places being turned to advantage in the fast-expanding trade of the Spaniards. The Ninth Book of Sahagún's Florentine Codex is clearly derived from merchant informants, most, from the bias, from Tlatelolco, and gives a merchant account of things, not only of the doings within the merchant calpullis, but of the merchants' preferred view of themselves. The other books of the Florentine Codex, where merchant influence is less dominant, provide a useful corrective.

40 *Florentine Codex*, 9: 4: 17.

41 *Florentine Codex*, 9: 2: 3.

42 *Florentine Codex*, 9: 2: 3–8.

43 *Florentine Codex*, 9: 2: 6–7.

44 The Mexica merchant corporation was perhaps independently organized only during the rule of Moctezoma the Younger. Chimalpahín Cuauhtlehuanitzin, *Anales* (Paris, 1889), p. 174.

45 Arthur J. O. Anderson, 'The Institution of Slave Bathing', esp. pp. 87–9.

46 *Florentine Codex*, 6: 14: 256.

47 Jacques Soustelle, *The Daily Life of the Aztecs on the Eve of the Spanish Conquest*, pp. 77–83.

48 *Florentine Codex*, 9: 13–14: 59–67. See also Chapter 3, 'Victims', section 2.

49 *Florentine Codex*, 4: 12: 45–58.

50 *Florentine Codex*, 4: 12: 45–8.

51 *Florentine Codex*, 4: 19: 69–70.

52 *Florentine Codex*, 9: 14: 67.

5. THE MASCULINE SELF DISCOVERED

1 *Florentine Codex*, 6: 10: 51.

2 Paul Radin points out that when the Winnebago speak of the 'apparel of men' which the vision-seeker sees spread out before him they mean not clothing, or not only clothing, but power and abilities of specific kinds embodied in the garments: for example, success on the war path. That which is 'spread before'

the seeker in his vision is only potentially his, being revealed to be within his capacity to obtain from the spirits. Paul Radin, *The Autobiography of a Winnebago Indian* (1920), p. 4, n. 7.

3 *Florentine Codex*, 8: 21: 75.

4 Victor Turner, 'Religious Paradigms and Political Action', in his *Dramas, Fields and Metaphors: Symbolic Actions in Human Society*, p. 64.

5 The game could also be played for augury, or 'sacrificially', the losing captain in some games of high importance being killed at centre court. For the forms of the ballcourt, see Jacinto Quirate, 'The Ballcourt in Mesoamerica: Its Architectural Development', in *Precolumbian Art History*. For human sacrifices associated with the ballgame, see Jeffrey K. Wilkerson, 'In Search of the Mountain of Foam'.

6 It is barely possible that the stone yokes found in association with the ballcourts were worn in play as counterweights to the impact of the ball and for protection, but that would make for a slow and lumbering performance.

7 Fr. Diego Durán, *Historia de las Indias de Nueva España e Islas de la Tierra Firme*, 1, chapter 23.

8 Durán, *Historia*, 1, chapter 23.

9 *Florentine Codex*, 8: 10: 30.

10 Bernal Díaz del Castillo, *Historia verdadera a de la conquista de la Nueva España*, chapter 97.

11 When after the conquest Indian gambling was prohibited, it almost completely ceased, while other prohibitions no easier to enforce proved ineffectual. Durán, *Historia*, 1, chapter 22. As yet I do not know what to make of that.

12 *Florentine Codex*, 5: 3: 157–8.

13 *Florentine Codex*, 9: 8: 39.

14 *Florentine Codex*, 5: Appendix chapter 5: 184.

15 Willard Gingerich, '*Chipahuacanemiliztli*, "The Purified Life"', Vol. 2, pp. 517–44. Note also his interesting thesis regarding shamanistic 'balance' informing the Mexica vision.

16 *Florentine Codex*, 4: 9: 34.

17 For mirrors and possible meanings, see James W. Fernandez, 'Reflections on Looking into Mirrors', *Semiotica* 30 (1980): 27–40.

18 John Bierhorst suggests scepticism can be identified in the 'Cantares Mexicanos', which he sees as products of a post-conquest revitalization movement. In my judgement the passages to which he points are melancholic rather than sceptical, and securely in the pre-contact mode. John Bierhorst, *Cantares Mexicanos: Songs of the Aztecs*, pp. 65–6.

19 John David Morley, *Pictures of the Water Trade: An Englishman in Japan*, speaks of this kind of moment in connection with the plunge of the ink-laden brush

on to unmarked paper in Japanese *shodo*, the Way of Writing. See esp. pp. 93–6, not least for Morley's final qualifier.

20 Díaz, *Historia*, chapter 152.

21 *Florentine Codex*, 2: 21: 49, 54, for Tlacaxipeualiztli and the cannibal feast; 2: 30: 125, for Ochpaniztli and Toci's service.

22 *Florentine Codex*, 6: 3: 13.

23 *Florentine Codex*, 6: 3: 14.

24 *Florentine Codex*, 5: 2: 154.

6. WIVES

1 *Florentine Codex*, 6: 33: 172–3.

2 *Florentine Codex*, 6: 31: 171.

3 *Florentine Codex*, 6: 37: 201; 6: 38: 205.

4 For commoner girls at the telpochcalli, see Edward Calnek, 'The Calmecac and Telpochcalli in Pre-Conquest Tenochtitlan'.

5 For a discussion of some strategies to retrieve something of female action and experience from recalcitrant sources, see Inga Clendinnen, 'Yucatec Maya Women and the Spanish Conquest: Role and Ritual in Historical Reconstruction'.

6 Donald Robertson, 'The Sixteenth-Century Mexican Encyclopedia of Fray Bernardino de Sahagún', esp. 624–6. References to the colonial period are also powerfully intrusive in this section: see *Florentine Codex*, 10, esp. chapters 1–20.

7 Fr. Bartolomé de las Casas, *Apologética historia sumaria cuanto a las cualidades, dispusición, cielo y suelo destas tierras*, 2, p. 417.

8 Fray Bernardino de Sahagún, *Historia general de las cosas de la Nueva España*, 1, p. 242.

9 Female 'hunchbacks and dwarfs' sang and played the small drum associated with women to amuse their mistresses, but only in the seclusion of the household, and presumably for an exclusively female audience. *Florentine Codex*, 8: 16: 49.

10 *Florentine Codex*, 4: 7: 23–5.

11 For incest rules see Jerome A. Offner, *Law and Politics in Aztec Texcoco*, pp. 173–5, and for laws relating to adultery in Texcoco, pp. 257–66. The punishment for adultery, as opposed to its definition, was egalitarian, both offenders being liable to death by stoning.

12 Contrast here the Yucatec Maya, who practised the usual exclusions, and the

strong concern among North American Indians with menstrual and parturitional blood.

13 *Florentine Codex*, 6, esp. chaps. 18 and 19.

14 *Florentine Codex*, 10: 13: 47.

15 Cf. the interpretations of, e.g., Colin MacLachlan, 'The Eagle and the Serpent: Male Over Female in Tenochtitlan', and on a broader canvas June Nash, 'The Aztecs and the Ideology of Male Dominance'.

16 *Florentine Codex*, 2: 36: 157–8.

17 *Florentine Codex*, 2: 23: 63–4. In Sahagún's Spanish version it is an 'old woman' who responds, but the female victory remains constant. Sahagún, *Historia general* 1, p. 151.

18 *Florentine Codex*, 4: 33: 108.

19 For example, the women's assessment of the physical charms of the Tezcatlipoca ixiptla, *Florentine Codex*, 2: 24: 66–8.

20 *Anales de Tlatelolco*, paras. 325–8, p. 67.

21 Fr. Diego Durán, *Historia de las Indias de Nueva España e Islas de la Tierra Firme*, 1, p. 77.

22 For example, a lord's address to the city people on the installation of a new ruler, *Florentine Codex*, 6: 15: 79–80; an exhortation to the ruler, 6: 10: 51, 54; as fond parent, 6: 10: 48–9. The ancient usage continues among the Quiché of Momostenango, Guatemala; Dennis Tedlock, *Popol Vuh: The Definitive Edition of the Mayan Book of the Dawn of Life and the Glories of Gods and Kings*, p. 61.

23 Durán, *Historia*, 1, chapter 20.

24 For details of marriage arrangements, see *Florentine Codex*, 2: chapters 39–41.

25 *Florentine Codex*, 6: 23: 132.

26 For market foods, see *Florentine Codex*, 8: 13: 37–9; for the ordering of the market, 8: 19: 67–9; for market stalls, 10: chapters 16–26: 60–94. In Sahagún's informants' account of the marketplace sellers, the tortilla seller, 'an owner of tortillas or a retailer', is described as a male; 10: 19: 69. This could mean he had a number of female suppliers, tortilla-making being a female monopoly. But as nearly all market sellers are described as male in this section of the Sahagún corpus, the term may be generic, not descriptive, especially as the accompanying drawings depict women as the usual sellers of non-exotic foods. Note the female seller of paper, 10, plate 132.

27 For what is almost certainly a traditional form of association reactivated to meet the Spanish demand for cochineal, see the developing organisation of cochineal gatherers and dealers described in a 1553 statement by the Cabildo of Tlaxcala. James Lockhart, Frances Berdan and Arthur J. O. Anderson (eds.), *The Tlaxcalan Actas*, pp. 79–84.

28 *Florentine Codex*, 8: 13: 37–9; 10: 14: 52–3.

29 *Florentine Codex*, 4: 2: 7.

30 *Florentine Codex*, 10: 15: 56, and chapter 1.

31 Fray Alonso de Molina, *Vocabulario en lengua castellana y mexicana*.

32 This is a vexed issue. Alfredo López Austin, while allowing that 'in the abstract' sexual relations were presented in Nahuatl sources as desirable and
good, identifies *tlāltipacayōtl* 'to have known the filth' (*in teuhtli, in tlazolli*) as
integral to the sexual act. He goes on to discuss the Nahuatl verb for 'to
conceive' or 'to impregnate', as in *itlacahui, itlacauhqui, itlacahuiliztli*. For
López Austin there are two ways by which men were joined to the earth and
incurred the stigma of mortality: by ingesting maize, and by having known 'the
filth'; that is, to have engaged in the sexual life. Alfredo López Austin, *The
Human Body and Ideology: Concepts of the Ancient Nahuas*, 1, p. 313–4. Only
new-born babes were free from these sullying bonds. (López Austin also
claims that the tonalli was understood to leave the body during the sexual act,
so adding to its dangers, but his evidence, derived from modern Indian understandings, can be applied to the ancient Nahua only speculatively. López
Austin, *The Human Body and Ideology*, 1, pp. 221–2, 293.) Here Karttunen's
attentiveness to Carochi's notation of the long vowel is telling. She identifies
the verbs *tlācati* 'to be born' and *tlācatiliā* 'to engender someone, to give birth
to someone' as deriving from the noun stem *tlāca* 'human being', with Molina's
entries noted above all belonging to the same derivational family; in this case
from *tlāca-* plus verbalizing *hui*, and all having to do with bringing a human
being into existence. She continues: 'On the other hand the vowel for the
syllable *tla* in intransitive *ihtlacahui* and transitive/reflexive *ihtlacoā* is short.
The verb means "to spoil" and has nothing to do with sex or procreation. It
just happened that Molina mentioned that one way that one can spoil oneself is
through sexual promiscuity'. Frances Karttunen, personal communication. I
am deeply grateful for her clarification. The incoming ruler was warned
against 'woman . . . for she is death, she is sickness', but this comes as the last
in a long catalogue of dangerous self-indulgences. *Florentine Codex*, 6: 51–4.

33 *Florentine Codex*, 1: 16: 73.

34 The association was headed by three titled office bearers. *Florentine Codex*, 2:
30: 119. Sahagún also comments on women physicians gaining professional
status by 'the results of examinations', which implies regulation, but it is not
clear that the reference is to the pre-conquest period. *Florentine Codex*, 10: 14:
53.

35 Fr. Diego de Landa, *Landa's Relación de las Cosas de Yucatán*, p. 125.

36 *Florentine Codex*, 6: 21: 117.

37 *Florentine Codex*, 6: 18: 93–6.

38 The woman urges Axayacatzin to exert himself and to use his weapons in the

play-battle she provokes, luring him on to the 'flowery mat, and singing of the desire for pleasure of her 'flowery vulva' and breasts. For this and another musical triumph, see Domingo Chimalpahín, *Relaciones originales de Chalco Amaquemecan escritas por Don Francisco de San Antón Muñón Chimalpahín Cuauhtlehuanitzin,* Séptima Relación, esp. pp. 211–14. One also notes the significance Chimalpahín accords the alliances and deaths of noble native women in both the pre-conquest and post-conquest periods. For the song (and a problematical translation), see John Bierhorst (ed.), *Cantares Mexicanos: Songs of the Aztecs,* Song 84, pp. 385–91.

39 *Florentine Codex,* 3: 5; 19–20.

40 *Florentine Codex,* 6: 21: 116–19.

41 *Florentine Codex,* 6: 22: 125–6. Macacoatl was also self-administered to heighten sexual appetite and enhance performance.

42 Arthur J. O. Anderson, 'Aztec Hymns of Life and Love', p. 45.

43 For the erections, see *Codex Borbonicus: Bibliothèque de l'Assemblée National, Paris (Y120),* 30; for the spindles, *Florentine Codex,* 2: 30: 122.

44 Ilama tecuhtli in the likeness of a young woman held her chalky shield pasted with eagle feathers in one hand, her weaving stick in the other, while her headdress was of eagle feathers. She wore the black mouth-paint of the insatiable earth goddesses, but her nose and forehead were painted in ochre yellow, the paint of the warrior who has taken a captive; *Florentine Codex,* 8: 21: 76. Toci was adorned by warriors as a warrior in her festival of Ochpaniztli. For the regalia see the several illustrations in the *Codex Borbonicus* and the description in the *Florentine Codex,* 2: 36: 155.

45 For an engrossing and most sensitive discussion of the permutations of such a comprehensive system in a modern Highland Maya society, see Barbara Tedlock, *Time and the Highland Maya.* Note especially the subtleties in the 'reading' of the locations of bodily sensations of the diviner, where Tedlock concludes that at least for her place of study 'what is operating . . . is not a simple binary opposition, but rather a dialectical complementarity in which the terms male–female and right–left encompass one another rather than opposing one another (male/female, right/left)'.

46 For example: 'It was said that in Mexico there used to be men who went dressed as women, and these were very humble [*sométicos*] and they used to fill the offices of women, spinning and weaving, and some lords kept one or two for their vices'; Federico Gómez de Orozco, 'Costumbres, fiestas, enterramientos y diversas formas de proceder de los indios de Nueva España', *Tlalocan,* 11, 1 (1945): 37–63, see esp. p. 58. (López Austin points out that the word *señores* for 'lords' has been supplied, with only the letter 's' appearing in the original.) Other (post-conquest acculturated native) writers insisted that

homosexuality attracted the death sentence: e.g., Don Fernando de Alva Ix-tlilxóchitl, *Obras históricas*, 1, p. 405. On lesbianism, see John Bierhorst, *Cantares Mexicanos*, pp. 95–6. For an insightful discussion see Harriet Whitehead, 'The Bow and the Burden-strap: A New Look at Institutionalized Homosexuality in Native North America'.

47 For example, Tlaloc's three 'sisters' Chalchihuitlicue, Uixcihuatl, and Chicomecoatl, goddesses respectively of fresh water, salt, and cultivated cereals, were sometimes represented as his wives, but always as 'the livelihood of the people; through them the people are satisfied; through them they can live'; *Florentine Codex*, 1: 11: 22.

48 There is perhaps a sex-and-violence dimension to the 'Legend of the Suns' story of the goddess Itzpapalotl, 'Obsidian Butterfly', recorded in the manuscript of 1558 (Part III of the *Códice Chimalpopoca*). For the full text, translated into English by Willard Gingerich, see Pat Carr and Willard Gingerich, 'The Vagina Dentata Motif in Nahuatl and Pueblo Mythic Narratives: A Comparative Study'. The *Histoyre du Mexique* tells us that Ehecatl–Quetzalcoatl provided men with the maguey, from which octli (pulque) was derived. Unlike maize, which was successfully stolen by Quetzalcoatl and the other gods from the custody of the Tlalocs, the maguey was freely given. *Histoyre du Mexique*, ed. Eduardo de Jonghe. The violence/violation theme could have something to do with the process of working with maguey for its sap, which involves the cutting out of the 'heart' of a mature plant with a knife, and then the steady collection of the fluid which slowly wells into the cavity. The Nahua choice of words indicates that the resonance with heart sacrifice was heard, and understood.

49 George Grinnell, *The Cheyenne Indians*, Vol. 1, esp. p. 168.

50 *Florentine Codex*, 4: 1: 2; 4: 16: 59.

51 *Florentine Codex*, 10: chap. 13 *passim*.

52 Note the Spanish-influenced denunciation of these activities as either spells-and-potions black magic or cynical deception, *Florentine Codex*, 10: 14: 53. For the activities of the physicians, see *Florentine Codex*, 10: 14. Just how the female and male physicians (who are described in much the same terms) divided their activities is not clear. *Florentine Codex*, book 10, chapter 8.

53 *Florentine Codex*, 4: 21: 79. The 'reckoned as a man' phrase recalls Oscar Lewis's seminal article on the Piegan 'manly-hearted woman': she who by her energy in female pursuits could build an authority in the tribe greater than that of many, perhaps most, males – although only by being very much better. Oscar Lewis, 'Manly-Hearted Women Among the North Piegan', *American Anthropologist*, 43(1941): 173–87.

54 *Florentine Codex*, 10: 14: 51.

55 Robert Lowie, *The Crow Indians*, p. 186.
56 Leyenda de los soles, fol. 75–6, appendix to *Anales de Cuauhtitlán*, in *Códice Chimalpopoca.*

7. MOTHERS

1 Erik Erikson, *Toys and Reasons: Stages in the Ritualization of Experience*, p. 54.
2 Fr. Bartolomé de las Casas, *Apologética historia sumaria cuanto a las cualidades, dispusición, cielo y suelo destas tierras*, 2, p. 417.
3 Arthur J. O. Anderson, 'Aztec Hymns of Life and Love', p. 36; revised translation of *Florentine Codex*, 6: 33: 179.
4 See Gordon Brotherston, 'Huitzilopochtli and What Was Made of Him'.
5 *Florentine Codex*, 6: 31: 171–2.
6 *Florentine Codex*, 6: 37: 204.
7 Peter Brown writes of the compelling force of this particular human association, the 'warm and nurturing solidarity between mother and child', as 'the last, vestigial right of all to a common human nature and so to a common claim to human love in a divided and inhumane world'; Peter Brown, 'The Notion of Virginity in the Early Church', p. 438. Atrocity stories both invented and enacted pay perverse tribute to its enduring potency, as indicated by the constancy of the theme of babies torn from the breast or womb by an inhuman soldiery.
8 *Florentine Codex*, 4: 35: 114.
9 *Florentine Codex*, 6: 27: 157.
10 Robert Hertz, 'The Collective Representation of Death', pp. 85–6.
11 Anderson, 'Aztec Hymns', p. 36.
12 Quoted in Fr. J. de Torquemada, *Monarquía indiana*, 1, pp. 80–1.
13 H. B. Nicholson, 'Religion in Pre-Hispanic Central Mexico', p. 422.
14 *Histoyre du Mexique*, ed. Edouard de Jonghe, esp. pp. 28–9; *Códice Chimalpopoca: anales de Cuauhtitlán y leyenda de los soles*, Appendix.
15 *Florentine Codex*, 4: 34: 111; 5: 11: 186.
16 *Florentine Codex*, 4: 31–3: 101–7. See also the discussion of evil sorcerers in Chapter 2, 'Local Perspectives', section 4.
17 For the funerary rites, see *Florentine Codex*, 6: 29: 161–5.
18 Thelma D. Sullivan, 'Pregnancy, Childbirth and the Deification of the Women who Died in Childbirth'.
19 *Florentine Codex*, 1: 10: 19; 4: 11: 41. Cf. *Historia de los mexicanos por sus pinturas:* 'in the second [level of] heaven there are a number of women who have no flesh, only bones, and they call them *tetzuahcihua* or *tzitzimime* and

they are there because if the world is to be destroyed it is their task to devour all the people'. For a striking visual representation, see H. B. Nicholson with Eloise Quiñones Keber, *Art of Ancient Mexico: Treasures of Tenochtitlan*, p. 67.

20 *Florentine Codex*, 5: 13: 187.

21 *Florentine Codex*, 4: 22: 81; Fray Diego Durán, *Historia de las Indias de Nueva España e Islas de la Tierra Firme*, 1, p. 143, for the crossroad shrines. The five days of the Cihuapipiltins' descent were One Deer, One Rain, One Monkey, One House, and One Eagle.

22 *Florentine Codex*, 7: 10: 27–8. Cf. Fr. Toribio de Motolinía, *Memoriales e historia de los indios de la Nueva España*, chapter 49, p. 67, for the intimate and terrible connection between a pregnant woman and the earth powers: 'Cuando temblaba la tierra à do habia mujer preñada, cubrian de presto las ollas, é quebrántan las porque no amoviese.'

23 Melissa Llewelyn-Davies, 'Women, Warriors and Patriarchs', p. 353.

24 For example, *Borbonicus* 13 represents the goddess Tlazolteotl and Tezcatlipoca. The goddess is seen from the front, seated on the floor with her legs apart. A fully formed baby is descending from the heavens into her womb. The act is watched over by Tezcatlipoca in his vulture guise, with his crown of stars; *Codex Borbonicus: Bibliothèque de l'Assemblée National, Paris (Y120)*. On the 'seating in the womb', see Alfredo López Austin, *The Human Body and Ideology: Concepts of the Ancient Nahuas*, 1, p. 297.

25 On semen, *omjcetl*, see *Florentine Codex*, 10: 27: twelfth paragraph, 130. The pregnant girl was exhorted to guard the child growing in her womb carefully, as 'perhaps our lord wishes to make likenesses [ixiptla] of those whom he hath destroyed, whom he has hidden [by death].' *Florentine Codex*, 6: 25: 142.

26 Cf. contemporaneous European preformationists, who saw intercourse as essential to 'grow' an existing and preformed entity. It seems that one Nahuatl term, *tlacaxinachtli*, or 'human seed', covered both semen and vaginal fluid. López Austin, *The Human Body and Ideology*, 1, p. 176.

27 *Florentine Codex*, 6: 25: 142; 6: 37: 204. For the possibility that semen was seen as necessary for the formation of bone, see Inga Clendinnen, 'The Cost of Courage in Aztec Society'.

28 For the fullest description of the care of the woman during the gestation and the birth process see *Florentine Codex*, 6, chapters 27, 28. The cessation of the menstrual flow for the duration of the pregnancy seems to have been given no particular significance.

29 *Florentine Codex*, 6: 37: 202.

30 For the horticulture, see *Florentine Codex*, 11: 13: 283–4. For the role of the sun, p. 284. 'Sustenance Woman' combined both rain and sun themes in her

regalia, wearing a shift painted with water flowers, and a shield with the sun sign.

31 *Florentine Codex,* 1: 4: 7.

32 *Florentine Codex,* 6: 8: 35.

33 *Florentine Codex,* 6: 8: 36.

34 For an elegantly concise account of the ways in which metaphors scavenged from a developing technology have transformed European biological understandings, see Jonathon Miller, *The Body in Question,* esp. chapter 5, 'The Pump'.

35 *Florentine Codex,* 10: 27: 128–32. This section of the Codex is heavily marked by European influences, but not in the cited particulars.

36 See Clendinnen, 'The Cost of Courage', esp. pp. 80–3; Jill Furst, *Codex Vindobonensis Mexicanus I, A Commentary.*

37 The notion of the fertilizing power of human (especially warrior) blood voluntarily or involuntarily shed has a long history in Mesoamerica. For related themes in related territory, see Linda Schele and Mary Ellen Miller, *The Blood of Kings: Dynasty and Ritual in Maya Art.*

38 *Histoyre du Mexique,* esp. 28–9; *Códice Chimalpopoca: anales de Cuauhtitlán; Florentine Codex,* 3: 1; 7: Appendix.

39 For a brief description of the Coatlicue statue, see Chapter 9, 'Aesthetics', section 6. For the conceptualization of the human body derived from this analogy, see *Florentine Codex,* 10: 27: 128, 130–2. Frances Karttunen mounts a telling critique against the conventional linguistic identification of the word *tonacayo,* 'our flesh', with the word describing the fruits of the earth. She offers *tonacayotl* as human sustenance or the fruits of the earth, contrasting this with tonacayo, which she identifies as the first-person plural inalienably possessed form of *nacatl,* 'flesh'; Frances Karttunen, private communication.

40 For a gallant attempt to pursue some of these deeper preoccupations see Carol Walker Bynum, 'Fast, Feast, and Flesh: The Religious Significance of Food to Medieval Women'. See also her *Holy Feast and Holy Fast: The Religious Significance of Food to Medieval Women.*

41 The theory of dreaming to which I attach myself is that recently mapped by Allan Hobson in *The Dreaming Brain.* Its strength is that it is in accord with and built from current thinking in neurophysiology; it takes the meaning of dreams as residing in their manifest content, characterized as the attempt of the dreamer to draw out of daily preoccupations the strategies to make sense out of random incoming stimuli; and it permits the dismissal of the over-staffed Freudian dream-bureaucracy. However, its capacity to incorporate the layered, occluded, nomad quality of human memory, which is the Freudians' greatest asset, is doubtful. Cf. Hobson's theory with the powerful argument for the

cultural and collective interpretation of a sequence of phosephenes generated by the intake of the hallucinogen *yajé* by the Barasana Indians of the Piraparaná in G. Reichel-Dolmatoff, *The Shaman and the Jaguar: A Study of Narcotic Drugs Among the Indians of Colombia*, pp. 157–81.

42 Motolinía, *Memoriales e historia*, chapter 49, p. 67; Sahagún, *Augurios y abusiones* trans. Alfredo López Austin (from 'Primeros memoriales', 1969), pp. 100–3. See also the dedicatory letter, p. 2; Durán, *Historia*, 1, chapter 13; 2, chapter 68, for dreams as augury and as intimations of the sacred. For a more developed discussion of the passion for augury, see Chapter 5, 'The Masculine Self Discovered', *passim*.

43 See *Florentine Codex*, 5: 3: 157–9 for Night Axe; book 5 *passim* for 'omens', which include night terrors. See also Alfredo López Austin, 'El hacha nocturna'.

44 Anthony F. Wallace, *The Death and Rebirth of the Seneca*, p. 77.

45 Wallace, *The Death and Rebirth of the Seneca*, p. 75.

46 Wallace, *The Death and Rebirth of the Seneca*, p. 35.

47 *Florentine Codex*, 6: 10: 49.

48 *Florentine Codex*, 6: 7: 32; 6: 8: 35–6. Infants also had the company of livelier toys. One of the Mexica riddle-me-rees asks 'What it is that stands at the edge of the hearth, rising with a curve at the end?' and answers 'The dog's tail'; *Florentine Codex*, 6: 42: 239.

49 *Florentine Codex*, 6: 40: 214.

50 Alfred Crosby claims that few adult indigenes of the Americas can tolerate animal milk beyond infancy, but the difficulty of managing the weaning transition stands. Alfred W. Crosby, *Ecological Imperialism: The Biological Expansion of Europe, 900–1900*, p. 27.

51 *Florentine Codex*, 5: 31: 193.

52 Fray Alonso de Molina, *Vocabulario en lengua castellana y mexicana;* see *tzipitl, tzipitlatoa, tzipinalhuia, tzipinoa, tzipicuazaloa*.

53 *Codex Mendoza*, part 3.

54 It is possible that among the consciousness-altering drugs only pulque was available to the commoners, Muñoz Camargo claiming the use of psychotropic drugs like peyote, mushrooms and tlapatl (a form of datura) was restricted to the lords. Diego Muñoz Camargo, *Historia de Tlaxcalla*, pp. 134–5.

55 *Florentine Codex*, 2; Appendix: 203.

56 Miguel León-Portilla, *Aztec Thought and Culture: A Study of the Ancient Nahuatl Mind*, p. 127: 'It is said that the little children who died, like jade, turquoise and jewels, do not go to the frightful and cold region of the dead. They go to the house of Tonacatecutli; they live by the 'tree of our flesh'. They nourish themselves on the tree of our sustenance . . . from it do they feed themselves.'

The Florentine Codex sets Chichihuacuauhco in the house of Tonacatecutli, 'Lord of Our Flesh'. *Florentine Codex*, 6: 21: 115.

57 *Codex Mendoza*, part 3, physical punishments from eight to thirteen years as administered by parents. For the claim that the harshness was exaggerated, see George C. Vaillant, *Aztecs of Mexico: Origin, Rise and Fall of the Aztec Nation*, p. 124.

58 *Florentine Codex*, 6: 40: 213–4.

59 *Florentine Codex*, 6: 42: 238. The Mexica's largely vegetable diet meant foods were eaten with the fingers, scooped up in tortillas, or drunk from cup or spoon. (Meat, something of a luxury, was typically pre-cut.) The flint knife (*tecpatl*) was primarily associated with the ritual killing of humans.

60 *Florentine Codex*, 6: 19: 101.

61 *Florentine Codex*, 10: 24: 89–90.

62 At least to judge from the advice of a father to his son; *Florentine Codex*, 6: 22: esp. 124.

63 *Florentine Codex*, 3: 2: 5–7.

64 López Austin, *The Human Body and Ideology*, 1, p. 178.

65 Louise M. Burkhart, *The Slippery Earth: Nahua–Christian Moral Dialogue in Sixteenth-Century Mexico*, p. 55.

66 Stanley Walens, *Feasting with Cannibals: An Essay on Kwakiutl Cosmology*, p. 6. For the uncomfortable consequences of this view for the 'greedy' child, see p. 15. We see something of the same conceptualization in a form at once intensified and softened among the ecologically sensitive today.

67 Durán, *Historia*, 2, chapter 13.

68 *Florentine Codex*, 6: 1: 4.

69 *Florentine Codex*, 6: 3: 13.

70 Durán, *Historia*, chapter 34.

71 *Florentine Codex*, 3: 1: 1–5.

72 Clearly no single (or indeed multiple) theme will fully explain the Mexica cultural preference for the excitements of one-to-one-contest. The towns of the Mexican valley, their agonistic histories providing the justification for the intensities of primordial loyalties, acted out their rivalries in a Lilliputian landscape, being largely in sight of each other, which possibly exacerbated competition.

73 See Chapter 4, 'Warriors', section 2.

74 *Florentine Codex*, 7: 2: 3–8.

75 *Florentine Codex*, 2: Appendix, 207.

76 See Thelma Sullivan's intriguing reference to the warrior emblem of the 'hungry child'; Thelma Sullivan, 'The Arms and Insignia of the Mexica'.

77 Durán, *Historia* 1, chapter 13, pp. 125–6.

78 For accounts of another upstart elder sister who interfered with Huitzilopochtli's plans, enlisting her son in the project, and for the characterization of Coyolxauhqui not as Huitzilopochtli's sister, but his mother, see the story of Malinalxochitl; Thelma Sullivan, 'The Finding and Founding of Mexico-Tenochtitlan'.

79 For the porphyry head and a Coyolxauhqui bibliography, see H. B. Nicholson with Eloise Quiñones Keber, *Art of Ancient Mexico: Treasures of Tenochtitlan*, pp. 48–50. For the story, *Florentine Codex*, 3: 1: 1–5. For discussions of the relief carving, see Esther Pasztory, *Aztec Art*, pp. 154–5; Cecelia Klein, 'Rethinking Cihuacoatl: Aztec Political Imagery of the Conquered Woman'; H. B. Nicholson, 'The New Tenochtitlan Templo Mayor Coyolxauhqui-Chantico Monument', in *Genenkschrift Gerd Kutscher, Indiana* 10: 77–98. For more on the implication of goddesses in war, Jane Berlo, 'The Warrior and the Butterfly: Central Mexican Ideologies of Sacred Warfare and Teotihuacan Iconography', esp. 87–95.

80 For the Coyolxauhqui carving, see the illustrations following page 240.

81 Pace Coyolxauhqui, the most intense rivalry probably invested male sibling relations. For a hint of this, note that the 'ruler's address to his sons' envisions three boys lined up before him. The speech is strung on a thread of competition and ranking: 'which one is my sluggard, which my incoherent one? . . . which one of you will profit?' *Florentine Codex*, 6: 17: 87, 92.

82 The festival was dated by Sahagún as falling between 31 August and 19 September; by Durán between 2 September and 21 September. The following account essentially derives from the *Florentine Codex*, 2: 30: 118–26. Durán, *Historia*, 1, chapter 15, offers a description which fits Sahagún's where it touches, but which describes the killing of victims very differently (having them forced to crash down from very high poles) and overall is very much an outsider's account, which makes the action appear disjunctive and notably 'exotic'. Nonetheless, the emotional ambience is very similar to the Sahagún account.

83 As the action in Ochpaniztli makes clear, the Teteo Innan complex incorporated earth deity and fertility notions ('Our Mother', 'Heart of the Earth', 'Mother of the Sacred Ones') and the 'sustenance' aspects, as with Chicomecoatl, the goddess of cultivated foods. Another aspect was differentiated by the name Tlazolteotl, 'Filth Goddess', She who cleansed from carnal pollution.

84 This would not be easy to do without damage to the supporting priest unless the woman's hair, and so her neck, was stretched taut, and the blow came from below, which would mimic the cutting of the maize cob. That appears to be the model here.

85 The bodies were typically flayed by the separate removal of the head skin, and the slitting of the skin from nape to coccyx. I have been assured by surgeons that the fatty tissue of the breasts would adhere to the skin.

86 'Toci' is usually said to be 'identical' with Teteo Innan (e.g. *Florentine Codex*, 2: 30; 119, n. 6) but the Ochpaniztli sequence, where the living woman is named 'Teteo Innan', and the priest in the flayed skin 'Toci', and where each figure has specific areas of control, suggests they were differentiated.

87 Borbonicus 31; see 'The festival of Ochpaniztli' in the illustrations following page 240 for reproduction. With the rampant Huaxtecs we return to the but unclarified role of sexuality in agricultural fertility. I suspect the metaphor is simply being worked the other way: sexual intercourse is necessary for human reproduction, and so in some way is also necessary for plant reproduction. Therefore Toci has her Huaxtecs. The Arrow Sacrifice, in which captives were tied to poles, raised, and shot with arrows so that their blood dripped down, was unequivocally associated with sexual congress with the earth in the account given of its introduction to Central Mexico from the eastern coast; see *Annals of Quauhtitlan*, quoted by Anderson, 'Aztec Hymns of Life and Love', p. 26.

88 The Mexica maintained an 'as if' map of significant ceremonial locations within the city and its environs, so the delivery of the war sign 'to enemy lands' may have been symbolic, not actual.

89 See, e.g., Betty Ann Brown, 'Ochpaniztli in Historical Perspective'.

8. THE FEMALE BEING REVEALED

1 On the decline of old age, see Alfredo Lopéz Austin, *The Human Body and Ideology: Concepts of the Ancient Nahuas*, 1, p. 290.

2 There were 'women priests' who were not fully subsumed under the maidens' 'retreat-before-marriage' rubric: e.g., *Florentine Codex*, 6: 40: 216. The Chicomecoatl 'priestesses', described as 'maidens' (priestly authority usually being a concomitant of age), were represented ideologically as the custodians of fertility. Cf. the midwife–curers in Ochpaniztli who inverted gender relationship by being the agents, with the phallic Huaxtecs presented as the icons. *Florentine Codex*, 10: 14.

3 *Florentine Codex*, 2: 22: 58–60. See also Inga Clendinnen, 'The Cost of Courage in Aztec Society', esp. pp. 80–3.

9. AESTHETICS

1 *Florentine Codex*, 10: 29: 165–9. See also *Anales de Cuauhtitlán*, fol. 7.

2 Miguel León-Portilla, *Aztec Thought and Culture*, p. 166. Twenty years ago

León-Portilla urged a renewed attempt by students of the Mexica 'to formulate an indigenous aesthetic'. His own work has constituted an incomparable contribution to that undertaking.

3 *Los Romances de los Señores de Nueva España*, fol. 9v.–10r., trans. Miguel León-Portilla, in 'Translating Amerindian Texts', p. 119.

4 *Florentine Codex*, 10: 29: 165–70.

5 Fr. Bernardino de Sahagún, *Códice matritense de la Real Academia*, 8, fol. 115v, trans. Miguel León-Portilla, in his *Pre-Columbian Literatures of Mexico*, p. 174.

6 Sahagún, *Códice matritense de la Real Academia*, 8, fol. 192r, trans. Miguel León-Portilla, in his *Aztec Thought and Culture: A Study of the Ancient Nahuatl Mind*, p. 23.

7 Dennis Tedlock, *The Spoken Word and the Work of Interpretation*, p. 280. See also his magnificent translation, *Popol Vuh: The Definitive Edition of the Mayan Book of the Dawn of Life and the Glories of Gods and Kings*, pp. 165–7.

8 Animals of particular 'power' were identified as the 'nahualli' or special associates of particular gods. For a general discussion of the concept, see L. Marie Musgrave-Portilla, 'The Nahualli or Transforming Wizard in Pre- and Postconquest Mesoamerica', *Journal of Latin American Lore*, 8, 1 (1982): 3–62.

9 *Florentine Codex*, 9: 1: 1–2.

10 *Florentine Codex*, 11: 2: 20.

11 The male children of the featherworkers were pledged to the priest houses to develop some knowledge of the sacred writing before embarking on intensive family training in their craft; *Florentine Codex*, 9: 19: 88, 93. The *Matrícula de Tributos* gives feathers and skins of the lovely cotinga (*xiuhtototl*) as coming from Lowland Veracruz to Chiapas, the Mexican trogon (*tzinitzcan*) in highlands from northern Mexico to Chiapas, the yellow-headed parrot (*toztli*) from the east coast, and the roseate spoonbill (*tlauhquechol*) from along the Gulf Coast. The green Pacific parakeet supplied green feathers, the scarlet macaw (alo) red. Most featherwork warrior costumes and shields were required from the provinces closest to the imperial centre, naturally enough given the necessity for the close control of the design. See Frances Berdan, 'The Economics of Aztec Luxury Trade and Tribute', map 4, p. 172. For the surviving examples of Mexican featherwork – a meagre eight – see Esther Pasztory, *Aztec Art*, pp. 278–90. Only eight of the provinces listed in the *Matrícula de Tributos* were not required to send feathers or featherwork in tribute. The passion and delight in feathers is unabashedly expressed in the detailed account of the decking of the human offerings presented to their special deity by the featherworkers. *Florentine Codex*, 9: 18: 83–5. For the birds, see L. Irby Davis, *A Field Guide to the Birds of Mexico and Central America*.

12 If Bernal Díaz had it right, the Mexica were able to breed the quetzal in

Moctezoma's aviary. Bernal Díaz del Castillo, *Historia verdadera de la conquista de la Nueva España*, chapter 91.

13 Alexander Skutch, cited in Jonathon Evan Maslow, *Bird of Life, Bird of Death*, p. 50.

14 *Florentine Codex*, 11: 2: 19.

15 Fr. Diego Durán, *Historia de las Indias de Nueva España e Islas de la Tierra Firme*, 2, chapter 25.

16 See Gordon Brotherston, 'Sacred Sand in Mexican Picture-Writing and Later Literature'. Cf. Charles E. Dibble, 'The *Xalaquia* Ceremony'. For the close identification between the victims' 'entering the sand' and the drinking of obsidian-knife-water, see Arthur J. O. Anderson, 'The Institution of Slave Bathing', p. 84.

17 *Florentine Codex*, 8: 7: 26.

18 *Florentine Codex*, 3: 7: 23–4.

19 Bierhorst's claim that the bulk of the songs were composed in the latter half of the sixteenth century has not won scholarly assent, although Christian allusions place some in the post-conquest period; John Bierhorst (trans.), *Cantares Mexicanos: Songs of the Aztecs*, p. 4.

20 Miguel León-Portilla, *Pre-Columbian Literatures of Mexico*, p. 94, translation of *Cantares Mexicanos*, fol. 3r. The deity invoked as Tloque Nahuaque, 'Lord of the Close and Near' (or 'the Here and Now'), is generally taken to be the equivocal Tezcatlipoca. While his name does not appear in the surviving songs, the same epithets applied to the Cantares' 'Life-Giver' are used for Tezcatlipoca throughout the Florentine Codex. In the songs the Mexica exhibit the usual flexibility, not to say confusion, as to the nature and the location of warrior afterlife, the warrior paradise seeming sometimes to be identified with Tlalocan, and with Tamoanchan. Bierhorst categorizes all the *Cantares* and the *Romances* as 'ghost songs' of the late-nineteenth-century type, in which the singers seek to 'sing back' dead warriors to renew the struggle; a notably contentious interpretation. Bierhorst, *Cantares, passim*, but especially pp. 16–37. For a magisterial survey of the categories and characteristics of Nahuatl literature, see Miguel León-Portilla, 'Nahuatl Literature'.

21 Andrew O. Wiget, 'Aztec Lyrics: Poetry in a World of Continually Perishing Flowers', p. 7.

22 Bierhorst, *Cantares*, p. 195.

23 *Cantares Mexicanos*, ff. 26v–27v, trans. Gordon Brotherston in collaboration with Ed Dorn, in *Image of the New World: The American Continent Portrayed in Native Texts*, p. 274.

24 Bierhorst, *Cantares*, p. 319.

25 Bierhorst, *Cantares*, p. 353.

26 Bierhorst, *Cantares*, p. 175.

27 Wiget, 'Aztec Lyrics', p. 9.

28 Brotherston, *Image of the New World*, p. 273. Cf. Bierhorst, *Cantares*, p. 221. In the Nahuatl text the 'mother' is identified as Santa María. Bierhorst chose the hard path of full consistency in his translations, the Nahuatl always being rendered by the same English word, so I have tended to prefer more mellifluous and accessible renderings.

29 Dennis Tedlock, *The Spoken Word and the Work of Interpretation*, esp. pp. 266–7, 270–1.

30 *Florentine Codex*, 7: 2: 4.

31 Wiget, 'Aztec Lyrics', p. 3.

32 The identification of the transforming sorcerer with the night-stalking jaguar is near-ubiquitous in Indian America. See, e.g., Peter T. Furst, 'The Olmec Were–Jaguar Motif in the Light of Ethnographic Reality'. That the jaguar is notably good to think with is powerfully demonstrated in Ted Hughes's poem, 'Second Glance at a Jaguar'.

33 Although the might of the Empire could be at their disposal. Moctezoma sent for a special abrasive sand from the Gulf Coast at the request of his stone carvers. The people of whom the requests were made were not immediately co-operative, so Moctezoma sent out his army. Durán *Historia*, 2, chapter 56.

34 The standard reference works for 'Aztec' art are Dudley T. Easby, Elizabeth Kennedy Easby, John F. Scott, and Thomas Hoving, *Before Cortés; Sculpture of Middle America: A Centennial Exhibition at the Metropolitan Museum of Art*; H. B. Nicholson with Eloise Quiñones Keber, *Art of Ancient Mexico: Treasures of Tenochtitlán*; Esther Pasztory, *Aztec Art*. For the vegetable representations, see Nicholson and Quiñones Keber, *Art of Ancient Mexico*, pp. 112–19, with associated plates.

35 For example, 'Toad', in Nicholson and Quiñones Keber, *Art of Ancient Mexico*, pl. 42, p. 115.

36 Pasztory, *Aztec Art*, p. 209. The monumental sculptures, a Tenochtitlan phenomenon, are more straightforward, as direct expressions of Mexica conviction of their predestined power, and the desire to memorialize (and explore) their imperial role, marked by a consciously archaizing inclination to emphasize the connection with Tula and Teotihuacan. Pasztory, *Aztec Art*, p. 141; Richard Fraser Townsend, *State and Cosmos in the Art of Tenochtitlán*, esp. p. 17.

37 "Jaguar crouching," in Nicholson and Quiñones Keber, *Art of Ancient Mexico*, cover, and pl. 44, p. 119. For a rare stone eagle, looking like a sick vulture, Pasztory, *Aztec Art*, pl. 223, p. 236; for a stylized eagle head, pl. 279, p. 258, and

pl. 40, p. 83. See Nicholson and Quiñones Keber, *Art of Ancient Mexico*, pl. 61, pp. 145–7 for magnificent but most unnaturalistic carvings of eagles in wood.

38 Nicholson and Quiñones Keber, *Art of Ancient Mexico*, pl. 45, p. 121.

39 Sahagún, quoted in Elizabeth Wilder Weismann, *Mexico in Sculpture 1521–1821*, p. 33. For some of the techniques, see Sahagún, *Florentine Codex*, 10: 20–4: 73–88.

40 For example, the doings of the pelican, ruler of the water birds, *Florentine Codex*, 11: 2: 30–1.

41 *Florentine Codex*, 11: 1: 9.

42 *Florentine Codex*, 11: 1: 11–12.

43 *Florentine Codex*, 11: 2: 43–44.

44 *Florentine Codex*, 11: 1: 2–3.

45 *Florentine Codex*, 9: 3: 13; 11: 12: 266–9.

46 *Florentine Codex*, 11: 5: 75–87.

47 *Florentine Codex*, 5: Appendix: 184.

48 *Florentine Codex*, 5: 9: 171.

49 There is of course the risk of over-ingenuity. A carved disk represents a squash blossom with a bee with the buccal mask of Quetzalcoatl as Wind God on the obverse. Pasztory, *Aztec Art*, pl. 233, p. 238. Is this a supremely laconic comment in stone on the role of bees and of wind in pollination (maize being wind-pollinated)? Almost certainly not: there is nothing in the Nahuatl accounts of maize or of bees to suggest any awareness of the process of pollination. But in the small hours of the morning it is possible to think so.

50 George Catlin, *Letters and Notes on the Manners, Customs, and Conditions of the North American Indians*, Vol. 1, p. 40.

51 *Ehuatl*, the sleeveless feathered warrior garment, is commonly rendered as 'shirt' or 'tunic': e.g. Thelma Sullivan, 'The Arms and Insignia of the Mexica', *passim*. It is translated by Molina as an animal pelt for tanning or the rind of a fruit, while Sahagún uses ehuatl (eoatl) to mean the human skin. Fr. Alonso de Molina, *Vocabulario en lengua castellana y mexicana; Florentine Codex*, 10: 27: 95. See also Alfredo López Austin, *The Human Body and Ideology*, 1, p. 130. The full warrior costume, the *tlahuiztli*, which enveloped the whole body closely, was open down the back and secured by ties (see, e.g., *Lienzo de Tlaxcala*, ed. Alfredo Chavez, Fig. 16), as was the flayed human skin which constituted Xipe Totec.

52 *Florentine Codex*, 11: 1: 3.

53 Berdan, 'The Economics of Aztec Luxury Trade'; *Matrícula de Tributos;* Johanna Broda, 'El tributo en trajes guerreros y la estructura del sistema tributario mexica'.

54 Cf. Richard Townsend, *State and Cosmos in the Art of Tenochtitlán*, p. 15, for the

identification of the pictorial manuscript tradition as 'the most likely vehicle for transmitting ideological principles of great antiquity', and the exchange of influence between the pictorial mode and Mexica sculptural relief. I am arguing for a rather more thorough-going priority than that.

55 For a discussion, see Robertson, *Mexican Manuscript Painting of the Early Colonial Period*. For intriguing implications of a related contrast see Flora S. Clancy, 'A Comparison of Highland Zapotec and Lowland Maya Graphic Styles'.

56 Walter Ong, *Orality and Literacy: The Technologizing of the Word*, p. 8. Ong is disappointingly laconic on character-based modes. Among Ong's bulky writings this overview volume provides the best beginning point and a useful bibliography. For a lucid account of Nahuatl writing before and after the conquest see Frances Karttunen, 'Nahuatl Literacy'. The issue of the shaping of different sensibilities through primary dependence on particular forms of communication has generated a daunting literature. Walter Ong has set the terms of much of the debate. See his *The Presence of the Word* and his *Rhetoric, Romance, and Technology: Studies on the Interaction of Expression and Culture*. For a sophisticated discussion of recent argument (and a useful bibliography), see James Clifford, 'On Ethnographic Allegory', esp. pp. 117–18.

57 For the Valley of Mexico there survives probably only one pre-contact codex, the *Codex Borbonicus*. For an impressive, if not finally decisive, argument against its Tenochtitlan-Tlatelolcan provenance, see H. B. Nicholson, 'The Provenience of the *Codex Borbonicus*: A Hypothesis', in *Smoke and Mist: Mesoamerican Studies in Memory of Thelma D. Sullivan*, ed. J. Kathryn Josserand and Karen Dakin, 1, pp. 77–97. For general analyses of the Central Mexican codices, Robertson, *Mexican Manuscript Painting of the Early Colonial Period;* for a recent evaluation, N. C. Christopher Couch, *The Festival Cycle of the Aztec Codex Borbonicus*, chapters 1–7.

58 There was possibly a further dimension of divination, less a reading than a 'seeing', the divining and pronouncing of a meaning beyond the signs but implicit in them. For a magnificent example of 'interpretation' of such a text, and a lucid discussion of the process of transcription and translation, see Dennis Tedlock, *The Spoken Word and the Work of Interpretation*, esp. chapter 4.

59 Note the extraordinary continuity of the codex style, exemplified in the body-in-bits of the Franciscan baptismal font from Acatzingo, dated Four Rabbit (1574), and reproduced in Weismann, *Mexico in Sculpture*, plate 61, p. 66. Weismann comments: 'The flying angels, with their Indian masks, are cutouts supreme: the disconnected wings, the single arm, and the zigzag drapery respond to no anatomical criticism' – precisely like the codex figures.

60 Such figures have often been taken to be representations of the ixiptlas, the

living 'god-presenters' earlier discussed (e.g. Townsend, *State and Cosmos in the Art of Tenochtitlán*, p. 23) but the stone representations are usually more formidably abstract and complete than the more partial representations built on a living human frame, as so precisely represented in the screenfold manuscripts. Esther Pasztory has pointed to the possibility that the monumental sculptures like the Coatlicue were not visual representations of theologically ratified conceptualizations, but rather explorations or musings on possible connections and associations: as much invitations to speculation as to habituated worship. Esther Pasztory, 'Masterpieces in Pre-Columbian Art'; *Aztec Art*, p. 141.

61 Weismann, *Mexico in Sculpture*, p. 11. One set of exceptions has to do with maize, which was represented at each stage of its growth by a human of the appropriate age and stage, while the images which represented the fruitful or more benign aspects of Earth Mother, in her role as Sustenance Woman or as Jade Skirt, goddess of fresh waters, were commonly of mature women. The faces are typically impassive and the images dwarfed by their regalia, most especially their vastly elaborate headdresses, but they remain indubitably human for all that: e.g. Nicholson and Quiñones Keber, *Art of Aztec Mexico*, pl. 17–20, pp. 69–77; Pasztory, *Aztec Art*, pl. 158, 159, 182–5; pp. 211, 219–21. The small seated deities identified as variations on the God of Fire, or the enigmatic Tepeyollotl, 'Hill Heart' or 'Heart of the Mountain', are also unequivocally men. There is no known stone sculpture of Huitzilopochtli, who was rarely imaged in any permanent public medium: the figures processed in his great ceremonies were constructed on a skeleton of seed-dough, the construction as much a part of the ritual action as the processing, and appropriately ephemeral. In a justly influential article H. B. Nicholson has discerned three great themes or clusters in the ritual round and the powers invoked: celestial creativity/paternalism; rain/moisture/agricultural fertility; war/sacrifice/sanguinary nourishment of sun and earth; 'Religion in Pre-Hispanic Central Mexico', pp. 395–446.

62 Nicholson and Quiñones Keber, *Art of Aztec Mexico*, pl. 16, pp. 67–8. For Coatlicue, see Pasztory, *Aztec Art*, pl. 110, p. 159; Townsend, *State and Cosmos in the Art of Tenochtitlán*, esp. pp. 28–30; Paul Westheim, *The Art of Ancient Mexico*, esp. pp. 226–31. For a more 'human' representation, see Chapter 7, 'Mothers', section 5.

63 These have been arranged in illuminating sequence from 'snake' to 'sacred' in Nicholson and Quiñones Keber, *Art of Aztec Mexico*, pl. 56–60, pp. 138–44.

64 See, e.g., Pasztory, *Aztec Art*, pl. 268, 269, p. 254; Nicholson and Quiñones Keber, *Art of Aztec Mexico*, pl. 32–7, pp. 100–9. Note especially pl. 36 and 37 of Xipe Totec.

65 A. L. Becker, 'Biography of a Sentence: A Burmese Proverb', *Construction and Reconstruction of Self and Society,* pp. 143–5.

66 On the shaping and administration of the city, see David Carrasco, *Quetzalcoatl and the Irony of Empire,* pp. 162–70, and Wayne Elzey, 'The Nahua Myth of the Suns', *Numen* (August, 1976); for the shape of codex representations and for the isomorphic structuring of time, Brotherston, *Image of the New World;* for the analysis of surviving ancient codices as records of Mexican myths dramatized into ritual enactment, Karl Nowotny, *Tlacuilolli;* for the 'parallel couplet' or *difrasismo,* Angel María Garibay K., *Historia de la literatura náhuatl,* 2, pp. 19, 65–7; for the architectural statements, Townsend, *State and Cosmos in the Art of Tenochtitlán.* (Verbs in Nahuatl distinguish direction, which implies a profound cultural concern for spatial arrangements.) The great Stone of Tizoc draws on manuscript painting for its symbolic representations and warrior–captive pairings in its procession of repeating units between framing borders, very much on the Toltec model. Just how complex and all-inclusive the organizing idea might have been is argued by Rudolph van Zantwijk, *The Aztec Arrangement: The Social History of Pre-Spanish Mexico.*

67 James Lockhart has written of a ubiquitous preference in pre- and post-Columbian America for what he has called the 'cellular' as opposed to a linear or hierarchical type of organization, expressed in land allocation and political organization as in oratical expression; James Lockhart, 'Some Nahua Concepts in Postconquest Guise'. He and Frances Karttunen find the same distinctive patterning in the structuring of songs; Frances Karttunen and James Lockhart, 'La estructura de la poesía náhuatl vista por sus variantes', esp. pp. 16–21.

68 I have not directly pursued possible European analogies and antitheses with my construction of the Mexica aesthetic, save as the inescapable because familiar touchstone for all statements and claims. Anyone who knows anything of North American Indians will have had a hard time restraining their impatience during my laborious analysis, with so much familiar in its general contours: worlds sung into existence, 'natural' things as shadows of the sacred, creatures of power, the disruptive glamour of the sacred, the passion for figuring pre-figured destinies. To those readers I apologize. But it is the details, not the contours, which count.

10. RITUAL: THE WORLD TRANSFORMED, THE WORLD REVEALED

1 Stephen Greenblatt, 'Exorcism into Art', p. 15.

2 Bronislaw Malinowski, *Magic, Science and Religion: and other essays.* For an

overly bleak recent view see George Marcus and Michael Fischer, who identify
'an especially modern condition': 'rituals are not seen by their "knowing"
participants or observers to be invested with cosmic or sacred truth, but merely
as one among many equally valid group displays that may engender momentary
cartharsis, but have little enduring hold on their performers or audiences'.
George E. Marcus and Michael M. J. Fischer, *Anthropology as Cultural Critique: An Experimental Moment in the Human Sciences.* p. 45. This is easier to
believe in a non-presidential election year.

3 For the discussion see Chapter 1, 'Tenochtitlan: The Public Image', section 8.

4 I am indebted to Mr. Ray Hargrave, unpublished paper 1986, for much of the
following discussion regarding agency.

5 *Florentine Codex,* 4: Appendix: 143.

6 *Florentine Codex,* 7: 10: 27.

7 The wording could be thought to imply the human assumption of control when
it was said that 'the years were newly laid hold of . . . everyone took hold of
them'. *Florentine Codex,* 7: 9: 25–7. However, we must take the constant equation of the bearing of the 'Bundle of Years' as a heavy burden seriously. Humans
must take it up, with no element of choice. That is part of their god-given
affliction.

8 Here Clifford Geertz and his famous cockfight remain the model, because
through his exemplary analysis we are brought to see something of the complexity of the gratifications of ritualized performances, with the modelling of chronic
rivalries, the purging of the bitter residue of daily politesse, the inversion of
aesthetics, the avowal of the unavowable. Clifford Geertz, 'Deep Play: Notes on
the Balinese Cockfight', in *The Interpretation of Cultures* pp. 412–53, esp. 449.
For a theoretical statement, see his 'Thick Description: Towards an Interpretive
Theory of Culture', in *The Interpretation of Cultures,* pp. 3–30. While it is true
that 'women's culture' can differ in some regards from 'men's culture', it is
difficult to imagine each operating out of a radically different metaphysical
context.

9 Cf. Maurice Bloch, who has argued that Madagascan royal ceremonials owed
their magic to their development and extension of 'ordinary, widespread, and
commonplace rituals', a variation on the 'enlargement' effect significantly present in the Mexica process of enchantment. Maurice Bloch, 'The Ritual of the
Royal Bath in Madagascar: The Dissolution of Birth, Death and Fertility into
Authority'. Victor Turner has claimed that the process of distillation and intensification through ritual performance, and the transformation wrought through
elevation to higher visibility, is particularly necessary when 'societies advance in
scale and complexity, often with sharp increases in the rates of spatial and social
mobility'. This would seem to fit the case of expanding, differentiating Ten-

ochtitlan. Victor Turner, *From Ritual to Theatre: The Human Seriousness of Play*, p. 26.

10 See discussion in 'Introduction', and for the relevant passages by Turner his 'Religious Paradigms and Political Action', in his *Dramas, Fields and Metaphors: Symbolic Actions in Human Society*, p. 64, and chapter 1, 'Social Dramas and Ritual Metaphors'. For the original model of 'social dramas', see his *Schism and Continuity in African Society: A Study of Ndembu Village Life*.

11 Stephen Greenblatt, *Shakespearean Negotiations: The Circulation of Social Energy in Renaissance England*, esp. chapter 1. For an expanded argument for what follows, see Inga Clendinnen, 'Ways to the Sacred: Reconstructing "Religion" in Sixteenth-Century Mexico'.

12 Cf. Stanley Walens's Kwakiutl: 'Kwakiutl principles of causal relationship operate not through systemic, syntagmic contiguities, but through metaphorical, paradigmatic correspondences.' Stanley Walens, *Feasting with Cannibals: An Essay on Kwakiutl Cosmology*, p. 22.

13 *Florentine Codex*, 2: 27: 104. Warrior dances ought ideally be discussed here, as avenues to the sacred. For a glimpse of their power and import, see Domingo Francisco Chimalpahín Cuauhtlehuanitzin, *Relaciones originales de Chalco Amaquemecan*, Séptima Relación, pp. 211–14.

14 Johanna Broda, 'Los estamentos en el ceremonial mexica', p. 45.

15 Even where costliness was the criterion, as with the offerings to the Fire God on the day One Dog, with the rich giving the Fire whole baskets of 'clean, white incense', the commoners handfuls of 'coarse incense', and 'the extremely poor, the poverty-stricken, the needy, the discontented' no more than aromatic herbs, the intention of the offerers and the aromatic nature of the gifts were clearly similar. *Florentine Codex*, 4: 25: 88.

16 For example the Xipe Totec figures in their warriors' skins and garlanded with maize cobs at the Feast of the Flaying of Men.

17 *Florentine Codex*, 2: 23: 61–2.

18 Fr. Bernardino de Sahagún, *Historia general de las cosas de la Nueva España* 1, p. 203; *Florentine Codex*, 2: 33: 136.

19 For a fine analysis of the Coatlicue figure, see Justino Fernández, *Coatlicue, estética del arte indígena antigua*, esp. pp. 265–6.

20 *Florentine Codex*, 10: 29: 193.

21 The Anonymous Conquistador, in *The Conquistadores: First-Person Accounts of the Conquest of Mexico*, ed. Patricia de Fuentes, p. 173; for Izcalli, see *Florentine Codex*, 2: 37, 38: 159–71; for the maguey, p. 169.

22 For an expansion of the sex-and-violence aspect, see Pat Carr and Willard Gingerich, 'The Vagina Dentata Motif in Nahuatl and Pueblo Mythic Narratives: A Comparative Study'.

23 For the rituals attending the making of the pulque, see *Florentine Codex*, 2: 21: 47–99; for the dangerous aspect, 2: 22: 51.

24 *Florentine Codex*, 2: 29: 115.

25 See for example the processing and the burning of the incense and rubber 'gods' in the invocation phase of Etzalqualiztli, *Florentine Codex*, 2: 25: 85.

26 *Florentine Codex*, 2: 23: 61–2. The women then presented the flesh-like atole to 'the young men and the priests', which is as it should be.

27 *Florentine Codex*, 2: 37: 159–62.

28 Fernando Alvarado Tezozómoc, 'The Finding and Founding of Mexico-Tenochtitlan' (from the *Crónica mexicáyotl*, 1609), esp. p. 318.

29 The cooking protocols for this singularly rich festival involved the highly conscious management of fire and water, with 'dry' heat being distinguished from heat as mediated by water. Even the maize husk wrappings of the tamales had to be 'strewed in the water' instead of being dropped in the fire, their usual fate. *Florentine Codex*, 2: 37: 161. See also *Florentine Codex*, 2: 37–8: 159–72.

30 Disagreements over identifications abound. On, for example, the 'horned deity' and his various interpreters, see Esther Pasztory, 'Texts, Archeology, Art, and History in the Templo Mayor: Reflections', p. 453. See also Cecelia Klein, 'The Identity of the Central Deity on the Aztec Calendar Stone', and 'Who was Tlaloc?' ·

31 *Florentine Codex*, 2: 26: 91–2.

32 See Chapter 6, 'Wives', section 5.

33 Captives who died on the stone were not ixiptlas, unless some other process (e.g., the taking of their skins to concoct Xipe Totec) took place, or unless, like the Tezcatlipoca impersonator, they had been adorned and given the name of a deity.

34 For priestly representations, see *Florentine Codex* 1: 16: 35; 1: 20: 45–6.

35 Sahagún, telling of the Tlillan calmecac, the 'Black House' where Moctezoma so often withdrew, describes it as a chapel made in honour of the goddess Cihuacoatl and tended by three priests, before whom the goddess 'would visibly appear and reside in that place, and from there visibly would emerge to go where she wished', but it is not clear just what should be made of that. Sahagún, *Historia general*, 1, p. 234.

36 *Florentine Codex*, 2: 21: 51

37 *Florentine Codex*, 1: 13: 29.

38 For example, *Florentine Codex*, 2: 26: 93–4; 36:155–6.

39 *Florentine Codex*, 2: 36: 156; 2: 26: 93.

40 For even more delirious doubling: the priests who donned the skins of those

who had been killed during Ochpaniztli when Toci's ixiptla had died are described as their ixiptlas, while the word *tototecti* appears to be used interchangeably both for the victims who were flayed and the warriors who then wore the flayed skins; *Florentine Codex*, 2: 30: 124; 2: 21: 47, n. 4; 8: Appendix 8: 85.

41 *Florentine Codex*, 2: 36: 155–8; 8: 21: 76.

42 *Florentine Codex*, 1: 21: 47; 2: 32: 133; 2: 35: 151–4. The narrative is a composite from these several accounts.

43 *Florentine Codex*, 2: 32: 131–3.

44 *Florentine Codex*, 1: 15: 45; 1: 11: 21; 2: 32: 131–3.

45 'At this time [One Wind] they made offerings to the one called Quetzalcoatl, who was the representative of the wind, the whirlwind', which adds another level of complexity; *Florentine Codex*, 4: 31: 101.

46 *Florentine Codex*, 1: 7: 13; 1: 11: 21. On Chicomecoatl's feast day in Uey Tocoztli 'they formed her image as a woman', offering before it all the abundance which constituted the deity.

47 Both the *Historia general* and the *Florentine Codex* versions emphasize the care with which this effect was achieved. Sahagún, *Historia general*, 1, pp. 17–24; *Florentine Codex*, 2: 26: 89.

48 *Florentine Codex*, 2: 23: 63–4. But note Arild Hvidfeldt's interesting argument that the 'Chicomecoatls', the bundles of seed-maize cobs carried on the backs of Mexica girls during this festival, *were* considered as ixiptlas, with the concept probably including the girls themselves. Hvidfeldt, *Teotl and *Ixiptlatli*, pp. 91–2.

49 *Florentine Codex*, 2: 23: 62. Cf. 'Tzapotlan tenen', goddess of turpentine, who was herself the unguent: 'she was represented as a woman. From her substance was made turpentine . . .'; *Florentine Codex*, 1: 16: 71.

50 *Florentine Codex*, 3: 1: 4–6. See also Panquetzaliztli, *Florentine Codex* 2: 34: 147, n. 22. It is possible that Sahagún or his informants confused the great image of Huitzilopochtli they described as being constructed during the festival of the fifth month with the Panquetzaliztli image; *Florentine Codex*, 2: 24: 71–3. Possible, but unlikely, the phallicism of the Toxcatl figure being fully appropriate in the fertility theme as described in the rest of the action. Clavijero asserts the dough flesh of the image was first distributed between the four subsections of the city, and so to each male. Sahagún's informants suggest that only the men attached to two warrior houses, who had spent a year of preparatory fasting, 'ate the god'. Francisco Javier Clavijero, *Historia antigua de México*, Vol. 3, pp. 168–70.

51 The great jewel-encrusted statue described by Bernal Díaz stood within the

shrine, and was not on general view; Bernal Díaz del Castillo, *Historia ver-dadera de la conquista de la Nueva España*, chapter 92. Huitzilopochtli may have retained his most complete representation as the sacred bundle de-picted in the early painted representations and descriptions. He was a swad-dled *bulto* when he was smuggled out of Tenochtitlan during the Spanish assault; *Procesos de indios idólatras y hechiceros*. 'Proceso del Santo Oficio con-tra los indios de Azcapotzalco por idólatras' (1538), pp. 99–105; 'Proceso del Santo Oficio contra Miguel, indio, por idólatras' (1540), pp. 115–140; Zelia Nuttall, 'L'évêque Zumarraga et les idoles principales du Templo Grande de Mexico'.

52 *Florentine Codex*, 3: 1: 6–7. Cf. the translation offered by van Zantwijk, *The Aztec Arrangement: The Social History of Pre-Spanish Mexico*, p. 248; 'those who have finished eating are said to be "god-possessing" '.

53 James Clifford, *Person and Myth: Maurice Leenhardt in the Melanesian World*, p. 33.

54 For the myth, see *Florentine Codex*, 3: 1: 1–5. There is an elaborate literature on the relation of the Huitzilopochtli myth to Mexica history, and to the ritual. The birth myth emerged late, and pertained to the Mexica alone. See Gordon Brotherston, 'Huitzilopochtli and What Was Made of Him'; Alfredo López Austin, *Hombre–Dios: religión y política en el mundo náhuatl*; Nigel Davies, *Los Mexicas: primeros pasos hacia el imperio*, pp. 35–8; Rudolph van Zantwijk, 'El parentesco y la afiliación étnica de Huitzilopochtli'.

55 For the wider action of Panquetzaliztli, see *Florentine Codex*, 1: 2: 3; 2: 34: 141–50; 2: Appendix: 175–6. For merchant participation see ibid., 9, esp. chapters 10–14.

56 See account of the Izcalli 'presentation of the children' ceremony in Chapter 7, 'Mothers', section 3.

57 Along, of course, with others, some apparently incompatible. To grasp the dominant themes (which is probably all that can be done at our temporal and cultural distance), one needs to scan the whole spectrum of ritual action, and the unobvious resonances between the performances. For another episode of aggressive and obligatory drunkenness, this time among the salt-farmers, see Tecuilhuitl, *Florentine Codex* 2: 26: 94. A beguiling little ceramic sculpture from Nayarit, now in the American Museum of Natural History in New York, gives some sense of such occasions, if on a midget scale. A man equipped with a conch trumpet and a cup, presumably the ritual pourer, stands beside a large jar, with villagers clustered around. A couple is boozily amorous; one man sprawls insensible; another hangs vomiting over the low wall bounding the sculpture.

58 Part of the following discussion has been rehearsed in Clendinnen, 'Ways to the Sacred'.

59 *Florentine Codex*, 2: Appendix: 193, 197.

60 Fr. Toribio Motolinía, *Historia*, 1, chapter 10. See also chapter 11 for the rigours of 'waiting on the god' in an eighty-day vigil. The priests' habitual instrument was the maguey spine, the accumulated spines being stuck in a ball of grass and set forth as an offering, while the laity more usually cut their ears during periods of fasting, flicking the blood towards the sun or letting it fall to spread on highly absorbent sacrificial 'papers', or painting their faces with the sticky stuff. Fr. Bernardino de Sahagún, *Historia general de las cosas de la Nueva España*, 1, p. 244.

61 Motolinía, *Historia* 1, chapter 9.

62 *Florentine Codex*, 9: 15: 69–70.

63 Cf. this slow construction of the persona by socially agreed steps – the compilation of a conventional icon – with the 'self-fashioning' described by Stephen Greenblatt, *Renaissance Self-Fashioning: From More to Shakespeare*: the conscious representation of a chosen 'self'. Greenblatt usefully comments: 'We wall off literary symbolism from the symbolic structures operative elsewhere, as if art alone were a human creation, as if humans themselves were not, in Clifford Geertz's phrase, cultural artifacts'; Greenblatt, *Renaissance Self-Fashioning*, p. 3.

64 For example *Florentine Codex*, 2: 27: 101. For the 'winding dance' of the Toxcatl feast, the warriors who had fasted for twenty days, or those specially selected 'elder brothers of Huitzilopochtli' who had fasted for a year, vigorously policed the dancers, allowing them to leave the dance zone only to urinate. *Florentine Codex*, 12: 19: 53. Cf. the dance-whippers of the Plains Indians.

65 I assume high precision because of the careful training of the lead dancers, the strong penalties, and the complexities of the interlocking patterns of collective dance. *Florentine Codex*, 2: 8: 56. Pre-Hispanic precision contrasts with the slouched shuffling of much Mexican 'folk' dance now. The standard text on pre-Columbian dance remains Gertrude Prokosch Kurath and Samuel Martí, *Dances of Anáhuac: The Choreography and Music of Precortesian Dances*. See also José de Acosta, *Historia natural y moral de las Indias*, esp. book 6, chapter 28. Barbara Tedlock's punctilious assessment of Zuñi song and of its compositional complexity amplifies the meagre clues regarding Mexica song; 'Songs of the Zuñi Kachina Society: Composition, Rehearsal, Performance'.

66 *Florentine Codex*, 8: 17: 56; Diego Durán, *Historia de las Indias de Nueva España e Islas de la Tierra Firme*, 1, chapter 10. Certain priests had the responsibility 'to

teach the people the holy songs throughout the wards . . . so they would learn the songs well'. Dance and song could be performed as a 'penance', a notion which had little to do with our sin-purging sense, but rather as something due to the deities, and as possibly influencing their actions. Even on 'secular' occasions, if any Mexica occasion can be so described, a singer took a pinch of incense from the incense gourd and tossed it into the fire as prelude to the song. So did a judge before making a formal pronouncement, which suggests the world-changing capacity of each statement: performative utterances indeed.

67 See, e.g., *Florentine Codex*, 2: 25: 84. Dance was ultimately part of Moctezoma's jurisdiction: *Florentine Codex*, 8: 7: 25–6. For non-obligatory participation, ibid. 2: 21: 56.

68 Motolinía, *Memoriales*, 2, chapter 27.

69 'In play, subjectivity forgets itself'; Paul Ricoeur, 'Appropriation', p. 186.

70 Given the different drugs administered, a range of abnormal behaviours is to be expected.

71 For the pyramids from a deity's eye view see, for example, Rudolph van Zantwijk, 'The Great Temple of Tenochtitlan: Model of Aztec Cosmovision', and, more elaborately, his *The Aztec Arrangement*. For the movements on high ceremonial, and their relationship to the conceptualization, order and use of space in codex representations, see Gordon Brotherston with Ed Dorn, *Image of the New World*, chapter 3; Karl Nowotny, *Tlacuilolli*.

72 Victor Turner draws the distinction between societies 'long in place' which have had time to consolidate their commonsense structures into plausible semblances of 'natural systems' and where 'understandings are widely and deeply shared', in which even the liminal periods of ritual 'do not contravene or criticize the mundane order . . . but present it as based in the primordial cosmogonic process', as opposed to those in which the ludic and potentially transforming aspect of ritual is dominant; 'Process, System and Symbol: A New Anthropological Synthesis', esp. pp. 70–1, 77. Hence the useful distinction between 'ritual' and 'ceremony', ritual being a 'transformative performance revealing major classifications, categories, and contradictions of cultural processes', and therefore 'by definition associated with social transitions', while ceremony is 'linked to social state and statuses'.

73 See Clendinnen, 'The Cost of Courage', *passim*.

74 For example, 'at the top [of the pyramid] were circular stones, very large, called *techcatl*, upon which they slew victims in order to pay honour to their gods. And the blood, the blood of those who died, indeed reached the base; so did it flow off.' *Florentine Codex*, 2: Appendix: 179. Durán, describing the killings which marked the dedication of the temple of Huitzilopochtli by

Ahuitzotl (admittedly the largest holocaust known, where Durán claims, almost certainly wrongly, that 'eighty thousand four hundred men from different cities' died), speaks of the blood running down the steps of the temple to form fat clots at the bottom, which were gathered up by the priests in gourds, and smeared on the walls, lintels, and doorways of the other temples, so that the city was filled with the sour reek of blood. Durán, *Historia*, 2, chapter 44.

75 No surgical precision, but significant and practised skill. For the most likely techniques see Francis Robicsek and Donald Hales, 'Maya Heart Sacrifice: Cultural Perspective and Surgical Technique'.

76 That constraint must also weigh equally on those who assert that what the Mexica were shown, what they saw, and so what they experienced, was the legitimation of the ideology of the ruling caste: for example, Warwick Bray, 'Civilizing the Aztecs', Donald V. Kurtz, 'The Legitimation of the Aztec State', and the earlier works of Johanna Broda as cited in the bibliography.

77 Tim Knab, 'Words Great and Small: Sierra Nahuatl Narrative Discourse in Everyday Life', unpublished manuscript, 1983, quoted in Johanna Broda, 'Templo Mayor as Ritual Space', in *The Great Temple of Tenochtitlan: Center and Periphery in the Aztec World*, p. 107.

11. DEFEAT

1 The problem of interpreters had been partially solved by two fortuitous (or providential) events: the rescue of a shipwrecked Spaniard, Jerónimo de Aguilar, who had spent eight years among the Maya Indians of Yucatán, and spoke their tongue, and the recognition of the talents of one of the girls given to Cortés at Tabasco. 'Doña Marina', as the Spaniards dubbed her, a Nahuatl-speaker, could also speak a Mayan intelligible to Aguilar. So the clumsy chain was forged. Bernal Díaz del Castillo, *Historia verdadera de la conquista de la Nueva España*, chapter 37.

2 See, e.g., for a recent version, Tzvetan Todorov, *The Conquest of America: The Question of the Other, passim*.

3 H. Cortés, *Hernán Cortés: Letters from Mexico*. See also J. H. Elliott, 'The Mental World of Hernán Cortés', What emerges from the Pagden–Elliott analyses is an an account of one adventurer, Cortés, hanging on by his fingernails, desperate not to be dislodged by Narvaez, who was a better equipped and marginally more legitimate one.

4 Inga Clendinnen, ' "Fierce and Unnatural Cruelty": Cortés and the Conquest of Mexico'.

5 Díaz, *Historia*, chapter 38.

6 Díaz, *Historia,* chapter 39.

7 *Florentine Codex,* 12: 11: 30.

8 Ibid.

9 Alfredo López Austin, *The Human Body and Ideology: Concepts of the Ancient Nahuas,* 1, pp. 178–9.

10 *Florentine Codex,* 12: 15: 40.

11 For example, *Florentine Codex,* 12: 11: 29, 31; Cortés, *Letters,* pp. 60–2.

12 *Florentine Codex,* 12: 29: 83.

13 *Anales de Tlatelolco: Unos annales* [sic] *históricos de la nación mexicana,* pp. 309–17, 65–6.

14 *Florentine Codex,* 12: 25: 72.

15 See Chapter 2, 'Local Perspectives', Section 7.

16 *Florentine Codex,* 12: 38: 117–18.

17 The Nahuatl poem was written down in European script perhaps as early as 1528, a mere seven years after the fall of the city. I offer León-Portilla's version as the one most likely to be familiar; *The Broken Spears: The Aztec Account of the Conquest of Mexico,* pp. 137–8. Cf. Miguel León-Portilla, *Pre-Columbian Literatures of Mexico,* pp. 150–1, and Gordon Brotherston, with translations by Ed Dorn, *Image of the New World,* pp. 34–5. For other songs in traditional form to do with the Conquest, see John Bierhorst, *Cantares Mexicanos,* esp. no. 13, pp. 151–3; no. 60, p. 279 (obscurely); no. 66, pp. 319–23; no. 68 (for its early stanzas), pp. 327–41; no. 91, pp. 419–25.

18 Berlin and Barlow, *Anales de Tlatelolco,* 371–89, pp. 74–6. For the moving address the surviving priests of Tenochtitlan made in response to the first formal statement of the incoming missionary friars in 1524 (reconstructed by Sahagún in 1564), see Fr. Bernardino de Sahagún, 'The Aztec–Spanish Dialogues of 1524; for the terms of the reconstruction, 52–4.

A QUESTION OF SOURCES

1 Bernal Díaz del Castillo, *Historia verdadera de la conquista de la Nueva España;* H. Cortés, *Hernán Cortés: Letters from Mexico.* A near-complete bibliography of sixteenth-century Mexican materials will be found in the *Handbook of Middle American Indians,* ed. Robert Wauchope, Vols. 12–15, and in Supplementary Vols. 1–4. For a handy collection of conquistador reports relating to Tenochtitlan and translated into English, see Patricia de Fuentes (ed. and trans.). *The Conquistadores: First-Person Accounts of the Conquest of Mexico.*

2 *Codex Borbonicus: Bibliothèque de l'Assemblée national. Paris (Y120).* For an at-

tempt to identify the place of origin of the Borbonicus more precisely, see H. B. Nicholson, 'The Provenience of the Codex Borbonicus: A Hypothesis', in *Smoke and Mist: Mesoamerican Studies in Memory of Thelma D. Sullivan,* Josserand and Karen Dakin (eds.), 1, pp. 77–97. For an illuminating discussion of the provenience and dating of the Codex, and a determined attempt to read the Borbonicus images in their own terms, see N. C. Christopher Couch, *The Festival Cycle of the Aztec Codex Borbonicus.*

3 For example: the *Codex Boturini* (also called the *Tira de la Peregrinación,* or the *Tira del Museo*); *Codex Aubin: Historia de la nación mexicana: reproducción a todo color del códice de 1576; Matrícula de Tributos, Commentary on Matrícula de Tributos (Códice de Moctezuma),* ed. Frances Berdan and Jacqueline Durand-Forest.

4 *Anales de Tlatelolco: Unos annales* [sic] *históricos de la nación mexicana.*

5 *The Codex Mendoza.* For a survey of pre- and post-conquest pictorial material, see John B. Glass, 'A Survey of Native Middle American Pictorial Manuscripts'. See also Donald Robertson, *Mexican Manuscript Painting of the Early Colonial Period: The Metropolitan Schools.* For recent evaluations, see *Text and Image in Pre-Columbian Art: Essays on the Interrelationship of the Verbal and the Visual Arts,* ed. Jane Catherine Berlo. For a gifted analysis of one codex, see Jill Leslie Furst, *Codex Vindobonensis Mexicanus I, A Commentary.* For a brisk overview of recent work and present thinking, see Edward B. Sisson, 'Recent Work on the Borgia Group Codices'. For a glimpse of the Christian intrusions, and a useful short bibliography of their clustering around the Quetzalcoatl story, see Eloise Quiñones Keber, 'Central Mexican Pictorial Manuscripts. From Tollan to Tlapallan: The Tale of Topiltzin Quetzalcoatl in the Codex Vaticanus A'. For a sensitive enquiry into how pre-Hispanic historical texts might best be read, Edward Calnek, 'The Analysis of Prehispanic Historical Texts'.

6 The three main collections are the 'Cantares mexicanos', the 'Cantares a los Dioses' (both probably collected by Bernardino de Sahagún), and the 'Romances de los señores de Nueva España'. See *Poesía náhuatl,* Angel María Garibay K., (ed.). For a recent annotated edition of the 'Cantares', see trans. John Bierhorst, *Cantares Mexicanos: Songs of the Aztecs,* and Bierhorst's *A Nahuatl–Spanish Dictionary and Concordance to the Cantares Mexicanos.*

7 For example, Hernando de Alvarado Tezozómoc *Crónica mexicana escrita hacia el año de 1598;* Fernando de Alva Ixtlilxóchitl, *Obras históricas;* Domingo Francisco Chimalpahín Cuauhtlehuanitzin *Relaciones originales de Chalco Amaquemecan;* Diego Muñoz Camargo, *Historia de Tlaxcalla;* Juan Bautista Pomar, 'Relación de Tezcoco'. For an overview, see Charles Gibson, 'Survey of Middle American Prose Manuscripts in the Native Historical Tradition'. For at-

tempted 'histories' in our sense, see, e.g., Nigel Davies, *The Aztecs: A History; The Toltec Heritage: From the Fall of Tula to the Rise of Tenochtitlan;* and *The Aztec Empire: The Toltec Resurgence.*

8 For a full discussion see Wauchope, *Handbook of Middle American Indians,* Vol. 12, part 1.

9 A difficulty of much of the missionary material for a Tenochtitlan-based study is the wide geographical base on which different observers drew (e.g., the Franciscan Motolinía into Tlaxcala, Durán into the Puebla valley) and the free trade in information, so that works are often cited as confirmation of earlier statements when they are in fact merely reiterating them. For example, The 'Tovar Calendar' of the Mexican Jesuit Juan de Tovar includes a version of the Mexican historical text known as the 'Relación del origen de los indios' or the 'Códice Ramírez', together with a series of paintings. Large sections of the Relación were incorporated in the *Historia natural y moral* of the Spanish Jesuit José de Acosta, completed in 1589, while the whole Tovar Relación is in its turn a condensed version of the Dominican Diego Durán's *Historia* (ca. 1580), with the historical paintings versions of the Durán 'Atlas'. (The Tovar Calendar itself is judged to be an independent work.) For a lucid discussion of the dizzying borrowings and leapfrogging, see the commentaries of George Kubler and Charles Gibson in *The Tovar Calendar: An Illustrated Mexican Manuscript ca. 1585.* The sequence of pre-contact Mexica rulers became an issue in clerical politics, with Tovar's version of the dynasty adopted by de Acosta as the Jesuit version, in contrast to the Franciscan tradition of Motolinía, Sahagún, Mendieta, and Torquemada; p. 17.

10 The major publications of the Florentine Codex are Fr. Bernardino de Sahagún, *Historia general de las cosas de la Nueva España;* Fr. Bernardino de Sahagún, *The Florentine Codex: General History of the Things of New Spain;* Fr. Bernardino de Sahagún, *El Códice Florentino de Fray Bernardino de Sahagún,* facsimile photographic reproduction of original manuscript in the Biblioteca Medicea Laurenziana, Florence. For earlier drafts see Fr. Bernardino de Sahagún *'Primeros Memoriales' de Fray Bernardino de Sahagún; Códices matritenses de la historia general de las cosas de la Nueva España de Fr. Bernardino de Sahagún,* 2 vols., ed. Manuel Ballesteros Gaibrois (Madrid: Ediciones Jóse Porrúa Turanzas, 1964).

11 For an influential discussion of the illustrations see Robertson, *Mexican Manuscript Painting of the Early Colonial Period,* p. 178, and his 'The Treatment of Architecture in the Florentine Codex of Sahagún'. For more recent work, see 'The Illustrations of the Sahaguntine Corpus', in *The Work of Bernardino de Sahagún, Pioneer Ethnographer of Sixteenth-Century Aztec Mexico,* section 4, ed. J.

Jorge Klor de Alva, H. B. Nicholson, and Eloise Quiñones Keber, pp. 199–202.

12 For an overview of investigations into the structure and nature of the Great Temple, see Elizabeth Hill Boone, 'Templo Mayor Research, 1521–1978', being papers from a 1983 symposium on the Templo Mayor.

13 Vladimir Nabokov, *Transparent Things: A Novel*, p. 1.

14 Ibid.

15 Veyne continues: 'Other than the techniques of handling and checking documents, there is no more a method of history than one of ethnography or of the art of travelling', a statement which could well be true if the notion of 'checking' is sufficiently expanded. Paul Veyne, *Writing History: Essay on Epistemology*, p. 12.

16 Pat Carr and Willard Gingerich, 'The Vagina Dentata Motif in Nahuatl and Pueblo Mythic Narratives: A Comparative Study'.

17 For a notably lucid account of Nahuatl writing before and after the conquest see Frances Karttunen, 'Nahuatl Literacy'. On the 'utopian art' of translation, see José Ortega y Gasset, 'The Difficulty of Reading'. For the comment, see *Beyond the Codices: The Nahua View of Colonial Mexico*, ed. Arthur J. O. Anderson, Frances Berdan, and James Lockhart, Appendix 1, p. 221, n. 2.

18 Miguel León-Portilla, 'The Problematics of Sahagún: Certain Topics Needing Investigation'. For the 'seeing device' or *tlachialoni*, see those pertaining to Huitzilopochtli in the festival of Panquetzaliztli, *Florentine Codex*, 2: 33: 146.

19 Miguel León-Portilla, 'Topics Needing Investigation', pp. 251–2; A. L. Becker, 'Literacy and Cultural Change', and his 'Biography of a Sentence: A Burmese Proverb'. Reading Becker transforms one's understanding of language and its dimensions.

20 José Ortega y Gasset, *Man and People*, p. 246. In that same rich discussion he reminds us of the importance of gesture: 'There are Central African peoples among whom individuals cannot converse at night, when it is completely dark, because they cannot see each other and not seeing each other leaves their speech gestureless', p. 254. In Tzvetan Todorov's intriguing and influential study of the conquest of the Mexica as a struggle for control over sign systems there is too little awareness of the language of gift exchange, as for the Indian talent for disguised speech; Tzvetan Todorov, *The Conquest of America: The Question of the Other*. For an extended discussion of that issue, see Inga Clendinnen, ' "Fierce and Unnatural Cruelty": Cortés and the Conquest of Mexico'.

21 On this issue the writings of Erving Goffman are fundamental. See especially his last book, *Forms of Talk*.

22 Annette B. Weiner, *Women of Value, Men of Renown: New Perspectives in Trobriand Exchange*, pp. 213–14.

23 Manning Nash, *Machine Age Maya*.

24 For post-conquest examples, see Karttunen and Lockhart (eds.), *The Art of Nahuatl Speech: The Bancroft Dialogues*.

25 *Florentine Codex*, 6: 35: 192.

26 Clifford Geertz, 'Thick Description: Towards an Interpretive Theory of Culture', pp. 6–7. Compare Edward Schieffelin watching Papuans sing what sounded like simple, nostalgic songs to visitors from another village, and seeing individuals in the audience first reduced to tears, and then to violence, leaping up to belabour the singer with the burning brands used to light the occasion – to the gratification of the burnt one, who duly paid compensation to the burner. Edward L. Schieffelin, 'Mediators as Metaphors: Moving a Man to Tears in Papua New Guinea'. With patient watching, thinking, and asking, Schieffelin came in time to 'hear' something of what the targeted individual had heard in those artfully simple little songs.

27 Keith Basso reports that unravelling the riddling meanings artfully tucked away in the 'wise words' coined by specially talented elders took even fellow Apaches long and hard thinking'; Keith Basso, ' "Wise Words" of the Western Apache: Metaphor and Semantic Theory'.

28 See Gordon Brotherston with Ed Dorn, *Image of the New World: The American Continent Portrayed in Native Texts*.

29 See Chapter 9, 'Aesthetics', section 5, and Chapter 10, 'Ritual', section 4.

30 Of the many magnificent publications on Mexica objects perhaps one of the most compelling is H. B. Nicholson with Eloise Quiñones Keber, *Art of Ancient Mexico: Treasures of Tenochtitlán*. The publication includes photographs of major objects from the recently completed excavation of the Great Temple of Tenochtitlan. See also Esther Pasztory, *Aztec Art*.

31 Fr. Diego Durán, *Historia de las Indias de Nueva España e Islas de la Tierra Firme* Vol. 1, Libro de los Ritos y Fiestas de los antiguos mexicanos, 1570, and El Calendario Antiguo, 1579; Vol. 2, Historia de las Indias de Nueva España e Islas de la Tierra Firme, 1581(?); Fr. Toribio Motolinía, O. F. M., *Memoriales e historia de los indios de la Nueva España*.

32 Ixtlilxóchitl claims that in ancient times there were 'writers for each branch of knowledge', some composing histories, some genealogies ('making a note of those born and cancelling the dead'), others mapping boundaries and borderstones of the villages, towns and fields, while yet others 'made records of the laws and the rites and ceremonies performed in pagan times. The priests made records regarding the temples of the idols, of their idolatrous doctrines

and the feasts of their false gods and their calendars'. The *Codex Borbonicus* is presumably an example of the last, but there the representation of the action (e.g., for Ochpaniztli, p. 30) is very much in shorthand. However Miguel León-Portilla has suggested that the 'Primeros Memoriales' of the *Códices matritenses* contained 'descriptions, probably learned by heart in *calmecac* or priestly schools, of ceremonies, sacred rituals, the attributes of the various priests by rank, the characteristic clothing of the principal gods, the clothing, food, drink and pastimes of the lords'. Miguel León-Portilla, 'Nahuatl Literature', p. 37.

33 For a gallant attempt to reconstruct festival choreography, see Gertrude Prokosch Kurath and Samuel Martí, *Dances of Anáhuac: The Choreography and Music of Precortesian Dances.*

34 For an attractive introduction, see Johanna Broda, David Carrasco, and Eduardo Matos Moctezuma, *The Great Temple of Tenochtitlan: Center and Periphery in the Aztec World;* also Elizabeth Hill Boone (ed.), *The Aztec Templo Mayor.* For reports, see Eduardo Matos Moctezuma, (ed.) *El Templo Mayor: Excavaciones y Estudios;* for maps and sketches, his *El Templo Mayor: Planos, cortes y perspectivas,* illustrations by Victor Rangel. Earlier studies on the Templo Mayor have been reissued in his *Trabajos Arqueológicos en el Centro de la Ciudad de México.*

35 Debra Nagao, *Mexica Buried Offerings: A Historical and Contextual Analysis* 13, pp. 107–12.

36 Nagao, *Mexica Buried Offerings,* pp. 114–15.

37 For example, James Lockhart, 'Some Nahua Concepts in Postconquest Guise'.

38 For example, for a tracing of change where others have too readily assumed continuity, see John K. Chance and William B. Taylor, 'Cofradías and Cargos: An Historical Perspective on the Mesoamerican Civil–Religious Hierarchy'.

39 Alexander Lesser, *The Pawnee Ghost Dance Hand Game: A Study of Cultural Change,* pp. 179–210. Note the fine observation: The smoker in one phase faces east, draws in smoke, puffs it upwards and outwards to the east, at the same time turning the pipe to present the mouthpiece to the east, in the 'presentation' pose adopted when offering the pipe to a smoker: 'In other words, the power of the orientation to which the smoke is directed is offered the pipe to smoke, not symbolically, but actually, while the smoker exhales the smoke for him' (p. 192). Here at least close observation and identification of a patterned gestural sequence would seem to identify intention. We know from James Murie, of the twenty distinct songs, some with up to a dozen stanzas, sung at one Pawnee ceremony, each song capable of being developed through 56 variations by a sequence of word-substitutions or 'steps'. James R. Murie,

Ceremonies of the Pawnee, Part 1, pp. 125–36. For the Morning Star sacrifice among the Pawnee, see Murie, 'Human Sacrifice to the Morning Star', *Ceremonies of the Pawnee*, Part 1, pp. 114–24.

40 Gregory Bateson, *Naven*, p. 259.

Select Bibliography

Acosta, José de, 1962. *Historia natural y moral de las Indias,* Prepared by Edmundo O'Gorman. Mexico City: Fondo de Cultura Económica.

Alva Ixtlilxóchitl, Fernando de, 1965. *Obras históricas de Don Fernando de Alva Ixtlilxóchitl,* 2 vols. Notes by Alfredo Chavero. Mexico City: Editorial Nacional.

Alvarado Tezozómoc, Hernando de, 1944, *Crónica mexicana escrita hacia el año de 1598.* Notes by Manuel Orozco y Berra. Mexico City: Editorial Leyenda.

Alvarado Tezozómoc, F., 1949. *Crónica mexicáyotl.* Mexico City: Imprenta Universitaria.

Anales de Cuauhtitlán, 1975. In *Códice Chimalpopoca,* translated by Primo Feliciano Velásquez. Mexico City: Imprenta Universitaria.

Anales de Tlatelolco: Unos annales [sic] *históricos de la nación mexicana* (1528), 1948. Edited and translated into Spanish by Heinrich Berlin and Robert H. Barlow. Mexico City: Editorial Porrúa.

Anderson, Arthur J. O., 1982. The Institution of Slave Bathing. In *Indiana 7: Gedenkschrift Walter Lehmann Teil 2,* pp. 81–92. Berlin: Gebr. Mann Verlag.

1982. Aztec Hymns of Life and Love. *New Scholar* 8: 1–74.

Anderson, Arthur J. O., Berdan, Frances, and Lockhart, James, eds. and trans., 1976. *Beyond the Codices: The Nahua View of Colonial Mexico.* Berkeley: University of California Press.

Anonymous Conqueror, The, 1971. Relación de algunas cosas de la Nueva España y de la gran ciudad de Temestitan Mexico: escrita por un compañero de Hernán Cortés. In *Colección de documentos para la historia de México,* 3 vols., edited by Joaquín García Icazbalceta, Vol. 1. Mexico City: Editorial Porrúa.

Aveni, Anthony A., and Brotherston, Gordon, 1983. *Calendars in Mexico and Peru and Native American Computations of Time.* Oxford: British Archaeological Reports.

Badianus Manuscript: An Aztec Herbal of 1552, The, 1940. Introduced, translated, and annotated by Emily Walcott Emmart. Baltimore: Johns Hopkins University Press.

Basso, Keith, 1976. 'Wise Words' of the Western Apache: Metaphor and Semantic Theory. In *Meaning of Anthropology*, edited by Keith H. Basso and Henry A. Selby, pp. 93–121. Albuquerque: University of New Mexico Press.

Bateson, Gregory, 1958. *Naven* (1936). Stanford: Stanford University Press.

Becker, A. L., 1983. Literacy and Cultural Change. In *Literacy for Life: the Demand for Reading and Writing*, edited by Richard W. Bailey and Robin M. Forsheim. New York: The Modern Language Association of America.

— 1984. Biography of a Sentence: A Burmese Proverb. In *Text, Play and Story: The Construction and Reconstruction of Self and Society*, edited by Edward M. Bruner, pp. 135–55. Washington, D.C.: American Ethnological Society.

Benson, Elizabeth P., ed. 1981. *Mesoamerican Sites and World-Views*. Washington, D.C.: Dumbarton Oaks.

Berdan, Frances, 1983. The Economics of Aztec Luxury Trade and Tribute. In *The Aztec Templo Mayor*, edited by Elizabeth Hill Boone, pp. 161–83. Washington, D.C.: Dumbarton Oaks.

Berdan, Frances, and Durand-Forest, Jacqueline de, eds., 1980. *Commentary on Matrícula de Tributos* (*Códice de Moctezuma*), pp. 27–45. Graz: Akademische Druck-u. Verlagsanstalt.

Berger, John, 1979. Historical Afterword, in his *Pig Earth*, pp. 195–213. New York: Pantheon.

Berlo, Jane, 1983. The Warrior and the Butterfly: Central Mexican Ideologies of Sacred Warfare and Teotihuacan Iconography. In *Text and Image in Pre-Columbian Art: Essays on the Interrelationship of the Verbal and the Visual Arts*, edited by Jane Berlo, pp. 79–117. Oxford: British Archaeological Reports.

Bierhorst, John, trans., 1985. *Cantares Mexicanos: Songs of the Aztecs*. Stanford: Stanford University Press.

— 1985. *A Nahuatl–Spanish Dictionary and Concordance to the Cantares Mexicanos*. Stanford: Stanford University Press.

Bloch, Maurice, 1987. The Ritual of the Royal Bath in Madagascar: The Dissolution of Birth, Death and Fertility into Authority. In *Rituals of Royalty: Power and Ceremonial in Traditional Societies*, edited by David Cannadine and Simon Price, pp. 271–97. Cambridge: Cambridge University Press.

Boon, James A., 1982. *Other Tribes, Other Scribes: Symbolic Anthropology in the Comparative Study of Cultures, Histories and Texts*. Cambridge: Cambridge University Press.

Boone, Elizabeth Hill, ed., 1982. *The Art and Iconography of Late Post-Classic Central Mexico*. Washington, D.C.: Dumbarton Oaks.

1983. *The Codex Magliabechiano and the Lost Prototype of the Magliabechiano Group.* Berkeley and Los Angeles: University of California Press.

Ed., 1984. *Ritual Human Sacrifice in Mesoamerica.* Washington, D.C.: Dumbarton Oaks.

1987. Templo Mayor Research, 1521–1978. In *The Aztec Templo Mayor,* edited by Elizabeth Hill Boone, pp. 5–69. Washington, D.C.: Dumbarton Oaks.

Ed., 1987. *The Aztec Templo Mayor.* Washington, D.C.: Dumbarton Oaks.

Bray, Warwick, 1978. Civilizing the Aztecs. In *The Evolution of Social Systems,* edited by J. Friedman and M. J. Rowlands, pp. 373–98. London: Duckworth.

Broda, Johanna, 1976. Los estamentos en el ceremonial mexica. In *Estratificación social en la Mesoamérica prehispanica,* edited by Johanna Broda and Pedro Carrasco, pp. 37–66. Mexico City: INAH.

1978. Relaciones políticas ritualizadas: El ritual como expresión de una ideología. In *Economía política e ideología en el México prehispánico,* edited by Pedro Carrasco and Johanna Broda, pp. 221–55. Mexico City: Editorial Nueva Imagen.

1978. El tributo en trajes guerreros y la estructura del sistema tributario mexica. In *Economía política e ideología en el México prehispánico,* edited by Pedro Carrasco and Johanna Broda, pp. 113–73. Mexico City: Editorial Nueva Imagen.

1978. Consideraciones sobre historiografía e ideología mexicas: Las crónicas indígenas y el estudio de los ritos y sacrificios. *Estudios de cultura náhuatl* 13: 23–43.

1982. La fiesta azteca del Fuego Nuevo y el culto de las Pléyades, *Lateinamerika-Studien* 10: 129–57.

1987. The Provenience of the Offerings: Tribute and *Cosmovisión.* In *The Aztec Templo Mayor,* edited by Elizabeth Hill Boone, pp. 246–8. Washington, D.C.: Dumbarton Oaks.

Broda, Johanna, and Carrasco, Pedro, eds., 1976. *Estratificación social en la Mesoamérica prehispanica.* Mexico City: INAH.

Eds., 1978. *Economía política e ideología en el México prehispánico.* Mexico City: Editorial Nueva Imagen.

Broda, Johanna, Carrasco, David, and Matos Moctezuma, Eduardo, 1987. *The Great Temple of Tenochtitlan: Center and Periphery in the Aztec World.* Berkeley and Los Angeles: University of California Press.

Brotherston, Gordon, 1974. Huitzilopochtli and What Was Made of Him. In *Mesoamerican Archeology: New Approaches,* edited by Norman Hammond, pp. 155–66. London: Duckworth.

1974. Sacred Sand in Mexican Picture-Writing and Later Literature. *Estudios de cultura náhuatl* 11: 303–9.

Brotherston, Gordon, and Aveni, Anthony A., eds., 1983. *Calendars in Mexico and Peru and Native American Computations of Time.* Oxford: British Archaeological Reports.

Brotherston, Gordon, with Dorn, Ed, 1979. *Image of the New World: The American Continent Portrayed in Native Texts.* London: Thames and Hudson.

Brown, Betty Ann, 1983. Seen But Not Heard: Women in Aztec Ritual: The Sahagún Texts. In *Text and Image in Pre-Columbian Art: Essays on the Interrelationship of the Verbal and the Visual Arts,* edited by Jane Berlo, pp. 119–53. Oxford: British Archaeological Reports.

1984. Ochpaniztli in Historical Perspective. In *Ritual Human Sacrifice in Mesoamerica,* edited by Elizabeth Hill Boone, pp. 195–210. Washington, D.C.: Dumbarton Oaks.

Brown, Peter, 1981. *The Cult of the Saints: Its Rise and Function in Latin Christianity.* Chicago: University of Chicago Press.

1982. Learning and Imagination. In his *Society and the Holy in Late Antiquity.* London: Faber and Faber.

1985. The Notion of Virginity in the Early Church. In *Christian Spirituality: Origins to the Twelfth Century,* edited by Bernard McGinn and John Meyerdorff, pp. 427–43. New York: Crossroad.

Brundage, Burr Cartwright, 1979. *The Fifth Sun: Aztec Gods, Aztec World.* Austin: University of Texas Press.

1985. *The Jade Steps: A Ritual Life of the Aztecs.* Salt Lake City: University of Utah Press.

Burke, Kenneth, 1984. *Permanence and Change: An Anatomy of Purpose,* 2nd edition. Indianapolis: Bobbs Merrill.

Burkhart, Louise M., 1985. *The Slippery Earth: Nahua–Christian Moral Dialogue in Sixteenth-Century Mexico.* Tucson: University of Arizona Press.

1986. Sahagún's *Tlauculcuicatl,* a Nahuatl Lament. *Estudios de cultura náhuatl* 18: 181–215.

Bynum, Carol Walker, 1985. Fast, Feast and Flesh: The Religious Significance of Food to Medieval Women. *Representations* 11: 1–25.

1987. *Holy Feast and Holy Fast: The Religious Significance of Food to Medieval Women.* Berkeley and Los Angeles: University of California Press.

Calnek, Edward, 1972. Settlement Patterns and Chinampa Agriculture at Tenochtitlan. *American Antiquity* 37: 104–15.

1976. The Internal Structure of Tenochtitlan. In *The Valley of Mexico,* edited by E. R. Wolf, pp. 287–302. Albuquerque: University of New Mexico Press.

1976. Organización de los sistemas de abastecimiento urbano de alimentos: el caso de Tenochtitlan. In *Las ciudades de América Latina y sus areas de influencia*, edited by Jorge E. Hardoy and Richard P. Schaedel. Buenos Aires: Hardoy.

1978. The City-State in the Basin of Mexico. In *Urbanization in the Americas from its Beginnings to the Present*, edited by R. P. Schaedel, J. E. Hardoy, and N. Scott Kinzer. The Hague: Mouton.

1978. El sistema de mercado en Tenochtitlan. In *Economia política e ideología en el México prehispánico*, edited by Pedro Carrasco and Johanna Broda, pp. 97–114. Mexico City: Editorial Nueva Imagen.

1978. The Analysis of Prehispanic Historical Texts. *Estudios de cultura náhuatl* 13: 239–66.

1982. Patterns of Empire Formation in the Valley of Mexico, Late Postclassic Period, 1200–1521. In *The Inca and Aztec States, 1400–1800: Anthropology and History*, edited by George A. Collier, Renato I. Rosaldo, and John D. Wirth, pp. 43–62. New York and London: Academic Press.

1988. The Calmecac and Telpochcalli in Pre-Conquest Tenochtitlan. In *The Work of Bernardino de Sahagún, Pioneer Ethnographer of Sixteenth-Century Aztec Mexico*, edited by J. Jorge Klor de Alva, H. B. Nicholson, and Eloise Quiñones Keber, pp. 169–77. Albany: Institute for Mesoamerican Studies, State University of New York.

Cannadine, David, and Price, Simon, eds., 1987. *Rituals of Royalty: Power and Ceremonial in Traditional Societies*. Cambridge: Cambridge University Press.

Carr, Pat, and Gingerich, Willard, 1982. The Vagina Dentata Motif in Nahuatl and Pueblo Mythic Narratives: A Comparative Study. *New Scholar* 8: 85–101.

Carrasco, David, 1982. *Quetzalcoatl and the Irony of Empire*. Chicago and London: University of Chicago Press.

Carrasco, Pedro, 1971. Social Organization in Ancient Mexico. In *Handbook of Middle American Indians*, Vol. 10, pp. 349–75. Austin: University of Texas Press.

1978. La economía del Mexico prehispánico. In *Economía política e ideología en el México prehispánico*, edited by Pedro Carrasco and Johanna Broda, pp. 13–76. Mexico City: Editorial Nueva Imagen.

1980. Markets and Merchants in the Aztec Economy. *Journal of the Steward Anthropological Society* 2: 249–69.

Catlin, George, 1973. *Letters and Notes on the Manners, Customs, and Conditions of the North American Indians (1844)*. 2 vols. New York: Dover.

Chance, John K., and Taylor, William B., 1985. Cofradías and Cargos: An Historical Perspective on the Mesoamerican Civil–Religious Hierarchy. *American Ethnologist* 12: 1–26.

Chartier, Roger, 1984. Culture as Appropriation: Popular Cultural Uses in Early Modern France. In *Understanding Popular Culture: Europe from the Middle Ages to the Nineteenth Century*, edited by Steven L. Kaplan. Berlin, New York, and Amsterdam: Mouton.

1988. *Cultural History: Between Practices and Representations*. Translated by Lydia G. Cochrane. Oxford: Polity Press.

Chimalpahín Cuauhtlehuanitzin, Domingo Francisco, 1965. *Relaciones originales de Chalco Amaquemecan escritas por Don Francisco de San Antón Muñón Chimalpahín Cuauhtlehuanitzin*. Edited by S. Rendón. Mexico City: Fondo de Cultura Económica.

Christian, William A., 1981. *Local Religion in Sixteenth-Century Spain*. Princeton: Princeton University Press.

Clancy, Flora S., 1983. A Comparison of Highland Zapotec and Lowland Maya Graphic Styles. In *Highland–Lowland Interaction in Mesoamerica: Interdisciplinary Approaches*, edited by Arthur G. Miller, pp. 223–40. Washington, D.C.: Dumbarton Oaks.

Clavijero, Francisco Javier, 1945. *Historia antigua de México*. 4 vols. Edited by Mariano Cuevas. Mexico City: Editorial Porrúa.

Clendinnen, Inga, 1982. Yucatec Maya Women and the Spanish Conquest: Role and Ritual in Historical Reconstruction. *Journal of Social History* 15: 427–42.

1982. The Cost of Courage in Aztec Society. *Past and Present* 94 (Feb.): 44–89.

1987. *Ambivalent Conquests: Maya and Spaniard in Yucatan, 1517–1570*. Cambridge: Cambridge University Press.

1987. Franciscan Missionaries in Sixteenth-Century Mexico. In *Disciplines of Faith: Studies in Religion, Politics and Patriarchy*, edited by J. Obelkevich, L. Roper, and R. Samuel, pp. 229–45. London and New York: Routledge and Kegan Paul.

1990. Ways to the Sacred: Reconstructing 'Religion' in Sixteenth-Century Mexico. *History and Anthropology* 5, pp. 105–41.

1991. 'Fierce and Unnatural Cruelty': Cortés and the Conquest of Mexico. *Representations* 33: 65–100.

Clifford, James, 1982. *Person and Myth: Maurice Leenhardt in the Melanesian World*. Berkeley and Los Angeles: University of California Press.

1986. On Ethnographic Allegory. In *Writing Culture: The Poetics and Politics of Ethnography*, edited by James Clifford and George E. Marcus. Berkeley and Los Angeles: University of California Press.

Cline, S. L., 1984. Land Tenure and Land Inheritance in Late Sixteenth-Century Culhuacan. In *Explorations in Ethnohistory: Indian Mexico in the Six-teenth Century*, edited by H. R. Harvey and H. Prem. Albuquerque: University of New Mexico Press.

Codex Aubin (Codex of 1576), 1903. *Colección de documentos para la historia de México*. Mexico City: Antonio Peñafiel.

Codex Aubin: Historia de la nación mexicana: reproducción a todo color del códice de 1576, 1963. Edited, introduced, and translated by Charles E. Dibble. Madrid: J. Porrúa Turanzas.

Codex Borbonicus: Bibliothèque de l'Assemblée national, Paris (Y120), 1974. Faksimile. Ausgabe de Codex im Original format. Edited by Karl Nowotny. Vollstandige. Graz: Akademische Druck-u. Verlagsanstalt.

*Codex Boturini (*also called *Tira de la Peregrinación)*, 1944. Mexico City: Librería Anticuaria.

Codex Magliabechiano, 1983. Edited by Elizabeth Hill Boone and Zelia Nuttall. Berkeley: University of California Press.

Codex Mendoza (1541?), 1938. 3 vols. Translated and edited by James Cooper Clark. London: Waterlow and Sons.

Codex Mendoza, 1978. Commentaries by Kurt Ross. Fribourg: Productions Liber S. A., Miller Graphics.

Códice Ramírez, 1944. Relación del origen de los indios que habitan esta Nueva España, según sus historias. Mexico City: Editorial Leyenda.

Codex Rios, 1964. Códice Vaticano Latino 3738. In *Antigüedades de México basadas en la recompilación de Lord Kingsborough*, Vol. 3. Mexico City: Secretaría de Haciendo y Crédito Público.

Codex Telleriano–Remensis, 1964. In *Antigüedades de México basadas en la recompilación de Lord Kingsborough*, Vol. 1. Mexico City: Secretaría de Haciendo y Crédito Público.

Códice Chimalpopoca: anales de Cuauhtitlán y leyenda de los soles, 1945. Translated by Primo Feliciano Velázquez. Mexico City: Imprenta Universitaria.

Códice Ixtlilxóchitl (1582) (Bibliothèque National, Paris, Ms. A. Mex. 65–71) (new ser.), 2 vols. in 1. Commentary by J. de Durand-Forest. Reproduktion des Manuskriptes in Original format. Graz: Akademische Druck-u. Verlagsanstalt.

Cohen, David, 1985. From PIM's Doorway. In *Reliving the Past: Essays in Social History*, edited by Oliver Zunz. Chapel Hill: University of North Carolina Press.

Colson, Elizabeth and Soudder, Thayer, 1987. *For Prayer and Profit: The Ritual, Economic and Social Importance of Beer in Gwembe District, Zambia, 1950–1982*. Stanford: Stanford University Press.

Conrad, Geoffrey W., and Demarest, Arthur A., 1984. *Religion and Empire: The*

Dynamics of Aztec and Inca Expansionism. Cambridge: Cambridge University Press.

Cortés, Hernando, 1986. *Hernán Cortés: Letters from Mexico.* Edited and translated by Anthony Pagden, with an introduction by J. H. Elliott. New Haven and London: Yale University Press.

Costumbres, fiestas, enterramientos y diversas formas de proceder de los indios de Nueva España (1553?), 1945. Prepared by Federico Gómez de Orozco. *Tlalocán* 11: 37–63.

Couch, N. C. Christopher, 1985. *The Festival Cycle of the Aztec Codex Borbonicus.* Oxford: British Archaeological Reports.

Crosby, Alfred W., 1986. *Ecological Imperialism: The Biological Expansion of Europe, 900–1900.* Cambridge: Cambridge University Press.

Davies, Nigel, 1973. *The Aztecs: A History.* New York: Putnam.

1973. *Los Mexicas: primeros pasos hacia el imperio.* Mexico City: UNAM.

1980. *The Toltec Heritage: From the Fall of Tula to the Rise of Tenochtitlan.* Norman and London: University of Oklahoma Press.

1987. *The Aztec Empire: The Toltec Resurgence.* Norman and London: University of Oklahoma Press.

Davis, L. Irby, 1972. *A Field Guide to the Birds of Mexico and Central America.* Austin: University of Texas Press.

Demarest, Arthur, 1984. Overview: Mesoamerican Human Sacrifice in Evolutionary Perspective. In *Ritual Human Sacrifice in Mesoamerica,* edited by Elizabeth H. Boone, pp. 227–47. Washington, D.C.: Dumbarton Oaks.

Díaz del Castillo, Bernal, 1966. *Historia verdadera de la conquista de la Nueva España.* Introduction and notes by Joaquín Ramírez Cabañas. Mexico City: Editorial Porrúa.

Dibble, Charles E., 1980. The *Xalaquia* Ceremony. *Estudios de cultura náhuatl* 4: 197–202.

Douglas, Mary, 1966. *Purity and Danger: An Analysis of the Concepts of Pollution and Taboo.* London: Routledge and Kegan Paul.

Ed., 1987. *Constructive Drinking: Perspectives on Drink from Anthropology.* Cambridge: Cambridge University Press.

Durán, Fr. Diego, 1964. *The Aztecs: The History of the Indies of New Spain (1581).* Translated by Doris Heyden and Fernando Horcasitas. London: Cassell.

1967. *Historia de las Indias de Nueva España e Islas de la Tierra Firme.* 2 vols. and atlas. Edited by Angel María Garibay K. Mexico City: Editorial Porrúa.

1971. *The Book of the Gods and The Ancient Calendar (1570, 1579).* Translated by Doris Heyden and Fernando Horcasitas. Lincoln: University of Oklahoma Press.

Durand-Forest, Jacqueline de, ed., 1984. *The Native Sources and the History of the Valley of Mexico*. Oxford: British Archaeological Reports.

Duverger, Christian, 1978. *La fleur létale: Economie du sacrifice aztèque*. Paris: Editions du Seuil.

Easby, Dudley T., Easby, Elizabeth Kennedy, Scott, John F., and Hoving, Thomas, 1970. *Before Cortés; Sculpture of Middle America: A Centennial Exhibition at the Metropolitan Museum of Art*. New York: Metropolitan Museum of Art.

Edmonson, Munro S., ed., 1974. *Sixteenth-Century Mexico: The Work of Sahagún*. Albuquerque: School of American Research and University of New Mexico Press.

Elliott, J. H., 1967. The Mental World of Hernán Cortés. *Transactions of the Royal Historical Society*, Fifth Series, 17: 41–58.

Elzey, Wayne, 1976. Some Remarks on the Space and Time of the 'Center' in Aztec Religion. *Estudios de cultura náhuatl* 12: 315–34.

Erikson, Erik, 1978. *Toys and Reasons: Stages in the Ritualization of Experience*. London: Marion Boyars.

Fernandez, James W., 1980. Reflections on Looking into Mirrors. *Semiotica* 30: 27–40.

Fernández, Justino, 1954. *Coatlicue, estética del arte indígena antigua*. Prologue by Samuel Ramos. Mexico City: Centro de Estudios Filosóficos.

Fuentes, Patricia de, ed. and trans., 1963. *The Conquistadores: First-Person Accounts of the Conquest of Mexico*. London: Cassell.

Furst, Jill Leslie, 1978. *Codex Vindobonensis Mexicanus I, A Commentary*. Institute for Mesoamerican Studies Publication 4. Albany: State University of New York Press.

Furst, Peter T., 1968. The Olmec Were–Jaguar Motif in the Light of Ethnographic Reality. In *Dumbarton Oaks Conference on the Olmec*, edited by Elizabeth P. Benson, pp. 143–78. Washington, D.C.: Dumbarton Oaks.

  Ed., 1972. *Flesh of the Gods: The Ritual Use of Hallucinogens*. London: Allen and Unwin.

  1976. *Hallucinogens and Culture*. San Francisco: Chandler and Sharp.

Garibay K., Angel María, 1953. *Historia de la literatura náhuatl*, 2 vols. Mexico City: Editorial Porrúa.

Garibay K., Angel María, ed., 1964–68. *Poesía náhuatl*, 3 vols. Vol. 1, Romances de los señores de Nueva España; Vols. 2 & 3, Cantares mexicanos (incomplete). complete). Mexico City: UNAM.

Geary, Patrick, 1983. Humiliation of Saints. In *Saints and their Cults: Studies in Religious Sociology, Folklore and History*, edited and introduced by Stephen Wilson, pp. 123–40. Cambridge: Cambridge University Press.

Geertz, Clifford, 1960. *The Religion of Java*. New York: The Free Press.

1973. Thick Description: Towards an Interpretive Theory of Culture. In his *The Interpretation of Cultures*, pp. 3–30. New York: Basic Books.

1975. Deep Play: Notes on the Balinese Cockfight. In his *The Interpretation of Cultures*, pp. 412–53. New York: Basic Books.

1975. Ritual and Social Change: A Javanese Example. In his *The Interpretation of Cultures*, pp. 142–69. New York: Basic Books.

1980. *Negara: The Theatre State in Nineteenth-Century Bali*. Princeton: Princeton University Press.

Geertz, H., 1975. An Anthropology of Religion and Magic. *Journal of Interdisciplinary History* 6: 71–89.

Gibson, Charles, 1964. *The Aztecs under Spanish Rule*. Stanford: Stanford University Press.

1971. The Structure of the Aztec Empire. *Handbook of Middle American Indians*, Vol. 10, pp. 322–400. Austin: University of Texas Press.

1975. Survey of Middle American Prose Manuscripts in the Native Historical Tradition. *Handbook of Middle American Indians*, Vol. 15, 311–21. Austin: University of Texas Press.

Gibson, Charles, and Kubler, George, 1951. *The Tovar Calendar: An Illustrated Mexican Manuscript ca. 1585*, pp. 9–21. New Haven, Conn.: Memoirs of the Connecticut Academy of Arts and Science.

Gilbert, Michelle, 1987. The Person of the King: Ritual and Power in a Ghanaian State. In *Rituals of Royalty: Power and Ceremonial in Traditional Societies*, edited by David Cannadine and Simon Price, pp. 298–330. Cambridge: Cambridge University Press.

Gingerich, Willard, 1977. Tlaloc, His Song. *Latin American Indian Literatures* 1, 79–88.

1988. *Chipahuacanemiliztli*, 'The Purified Life', in the Discourses of Book VI, Florentine Codex. In *Smoke and Mist: Mesoamerican Studies in Memory of Thelma D. Sullivan*, 2 vols., edited by J. Kathryn Josserand and Karen Dakin, Vol. 1, pp. 517–44. Oxford: British Archaeological Reports.

Glass, John B., 1975. A Survey of Native Middle American Pictorial Manuscripts. In *Handbook of Middle American Indians*, edited by Robert Wauchope, Vol. 14, pp. 3–81. Austin: University of Texas Press.

Goffman, Erving, 1981. *Forms of Talk*. Philadelphia: University of Pennsylvania Press.

Graulich, Michel, 1981. The Metaphor of the Day in Ancient Mexican Myth and Ritual. *Current Anthropology* 22: 45–60.

1982. Quecholli et Panquetzaliztli: une nouvelle interprétation. *Lateinamerika-Studien* 10: 159–73.

1984. Aspects mythiques des peregrinations Mexicas. In *The Native Sources and the History of the Valley of Mexico,* edited by Jacqueline de Durand-Forest, pp. 25–71. Oxford: British Archaeological Reports.

Greenblatt, Stephen, 1980. *Renaissance Self-Fashioning: From More to Shakespeare.* Chicago and London: University of Chicago Press.

1985. Exorcism into Art. *Representations* 12: 15–23.

1988. *Shakespearean Negotiations: The Circulation of Social Energy in Renaissance England.* Oxford: Clarendon Press.

Grinnell, George B., 1961. *Pawnee Hero Stories and Folk Tales* (reprint). Lincoln: University of Nebraska Press.

Grinnell, George, 1972. *The Cheyenne Indians* (1923). 2 vols. Lincoln: University of Nebraska Press.

Gruzinski, Serge, 1989. *Man-Gods in the Mexican Highlands: Indian Power and Colonial Society 1520–1800.* Translated by Eileen Corrigan. Stanford: Stanford University Press.

Hall, David, 1984. Introduction. In *Understanding Popular Culture: Europe from the Middle Ages to the Nineteenth Century,* edited by Steven L. Kaplan. Berlin, New York, and Amsterdam: Mouton.

Harner, Michael, 1977. The Ecological Basis for Aztec Sacrifice. *American Ethnologist* 4: 117–35.

1977. The Enigma of Aztec Sacrifice. *Natural History* 86: 47–52.

Harris, Marvin, 1977. *Cannibals and Kings: The Origins of Cultures.* New York: Random House.

Harvey, H. R., 1984. Aspects of Land Tenure in Ancient Mexico. In *Explorations in Ethnohistory: Indian Mexico in the Sixteenth Century,* edited by H. R. Harvey and H. Prem, pp. 83–102. Albuquerque: University of New Mexico Press.

Harvey, H. R., and Prem, H., eds. 1984. *Explorations in Ethnohistory: Indian Mexico in the Sixteenth Century.* Albuquerque: University of New Mexico Press.

Hassig, Ross, 1985. *Trade, Tribute, and Transportation: The Sixteenth-Century Political Economy of Mexico.* Norman: University of Oklahoma Press.

1988. *Aztec Warfare: Imperial Expansion and Political Control.* Norman: University of Oklahoma Press.

Hemingway, Ernest, 1932. *Death in the Afternoon.* New York: Scribner.

Hertz, Robert, 1960. The Collective Representation of Death (1907). In *Death on the Right Hand,* translated by Rodney and Claudia Needham. Aberdeen: Cohen and West.

Hicks, Frederick, 1975. Dependent Labor in Prehispanic Mexico. *Estudios de cultura náhuatl* 11: 243–66.

1979. Flowery War in Aztec History. *American Ethnologist* 6: 87–93.

1984. Rotational Labor and Urban Development in Prehispanic Tetzcoco. In *Explorations in Ethnohistory: Indian Mexico in the Sixteenth Century*, edited by H. R. Harvey and H. Prem. Albuquerque: University of New Mexico Press.

Historia de los mexicanos por sus pinturas, 1965. In *Teogonía e historia de los mexicanos. Tres opúsculos del siglo XVI*, edited by Angel María Garibay K., pp. 21–90. Mexico City: Editorial Porrúa.

Historia tolteca–chichimeca, 1976. Facsimile edition, with studies, pictures, and maps by Paul Kirchoff, Lina Odena Güemes and Luis Reyes García. Mexico City: INAH.

Histoyre du Mexique, 1905. Edited by E. de Jonghe. *Journal de Société de Americainistes* (new ser.), Paris, 1–42.

Hobson, J. Allan, 1988. *The Dreaming Brain*. New York: Basic Books.

Holmes, Clive, 1984. Popular Culture? Witches, Magistrates and Divines. In *Understanding Popular Culture: Europe from the Middle Ages to the Nineteenth Century*, edited by Steven L. Kaplan. Berlin, New York, and Amsterdam: Mouton.

Hvidtfeldt, Arild, 1958. *Teotl and *Ixiptlatli: Some Central Conceptions in Ancient Mexican Religion*. Copenhagen: Munksgaard.

Información sobre los tributos que los indios pagaban a Moctezuma: Año de 1554, 1957. Documentos para la Historia de Mexico Colonial, 4, edited by France V. Scholes and Eleanor B. Adams. Mexico City: Editorial Porrúa.

Josserand, J. Kathryn, and Dakin, Karen, eds., 1988. *Smoke and Mist: Mesoamerican Studies in Memory of Thelma D. Sullivan*, 2 vols. Oxford: British Archaeological Reports.

Kaplan, Steven L., ed., 1984. *Understanding Popular Culture: Europe from the Middle Ages to the Nineteenth Century*. Berlin, New York, and Amsterdam: Mouton.

Karttunen, Frances, 1982. Nahuatl Literacy. In *The Inca and Mexica States 1400–1800: Anthropology and History*, edited by George A. Collier, Renato I. Rosaldo and John D. Wirth. London and New York: Academic Press.

1983. *An Analytical Dictionary of Nahuatl*. Austin: University of Texas Press.

Karttunen, Frances, and Lockhart, James, 1980. La estructura de la poesía náhuatl vista por sus variantes. *Estudios de cultura náhuatl* 14: 15–64.

Eds. and trans., 1987. *The Art of Nahuatl Speech: The Bancroft Dialogues*. UCLA Latin American Studies, Vol. 65. Los Angeles: University of California Press.

Keber, Eloise Quiñones, 1987. Central Mexican Pictorial Manuscripts. From Tollan to Tlapallan: The Tale of Topiltzin Quetzalcoatl in the Codex Vaticanus A. *Latin American Indian Literatures Journal* 3: 76–91.

Kellog, Susan M., 1986. Kinship and Social Organization in Early Colonial

Tenochtitlan. In *Ethnohistory: Supplement to the Handbook of Middle American Indians*, Vol. 4. Austin: University of Texas Press.

1988. Cognatic Kinship and Religion: Women in Aztec Society. In *Smoke and Mist: Mesoamerican Studies in Memory of Thelma D. Sullivan*, 2 vols., edited by J. Kathryn Josserand and Karen Dakin, Vol. 2, pp. 666–81. Oxford: British Archaeological Reports.

Klein, Cecelia F., 1976. The Identity of the Central Deity on the Aztec Calendar Stone. *Art Bulletin* 58: 1–12.

1980. Who was Tlaloc? *Journal of Latin American Lore* 6: 155–204.

1987. The Ideology of Autosacrifice at the Templo Mayor. In *The Aztec Templo Mayor*, edited by Elizabeth Hill Boone, pp. 293–370. Washington, D.C.: Dumbarton Oaks.

1988. Rethinking Cihuacoatl: Aztec Political Imagery of the Conquered Woman. In *Smoke and Mist: Mesoamerican Studies in Memory of Thelma D. Sullivan*, 2 vols., edited by J. Kathryn Josserand and Karen Dakin, Vol. 1, pp. 237–77. Oxford: British Archaeological Reports.

Klor de Alva, J. Jorge, trans., 1978. The Aztec–Spanish Dialogues of 1524. *Alcheringa: Ethnopoetics* N.S., 4: 52–193.

1981. Martín Ocelotl: Clandestine Cult Leader. In *Struggle and Survival in Colonial America*, edited by David G. Sweet and Gary B. Nash, pp. 128–41. Berkeley: University of California Press.

1982. Spiritual Conflict and Accommodation in New Spain: Towards a Typology of Aztec Responses to Christianity. In *The Inca and Aztec States 1400–1800*, edited by George A. Collier, Renato I. Rosaldo, and John D. Wirth. New York: Academic Press.

Klor de Alva, J. Jorge, Nicholson, H. B., and Keber, Eloise Quiñones, eds., 1988. *The Work of Bernardino de Sahagún, Pioneer Ethnographer of Sixteenth-Century Aztec Mexico*. Albany: Institute for Mesoamerican Studies, State University of New York Press.

Kubler, George, and Gibson, Charles, 1951. *The Tovar Calendar: An Illustrated Mexican Manuscript ca. 1585*. Vol. 11, pp. 9–21. New Haven, Conn.: Memoirs of the Connecticut Academy of Arts and Science.

Kurath, Gertrude Prokosch, and Martí, Samuel, 1964. *Dances of Anáhuac: The Choreography and Music of Precortesian Dances*. Chicago: Aldine.

Kurtz, Donald V., 1978. The Legitimation of the Aztec State. In *The Early State*, edited by H. Claessen and P. Skalnik, pp. 168–89. The Hague: Mouton.

La orden que tenían los indios en suceder en las tierras y baldíos, 1939–42. In *Epistolario de Nueva España, 1505–1818*, 16 vols., edited by Francisco del Paso y Troncoso, Vol. 14, pp. 145–8. Mexico City: Biblioteca Historica Mexicana de Obras Inéditas, 2nd. ser.

Lafaye, Jacques, 1976. *Quetzalcoatl and Guadalupe.* Chicago: University of Chicago Press.

Landa, Fr. Diego de, 1941. *Landa's Relación de las Cosas de Yucatán.* Translated and edited by Alfred M. Tozzer. Cambridge: Peabody Museum, Harvard University.

las Casas, Fr. Bartolomé de, 1967. *Apologética historia sumaria cuanto a las cualidades, dispusición, cielo y suelo destas tierras,* 2 vols. Edited and prepared by Edmundo O'Gorman. Mexico City: UNAM.

León-Portilla, Miguel, 1963. *Aztec Thought and Culture: A Study of the Ancient Nahuatl Mind.* Translated by Jack Emory Davis. Norman: University of Oklahoma Press.

1966. *The Broken Spears: The Aztec Account of the Conquest of Mexico.* Boston: Beacon Press.

1969. *Pre-Columbian Literatures of Mexico.* Translated by Grace Lobanov and Miguel León-Portilla. Norman: University of Oklahoma Press.

1974. The Problematics of Sahagún: Certain Topics Needing Investigation. In *Sixteenth-Century Mexico: The Work of Sahagún,* edited by Munro S. Edmonson, pp. 235–55. Albuquerque: University of New Mexico Press.

1980. *Native Mesoamerican Spirituality: Ancient Myths, Discourses, Stories, Doctrines, Hymns, Poems from the Aztec, Yucatec, Quiché-Maya and Other Sacred Traditions.* New York: Paulist Press.

1983. Translating Amerindian Texts. *Latin American Indian Literatures* 7: 101–22.

1986. Nahuatl Literature. In *Literatures: Supplement to the Handbook of Middle American Indians,* edited by Munro S. Edmonson, pp. 7–43. Austin: University of Texas Press.

Lesser, Alexander, 1933. *The Pawnee Ghost Dance Hand Game: A Study of Cultural Change.* New York: Columbia University Press.

Lewis, Oscar, 1941. Manly-Hearted Women Among the North Piegan. *American Anthropologist* 43: 173–87.

Lienzo de Tlaxcala (1550), 1982. In *Antiguédes Mexicanas,* edited by Alfredo Chavez. Mexico: Secretaría de Fomento.

Llewelyn-Davies, Melissa, 1981. Women, Warriors and Patriarchs. In *Sexual Meanings: The Cultural Construction of Gender and Sexuality,* edited by Sherry B. Ortner and Harriet Whitehead, pp. 330–58. Cambridge: Cambridge University Press.

Lockhart, James, 1982. Views of Corporate Self and History in Some Valley of Mexico Towns: Late Seventeenth and Eighteenth Centuries. In *The Inca and Aztec States 1400–1800: Anthropology and History,* edited by George A.

Collier, Renato I. Rosaldo, and John D. Wirth, pp. 367–93. New York and London: Academic Press.

1985. Some Nahua Concepts in Postconquest Guise. *History of European Ideas* 16: 465–82.

Lockhart, James, Berdan, Frances, and Anderson, Arthur J. O., 1986. *The Tlaxcalan Actas.* Salt Lake City: University of Utah Press.

Lockhart, James, and Karttunen, Frances, eds. and trans., 1987. *The Art of Nahuatl Speech: The Bancroft Dialogues.* UCLA Latin American Studies Vol. 65. Los Angeles: University of California Press.

López Austin, Alfredo, 1963. El hacha nocturna. *Estudios de cultura náhuatl* 4: 179–86.

1967. *Juegos rituales aztecas.* Mexico City: UNAM.

1973. *Hombre–Dios: religión y política en el mundo náhuatl.* Mexico City: UNAM.

1988. *Cuerpo humano e ideología: Las concepciones de los antiguos Nahuas,* 2 vols. Mexico City: UNAM. Translated into English as *The Human Body and Ideology: Concepts of the Ancient Nahuas,* 2 vols., by Thelma Ortiz de Montellano and Bernard Ortiz de Montellano. Salt Lake City: University of Utah Press.

Lowie, Robert H., 1916. Military Societies of the Crow Indians. In *Societies of the Plains Indians: Anthropological Papers of the American Museum of Natural History,* edited by Clark Wissler, Vol. 10. New York: American Museum of Natural History.

1935. *The Crow Indians.* New York: Farrar and Rinehart.

MacAloon, John J., ed., 1984. *Rite, Drama, Festival, Spectacle: Rehearsals Towards a Theory of Cultural Performance.* Philadelphia: ISHI.

MacAndrew, Craig, and Edgerton, Robert, 1969. *Drunken Comportment: A Social Explanation.* Chicago: Aldine.

MacLachlan, Colin, 1976. The Eagle and the Serpent: Male Over Female in Tenochtitlan. *Proceedings of the Pacific Coast Council of Latin American Studies* 5: 45–56.

Malinowski, Bronislaw, 1974. *Magic, Science, and Religion and Other Essays.* London: Souvenir Press.

Marcus, George E., and Fischer, Michael M. J., 1986. *Anthropology as Cultural Critique: An Experimental Moment in the Human Sciences.* Chicago: University of Chicago Press.

Maslow, Jonathon Evan, 1986. *Bird of Life, Bird of Death.* New York: Laurel.

Matos Moctezuma, Eduardo, ed., 1982. *El Templo Mayor: Excavaciones y Estudios.* Mexico City: INAH.

1982. *El Templo Mayor: Planos, cortes y perspectivas.* Illustrated by Victor Rangel. Mexico City: INAH.

1982. *Trabajos Arqueológicos en el Centro de la Ciudad de México.* Mexico City: INAH.

Miller, Arthur G., ed., 1983. *Highland–Lowland Interaction in Mesoamerica: Interdisciplinary Approaches.* Washington, D.C.: Dumbarton Oaks.

Miller, Jonathon, 1978. *The Body in Question.* London: Macmillan.

Millon, René, 1976. Social relations in Ancient Teotihuacán. In *The Valley of Mexico,* edited by Eric R. Wolf, pp. 205–48. Albuquerque: University of New Mexico Press.

Molina, Fr. Alonso de., 1970. *Vocabulario en lengua castellana y mexicana y mexicana y castellana.* Introductory study by Miguel León-Portilla. Mexico City: Editorial Porrúa.

Monzón, Arturo, 1949. *El calpulli en la organización social de los Tenochas.* Mexico City: Instituto de Historia.

Morley, John David. 1985. *Pictures of the Water Trade: An Englishman in Japan.* London: Deutsch.

Motolinía, Fr. Toribio, 1970. *Memoriales e historia de los indios de la Nueva España.* Introductory study by Fidel de Lejarza, O. F. M. Madrid: Ediciones Atlas.

Muñoz Camargo, Diego, 1972. *Historia de Tlaxcalla.* Edited and with notes by Alfredo Chavero. Facsimile of 1892 edition. Guadalajara, Jal., Mexico: Edmundo Aviña Levy.

Murie, James R., 1981. *Ceremonies of the Pawnee,* Parts 1 and 2. Edited by Douglas R. Parks. Washington, D.C.: Smithsonian Institution Press.

Musgrave-Portilla, L. Marie, 1982. The Nahualli or Transforming Wizard in Pre- and Postconquest Mesoamerica. *Journal of Latin American Lore* 8: 3–62.

Nabokov, Vladimir, 1972. *Transparent Things: A Novel.* New York: McGraw Hill.

Nagao, Debra, 1985. *Mexica Buried Offerings: A Historical and Contextual Analysis.* Oxford: British Archaeological Reports.

Nash, June, 1978. The Aztecs and the Ideology of Male Dominance. *Signs* 4: 349–62.

Nash, Manning, 1967. *Machine Age Maya* (1958). Chicago: University of Chicago Press.

Nicholson, H. B., 1971. Religion in Pre-Hispanic Central Mexico. *Handbook of Middle American Indians,* Vol. 10, pp. 395–446. Austin: University of Texas Press.

1974. Tepepolco, the Locale for the First Stage of Fr. Bernardino de Sahagún's Great Ethnographic Project: Historical and Cultural Notes. In

Mesoamerican Archeology: New Approaches, edited by Norman Hammond. London: Duckworth.

1988. Recent Sahaguntine Studies: A Review. In *The Work of Bernardino de Sahagún, Pioneer Ethnographer of Sixteenth-Century Aztec Mexico*, edited by J. Jorge Klor de Alva, H. B. Nicholson, and Eloise Quiñones Keber, pp. 13–30. Albany: Institute for Mesoamerican Studies, State University of New York Press.

Nicholson, H. B., with Quiñones Keber, Eloise, 1983. *Art of Ancient Mexico: Treasures of Tenochtitlán*. Washington, D.C.: National Gallery of Art.

Nicolau D'Olwer, Luis, 1987. *Fray Bernardino de Sahagún, 1499–1590* (1952). Translated by Mauricio J. Mixco. Salt Lake City: University of Utah Press.

Nowotny, Karl Anton, 1961. *Tlacuilolli*. Berlin: Gebr. Mann Verlag.

Nuttall, Zelia, 1903. *The Book of the Life of the Ancient Mexicans, Containing an Account of Their Rites and Superstitions* [Codex Magliabechiano]. Facsimile edition. Translated and with introduction and commentary by Zelia Nuttall. Berkeley: University of California Press.

1911. L'évêque Zumarraga et les idoles principales du Templo Grande de Mexico. *Journal de la Société des Américainistes* (new ser.), Paris, 8: 153–171.

Offner, Jerome A., 1983. *Law and Politics in Aztec Texcoco*. Cambridge: Cambridge University Press.

1984. Household Organization in the Texcocan Heartland: The Evidence in the *Codex Vergara*. In *Explorations in Ethnohistory*, edited by H. R. Harvey and H. Prem. Albuquerque: University of New Mexico Press.

Ong, Walter, 1967. *The Presence of the Word*. New Haven, Conn.: Yale University Press.

1977. *Rhetoric, Romance, and Technology: Studies on the Interaction of Expression and Culture*. Ithaca, N.Y.: Cornell University Press.

1982. *Orality and Literacy: The Technologizing of the Word*. London and New York: Methuen.

Ortega y Gasset, José, 1957. *Man and People*. New York: Norton.

1959. The Difficulty of Reading. *Diogenes* 28: 1–17.

Ortiz de Montellano, Bernard R., 1978. Aztec Cannibalism: An Ecological Necessity? *Science* 200: 611–17.

1983. Counting Skulls: Comment on the Aztec Cannibalism Theory of Harner–Harris. *American Anthropologist* 85: 403–6.

Ortner, Sherry B., and Whitehead, Harriet, eds., 1981. *Sexual Meanings: The Cultural Construction of Gender and Sexuality*. Cambridge: Cambridge University Press.

Padden, Robert C., 1967. *The Hummingbird and the Hawk*. Columbus: Ohio State University Press.

Pagden, Anthony, trans. and ed., 1986. *Hernán Cortés: Letters from Mexico*. With an introduction by J. H. Elliott. New Haven and London: Yale University Press.

1986. *The Fall of Natural Man: The American Indian and the Origins of Comparative Ethnology*. Cambridge: Cambridge University Press.

Pasztory, Esther, 1976. Masterpieces in Pre-Columbian Art. *Proceedings of the 42nd Congress of Americanists, Paris*. 7: 377–90.

1983. *Aztec Art*. New York: Harry Abrams.

1987. Texts, Archeology, Art, and History in the Templo Mayor: Reflections. In *The Aztec Templo Mayor*, edited by Elizabeth Hill Boone. Washington, D.C.: Dumbarton Oaks.

Peristiany, J. G., 1965. *Honour and Shame: The Values of Mediterranean Society*. London: Weidenfeld and Nicolson.

Pomar, Juan Bautista, 1981. Relación de Tezcoco. In *Nueva colección de documentos para la historia de México*, 3 vols., edited by Joaquín García de Icazbalceta, Vol. 3, pp. 1–69. Mexico City: Editorial Porrúa.

Popol Vuh: The Definitive Edition of the Mayan Book of the Dawn of Life and the Glories of Gods and Kings, 1985. Translated and introduced by Dennis Tedlock. New York: Simon and Schuster.

Prescott, W. H., (n.d.). *History of the Conquest of Mexico* (1843). New York: The Modern Library, Random House.

Price, Barbara, 1978. Demystification, Enriddlement, and Aztec Cannibalism: A Materialist Rejoinder to Harner. *American Ethnologist* 5: 98–115.

'Primeros Memoriales' de Fray Bernardino de Sahagún, 1974. Edited by Wigberto Jiménez Moreno. Mexico City: INAH.

Procesos de indios idólatras y hechiceros, 1912–13. Publicaciones del Archivo General de la Nación, Vols. 12 and 13. Mexico City: Boletín del Archivo de la Nación.

Quiñones Keber, Eloise, 1987. Central Mexican Pictorial Manuscripts. From Tollan to Tlapallan: the Tale of Topiltzin Quetzalcoatl in the Codex Vaticanus A. *Latin American Indian Literatures Journal* 3: 76–91.

Quirate, Jacinto, 1977. The Ballcourt in Mesoamerica: Its Architectural Development. In *Precolumbian Art History*, edited by Alana Cordy-Collins and Jean Stern. Palo Alto: Peek Publications.

Radin, Paul, 1920. *The Sources and Authenticity of the History of the Ancient Mexicans*, pp. 1–150. Berkeley: University of California Press.

1963. *The Autobiography of a Winnebago Indian* (1920). New York: Dover.

Reichel-Dolmatoff, G. 1975. *The Shaman and the Jaguar: A Study of Narcotic Drugs Among the Indians of Colombia.* Philadelphia: Temple University Press.

Relaciones Geográficas, 1905–6. In *Papeles de Nueva España,* 2nd. series, 8 vols., edited by Francisco Paso y Troncoso. Madrid: F. Paso y Troncoso.

Ricoeur, Paul, 1981. Appropriation. In *Hermeneutics and the Human Sciences: Essays on Language, Action and Interpretation,* edited and translated by John B. Thompson. Cambridge: Cambridge University Press.

Robertson, Donald, 1959. *Mexican Manuscript Painting of the Early Colonial Period: The Metropolitan Schools.* New Haven, Conn.: Yale University Press.

——— 1966. The Sixteenth-Century Mexican Encyclopedia of Fray Bernardino de Sahagún. *Cuadernos de Historia Mundial* 9: 617–28.

——— 1974. The Treatment of Architecture in the Florentine Codex of Sahagún. In *Sixteenth-Century Mexico: The Work of Sahagún,* edited by Munro S. Edmonson, pp. 617–28. Albuquerque: University of New Mexico Press.

Robicsek, Francis, and Hales, Donald, 1984. Maya Heart Sacrifice: Cultural Perspective and Surgical Technique. In *Ritual Human Sacrifice in Mesoamerica,* edited by Elizabeth H. Boone, pp. 49–87. Washington, D.C.: Dumbarton Oaks.

Román Berrelleza, Juan Alberto, 1987. Offering 48 of the Templo Mayor: A Case of Child Sacrifice. In *The Aztec Templo Mayor,* edited by Elizabeth Hill Boone, pp. 131–43. Washington, D.C.: Dumbarton Oaks.

Rosaldo, Michele Z., 1980. *Knowledge and Passion: Ilongot Notions of Self and Social Life.* Cambridge: Cambridge University Press.

Rounds, J., 1979. Lineage, Class and Power in the Aztec State. *American Ethnologist* 6: 73–87.

——— 1982. Dynastic Succession and the Centralization of Power in Tenochtitlan. In *The Inca and Aztec States 1400–1800: Anthropology and History,* edited by George A. Collier, Renato I. Rosaldo, and John D. Wirth, pp. 63–89. New York and London: Academic Press.

Ruiz de Alarcón, Hernando, 1984. *Treatise on the Heathen Superstitions that Today Live Among the Indians Native to This New Spain, 1629.* Edited by J. Richard Andrews and Ross Hassig. Albuquerque: University of Oklahoma Press.

Sabean, David, 1984. *Power in the Blood: Popular Culture and Village Discourse in Early Modern Germany.* Cambridge: Cambridge University Press.

Sahagún, Fr. Bernadino de, 1950–82. *The Florentine Codex: General History of the Things of New Spain.* 12 books in 13 vols. Translated by Arthur J. O. Anderson and Charles Dibble. Santa Fe: School of American Research and the University of Utah Press.

1956. *Historia general de las cosas de la Nueva España,* 4 vols. Edited by Angel María Garibay K. Mexico City: Editorial Porrúa.

1969. *Augurios y abusiones* (from 'Primeros memoriales'). Translation and commentary by Alfredo López Austin. Mexico City: UNAM.

1974. *'Primeros memoriales' de Fray Bernardino de Sahagún.* Edited and translated by Wigberto Jiménez Moreno. Mexico City: INAH.

1978. The Aztec–Spanish Dialogues of 1524. Translated by J. Jorge Klor de Alva, *Alcheringa: Ethnopoetics* (new ser.), 4: 52–193.

1979. *El Códice Florentino de Fray Bernardino de Sahagún,* 3 vols. Facsimile Edition. (Original manuscript in the Biblioteca Medicea Laurenziana, Florence.) Mexico City: Secretaría de Gobernación.

Sahlins, Marshall D., 1978. Culture as Protein and Profit. *New York Review of Books* 23 (November 1978): 45–53.

Sanders, William T., Parsons, Jeffrey, R., and Santley, Robert S., 1979. *The Basin of Mexico: Ecological Processes in the Evolution of a Civilization.* New York and London: Academic Press.

Schele, Linda, and Miller, Mary Ellen, 1986. *The Blood of Kings: Dynasty and Ritual in Maya Art.* Fort Worth: Kimball Art Museum.

Schieffelin, Edward L., 1979. Mediators as Metaphors: Moving a Man to Tears in Papua New Guinea. In *The Imagination of Reality,* edited by A. L. Becker and Aram A. Yengoyan, pp. 127–44. Norwood, N.J.: ABLEX.

Scholes, France, V., and Adams, Eleanor B., eds. 1957. *Información sobre los tributos que los indios pagaban a Moctezuma: año de 1554.* Documentos para la Historia de Mexico Colonial, 4. Mexico City: Editorial Porrúa.

Schultes, Richard Evans, and Hofmann, Albert, 1979. *Plants of the Gods: Origins of Hallucinogenic Use.* New York: McGraw Hill.

Sisson, Edward B., 1983. Recent Work on the Borgia Group Codices. *Current Anthropology* 24: 653–6.

Soustelle, Jacques, 1955. *La vie quotidienne des Aztéques en la veille de la conquête espagnole.* Paris: Le club du meilleur livre. Translated into English as *The Daily Life of the Aztecs on the Eve of the Spanish Conquest* by Patrick O'Brien (1964). London: Pelican Books.

Spierenburg, Pieter, 1984. *The Spectacle of Suffering.* Cambridge: Cambridge University Press.

Stenzel, Werner, 1976. The Military and Religious Orders of Ancient Mexico. *Proceedings of the 42nd International Congress of Americanists, Paris* 7: 179–87.

Sullivan, Thelma D., 1963. Náhuatl Proverbs, Conundrums and Metaphors Collected by Sahagún. *Estudios de cultura náhuatl* 4: 93–177.

1966. Pregnancy, Childbirth and the Deification of the Women who Died in Childbirth. *Estudios de cultura náhuatl* 6: 64–95.

1971. The Finding and Founding of Mexico-Tenochtitlan (selection from the *Crónica Mexicayotl* of Fernando Alvarado Tezozómoc). *Tlalocan* 6: 312–36.

1972. The Arms and Insignia of the Mexica. *Estudios de cultura náhuatl* 10: 156–93.

1980. Tlatoani and Tlatocayotl in the Sahagún Manuscripts. *Estudios de cultura náhuatl* 14: 225–38.

1982. Tlazolteotl–Ixcuina: The Great Spinner and Weaver. In *The Art and Iconography of Late Post-Classic Central Mexico*, edited by Elizabeth Hill Boone. Washington, D.C.: Dumbarton Oaks.

Taylor, William B., 1979. *Drinking, Homicide, and Rebellion in Colonial Mexican Villages*. Stanford: Stanford University Press.

Tedlock, Barbara, 1980. Songs of the Zuñi Kachina Society: Composition, Rehearsal, Performance. In *Southwestern Indian Ritual Drama*, edited by Charlotte J. Frisbie. Albuquerque: University of New Mexico Press.

1982. *Time and the Highland Maya*. Albuquerque: University of New Mexico Press.

Tedlock, Dennis, 1983. *The Spoken Word and the Work of Interpretation*. Philadelphia: University of Pennsylvania Press.

Trans., 1985. *Popol Vuh: The Definitive Edition of the Mayan Book of the Dawn of Life and the Glories of Gods and Kings*. New York: Simon and Schuster.

Thomas, Keith, 1971. *Religion and the Decline of Magic*. New York: Scribner.

Tira de la Peregrinación, see *Codex Boturini*.

Todorov, Tzvetan, 1984. *The Conquest of America: The Question of the Other* (1982). New York: Harper and Row.

Torquemada, Juan de, 1943–4. *Monarquía indiana*. 3 vols. Facsimile of 1723 edition; Vol 2, p. 299. Mexico City: S. Chávez Hayhoe.

Townsend, Richard Fraser, 1979. *State and Cosmos in the Art of Tenochtitlán*. Washington, D.C.: Dumbarton Oaks.

1987. Coronation at Tenochtitlan. In *The Aztec Templo Mayor*, edited by Elizabeth Hill Boone, pp. 371–409. Washington, D.C.: Dumbarton Oaks.

Turner, Victor, 1957. *Schism and Continuity in African Society: A Study of Ndembu Village Life*. Manchester: University of Manchester Press.

1974. *Dramas, Fields and Metaphors: Symbolic Actions in Human Society*. Ithaca, N.Y. and London: Cornell University Press.

1977. Process, System and Symbol: A New Anthropological Synthesis. *Daedalus* 106: 61–80.

1982. *From Ritual to Theatre: The Human Seriousness of Play*. New York: Performing Arts Journal, Inc.

1984. Liminality and the Performative Genres. In *Rite, Drama, Festival, Specta-*

cle: Rehearsals Towards a Theory of Cultural Performance, edited by John J. MacAloon. Philadelphia: ISHI.

Turner, Victor, and Bruner, Edward M., eds., 1986. *The Anthropology of Experience.* Urbana and Chicago: University of Illinois Press.

Umberger, Emily G., 1981. Aztec Sculptures, Hieroglyphs, and History. Ph.D. dissertation, Columbia University.

1984. El Trono de Moctezuma. *Estudios de cultura náhuatl* 17: 63–87.

Vaillant, George C., 1972. *Aztecs of Mexico: Origin, Rise and Fall of the Aztec Nation.* Revised edition. Harmondsworth: Pelican Books.

van Zantwijk, Rudolph, 1979. El parentesco y la afiliación étnica de Huitzilopochtli. *Proceedings of the 42nd International Congress of Americanists, Paris* 6: 63–8.

1981. The Great Temple of Tenochtitlan: Model of Aztec Cosmovision. In *Mesoamerican Sites and World-Views,* edited by Elizabeth P. Benson, pp. 71–86. Washington, D.C.: Dumbarton Oaks.

1985. *The Aztec Arrangement: The Social History of Pre-Spanish Mexico.* Norman: University of Oklahoma Press.

Veyne, Paul, 1984. *Writing History: Essay on Epistemology* (1971). Middletown, Conn.: Wesleyan University Press.

Walens, Stanley, 1981. *Feasting with Cannibals: An Essay on Kwakiutl Cosmology.* Princeton: Princeton University Press.

Wallace, Anthony F., 1970. *The Death and Rebirth of the Seneca.* New York: Knopf.

Wauchope, Robert, 1964–76. *Handbook of Middle American Indians.* Austin: University of Texas Press.

Weiner, Annette B., 1976. *Women of Value, Men of Renown: New Perspectives in Trobriand Exchange.* Austin: University of Texas Press.

Weismann, Elizabeth Wilder, 1950. *Mexico in Sculpture 1521–1821.* Cambridge: Harvard University Press.

Westheim, Paul, 1965. *The Art of Ancient Mexico.* Translated by Ursula Bernard. New York: Doubleday.

Whitehead, Harriet, 1981. The Bow and the Burden-strap: A New Look at Institutionalized Homosexuality in Native North America. In *Sexual Meanings: The Cultural Construction of Gender and Sexuality,* edited by Sherry B. Ortner and Harriet Whitehead, pp. 80–115. Cambridge: Cambridge University Press.

Wiget, Andrew O., 1980. Aztec Lyrics: Poetry in a World of Continually Perishing Flowers. *Latin American Indian Literatures* 4: 1–11.

Wilkerson, S. Jeffrey K., 1984. In Search of the Mountain of Foam. In *Ritual Human Sacrifice in Mesoamerica,* edited by Elizabeth H. Boone, pp. 101–32. Washington, D.C.: Dumbarton Oaks.

Wilson, Stephen, ed., 1983. *Saints and their Cults: Studies in Religious Sociology, Folklore and History.* Cambridge: Cambridge University Press.

Wissler, Clark, 1916. Societies and Ceremonial Associations of the Oglala Division of the Teton-Dakota. *Anthropological Papers of the American Museum of Natural History*, Vol. 11, pp. 114–25. New York: American Museum of Natural History.

Wolf, Eric, 1959. *Sons of the Shaking Earth.* Chicago: Chicago University Press.
Ed., 1976. *The Valley of Mexico.* Albuquerque: University of New Mexico Press.

Zunz, Oliver, ed., 1985. *Reliving the Past: Essays in Social History.* Chapel Hill: University of North Carolina Press.

Index

actions: analyses, 302n8; focus of Aztecs, 5, 6; meanings, 44, 238–9, 242, 245–9

afterlife: for mothers, 178–9; for sacrificial victims, 99, 104; for sucklings, 191, 339n56; for warriors, 151, 195–6, 220–1, 244

Ahuitzotl: mythic water creature, 226; ruler, 136

Alvarado, Pedro de, 145

arts, 213–35; compiling mode, 202–4, 232–3, 248–9, 252–3; dislocation, 232, 243; ephemerality, 214, 218; featherwork, 216–18, 229–30, 343n11; priests supreme artificers, 235, 242–4; song-poems, 213, 218–23, 272; speech, 51, 62–3, 171, 219, 311n2; vaunting, 123

auguries, 36, 144–6, 151, 179, 185, 191, 201, 237, 272, 330n5

Axayacatzin (ruler), 166

Aztecs, *see* Mexica; Tenochtitlan–Tlatelolco

battle: captives, not corpses, 94–5, 116, 271; exalted state, 51, 150, 207, 220; formal (flowery wars), 34, 97, 114, 116–17; one-to-one combat, 113–14, 115–16, 122, 340n72; *see also* war; warriors

Becker, A. L., 234

Berger, John, 28–9, 30, 32

blood: auto-sacrifice, 74–5, 255–6, 262–3; creative, fertile element, 92, 173, 182–4, 208, 243, 262

Broda, Johanna, 243

butterflies, 229; *see also* afterlife, for warriors

calendars: Book of Days (*tonalamatl*), 35, 55, 56, 154, 170; ritual (260-day; *tonalpoualli*), 35; seasonal (solar; *xiuitl*), 35, 295–7, (Nemontemi) 191; *see also* childbirth; time

calpullis (wards): clan-based? 302n12, 306n13, 307n15; controlled from palace, 21, 25, 32, 39–40; core units, 7, 20, 21, 57; craft, 20, 132; elders in 39, 120, 207; ethnic, 23, 33; merchant, 20, 33, 133; public buildings in, 17; ritual duties of, 42, 43, 63, 88, 89, 95; role of, 40, 49, 66, 187; strains within, 64; tribute obligations of, 41; warriors in, 40, 63, 91, 95, 113, 120, 129

Catlin, George, 119, 228

Celestial Princesses, 82, 179, 199

Centeotl (Young Lord Maize Cob), *see* maize

Chalchihuitlicue (Lake Waters Goddess), 31, 168, 251

Chicomecoatl (Sustenance Woman/ Tlaloc's sister), 182, 201, 203

childbirth: all-female affair, 156; assistance at, 175, 176; babies welcomed, 110, 155, 176, 187; of boy, 112, 175–6; daysigns, 42, 56–7, 98, 157, (*tonalli*: vigour and fate) 58, 206–7, 314n44; death in, 176–7, 178; emergencies, 176; of girl, 153, 173; rituals, 55, 58–9, 110, 112, 175–6, 178, 181; and the sacred, 51, 171, 175, 176, 178, 180, 184, 205, \206; Tlaloc victims chosen

Acknowledgements for Literary Material and Illustrations

Beacon Press for the Nahuatl lament on p. 272, from *The Broken Spears: The Aztec Account of the Conquest of Mexico*, by Miguel León-Portilla. Copyright 1966 by Beacon Press. Professor Gordon Brotherston, University of Essex, and Thames and Hudson Ltd. for the song-poems on pp. 221–3 and 223, from *Image of the New World: The American Continent as Portrayed in Native Texts*, by Gordon Brotherston with Ed Dorn. Copyright 1979 by Thames and Hudson Ltd. Dr. T. J. Knab, Shandaken, N.Y., for the Nahuatl poem on p. 263, from 'Words Great and Small: Sierra Nahuatl Narrative Discourse in Everyday Life', 1983. Unpublished manuscript. *Latin American Indian Literatures Journal*, for the song-poems on pp. 221 and 222, from Andrew O. Wiget, 'Aztec Lyrics: Poetry in a World of Continually Perishing Flowers', *Latin American Indian Literatures* 4: 1–11, 1980, and for the song-poem on pp. 213–4, from Miguel León-Portilla, 'Translating Amerindian Texts', *Latin American Indian Literatures* 7: 101–22, 1983. Copyright 1980 and 1983 by *Latin American Indian Literatures*. Stanford University Press for the song-poem on p. 221, from *Cantares Mexicanos: Songs of the Aztecs*, translated by John Bierhorst. Copyright 1985 by Stanford University Press. University of Oklahoma Press for the song-poem on p. 220, from *Pre-Columbian Literatures of Mexico*, by Miguel León-Portilla, translated from the Spanish by Grace Lobanov and Miguel León-Portilla. Copyright 1969 by the University of Oklahoma Press.

Color illustrations: New Fire Ceremony; a page from a *tonalamatl*; Quetzalcoatl and Tezcatlipoca; the festival of Ochpaniztli; Tlazolteotl giving birth: From the Codex Borbonicus, by courtesy of Akademische Druck-u. Verlagsanstalt: Codices Selecti (Series C, Mesoamerican Manuscript), Vol. 44, Complete true-colour facsimile edition, and the Bibliothèque de l'Assemblée Nationale Française, Paris. Feathered headdress: By courtesy of the Museum für Volkerkunde, Vienna. Warrior costumes: From Codex Mendoza, by courtesy of the Bodleian Library, Oxford. The 'Milk Tree': From Vaticanus Latinus 3738 (Codex Vaticanus A.,

'Rios'), photograph Biblioteca Vaticana, by courtesy of the Biblioteca Apostolica Vaticanus, Rome. Coatlicue; Coyolxauhqui Relief, Templo Mayor Project: By courtesy INAH.-CNCA.-MEX., Mexico. Seated Xipe Totec: By courtesy of the Museum für Volkerkunde und Schweizerisches Museum für Volkskunde, Basel. The red Xipe Totec: Courtesy of F. Hébert-Stevens and Claude Arthaud.

Black and white illustrations: The Spanish view of ritual killings: Codex Magliabechiano, by courtesy of the Biblioteca Nazionale Centrale of Florence. 'Tira de la peregrinación': By courtesy of the Biblioteca Nacional de Antropología e Historia, Mexico City. The Eagle Man flies upwards: Malinalco Drum, by courtesy of INAH.-CNCA.-MEX., Mexico. 'The Face of Battle', Tlazolteotl giving birth: By courtesy of the Dumbarton Oaks Research Library and Collections, Washington, D.C. Aragonite squash; granite rattlesnake: By courtesy of the Trustees of the British Museum, London. Quetzalcoatl figure: Upright Feathered Serpent: By courtesy of the Museum für Volkerkunde, Vienna. Red porphyry Quetzalcoatl: By courtesy of the Musée de l'Homme, Paris. Deerskin screenfold: By courtesy of the Board of Trustees of the National Museums and Galleries on Merseyside. The Spanish penetrate the main temple precinct of Tenochtitlan: Lienzo de Tlaxcala, by courtesy of the Bodleian Library, Oxford.

29- urbanites + nat. world
42-3 — ... of religion/ ritual
51 + — alcohol, "pollution"
60 — feast

95 — Hegel Captor/Captive